The Liberalization of Transportation Services in the EU and Turkey

The Liberalization of Transportation Services in the EU and Turkey

Sübidey Togan

OXFORD
UNIVERSITY PRESS

OXFORD

UNIVERSITY PRESS

Great Clarendon Street, Oxford, OX2 6DP,
United Kingdom

Oxford University Press is a department of the University of Oxford.
It furthers the University's objective of excellence in research, scholarship,
and education by publishing worldwide. Oxford is a registered trade mark of
Oxford University Press in the UK and in certain other countries

First Edition published in 2016
Impression: 1

Published in the United States of America by Oxford University Press
198 Madison Avenue, New York, NY 10016, United States of America

British Library Cataloguing in Publication Data
Data available

Library of Congress Control Number: 2015959278

ISBN 978–0–19–875340–7

Printed in Great Britain by
Clays Ltd, St Ives plc

To the memory of my parents and with love for Inci

Preface and Acknowledgements

This book is about the liberalization of transportation services. Since barriers to trade in services are typically regulatory in nature, and the outcomes of services liberalization depend heavily on the regulatory environments, the study concentrates on analysing the effects of changes in regulatory frameworks. It studies not only the effects of unilateral liberalization within the context of international trade but also the effects of liberalizing transport services within a regional context. The book provides a thorough discussion of international and regional rules and regulations in road transportation, rail transportation, maritime transportation, and air transportation. When considering the liberalization of transport services within a regional context, the study concentrates on the case of the European Union (EU) and makes reference to Turkey, a candidate to EU accession.

Chapter 1 begins with a discussion of the relations between trade costs and trade and economic growth, and explores the historical forces that created the present world trading system by concentrating on the economic history of the relation between trade costs and trade, emphasizing developments in transportation costs over the last millennium. Chapter 2 explores transport infrastructure, market structure, and competition in the Turkish road, rail, maritime, and air transportation sectors, and Chapter 3 through 6 concentrate on analysing the regulatory frameworks in the road, rail, maritime, and air transportation sectors by considering the international rules and regulations as well as the regulatory frameworks prevailing in the EU and Turkey. Since liberalizing transportation services between the EU and Turkey can be achieved only through harmonizing the respective regulatory frameworks (which requires Turkey to adopt the EU rules and regulations in different transportation sectors and strictly implement them), Chapter 7 quantitatively studies the effects of liberalization in those sectors. The chapter first provides an analysis of opening up the Turkish transport sectors and determines the tariff equivalents of barriers to trade in the different sectors. Then, the chapter analyses the effects of liberalization using a computable general equilibrium model. Finally, the chapter considers the economic impact of infrastructure development.

I would like to express my thanks to Bernard Hoekman of the Robert Schuman Center at the European University Institute in Florence for sparking my study of services liberalization. The present work started with the Forum Euromediterranéen des Instituts Sciences Economiques (FEMISE) project 'Impact of Liberalization of Trade in Services: Banking, Telecommunications and Maritime Transport in Egypt, Morocco, Tunisia and Turkey' (FEM22-02). That study was later extended with the Economic Research Forum (ERF) project 'Quantifying the Impact of Liberalization of Services and Network Industries within the Context of EU Integration in Turkey' (ERF Project No: ERF 03-TK-2002), the FEMISE project FEM32-02 'Liberalization of Services in Poland and Turkey: A Comparative Analysis', and the FEMISE project 'Facilitation of Transportation in Turkey and Poland: A Comparative Study' (FEM35-09). Financial support from FEMISE, supported by the European Commission, and from ERF is greatly appreciated. The views expressed in this book, however, do not necessarily represent the official position of the Commission nor that of FEMISE or ERF.

This book may carry my name alone, but its contents were shaped by the contributions and insights of Professor Jan Michalek of the University of Warsaw, Professor Nergiz Dinçer of TED University in Ankara, and Dr. Güzin Bayar of the Ministry of the Economy in Turkey. I am pleased to acknowledge their contributions here.

Contents

Contents

List of Figures

List of Tables

1

Transportation Costs, Trade, and Global Value Chains

A close relationship exists between trade costs and exports, as shown by Samuelson (1964) and Dornbush et al. (1977) within the framework of the Ricardian model of international trade. In that model, trade costs, by driving a wedge between origin and destination prices, affect the volume of trade, and thus trade increases as a result of drops in trade costs.[1] In the Melitz (2003) model, which combines economies of scale at the firm level with technological differences between firms, and in the model's theoretical extensions, trade costs also play important roles. In all models of 'new' trade theory, trade costs affect economic productivity as well as the aggregate volume of international trade as pointed out by Melitz and Treffler (2012) and Melitz and Ottoviano (2008).[2] Similar considerations apply to global value chain (GVC) trade, as emphasized by Baldwin (2014) and the OECD (2013).

In their seminal work, Anderson and van Wincoop (2004) define trade costs as costs related to policy barriers (such as tariffs and non-tariff barriers (NTBs)), transportation costs (consisting of freight and time costs), contract enforcement costs, costs associated with the use of different currencies, legal and regulatory costs, and local distribution costs (such as wholesale and retail costs). According to the authors, the tax equivalent of trade costs for industrialized countries is about 170 per cent, which breaks down as follows: 21 per cent transportation costs, 44 per cent border-related trade barriers, and 55 per cent retail and wholesale distribution costs. Transportation costs include directly measured trade costs and a 9 per cent tax equivalent of the time value of goods in transit; border-related costs break down into a 5 per cent tariff barrier, an 8 per cent NTB barrier, a 7 per cent language barrier,

---

[1] For a discussion of the Ricardian model of trade and transportation costs with many goods, see Annex 1 to this chapter.

[2] For a good discussion of the Melitz model and its extensions see Melitz and Redding (2013).

a 14 per cent currency barrier, a 6 per cent information cost barrier, and a 3 per cent security barrier.

Trade costs are usually reduced by increasing competition in the economy, which can be achieved in general through liberalizing trade that affects tariffs, NTBs, and transport costs. Liberalizing trade by removing distortions in the price system and increasing access to foreign markets boosts the economy's allocative efficiency, and thus improves the country's investment climate. Investments increase, as do foreign direct investment (FDI) inflows. Consequently, the allocative efficiency gains from liberalization are boosted by induced capital formation. When investment increases beyond its normal level, the economy experiences a growth effect. A country's gross domestic product (GDP) thus increases over time, but this does not mean an increase in the *rate* of economic growth over time, which depends on technological advances. However, trade may affect the rate of economic growth by reinforcing or dampening incentives for firms to innovate. The possibility of freely trading with other economies creates a larger market, increasing profitable opportunities, which in turn increases incentives to invest in research and development (R&D). Opening trade by increasing competition may force firms to invest more in R&D in an effort to come out on top. Hence, intense competition may lead to higher R&D investment, increasing the rate of economic growth. Finally, note that, lately, most innovations have taken place in a small number of advanced economies and later transferred to the rest of the world. Thus, the presence of international trade enriches the process of technology diffusion, and boosts the rate of economic growth in the developing world.

Reductions in trade costs lead not only to increases in economic growth but also to greater fragmentation of production, with firms parcelling out the different stages of their production processes geographically. This process is called vertical FDI, defined as investing in firm affiliates that replicate parts of the production process in a foreign country or as giving an independent firm in a foreign country license to replicate parts of the production process. In the economics literature, fragmenting the production process is called 'offshoring', which involves sourcing from a foreign affiliate through FDI or sourcing from a non-affiliate through arm's-length contracts. Manufacturing today is increasingly managed through GVCs, which, according to the World Trade Organization (WTO) (2013), is a major development in the world economy.

Empirical research confirms the existence of a negative relation between trade costs and GDP, indicating that decreases in trade costs lead to increases in volume of trade which in turn increases GDP. Jacks et al. (2008), who analyse the relation between trade costs and trade, report that trade cost declines explain roughly 55 per cent of the pre-World War I trade boom and 33 per cent of the post-World War II trade boom. According to the authors, the precipitous rise in trade costs experienced during the interwar period explains the entire trade bust.[3] On the relation between trade and GDP, Sachs and Warner (1995) report that a positive relation exists between the amount of international trade and size of GDP. Frankel and Romer (1999) confirm this result. Warziarg and Welch (2003) report a positive relation between trade liberalization and increases in GDP, and van Biesebroeck (2005), using firm-level data, shows that exporting is associated with a boost in firm productivity. Finally, regarding international knowledge spillovers, Coe and Helpman (1995) report that technological spillovers are higher when a country imports relatively more from high-knowledge rather than from low-knowledge countries.[4]

In this study we concentrate on transport costs.[5] Since transport costs are a major component of trade costs, they are one of the major determinants of a country's level of competitiveness and of its ability to participate in the world economy.[6] This chapter, setting out the purpose of the study, the importance of the subject, and the structure of the study is configured as follows: Section 1.1 discusses the development of historical forces that created the present world trading system by concentrating on the economic history of trade, trade costs, and transportation costs, with an emphasis on issues related to providing security for merchants engaged in inter-regional trade. Section 1.2 studies how transportation costs affect trade and economic activity in general, and concentrates on the determinants of transportation costs, emphasizing the roles of infrastructure and the regulatory framework. Section 1.3 explores GVCs. Finally, Section 1.4 concludes.

1.1 An Economic History of Trade and Trade Costs with Emphasis on Transportation Costs

The assertion that a major determinant of trade is trade costs (defined as costs related to tariffs, NTBs, transportation costs, enforcement costs, exchange rate costs, legal and regulatory costs, and local distribution costs) needs to be

[3] 'Interwar period' refers to the period between the end of World War I and the beginning of World War II.

[4] For a recent summary of these results, see the WTO (2008).

[5] When discussing transport costs it is almost impossible not to mention Krugman's work on 'New Economic Geography' (NEG). The NEG literature provides an integrated and micro-founded approach to spatial economics, and clarifies why economic activity at urban, regional, and international levels is distributed unevenly across space with centres of concentrated activity surrounded by peripheral regions of lower density. The NEG literature employing many of the assumptions of Krugman's (1979) 'new' trade theory, has been developed largely by Krugman (1991) and Krugman and Venables (1995). For a good survey of the literature see Fujita et al. (1999).

[6] The empirical models of Bougheas et al. (1999) and Limao and Venables (2001) confirm this conclusion.

modified when considering trade developments during the last millennium. The economic history of trade reveals that trade was also determined largely by conditions regarding security for merchants engaged in inter-regional trade. To emphasize this point, we consider in the following the developments in trade along the Silk Road during the period 1250–1350. Thereafter we concentrate on developments in transportation technology and trade costs until the present day.

Between 1250 and 1350, East–West trade flourished, a period that Findlay and O'Rourke (2007) call the first age of globalization. According to accounts of explorers such as Ibn Battuta and Marco Polo, travelling enormous distances in Eurasia was perfectly safe by day and night.[7] Abu-Lughod (1989, p. 177) states:

> It is difficult for us today to appreciate the extent to which trade depended on risk reduction, or the proportion of all costs that might have to be allocated to transit duties, tribute, or simple extortion. Unfortunately, there are no figures from the thirteenth century with which to estimate the proportion of transportation costs that went for protection. However, on the basis of evidence from the seventeenth century, over at least the westernmost part of the land route, Niels Steensgaard (1973: 37–40) has concluded that protection costs (including duties) far exceeded transport expenses themselves, which according to his calculations, were a great bargain. The spread between purchase/transport costs and gross sales prices might be considered enormous—until one calculates not only what was added in transit duties but the risks involved in shipments that were confiscated or lost, as well as in buying goods whose eventual market price could not really be estimated.

Thus, the flourishing trade between 1250 and 1350 was due mainly to reductions in 'transit duties, tribute, or simple extortion', achieved through earlier unification of Central Asia under Genghis Khan and his confederation of Mongol and Tatar tribes.[8] Prior to this unification, demands for protection money by different rival tribal groups could reach prohibitive levels.

During the thirteenth century, the journey from Crimea, on the Black Sea, to China by camels and horses took between eight and eleven months. Even then it was possible to make huge profits. As emphasized by Lopez (1987),

---

[7] As quoted by Findlay and O'Rourke (2007). For original accounts of their travels, see Ibn Battuta (died 1377, translated in 1929 by H. A. R. Gibb, quoted as Ibn Battuta (1929)) and Polo (various editions of 'Travels'. See the 1992 translation by H. Yule and H. Cordier, quoted as Polo (1992)).

Note that Marco Polo started his travels in 1271 and Ibn Battuta in 1328. Thus the statement that travelling enormous distances in Eurasia was perfectly safe by day and night refers to the periods after 1271 in the case of Marco Polo and the period after 1328 in the case of Ibn Battuta.

[8] In the early thirteenth century, Mongol tribes were forged into a union by Temüjin, who was proclaimed as Genghis Khan in 1206. Under his descendants a large part of the Eurasian landmass was conquered and *Pax Mongolica* was established, creating an environment conducive to trade and communication.

Chinese silk in Italy was selling for three times its purchase price in China. The East–West trade involved general items with a high ratio of value to weight, such as spices, silk, and furs. While China was exporting porcelain, silk, and other textiles, India was exporting spices such as black pepper, as well as cotton textiles. European imports were largely paid for by silver and copper, as well as by fine linen, woollen cloth, mechanical clocks, glassware, and beads.

There were many routes, called Silk Roads, connecting China and India with Europe, and these are shown in Figure 1.1. Although these roads consisted of a constantly shifting network of pathways, three of these routes dominated East–West trade. The northern route through the Black Sea was controlled by Genoa, whose merchants acted as middlemen between Western Europe and Asia. The middle route via the Persian Gulf was dominated by Baghdad. Finally, the southern route through the Red Sea gave life to Cairo and its Mediterranean partner, Venice.

The northern route passed through Constantinople via the Black Sea. From ports in Crimea and from ports towards the eastern end of the Black Sea, goods were transferred to the caravan route to China and India. This route, stretching some 8,000 km, crossed the newly unified Central Asian steppes and deserts. During this period the routes underwent substantial improvements as a result of steady horse movements by travelling Mongol troops as well as by those engaged in mail communications.[9] The road network included way stations and points around which *caravanserais* flourished, and it was the greater safety and stability of this area that facilitated the marked expansion of overland trade.[10] This period witnessed not only a series of Papal missions to the Mongols but also merchant trade missions, including those from Venice and Genoa by Marco Polo, who managed to reach the present Beijing.

The southern route started at the Egyptian port of Alexandria, from which connections were made via Cairo to the Red Sea and from there farther eastward through the Arabian Sea and Indian Ocean. While the Genovese controlled trade between Genoa and the different parts of the Black Sea, trade between Alexandria and Europe was controlled by the Venetians. European merchants were stopped in Egypt and not permitted to cross the Nile to the Red Sea. They had to transfer their goods to local *Karimi* (wholesale) merchants, who were engaged not only in Red Sea trade, but also in trade with the Far East. Towards the end of the thirteenth century, the connections between Egypt and Venice strengthened while the *Karimi* merchants virtually monopolized trade between Europe and India and between Europe and the Far East.

---

[9] The Mongol rulers developed a postal relay system designed to speed official communication. Those on the business of the ruler showed their badges of authority and received fresh mounts at regularly placed relay stations so that official communication could be efficiently carried out.

[10] *Caravanserais* were rest stops located a day's distance from each other and which accommodated large numbers of travellers and their animals.

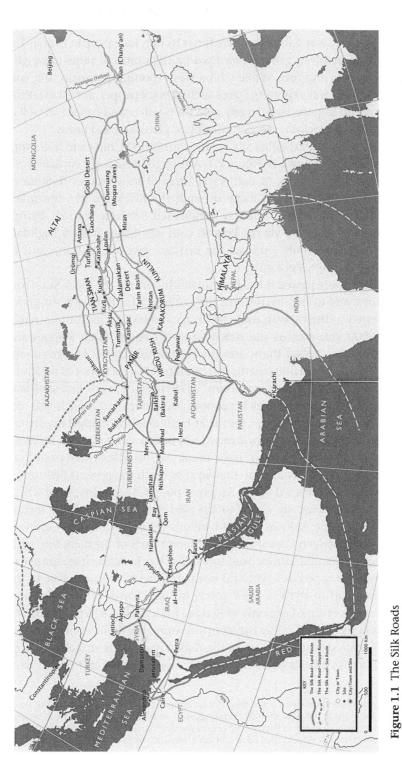

Figure 1.1 The Silk Roads

Source: Road Map by Emily Toner, *Expedition* 52,3 Winter 2010, p. 12. Courtesy of University of Pennsylvania Museum of Archeology & Anthropology.

Transport up the Red Sea was protected by Egyptian sultans, and Aden at the mouth of the Red Sea was the entrepôt for traffic heading to the East as well as for goods arriving from the East. The route to India from Aden was quite treacherous, requiring skilled knowledge of monsoon winds and careful navigation techniques to cross the open sea. As emphasized by Abu Lughod (1989), the winds imposed stringent schedules for sailing the Indian Ocean, the Bay of Bengal, and the South China Sea. Ships departing Aden sailed in the spring and fall, and in summer and winter merchants settled in ports to conduct business. They arrived in Gujarat (near present-day Mumbai) or on the Malabar Coast in India (at Quilon and Calicut). From there merchants had to cross the Bay of Bengal to the Strait of Malacca. Since monsoon winds reversed at the strait, long layovers were required for boats travelling to the East or West. In addition to the frustrations of optimal timing, merchants faced the risks of product and life loss from storms and piracy. There were also cultural divisions on the sea route. While the route from the Red Sea to Gujarat and the Malabar Coast was controlled by Muslim merchants, the route from the South Indian coast to Java and other Indonesian islands was controlled by Indian merchants. Finally, the Chinese section was controlled by the Chinese. But none of these three powers exercised dominance over the entire Asian sea transport system.

The middle Silk Road route started at the Mediterranean coast of Syria/ Palestine and crossed the Mesopotamian plain to Baghdad. From there one could follow either the land route or the sea route. The former crossed Persia and then branched off to either Northern India or eastward to Samarkand and then China. The sea route followed the Tigris River to Basra. From there it followed the Persian Gulf route and passed Oman to the Indian Ocean and beyond. Until the conquest of Baghdad by the Mongols in 1258, the middle route was the oldest, easiest, cheapest, and most enduring among the three options connecting West and East.

When part of the sea route, for example, the Indian Ocean and South China Sea, was controlled by a single unifying power, such as China, trade costs decreased and thus trade increased in that region. When China withdrew from the Indian Ocean and South China Sea, the risk of loss due to piracy in those regions increased and trade started to suffer.

During the time of the Umayyads (661–750 CE) Arab sailors were active in the Persian Gulf, in the Indian Ocean, and up to Canton. After the establishment of Mongol rule, Tabriz became the capital of Il-Khans. As Baghdad and Basra lost their privileged positions, international trade shifted to Tabriz, and Hormuz became the offshore port of Il-Khans. At the same time, Crusader ports on the Mediterranean, hosting Italian merchants who trans-shipped Eastern goods to Europe, were destabilizing, and the last one was gone by 1291. All these factors led to the decline of the middle route by the end of the thirteenth century.

After the death of Genghis Khan in 1227, his empire was divided among his sons. Successions between 1250 and 1350 took place rather smoothly, and political stability prevailed, which decreased trade costs and led to trade increases. During this time, much trade diverted from the sea route towards the overland route, which was more cost-efficient. The period ended with a pandemic, which started in the Himalayan mountain region between China, India, and Burma. The plague bacillus (or bubonic plague) spread to China and then to Central Asia. Since the populations exposed to the plague had little or no natural immunities to it, mortalities were very high, especially among Mongol soldiers. Demographically weakened, the Mongols were less able to exert control over their domains, which one by one began to revolt.[11]

In China, the political effects of the plague were dramatic. The Ming Rebellion of 1368 deposed the Yuan Dynasty of Kublai Khan, grandson of Genghis Khan, and replaced it with the indigenous Ming Dynasty. During the Ming reign, Chinese attitudes towards trade and maintaining a strong navy were subjects of heated debate. Some in the palace favoured withdrawing from the world system, which had facilitated a free flow of goods under the Mongols. Around the 1430s, the palace started to support opponents of free trade and as a result, China withdrew from the Indian Ocean and the South China Sea, leaving the area defenceless.

With the withdrawal of the Chinese from the thirteenth-century world system during the fifteenth century, the disintegration of Il-Khan's regime in Persia, and the internal conflicts of Mongol states in Central Asia, security problems in international trade began to arise, and trade was adversely affected. The increase in trade costs caused by increases in transit duties, tribute, and extortion lessened the free flow of goods. Caravan trade declined, and East–West trade reverted to the sea routes.

The transportation technology of the time did not change much over the first half of the second millenium. While overland transport was facilitated by horses and camels, sea transport was facilitated by sailing vessels. During the fifteenth century progress was achieved in shipbuilding techniques, such as adding additional masts with lateen sails to square-rigged ships.[12] As a result, in 1497 Vasco da Gama was able to round the southern tip of Africa—the Cape of Good Hope—and reach India in 1498. The sixteenth century saw the emergence of the Portuguese as important actors in the Indian Ocean and the South China Sea, largely due to the Chinese decision to withdraw from the

---

[11] The plague bacillus travelled along the caravan routes, reaching Crimea in 1346, and thereafter proceeded to penetrate almost all of Europe and the Near East, causing the death of large segments of European populations.

[12] While the ancient square sail permitted sailing only before the wind, the triangular lateen sail was capable of taking the wind on either side, and enabled the vessel to tack into the wind. It was of decisive importance to medieval navigation.

world system, and they enjoyed a monopoly of the Cape route throughout most of that century.

According to Gunder Frank (1998), the transcontinental caravan trade was not replaced by circum-Asian maritime trade, mainly because the maritime route around Africa did not lower transportation costs. Eventually, sea route trade again subsided in favour of the trans-Central and West Asian route. But a decline in caravan trade again occurred in the seventeenth century, mainly due to political upheavals, including the replacement of the Ming dynasty in 1644 by the Machu dynasty, the fall of the Timurid Empire in Western Central Asia, and problems with Mughal rule in Northern India, as well as the expansion of intra-regional trade in Asia.

Towards the end of the sixteenth century, the Portuguese were displaced by the Dutch, who formed the Vereenigde Oost-Indische Compangnie (VOC) in 1602. The company was awarded a monopoly east of the Cape of Good Hope and west of the Straits of Magellan. By the middle of the seventeenth century the Dutch were the dominant European power in trade between Asia and Europe, and like the Portuguese before them, they enjoyed almost a complete monopoly of the Cape route. The VOC established monopsonistic control for nutmeg and cloves, but not for black pepper or other spices.

The rise of the Dutch had been watched by the British with some jealousy. In 1600, an English joint-stock company was formed for pursuing trade with countries east of the Cape of Good Hope and west of the Straits of Magellan. During the same year, the company, called the British East India Company (EIC), was granted a Royal Charter. During the first years of its formation, the EIC struggled in the spice trade due to competition from the well-established VOC. In 1612, a mission was sent to the Mughal emperor to arrange for a commercial treaty. The mission was highly successful, and the EIC expanded its commercial trading operations in India. By 1630 the penetration of the Indian subcontinent was well underway. By the end of the seventeenth century, Bombay, Madras, and Calcutta became EIC trading stations, and EIC trade continued its exponential growth. Their main commodities included raw cotton, cotton textiles, silk, indigo dye, tea, and opium. Tea was imported mainly from China and purchases were financed mainly by Indian goods, including opium.

Although trade along the Cape route flourished, it did not displace the old trade routes. The Cape route did help to increase competition and lower profit margins. But during the sixteenth century substantial margins remained between Amsterdam prices and Southeast Asian prices. The sea routes through the Red Sea and the Persian Gulf were still extensively used because the Cape route, as mentioned above, brought no major cost advantages. Also as noted, the land route from 1500 onwards was affected by political disruptions, including instability in Central Asia and China. With Russian penetration into Siberia and the signing of the Treaty of Kiahta in 1727, the conduct of overland trade between China and Russia was regulated. As a result of these developments, trade between Western Europe and Asia was then largely diverted from the overland route towards the sea route.

During the period under consideration there was no systematic decline in freight rates because there were no major technological improvements in shipbuilding. Massive expansion of trade flows was triggered only by the industrial revolution in the early 1800s, and it was breakthroughs in transport technologies that facilitated the further opening up of economies. The first revolutionary technology transforming transportation was the invention of the steamship. During the first half of the nineteenth century steamships were used for maritime transport in rivers, North America's Great Lakes, and inland seas such as the Mediterranean, where ships could pick up coal or timber along the way. With the advent of the screw propeller, steamships were crossing the Atlantic by the 1830s. With the introduction of compound and turbine engines, improved hull designs, and more efficient ports, transoceanic steam-ship trade in bulk commodities began. But steamship trade to Asia was still not possible because ships could not carry enough coal to circumnavigate Africa, and there were no places to pick it up along the way. As a result, Far Eastern trade was still dominated by sail. In 1869, the Suez Canal was opened, which made it possible to pick up coal at Gibraltar, Malta, Port Said, and Aden. As a result, steamships became viable and cost-efficient for the route to the Far East.

In the late eighteenth century, canal and road construction in the United States intensified. Although better road surfaces sped up travel by horse-drawn carriages considerably, that option was still expensive. Canals offered a far more cost-effective way of transportation wherever they were practical. The length of navigable waterways in the US as well as in France and Germany increased rapidly. The Erie Canal, constructed between 1817 and 1825, cut the journey between Buffalo and New York from twenty-one to eight days, and reduced transportation costs by 85 per cent. Then, the Liverpool–Manchester railroad opened in 1830, and railways were soon adopted by Belgium, France, and Germany. By 1869, the East and West coasts of the US were connected by rail, and in Russia the Trans-Siberian Railway was completed in 1903. Thus, trains played a major role in creating national markets in the US and Russia. During that time, British companies also undertook extensive investments in railroad construction in India, Australia, Canada, and China. Finally, mech-anical refrigeration was developed in the 1830s, and refined over the next two decades, which meant that by the 1880s, beef was being exported from North America to Europe, meat from Australia to Europe, and butter from New Zealand to Europe.

As emphasized by Lundgren (1996), inland transport costs fell by 90 per cent between 1800 and 1910 and transatlantic transport costs by 60 per cent between 1870 and 1900. O'Rourke and Williamson (1999) note that the cost of shipping wheat from Chicago to New York decreased from 17.2 per cent of Chicago wheat prices between 1866 and 1870 to 5.5 per cent of Chicago wheat prices between 1909 and 1913. Similarly, the cost of shipping wheat from New York to Liverpool decreased from 11.6 per cent of Chicago prices between 1866 and 1870 to 4.7 per cent of those prices between 1909 and 1913. With falling transport costs, trade costs also decreased, which amounted to a 45 per cent drop in trade barriers between 1870 and 1913 due to transport improvements. As a result, trade increased considerably during the period under consideration.

When defining trade costs, Anderson and van Wincoop (2004) abstain from considering the costs of providing security for land and sea merchants, as over time, security began to be largely provided as a public good by governments. On the seas it was mainly Britain that provided security, starting in the nineteenth century; its Royal Navy provided a guarantee of open international trading conditions for vessels from all countries.

With the start of World War I, the globalization of the 1870–1914 period came under strain. Trade barriers shot up after 1914 and remained high and rising until the mid-1920s. The years following the 1929 US stock market crash were disastrous in terms of unemployment, declining production, business failures, and human suffering. In June 1930, the US passed the Smooth-Hawley tariff, which raised duties on imports by 23 per cent. Most countries retaliated by applying tariffs, quantitative restrictions, and other trade barriers to importing in an attempt to stimulate their economies.

On the transportation side, technological advances continued during World War I and into the interwar period. By the late 1920s, railroad steam engines were replaced by diesel and electric locomotives. The interwar period witnessed the development of the turboelectric transmission, the replacement of coal-fired plants with oil and diesel, improvements to boilers used to convert water to steam, as well as the mass adoption of the motor vehicle. Large motorized trucks started to compete with rail lines. The rapid expansion of air freight represented another major transportation breakthrough. During World War I, airborne military cargo dramatically increased, and by the mid-1920s aircraft manufacturers were designing and building dedicated cargo planes.

After World War II the world economy underwent a process of liberalization. On the transportation side the closure of the Suez Canal during 1956 forced the shipping industry to develop huge, specialized bulk carriers and the harbour facilities to handle these new vessels. A major innovation was introduced through containerization. A cargo container, Levinson (2006) notes, is a metal box of standardized dimensions developed during the 1950s. The value of containerization lies in the specifically built system of container ships, trucks, freight trains, and automated handling technology that grew around it. The system facilitated multi-modal transport and enabled the expansion of world trade during the second half of the last century, contributing to the rise of GVCs. Furthermore, advances in air transportation led to exponential growth in that industry. The introduction of jet aircraft in the 1950s created profound changes in the operating efficiency of commercial aircraft, as jet engines are faster and have lower maintenance and fuel costs. By 1980, the real costs of air freight had fallen to about a quarter of their levels at the beginning of World War II, and as a result, air freight has become a key component of international trade. Hummels (1999) notes that the average revenue per tonne-km shipped for all air traffic worldwide has fallen between 1955 and 2004 more than ten times. Since air transport used to be more expensive than ocean transport, it was generally only used for goods with a high value-to-weight ratio, and it was also used over long distances relatively more than over short distances.

1.2 Transport Costs and International Trade

According to Maddison (2005), world GDP and world trade increased between 1500 and 1820 by only 0.32 and 0.96 per cent per annum, respectively. The world's relatively recent remarkable rise in international trade only began in the early nineteenth century, when the growth rate of world GDP and world trade between 1820 and 1870 increased to 0.93 and 4.18 per cent, and to 2.11 and 3.4 per cent, respectively, between 1870 and 1913. This growth slowed with World War I and almost halted with the Great Depression. Between 1913 and 1950 the growth rate of world GDP and trade decreased to 1.82 and 0.9 per cent, respectively. World trade revived after World War II with the trade liberalization achieved through the General Agreement on Tariffs and Trade (GATT), and between 1950 and 1973 the growth rate of world GDP and trade amounted to 4.9 and 7.88 per cent, respectively. In 1973 the fixed but adjustable Bretton Woods exchange rate system, with its restrictions on international capital flows, broke down and was replaced with the flexible exchange rate system that allowed for the liberalization of international capital movements. Between 1973 and 2001 the growth rate of world GDP and world trade amounted to 3.05 and 5.22 per cent, respectively.

O'Rourke and Williamson (1999) and Jacks et al. (2008) maintain that the enormous rise in trade experienced between 1820 and 1913 was a consequence of sharply declining transport costs. During the interwar period, however, artificial barriers to trade were erected, which led to an increase in trade costs despite important technological breakthroughs in transportation technology. Findlay and O'Rourke (2007) point out that transport-cost declines during that period were not large enough to overcome the effects of rising trade barriers. Jacks et al. (2008) maintain that the 10 per cent rise in trade costs due to those barriers explains, as emphasized above, the entire interwar trade bust.

After World War II, freight rates in air transport declined dramatically, leading to a substantial increase in the share of air transport in exports. This faster transportation also had cost-saving advantages, as revealed by Hummels and Schaur (2013), who estimate that each additional day goods spend in transit equals a 0.6 per cent to 2.3 per cent *ad valorem* tariff barrier for manufactured goods. The authors point out that a delay of three days can reduce the probability of export by 13 per cent. Adverse developments have also occurred in the post-World War II period, such as a rise in ocean freight rates. When deflating nominal ocean freight rates by a commodity price deflator, Hummels (1999) finds that real tramp voyage freight rates remained constant between the 1950s and the 1990s. Other studies also reveal that the real costs of ocean transport have been stable or increasing in the post-war period due to rising costs of fuel, wages, and shipbuilding. Moreover, there have been sharp rises in port costs. Thus, the productivity increase in transportation was counteracted by rising factor prices. According to Jacks et al. (2008), 33 per cent of the trade boom experienced between 1950 and 2000 is explained by a 16 per cent fall in trade costs, while the contribution of growth in output during this period amounted to 66.8 per cent. As transportation costs were quite stable during that period, the fall in trade costs was due to other factors, such as decreases in tariffs and communication costs.

Studying the determinants of transport costs reveals that the main factors influencing them are infrastructure, the regulatory framework, geography, technological change, trade facilitation, fuel costs, and product characteristics.[13] A high-quality transport infrastructure with major international gateways, and corridor infrastructures such as airports, harbours, railways, and highways increases the competitiveness of a country's products, and restrictive land, air, and sea transport regulations that restrain competition add to exporters' transport costs. A country's geographical characteristics, such as being landlocked, or with long distances to other markets and main transportation routes, can also have a significant negative bearing on transportation costs. Similarly, innovations in the transportation sector, such as the 1950s' adoption of containerization in maritime transportation and the development of jet aircraft, help to bring down transportation costs, as do improvements in procedures and controls governing the movement of goods across and within national borders. While higher fuel costs increase transportation costs, product characteristics such as high value-to-weight ratios and

---

[13] See e.g. Behar and Venables (2011).

higher product quality may also lead to lower transportation costs.[14] Of the above determinants, we concentrate on only two factors, namely the infrastructure and regulatory framework, the topics of our study. But before starting the discussion of infrastructure and regulatory framework as determinants of transport costs we shall first explore some of the problems related to measuring transport costs.

1.2.1 Measuring Transport Costs

Transport cost is the price users pay for transportation services. Rodrigue et al. (2006) make a distinction between a variety of transport costs such as free on board (fob), cost-insurance-freight (cif), terminal costs, linehaul costs, and capital costs. While the value of bilateral trade reported by the exporter is fob (i.e. it does not include freight and insurance), the same trade as reported by the importer includes cif. Terminal costs are related to loading, transshipment, and unloading, and linehaul costs are a function of the distance over which a unit of freight or a passenger is carried. Finally, capital costs are costs applying to the physical assets of transportation, mainly infrastructures, terminals, and vehicles.

A source of data on transport costs often used by researchers is the International Monetary Fund's (IMF) Direction of Trade Statistics, which report bilateral trade data by the exporting country on fob, and by the importing country on a cif basis. The cif/fob ratio is then taken as a measure of transport costs, as Limao and Venables (2001) do. A problem with this measure of transport cost is the fact that a high proportion of observations have been imputed by the IMF. As emphasized by Golub and Tomasik (2008), cif/fob ratios are, due to the lack and unreliability of the underlying trade data, severely flawed measures both for cross-sectional and time series analyses of transport costs. Hence, researchers are generally left with proxies.

The *Doing Business* dataset of the World Bank reports the costs of document preparation, customs clearance and inspections, inland transport and handling, and port and terminal handling for exporting and importing goods. As shown in Table 1.1 *Doing Business* measures the time and cost of exporting and importing a 20-foot equivalent unit (TEU) container by sea transport with 10 tonnes of weight and $20,000 of value, but the time and cost of actual sea transport as well as tariffs are not included in the cost figures. Data are

---

[14] On the role of geography, see Limao and Venables (2001), Hummels (1998), and Hummels (2007); on technological change, see section 1.1 on 'Economic History of Trade and Transportation Costs'; on trade facilitation, see Wilson et al. (2003) and Wilson et al. (2005); on fuel costs see Mirza and Zitouna (2010); and on product characteristics, see Hummels (2007).

Table 1.1 Costs and handling time for a 20-foot container

	Time to export (days)	Cost to export (US$ per container)	Time to import (days)	Cost to import (US$ per container)
East Asia & Pacific	20.2	864	21.6	895.6
Europe & Central Asia	23.6	2,154.50	25.9	2,435.90
Latin America & Caribbean	16.8	1,299.10	18.7	1,691.10
Middle East & North Africa	19.4	1,166.30	23.8	1,307.00
OECD high income	10.5	1,080.30	9.6	1,100.40
South Asia	33.4	1,922.90	34.4	2,117.80
Sub-Saharan Africa	30.5	2,200.70	37.6	2,930.90

Source: Doing Business website, 2015 data.

obtained from local freight forwarders, shipping lines, customs brokers, port officials, and banks.

The table reveals that cost to export, cost to import, time to export, and time to import vary considerably among regions. Whereas cost to export (import) totals $864 ($895.6) in East Asia and the Pacific, the cost goes up to $2,200.7 ($2,930.9) in sub-Saharan Africa. While it takes 10.5 (9.6) days to export (import) in OECD high-income countries, the time to export (import) takes 33.4 (34.4) days in South Asia.

While container rates for actual sea transport per TEU on particular routes such as Shanghai–Northern Europe are reported by UNCTAD (2014), Limao and Venables (2001) use cif/fob ratio quotes for shipping a standard container from Baltimore to various destinations. Golub and Tomasik (2008) develop a new approach for estimating international transport costs, giving country-specific costs for a number of OECD countries over the period 1973–2005, based on direct measures of transport costs. Similarly, Combes and Lafourcade (2005) derive estimates of road transport costs for a number of French employment areas based on the real transport network.

1.2.2 *Infrastructure*

Adequate quantity and reliability of infrastructure are key factors in a country's ability to compete in international markets, and transport infrastructure is a powerful tool to connect to those economies. According to the World Bank (1994), transport infrastructure represents the wheels of economic activity, and this reality becomes painfully evident when natural disasters or wars destroy roads, bridges, and canals. Poor transport infrastructure or inefficient transport services are reflected in higher transport costs and longer delivery time, and improvements in a country's infrastructure make a difference to the trading costs. Noting that all goods a country exports travel first through the domestic transport system to reach export markets, Blyde (2010) points out that poor access from the place of production to the country's shipment platforms increases the exporter's operational costs and hence the product prices in export markets.

Over the last three decades, empirical work by Aschauer (1989), Canning (1999), Esfahani and Ramirez (2003), Calderón and Servén (2010), and Limao and Venables (2001) has found evidence of infrastructure's contribution to economic growth, productivity, and international trade. According to Calderon and Servén (2010), there is consensus that infrastructure development has the potential to promote growth. Limao and Venables (2001) show that infrastructure is an important determinant of transport costs.

Limao and Venables (2001) also reveal that the amount and quality of transportation infrastructure in source, destination, and transit countries have a major impact on transportation costs. To show that better transport infrastructure reduces transport costs and is hence associated with higher volumes of trade, the authors construct an infrastructure index for fifty-one countries from four variables: kilometres of road, kilometres of paved road, kilometres of rail, and telephone mainlines per person, where the first three variables are obtained per square kilometre of country area. These four items are normalized and averaged to construct the country's infrastructure index. For transport costs the authors use two different sets of data: first, shipping company quotes for the cost of transporting a standard container from Baltimore, Maryland, in the US to selected destinations around the world, and second, a cross section of the ratio of cif to fob values that the IMF reports for bilateral trade between countries. In addition to indices of infrastructure levels, the transport cost factor regression shows distance, per capita incomes, and geographical factors such as common borders and island dummies as explanatory variables. The empirical analysis reveals that infrastructure is quantitatively important in determining transport costs. In addition, Limao and Venables (2001) explain transport costs and bilateral trade flows in terms of the geography and infrastructure of the trading countries, and of countries through which their trade passes. According to the authors, a deterioration of infrastructure from the median to the seventy-fifth percentile raises transport costs by 12 per cent and reduces trade volumes by 28 per cent.

Clark et al. (2004) look at the relationship between port infrastructure and transportation costs, and the authors use data on all US imports transported by sea. Using official US statistics that annually record harmonized system (HS) six-digit commodity-based, via liner, port-to-port import values, weights, and import charges reflecting transport costs between ports, the authors run a regression analysis for cross-sectional data. While their dependent variable is the port-to-port via liner import charge per weight at the HS six-digit commodity level, the independent variables are bilateral (port-to-port) distance, port-to-port via liner trade value per weight at the HS six-digit level, total import volume from the exporting country, directional imbalance in total trade between the US and the exporting country, containerization ratio of the HS six-digit-based import from the exporting country, and various policy variables, as well as efficiency indicators of the sea ports of exporting countries to US ports. The data on port efficiency, based on a one-to-seven index (with seven being the best score), come from the World Economic Forum's (WEF) *Global Competitiveness Report*, various years (1996–2000). For seaport infrastructure, the authors use two different sets of data. The first is constructed as the square number of the largest seaports by country, normalized by the product between a foreign country's population and area, and the second is constructed using an approach similar to Limao and Venables' study (2001). According to Clark et al. (2004), improvement in port efficiency leads to a reduction in transport costs. The authors estimate that a country that improves its ranking in port efficiency from the twenty-fifth to the seventy-fifth percentile reduces its shipping costs by 12 per cent, which in turn implies an increase in bilateral trade of around 25 per cent. The authors show that if port efficiency in Brazil or India were at the level of France or Sweden their maritime transport costs would fall by over 15 per cent; and if Turkey was able to improve its sea port efficiency to the level of Australia's, it would be able to increase its trade by 25 per cent.

Blonigen and Wilson (2008) adopt quite a different methodology to estimate the efficiency of major ports in the world, including those in the US. The authors use the port-to-port HS, a US six-digit commodity-based import statistic reported in the country's census data, and derive data on import charges. They then aim to break import charges into three main components: (i) costs associated with loading freight and disembarking from a foreign port, such as Haifa in Israel; (ii) costs connected with transportation between ports, such as Antwerp, Belgium, and Baltimore, MD; and (iii) costs associated with US port arrival and unloading freight, such as in Boston, MA. To get the breakdown, they regress import charges on distance measures, weight and value of the product, and other observables. The regression helps remove second-component effects, leaving the first and third components in the error term. Identifying the first and third components is accomplished through the introduction of fixed effects for US and foreign ports. The authors note that as a port's contribution to import charges increases, costs increase, and thus the port's contribution will be inversely related to the port's efficiency. Hence, port fixed effects provide measures of port efficiencies. Blonigen and Wilson (2008) then test the estimated port efficiency measures by applying them to the regression of a port-to-port bilateral trade gravity model as an explanatory variable. They obtain a significant negative coefficient, confirming that their estimated port efficiency measurements reflect the transport costs, which have an explanatory power on bilateral trade.

17

Noting that data on direct transport costs are either unavailable or of poor quality, Nordas and Piermartini (2004) approximate transportation costs from information on distance, geography, and infrastructure quality in gravity equation regressions. The authors develop two types of indicators of infrastructure quality. First, they construct an index for each type of infrastructure (rail, road, port, airport, telecommunications, and time cost) that positions each country relative to the sample average. Second, the individual indicators are aggregated into one measure of overall infrastructure quality, following an approach similar to that of Limao and Venables (2001). For road quality, the authors consider the percentage of paved roads; for port quality they use the index developed by Clark et al. (2004); for airport quality they use the number of paved airports per 1,000 square kilometres; for telecommunications quality the main telephone lines per 1,000 people, and for time cost, the median port clearance time in terms of days. Data for the quality of roads, airports, and telecommunications are taken from the World Bank's World Development Indicators, and data for median port clearance time are based on surveys conducted by the World Bank on the imports of each country. All data refer to the year 2000. Econometric results indicate that a 10 per cent improvement in port efficiency in either exporting or importing increases bilateral trade by 6 per cent; that doubling the kilometres of paved roads per 100 square kilometres increases trade by 13 per cent; and that doubling the number of paved airports per square kilometres of territory in a country boosts trade by 14 per cent.

1.2.3 Regulatory Framework

Regulating the road freight transportation sector has been motivated in a large number of countries by concerns that competition could cause instability and lead to bankruptcies. Boylaud (2000) emphasizes that the main rationale for regulating the road freight business relates to road safety, the environment, and infrastructure congestion. Kunaka et al. (2013) maintain that market access regulations on road transport have their roots in the 1930s, when governments sought to protect railways from road competition by introducing a system of licenses, quotas, and tariffs. In this context, tight regulations were introduced in North America and Europe.

Historically, the road freight transportation sector has had many regulations with respect to entering and exiting the market, as in the case of Mexico. Prior to 1989, Mexico had extremely rigid regulations in the road freight transportation sector, with a high degree of government interference. As emphasized by Dutz et al. (2000, p. 1):

> Important government-imposed barriers to competition included entry restrictions to operate on federal highways, discretionary allocations of freight among

truckers, and strong restrictions on moving cargo outside the established transport corridors. Official tariffs applied to all cargo and a semipublic company held a monopoly in handling containers. Regulations did not allow companies to charge higher rates for better service and hence no incentive to offer better services. Neither did they allow them to compete with one another by offering lower rates. As a result, the trucking industry was characterized by a limited number of firms operating with minimal competition. Moreover, to maintain this highly inefficient and archaic system, the government employed a sizeable bureaucracy.

Thus, in Mexico, the effect of restrictions on itineraries or distances, the need to pass through freight centres, and the impossibility of transporting a load on the return journey diminished the productivity of the undertakings. These undertakings were protected from the full effects of competition, and as a result, they could enjoy higher returns. Hence, the consequence of quantitative regulations was to limit gains in productivity and technical and organizational innovations, thereby preventing a downward trend in transport prices, whether in relative or absolute terms.

To increase competition and the efficiency in road freight transport markets countries have to open up their road freight transport markets to competition not only in the internal market but also to competition from abroad. In a sense they have to liberalize the road freight transport services internally as well as externally. But how can countries liberalize when different countries have different regulatory regimes in the road freight transportation sector. In such cases countries often have little interest in each other's regulatory regimes, little confidence in the quality of other countries' regimes, and they are in general reluctant to change their own regulatory regimes. As long as the qualifications of different countries differ substantially and the associated complying costs are country specific, such factors become market-entry costs and may turn out to be prohibitive, thus hampering exports and investment.

In principle, countries can unilaterally choose to liberalize markets for road freight transportation services by adopting and implementing universally accepted norms and thereby achieving efficiency gains. Alternatively and also simultaneously, countries can use a multilateral engagement strategy, through negotiations under the World Trade Organization's (WTO) General Agreement on Trade in Services (GATS). Finally, the third alternative to road freight transport services liberalization is through regional cooperation.

The above considerations reveal that road freight transport services liberalization, whether pursued unilaterally or through multilateral engagement, and/or alternatively through regional cooperation, is a challenging task. To emphasize the problems related to trade liberalization of services trade within a regional context, consider the problems encountered in the recently proposed Transatlantic Trade and Investment Partnership (TTIP) between the EU and the US. Officially, the TTIP negotiations started in July 2013, and as of the end of June 2015 nine rounds of negotiation have taken place. The target year for ending the negotiations was set initially as 2015, although a large number of economists believed that negotiations could take longer.

According to the final report of the High Level Working Group on Jobs and Growth, TTIP negotiations should aim to achieve outcomes in (i) market access; (ii) regulatory issues and non-tariff barriers; and (iii) rules, principles, and new modes of cooperation to address shared global trade challenges and opportunities. Since each issue is rather challenging, we concentrate in this book only on services liberalization within TTIP, as in the rest of this study we analyse transportation services.

Recent research by Borchert et al. (2012a) indicates that barriers to services trade remain prevalent in EU countries and in the US. However, even among EU member countries, service barriers in different sectors vary considerably, as revealed by the OECD's Product Market Regulation indexes. Such barriers lead to inefficiencies in service sectors and to high costs of services. The TTIP agreement aims to eliminate these barriers by liberalizing services trade, which requires negotiating regulations shaping the functioning of these services markets.

There are essentially two ways to liberalize services trade: harmonization and mutual recognition of rules and regulations in different service sectors. The harmonization approach has been pursued intensively within the EU.[15] Under mutual recognition, countries agree to recognize the rules and regulations that determine the functioning of services markets in their respective economies. But this approach is based on mutual trust and requires, as a minimum, a relatively high degree of harmonization of rules and regulations in the relevant service sectors.

The US and the EU each has its own system of rules and regulations determining the functioning of its services sectors, and since both consider its own system superior to the other, and since there is no optimal system of rules and regulations, achieving harmonization between the two parties will be almost impossible. The only alternative is mutual recognition. But here the problem is to determine how high the minimum degree of harmonization of rules and regulations should be. A good example of mutual recognition is the Bilateral Aviation Safety Agreement (BASA) concluded between the US and the EU in 2011, which created a framework for bilateral cooperation on the certification of civil aircraft by focusing on (i) airworthiness approvals and monitoring civil aeronautical products; (ii) environmental testing; and (iii) approvals for monitoring maintenance facilities. Under BASA, the US Federal Aviation Administration and the European Aviation Safety Agency recognize each

---

[15] This issue is discussed in some detail in Chapters 3 to 6.

other's inspections and analyses so that two agencies can share information and avoid duplicating efforts. As emphasized by Akhtar and Jones (2014), BASA is expected to produce greater efficiency in transatlantic oversight of certification, continued airworthiness, and better maintenance by doing away with redundant certification activities through validating and accepting design approvals and repairs between the US and EU member states.

There is a third alternative to harmonization, which Messerlin (2014) calls mutual equivalence. Each party recognizes the other's implementation norms and procedures as fully equivalent to its own. As emphasized by Hoekman (2014), a necessary condition for mutual recognition is trust. Mutual equivalence requires as a preliminary step a joint process of mutual evaluation of the respective regulations by the two (or more) partners, and listing the goods and services to be excluded from mutual recognition in the sector in question. Thus, mutual equivalence requires regulatory bodies to participate in the negotiations. The procedure (in the TTIP case) is as follows: TTIP trade negotiators would draw up a list of sectors as candidates for mutual recognition. Then TTIP sectoral regulators would undertake a mutual evaluation of the regulations in question, and agree on which regulations could be considered as equivalent, possibly with some agreed-upon exceptions and reviews.

1.3 Global Value Chains

After World War II there was a tremendous increase in world trade, driven by lower trade costs achieved as a result of technological change, trade reforms, and the pursuit of outward-oriented policies. There were also important advances in the information and communication industries, developments in containerization, and improvements in logistics. Applied tariffs decreased substantially as a result of multilateral trade negotiations conducted within the context of GATT. Furthermore, developing countries, including China, started to liberalize their foreign trade regimes.

The reductions in trade costs achieved during the twentieth century led not only to increases in economic growth, but also to greater production fragmentation, with firms geographically spreading the different stages of their production processes. The developments in telecommunications and the Internet, together with organizational innovations and the development of international standards for product descriptions and business protocols, triggered a suite of information-management innovations that made it easier and cheaper to coordinate complex activities at a distance. Stages of production that previously had to be performed in close proximity within countries could now be dispersed from high-tech countries, a process called offshoring or international outsourcing: sourcing in low-wage nations without an enormous drop in efficiency and timeliness.[16]

The value chain describes the full range of activities to bring a product from its conception to its end use and beyond: design, production, marketing, and distribution and support to the final consumer. Those activities can, in general, be contained either in a single firm or divided among different firms. When the division takes place over geographic space, we talk of GVCs, which locate various stages of the production process in the world's most cost-efficient locations. In such cases multinational firms usually have to decide which activities to source outside the firm and which ones to keep internal. The decision to offshore depends on the difference between the cost advantage the firm receives from offshoring and the costs associated with the process of offshoring—called transaction costs or coordination costs. Recent research indicates that firms are inclined to relocate production aspects that require low skills and standard technologies (for example, component manufacturing and final assembly) to external providers, and that they are reluctant to source more complex and high-value-added activities externally. High-value activities turn out to be upstream activities such as R&D, product design, procurement, and human resource management, as well as downstream activities such as branding and advertising services.

Today, when firms set up production facilities abroad or form long-term ties with foreign suppliers, they expose their capital as well as their technical, managerial, and marketing know-how to new international risks. Bringing high-quality, competitively priced goods to customers in a timely manner requires international coordination of production facilities via the continuous two-way flow of goods, people, ideas, and investments. Such trade demands lower tariffs on parts and components as well as on final goods. The sharing of tacit and explicit technology and intellectual property requires that foreign knowledge-capital owners are treated fairly and that their property rights are respected. Hence, the FDI requires assurances on non-discrimination, rights of establishment, transferability of investment-related funds, investors' ability to choose top managers, anticompetitive practices, and the right to submit disputes with the host government to international arbitration as opposed to local courts. In addition, connecting factories in different counties often involves time-sensitive shipping, world-class telecommunication systems, and short-term movement of managers and technicians.

According to Baldwin (2013), the heart of GVC trade is an intertwining of (i) trade in goods, especially parts and components; (ii) international investment in production facilities, training, technology, and long-term business

---

[16] See Baldwin (2011a, 2011b).

relationships; (iii) the use of infrastructure services to coordinate dispersed production, especially services such as telecoms, Internet, express parcel delivery, air cargo, trade-related finance and customs clearance services; and (iv) cross-border flow of know-how, such as formal intellectual property know-how, as well as more-tacit forms such as managerial and marketing know-how. Baldwin (2006) calls this development the *trade-investment-services nexus*.

To clarify, consider the case of the Japanese company Toyota. In the past, Toyota produced all its car parts in Japan, either at Toyota itself or by sub-contracting some parts to other firms in Japan. Then, the company determined that developments in communication and coordination technology, together with low transportation costs, permitted the unbundling of production, and that it would be cheaper to produce some parts abroad. Today Toyota produces about 10 million cars worldwide, and each car consists of 20,000 to 30,000 parts. Some parts are produced in Thailand, and some in other countries. From Toyota's perspective, the problem is how to produce the parts cheaper in other locations but of the same quality or better.

Baldwin (2011b) emphasizes that recently, the most successful developing nations have joined GVCs from high-tech nations, namely the US, Japan, and Germany, and that rich-nation firms offshore segments of their value chains to developing nations. As a result, globalization's second unbundling has transformed industrialization. Before 1985, successful industrialization meant building a domestic supply chain, but today, developing countries join GVCs and grow rapidly. Offshore production quickly allows a firm to produce sophisticated manufactured goods that took Germany and Korea decades to develop domestically. Since GVCs are expected to expand further over time, developing countries are very much interested in joining them because they realize they can industrialize by doing so. But joining the GVCs requires fulfilling certain pre-conditions, and if these are not met, then companies such as Toyota will locate offshore stages elsewhere. How, then, should developing countries pursue active promotion of GVCs and support the process of upgrading towards higher value-added activities and thus diversify into higher value-added chains? What are the prerequisites for developing activities within value chains?

According to the UNCTAD (2013), the prerequisites for developing activities within value chains include (among others):

- Providing a conducive environment for trade and investment, which requires in addition to goods and services liberalization the adoption of appropriate competition policies, labour market regulations, and intellectual property rights protection;
- Trade facilitation, such as modernizing customs processes;
- Investment-facilitation measures related to procedures for FDI start-ups, registration and licensing, and to procedures for hiring key personnel;

- Providing reliable infrastructure (e.g. roads, ports, airports, telecommunications, broadband connectivity, and energy);
- Decreasing data transmission costs, facilitating data entry, R&D, or remotely supplied consultancy services;
- Harmonizing product standards and conformity-assessment procedures;
- Establishing a pool of relatively low-cost semi-skilled workers.

As mentioned above, goods in GVCs are traded across borders many times as intermediates and then as final products. A small tariff would then add up to a large tariff if applied several times in a production process. Similar considerations hold for transport costs every time the goods are shipped to another country for further processing. Administrative costs and delays incurred when intermediate goods cross borders are also cumulative in GVCs. Hence, in GVC trade it is very important that tariffs are eliminated, that transport and administrative costs are low, and that delays do not occur. On the other hand, lower barriers to investment are a must for participating in GVC trade, as they facilitate investments by lead firms, which result in economies being able to integrate into international production networks. Since services trade constitutes roughly one-third of trade on a value-added basis, services market efficiency is of prime importance for GVC trade. Furthermore, logistical operations, as pointed out by the OECD (2013), rely on port infrastructure efficiency and on the regulatory framework in the destination country. Thus, restrictive land, air, and sea transport regulations add to exporters' shipping costs. Delays in clearing customs and the time necessary to comply with various procedures at the border force firms to hold larger inventories, increasing costs.

The World Economic Forum (WEF (2012)) identifies four areas affecting supply chains: (i) market access, indicating the extent to which a country's policy framework welcomes foreign goods into the country's economy and enables access to foreign markets for its exports; (ii) border administration, indicating the extent to which it facilitates the entry and exit of goods; (iii) transport and communication infrastructures, indicating the extent to which a country has such infrastructures, which are necessary to facilitate the movement of goods within the economy and across borders; and (iv) business environment, indicating the quality of a country's government, including the regulatory and security environment affecting the business of importers and exporters active in the country. Since supply chain barriers add to operating and capital expenditure costs as well as increase risk, the market access, border administration, transport and communications infrastructures, and business environment need to be conducive to conducting trade. Thus, as emphasized by Hoekman (2014), reducing trade costs and improving connectivity to regional and global markets is a precondition for attracting GVC investments.

Returning to the case of Toyota, we note that the company is interested in producing parts cheaper but of the same quality or better quality in Thailand than when producing those parts in Japan. For Toyota to achieve this goal, Thailand has to satisfy the conditions specified above.

Looking at GVC trade from Thailand's point of view, the problem reduces to how this kind of trade can contribute to the country's economic and social performance. Such a formulation of the problem requires the measurement of GVC participation, which according to Koopman et al. (2011) and Kowalski et al. (2015), is defined in terms of the origin of the value added embodied in exports, looking both backward and forward from the reference country, which in our case is Thailand. While the backward participation index captures the extent to which domestic firms use foreign intermediate value added for exporting activities in a given country, the forward GVC participation index captures the extent to which the given country's exports are used by firms in partner countries as inputs into their own exports. By this construction, a high value of the backward participation index and a low value of the forward participation index, both expressed as shares of the reference country's exports, refer to a country that predominantly assembles products into final goods and exports them. On the other hand, a country that predominantly supplies intermediaries to an assembler will have a high forward participation measure but a small backward participation measure.

Kowalski et al. (2015) note that backward and forward linkages in GVCs tend to bring economic benefits such as enhanced productivity and sophistication and diversification of exports. On the other hand, the OECD, WTO, and the World Bank (2014) note that developing economies with the fastest-growing GVC participation have GDP per-capita growth rates 2 per cent above average. The authors show that in addition to countries' structural characteristics, the main determinants of GVC participation include trade and other policies pursued by the countries. While a country's main structural characteristics include market size, level of development, industrial structure, and location, its main trade and other policies include low import tariffs, inward FDI openness, logistics performance (including trade facilitation), intellectual property protection, infrastructure quality, and institutional quality. The results are more salient in the case of backward integration, as backward engagement is more closely linked to country characteristics such as market size and degree of industrialization. Forward integration, on the other hand, is concerned with the supply side of value chains, covering activities extending from the supply of natural resources by countries such as Russia and Australia, through high-tech intermediate inputs as in the cases of Germany and Japan, to specialized service providers such as the UK and the US.

Multinational enterprises (MNEs), such as Apple in electronics and Walmart in retailing, are called lead firms, and determine the location of GVC activities as well as the conditions under which other firms participate in GVCs. As emphasized by the WTO (2014), firms from developing countries mostly enter the GVC trade at the low-value-added manufacturing and assembly stages, where knowledge is often codifiable by standards and where capabilities required by the producers are relatively low. High-value-added activities such as research and development (R&D), design, marketing, and distribution are usually undertaken by lead firms, since those activities are not easily codifiable and brand value and recognition play a large role. From the perspective of developing countries that are part of GVC trade, the main issue is to how to upgrade and deepen their integration in GVCs. While upgrading refers to moving away from low-skill activities characterized by high competition and low entry barriers, deepening integration refers to the ability to establish backward linkages or transfer capabilities to new products and activities. According to the WTO (2014, p. 102) there are three different types of upgrading:

> The first is 'process upgrading', referring to improvements in the production process that result in more efficient transformation of inputs into outputs ... The second is 'product upgrading', consisting of introducing new products, changing designs, improving quality, and producing a more sophisticated final output. The third is 'functional upgrading', involving moving into different stages of production or functions beyond production within a given GVC.

In 2005 the OECD launched the Aid-for-Trade Initiative following the 2005 Hong Kong WTO Ministerial Conference. The survey conducted within this initiative asked developing country firms what the main barriers were that prevented their participation in value chains. The survey revealed that firms consider standards compliance, delays, cumbersome customs procedures, high price and poor quality of transport services, and inadequate transport infrastructures (among others) as the main barriers preventing their participation in value chains. A discussion of the prerequisites for developing activities within value chains revealed that a high-quality transport infrastructure with appropriate airports, harbours, railways, and roads is essential for participation in GVCs. Adopting appropriate regulations in the transport sector to increase competition within the country, and increased access to foreign markets would also help countries overcome such obstacles.

On the empirical side, estimating GVC trade is rather difficult. To measure amounts of offshoring, economists use the share of trade in parts and components in total trade. Data reveal that this share has been increasing very rapidly during the last decade. To measure offshoring in the case of services trade, economists use data on 'other business services' in the IMF's Balance of Payments Statistics. These studies reveal that trade in 'other business services' has also been increasing rather rapidly during the last decade. The increasing importance of offshoring provides an indication of GVC development.

In the case of GVC trade, an intermediate commodity may be exported by one country for further processing to another country. The second country may export the processed commodity to a third country, which may then export the manufactured product to a fourth country for final consumption. The exports of the third country will include the value of intermediate goods exported by the second country, and since the value of exports by the second country will include the value of intermediate goods exported by the first country, we note that trade in intermediate goods leads to a significant amount of double counting in global trade. Thus, export figures do not necessarily mean that a country creates and captures a large share of the value added by GVCs. To make the point clearer, WTO (2014) gives the following example: Suppose that Country A exports intermediate goods to Country B for a value of 100 units. Country B processes further the intermediate goods and exports a final product worth 110 units to Country C. While the total value of trade between these countries amounts to 210 units, the total value added among the three countries is only 110 units, of which 100 units have been generated by Country A and 10 units by Country B. While under conventional measures Country C has a trade deficit of 110 units with B and no trade with A, C's trade deficit with B in terms of the value added reduces to 10 units, and C's trade deficit with A measured in terms of value added increases to 100 units.

Since statistics on international trade flows are collected in gross terms, they record the value of intermediate inputs traded along the value chain multiple times. To capture the role of GVCs in international trade, adjustments must be made to trade data, and the most common method of measuring trade in GVCs is the use of input-output tables. By constructing these tables for different countries in a uniform manner, a value chain can be calculated for the final goods sold. Current GVC trade analysis along input-output tables relies mainly on the World Input-Output Database (WIOD), the UN Conference of Trade and Development's EORA GVC database, and on the Global Trade Analysis Project (GTAP) database.[17] But these results are based on single efforts. In 2012, the OECD and the WTO joined forces to develop a database of indicators based on trade in value-added goods (the TiVA database), the latest version of which was released in June 2013 and includes input-output tables for fifty-eight countries and thirty-seven sectors for the years 1995, 2000, 2005, 2008, and 2009.

The question of how much value value-added trade actually generates was recently answered by the UNCTAD (2013), using its EORA GVC database. The

---

[17] The WIOD database, funded by the European Commission, includes 27 EU members and 13 other major economies for the period 1995 to 2009 and covers 35 sectors. The UNCTAD-EORA database includes data for 187 countries for 1990 to 2011 and covers 25 sectors. Finally, the GTAP database includes input-output tables for 129 countries or regions and 57 sectors for the years 1992, 1995, 1997, 2001, 2004, 2007, and 2011.

study estimates that the average foreign value of exports at the global level is 28 per cent, implying that about US$5 trillion of the US$19 trillion of world exports of goods and services during 2010 was contributed by foreign countries. Thus, the value added in trade amounted to about US$14 trillion in 2010. The study further revealed that the electronics, automotive, and textiles sectors have been at the forefront of value chain segmentation, that GVC participation has varied considerably among countries, and that about 80 per cent of global trade is linked to transnational corporations' international production networks. Studies of the Chinese and Mexican cases reveal that while in Mexico, one-third of the export value derives from value-added activities, in China, that share reaches 66.2 per cent.[18]

Noting that services are part of almost every activity in an economy, we next turn to an empirical determination of their role in international trade. The WTO (2014) points out that while services are traded directly across borders, the more important trade occurs when goods are traded that embody services. In particular, the logistics services, domestic engineering services, and financial services used when producing a car will be exported indirectly when the car gets exported. Recently, using the OECD TiVA database, the WTO estimated that the share of commercial services in world trade amounted to 45 per cent in value-added terms and 23 per cent in gross terms.[19] Using the GTAP database, Francois et al. (2013) also estimate the share of services embodied in trade on a value-added basis, and show that services trade constitutes roughly one-third of trade on a value-added basis and that most exports of services on a value-added basis are embodied in goods exports. Thus, reforms in services trade across all services sectors are important to improve strategies for enhancing firms' competitiveness. Finally, note that one of the most important service sectors is transport together with trade, constituting in 2007 13.9 per cent of all exports on a value-added basis. Hence, particularly the reform of transport sectors, which is the topic of the present study, is of crucial importance for enhancing firm competitiveness.

Although value chains are said to be global, in fact they are not. They have a strong regional focus, as indicated by the fact that the foreign value added to economies' exports originates largely in neighbouring countries (OECD, 2013). In Asia, the majority of intermediate goods used in the production of other commodities and embodied in exports are sourced from Factory Asia, consisting of countries like Thailand, Vietnam, and China that supply the intermediates mainly to Japan. Similar considerations apply to the US (and thus to Factory North America) and to Germany (and hence to Factory Europe). This situation is related to the role of distance and trade costs because

---

[18] See De La Cruz et al. (2012) and Pilat et al. (2012).
[19] See Park et al. (2013) and Low (2013).

inputs are often shipped multiple times. International supply chains require face-to-face and face-to-machine interactions. Although transport costs have decreased substantially over the last few decades, the costs of moving technicians and managers increase with distance. Furthermore, timely deliveries of intermediates are crucial for the smooth functioning of GVCs, and the adoption of just-in-time techniques is pushing firms to locate the production of time-sensitive components closer to home.[20]

In Europe, 60 to 70 per cent of exports' foreign value-added content comes from other European countries (OECD, 2013). Similar considerations hold for the NAFTA region and Asia. In the former, almost half of the imported intermediates embodied in US exports originate from NAFTA countries, and in Asia components are produced by Japan and Korea and then exported to China (and increasingly to Vietnam and Cambodia), where they are assembled into finished products.

1.4 Conclusion

This book on transportation services, studying the effects of changes in infrastructure and regulatory frameworks in the transportation sector, examines not only the unilateral liberalization of transport services but also the liberalization of transport services within a regional context. The book provides a thorough discussion of international and regional rules and regulations in road transportation, rail transportation, maritime transportation, and air transportation, and analyses the effects of liberalization in the various transport sectors. When considering liberalization transport services within a regional context, we study the experience of the EU in detail and make reference to the case of Turkey, a candidate for EU accession. Turkey, when liberalizing the transport services, has to follow the harmonization approach which requires that the country adopts and strictly implements the EU rules and regulations of the EU in the transport sector. Therefore we devote quite a few chapters to the discussion of the EU and Turkish rules and regulations in the various transport sectors. Such an approach has the advantage of making it possible on the one hand to open up the prosperous EU market to Turkish producers of transport services and on the other hand to satisfy a precondition for attracting GVC investments by providing reliable transport infrastructure.

The book is structured as follows: Chapter 2 discusses the transport sectors in Turkey, with Section 2.1 providing a general overview of the Turkish road, rail, maritime, and air transport sectors, emphasizing the current state as well

---

[20] For the derivation of the above three results, see Table 1.A1 in Annex 2 to this chapter, showing the structure of a general input-output table with two countries and n-sectors.

future developments. Section 2.2 provides an analysis of inter-industry linkage effects. Using an input-output framework, the section shows how important the different transport sectors are for the economy. While Section 2.3 considers the market structure in the Turkish transport sectors using firm-level data, Section 2.4 studies the state of competition in the Turkish transport sectors using mark-ups. Finally, Section 2.5 concludes.

Chapter 3 explores the regulatory framework in road freight transportation. Section 3.1 discusses the functioning of the road freight transportation sector, Section 3.2 considers the bilateral and multilateral transport agreements, Section 3.3 covers the EU rules and regulations, and Section 3.4 the Turkish rules and regulations. In each case, the rules and regulations are explained under the headings of 'Market Access and Competition', 'Prices and Fiscal Conditions', 'Social Conditions', 'Technical Conditions', 'Road Safety', and 'International Transport Networks'.

Chapter 4 examines the regulatory framework in rail transport services. Section 4.1 introduces the basic characteristics of railway services, Section 4.2 considers the international regulatory regime in the rail sector, and Section 4.3 covers EU railway rules and regulations, which are studied under the headings of 'First Railway Package', 'Second Railway Package', 'Third Railway Package', 'The Fourth Railway Package', and 'Trans-European Rail Transport Networks and Rail Freight Corridors'. Finally, Section 4.4 studies regulatory issues in the Turkish railway sector.

In Chapter 5, we turn to maritime services and note that the sector is inherently international in character. Since vessels on most voyages must comply with the regulatory requirements of multiple jurisdictions, there is an inherent need for harmonization across countries. Thus, to liberalize the sector, countries must adopt not only international norms, but in the case of regional integrations, also the rules and regulations of countries with stricter regulations. Chapter 5 is structured as follows: Section 5.1 discusses the functioning of the maritime freight transport sector, Section 5.2 considers the international regulatory regime in the sector, Section 5.3 covers the EU rules and regulations, and Section 5.4 explains the Turkish rules and regulations. In each case, rules and regulations are studied under the headings of 'Internal Market', 'Port Infrastructure', 'Social Conditions', and 'Safety and Environment'.

Similar considerations hold for the air transport sector (Chapter 6), where the provision of air transport services is tightly linked to so-called ancillary services, consisting of air-traffic control, the booking system, ground handling, catering, and maintenance. Chapter 6 studies the regulatory framework in the air transportation sector, with Section 6.1 providing a brief introduction to its functioning, Section 6.2 discussing international rules and regulations, and Section 6.3 focusing on EU rules and regulations under the headings of 'Economic Policy', 'Air Safety', 'Air Traffic Management', and 'External Policy'.

While Section 6.4 concentrates on the study of the regulatory framework in the Turkish air freight transport sector, Section 6.5 concludes.

The final chapter studies the effects of liberalization in Turkish transportation sectors. The chapter is structured as follows. Section 7.1 analyses how the Turkish transport sectors opened up. Section 7.2 discusses the World Bank's new Services Restrictions Database as well as the OECD's Services Trade Restrictiveness Index and the OECD's Indicators of Product Market Regulation. Section 7.3 quantitatively determines the tariff equivalents of barriers to trade in the different transport sectors in Turkey and in the country's major export markets using the approach developed by Chen and Novy (2011). Section 7.4 discusses the quantification of policy restrictiveness and Section 7.5 analyses the effects of liberalization in transport service sectors using a computable general equilibrium model. Finally, Section 7.6 discusses the economic impacts of infrastructure development, and Section 7.7 concludes.

Annex 1: Trade and Transportation Costs in the Ricardian Model

Consider the two-country (home and foreign), multiple commodity, and one-factor of production (labour) model of international trade. Let the constant unit labour requirements for goods in the home country be given by $(l_1, \ldots, l_i, \ldots, l_n)$, and let the constant unit labour requirements for goods in the foreign country be given by $(l_1^*, .., l_i^*, .. l_n^*)$. The relative labour productivity ratio in sector i, defined as labour productivity in sector i of the home country over the labour productivity in sector i of the foreign country, is given by $a(i) = \frac{l_i^*}{l_i}$ $(i = 1, \ldots, n)$. Order the commodities in descending order when the first commodity equals max{a(1),.., a(i),..,a(n)} and the last commodity equals min {a(1),.., a(i),..,a(n)}. Denote the strictly decreasing relative labour productivity schedule by the relation A(i). Total labour supply in the home country is L units, and total labour supply in the foreign country is L* units.

Choose Commodity 1 as the numeraire so that all variables are measured in terms of Commodity 1, that is, $p_1 = p_1^* = 1$. Suppose that both economies operate under perfectly competitive conditions. Assume that the home country and the foreign country have the same preferences, given by the Cobb-Douglas function:

$$u = D_1^{a_1}..D_n^{a_n},$$

where D_i denotes consumption of Commodity i, and $a_i > 0$ so that $\sum_{i=1}^{i=n} a_i = 1$ are constant parameters. Given the prices of the commodities p_i (i=1,..,n) we assume that consumers maximize the utility function subject to the budget constraint.

Let w and w* denote the wage rates at home and foreign country respectively, wL the income of the home country, and w*L* the income of the foreign country. Assume that consumers purchase goods from the lowest-cost producers. When trade costs are zero the price of each good under free trade will be equal in the two countries and will be given by $p(i) = p^*(i) = \min\{wl_i, w^*l_i^*\}$. Then for a given relative wage rate (w/w^*), there is a marginal good z, defined by the relation:

$$a(z) \geq (w/w^*) > a(z+1),$$

so that the home country produces goods in $[1, z]$, and the foreign country produces goods in $[z+1, n]$. The prices of the n-commodities now become $p(i) = p^*(i) = w\,l_i$ for $i \in [1, z]$ and $p(i) = p^*(i) = w^*l_i^*$ for $i \in (z+1, n]$.

Under the given assumptions, income equals total expenditure in each country so that:

$$wL = \sum_{i=1}^{i=n} p_i\, D_i \text{ and } w^*L^* = \sum_{i=1}^{i=n} p_i^*\, D_i^*,$$

where D_i denotes consumption of Commodity i in the home country and D_i^* consumption of Commodity i in the foreign country. Given the total world income $(w\,L + w^*\,L^*)$, we note that it equals the total world expenditure $\sum_{i=1}^{i=n}(p_i\, D_i + p_i^* D_i^*)$. Define a new variable $h(j)$ so that:

$$h(j) = a_1 + a_2 + .. + a_j.$$

Since home produces the goods $[1, z]$ the total expenditure on home goods equals:

$$h(z)(w\,L + w^*\,L^*),$$

which must be equal to home income, $w\,L$, in equilibrium. Thus, we have:

$$h(z)(w\,L + w^*\,L^*) = w\,L,$$

yielding the relation:

$$(w/w^*) = \left[\frac{h(z)}{(1 - h(z))}\right]\left[\frac{L^*}{L}\right]$$

Note that this relation, shown by B(i) in Figure 1.A1, is upward sloping, which Matsuyama (2009) explains as follows: since higher z means that a larger fraction of the world expenditure goes to goods by home country labour, relative wage (w/w^*) goes up.

The intersection of the curves A(i) and B(i) determines the equilibrium relative wage rate, w/w^*, and thus the equilibrium pattern of trade and specialization. The home country exports and the foreign country imports commodities $[1, z]$ and the foreign country exports and the home country imports goods $[z+1, n]$. Thus, each country exports those commodities in the production of which they have a comparative advantage measured in terms of relative productivities.

Consider now the effects of introducing trade costs into the simple Ricardian model of international trade. Trade costs are introduced into the model assuming that each good, when shipped abroad, melts away in transit and only a fraction $g < 1$ arrives to the destination. This Iceberg formulation of transportation costs employed by Samuelson (1952) assumes that in order to supply one unit of a good, the exporter must produce $1/g$ units of the good. In such a case home country will export the good i as long as $l_i\, w/g < l_i^*\, w^*$ or $\left(\dfrac{w}{w^*g}\right) < a(i)$. On the other hand, the foreign country will export commodity i to the home country as long as $l_i\, w > (l_i^*\, w^*/g)$ or $\left(\dfrac{wg}{w^*}\right) > a(i)$.

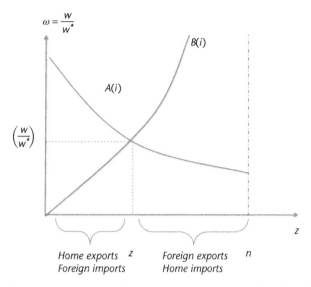

Figure 1.A1 Determination of equilibrium pattern of trade in the Ricardian model of international trade

Source: Matsuyama (2009).

The above considerations reveal that there are two marginal goods z_1 and z_2 defined by:

$$\left(\frac{w}{w^* g}\right) = a(z_1), \tag{1}$$

$$\left(\frac{w g}{w^*}\right) = a(z_2). \tag{2}$$

In this case home country produces all goods in the interval $[1, z_1)$ for both countries, and foreign country produces all commodities in the interval $(z_2, n]$ for both countries, and the commodities in $[z_1, z_2]$ become non-traded goods so that each country produces all goods (z_1, z_2) locally. Total expenditure on the goods produced at home country equals:

$$h(z_1)[w L + w^* L^*] + [h(z_2) - h(z_1)] w L,$$

which must be equal to the home country income wL in equilibrium. From the relation:

$$h(z_1)[w L + w^* L^*] + [h(z_2) - h(z_1)] w L = w L.$$

This equation yields the condition:

$$(w/w^*) = \left[\frac{h(z_1)}{(1 - h(z_2))}\right]\left[\frac{L^*}{L}\right]. \tag{3}$$

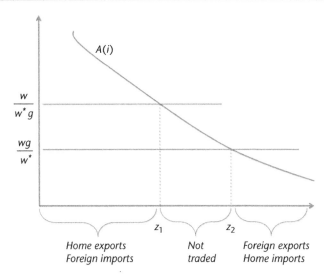

Figure 1.A2 Determination of equilibrium pattern of trade in the Ricardian model of international trade with transport costs

Source: Matsuyama (2009).

For given value of g these three equations determine the three endogenous variables z_1, z_2, and (w/w*) shown in Figure 1.A2.

This model originally developed by Dornbush et al. (1977) for a continuum of goods can be used to study the effects of decreases in transportation costs shown by increases in g. The model indicates that an increase in g leads to an increase z_1 and a decrease in z_2. Thus decreases in transportation costs leads to decreases in non-traded goods and increases in trade.

Annex 2: Global Value Chain Analysis

Consider Table 1.A1 based on Powers (2012) and Jones et al. (2013). Following Powers (2012), we note that the rows in the table indicate how and where products are used and the columns show total inputs from Country 1 and Country 2, plus value added in the related country that must be supplied to produce the total product output in the related country. Let X_1 be the nx1 vector of gross outputs of Country 1, X_2 the nx1 vector of gross outputs of Country 2,

$$X = \begin{bmatrix} X_1 \\ X_2 \end{bmatrix}$$

the 2nx1 vector of gross outputs, and $\hat{X}$ the diagonalized 2nx2n matrix of gross outputs. $A_1 = (a_{ij}^1)$, the nxn matrix of direct intermediate domestic input-output coefficients a_{ij}^1, indicating the intermediate input use of Domestic Sector i output in the production of one unit of output of Sector j in Country 1, $A_2 = (a_{ij}^2)$, the nxn matrix of direct intermediate domestic input-output coefficients a_{ij}^2 indicating the intermediate

34

Table 1.A1 A two-country input-output table with n-sectors

		Intermediate use					Final use		Total use
		Country 1			Country 2		Country 1	Country 2	
		Industry 1	....	Industry n	Industry 1	.... Industry n			
Country 1	Industry 1 . . Industry n	Country 1's use of its own inputs			Country 2's use of inputs from country 1		Country 1's use of own final goods	Country 2's use of final goods from Country 1	Country 1's total output
Country 2	Industry 1 . . Industry n	Country 1's use of inputs from country 2			Country 2's use of its own inputs		Country 1's use of final goods from Country 2	Country 2's use of own final goods	Country 2's total output
Value added		Country 1's value added			Country 2's value added				
Total Supply		Country 1's total output			Country 2's total output				

Source: Powers (2012).

input use of Domestic Sector i output in the production of one unit of output of Sector j in Country 2, $M_1 = m^1_{ij}$, the nxn matrix of direct intermediate imported input-output coefficients m^1_{ij} indicating the intermediate input use of Imported Sector i output from Country 2 in the production of one unit of output of Sector j in Country 1, and $M_2 = (m^2_{ij})$, the nxn matrix of direct intermediate imported input-output coefficients m^2_{ij}, indicating the intermediate input use of Imported Sector i output from Country 1 in the production of one unit of output of Sector j in Country 2. Let:

$$A = \begin{bmatrix} A_1 & M_2 \\ M_1 & A_2 \end{bmatrix}$$

be the input-output coefficient matrix, F_1 the nx1 vector of Country 1's use of its final demand for domestic goods, F_2 the nx1 vector of Country 2's use of its final demand for domestic goods,

$$F = \begin{bmatrix} F_1 \\ F_2 \end{bmatrix}$$

be the 2nx1 vector of final demands for domestic goods by the two countries, and $\hat{F}$ be the diagonalized 2nx2n matrix of final demands. Then, the relations in Table 1.A1 can be written as:

$$\hat{X} = A\hat{X} + \hat{F}.$$

Solving for $\hat{X}$, we can express this equation as:

$$\hat{X} = (I - A)^{-1}\hat{F} = B\hat{F},$$

where B 2nx2n is the 'Leontief inverse' matrix. Elements of this matrix show the total output both directly and indirectly required to produce one unit of final goods and services.

Let V_1 denote the 1xn vector of unit value-added coefficients, indicating the amount of value contributed directly by primary factors per unit of output in Country 1, V_2 the 1xn vector of unit value-added coefficients, indicating the amount of value contributed directly by primary factors per unit of output in Country 2, and:

$$V = [V_1 V_2]$$

the unit value-added vector. Pre-multiplying $\hat{X}$ by V produces the global GDP for the world economy, that is,

$$V\hat{X} = VB\hat{F}.$$

To study how much value value-added trade actually generates, consider the two-country case and assume that the first country is the EU and the second country is the rest of the world. Then set F_1 equal to EU exports and F_2 equal to rest of the world's exports. Let u be the 2nx1 unit column vector. Then $VB\hat{F}u$ yields the value added contained in the total exports of Countries 1 and 2. By comparing this number with the value of total actual exports by Countries 1 and 2, one could state that the average domestic value of value-added exports at the global level is a per cent and that the foreign value of value-added of exports at the global level is $(1 - a)$ per cent.

2

Transport Sectors in Turkey

Co-authored with Nergiz Dinçer

This chapter, exploring the road, rail, maritime, and air transport sectors in Turkey, is structured as follows: Section 2.1 provides a general overview of the Turkish road, rail, maritime, and air transport sectors. Section 2.2 analyses inter-industry linkage effects using an input-output framework, Section 2.3 considers the market structure in the Turkish transport sectors using firm-level data, and Section 2.4 studies the state of competition in the Turkish transport sectors using mark-ups. Finally, Section 2.5 concludes.

2.1 An Overview of Turkish Transport Sectors

Turkey is a large country with mountainous terrain and harsh winter conditions, and distances across the country are relatively long: from the Bulgarian border in the west to Iran in the east is 1,750 km and from the Bulgarian border to Iraq is 1,900 km. Transportation connecting different parts of the country lies at the core of recent developments in the international integration of economic activity. The transport sector accounted for more than 5 per cent of the gross domestic product (GDP) and of employment in Organisation for Economic Co-operation and Development (OECD) countries during 2010. In Turkey, transport together with storage contributed 11.96 per cent to the GDP in 2013.

The main institution responsible for the transport sector at the central government level in Turkey is the Ministry of Transport, Maritime Affairs, and Communications (MoTMC). The ministry is responsible for developing the infrastructure for road, rail, maritime, and air transport modes; for the regulation of transport operations in the various modes; and for supervising state economic enterprises (SEEs) in the transport sector. Institutions attached to the MoTMC include the Directorate General of Highways (KGM) and the Directorate General of Civil Aviation (DGCA). Related institutions consist of the Directorate General of State Railways (TCDD), the Directorate General of State Airports Authority (DHMI), and the Directorate General of Coastal Safety (KEGM). The KGM is responsible for developing and maintaining state and provincial roads and motorways, the TCDD is responsible for operating the railways and some of the country's major ports, the DGCA supervises and monitors the air transport sector, the DHMI manages air navigation systems and most airports, and the KEGM is concerned with coastal safety in Turkish waters.

The backbone of Turkey's transport system consists of 65,909 km of roads (as of January 2015) and 12,485 km of rail (as of 2014). Surrounded by seas on three sides, Turkey has a coastline of 8,323 km. Turkey's transport system relies essentially on road transportation. In 2012, while the share of road transportation in freight transport according to Eurostat was 75.1 per cent in the European Union-28 (EU-28), that share amounted to 94.7 per cent in Turkey. Similarly, while the share of rail transportation in freight transport was 18.2 per cent in the EU-28, that share amounted to 5.3 per cent in Turkey. Finally, while the share of inland waterways in freight transport was 6.7 per cent in the EU-28, it amounted to almost zero per cent in Turkey. On the other hand, the share of passenger cars in passenger transport was 83.3 per cent in the EU-28, and 61.6 per cent in Turkey. Similarly, while the share of trains in passenger transport was 7.4 per cent in the EU-28, it was 1.7 per cent in Turkey. Finally, the share of motor coaches, buses, and trolleys in passenger transport was 9.2 per cent in the EU-28 and 36.6 per cent in Turkey.[1]

An examination of Turkish exports and imports by transport mode reveals that in the case of foreign trade, the Turkish transport system relies essentially on sea and road modes. In 2014, the share of sea transportation in exports amounted to 54.76 per cent, the share of road 35.07 per cent, air 8.95 per cent, and rail 0.6 per cent. On the other hand, the share of sea transportation in imports amounted to 58.4 per cent, roads 15.4 per cent, air 10.2 per cent, and rail 0.5 per cent.

Turkey's transport sector has been growing relatively quickly. Road freight traffic increased from 151.4 billion tonne-km in 2001 to 234.5 billion tonne-km in 2014 and rail freight increased from 7.6 billion tonne-km in 2001 to 11.2 billion tonne-km in 2013. Similarly, maritime container freight transport increased from 1.2 thousand TEUs in 2003 to 3.4 thousand TEUs in 2013, and

---

[1] According to the Ministry of Transport, Maritime Affairs, and Communications (2015), the share of roads in Turkish passenger transport is 90.3 per cent, the share of air 7.9 per cent, rail 1.3 per cent, and sea 0.6 per cent. The share of roads in Turkish freight transport is 88.7 per cent, rail 4.4 per cent, and sea 6.9 per cent.

air freight traffic increased from 763.2 thousand tonnes in 2001 to 2.6 million tonnes in 2013.[2] Between 2001 and 2013 annual demand growth rates were 3.3 per cent for road freight transport, 3.8 per cent for rail freight transport, 2.4 per cent for maritime freight transport, and 10 per cent for air freight transport.[3]

To assess the quality of the transport network we consider the World Economic Forum's (2014a and 2006) *Global Competitiveness Report*. According to the 2014 report, Turkey ranks fortieth country out of 144 countries in the quality index for roads, with a score of 4.9. In 2006, Turkey ranked fifty-third in the quality index for roads among 125 countries, with a score of 3.7. Both rankings are based on survey questions that ask respondents to rate the quality of roads in their country from 1 (extremely underdeveloped) to 7 (extensive, efficient, and among the best in the world). Both in 2006 and 2014 Turkey ranked below Malaysia, Korea, and South Africa. Regarding railroad infrastructure quality, Turkey was forty-ninth out of 144 countries in 2014, with a score of 3.1. In 2006, it ranked sixty-seventh, with a score of 2.3, and in both those years it ranked below Korea, Malaysia, and China. The figures indicate, however, that there was some improvement in the quality of rail infrastructure in the time between the two surveys. According to the quality of port infrastructure, in 2014 Turkey was fifty-seventh out of 144 countries, with a score of 4.4, and seventy-sixth among 125 countries in 2006, with a score of 3.1. Both times, it again ranked below Malaysia, Korea, and China. Finally, regarding air transport infrastructure quality, Turkey was thirty-fourth among 144 countries in 2014, and fifty-fourth among 125 countries in 2006. In both 2006 and 2014 Turkey ranked below Korea, Malaysia, and South Africa. The above results do reveal that there was considerable improvement between 2006 and 2014 in road, rail, port, and air transport infrastructure.

According to the WEF's (2014b) *Global Enabling Trade Report*, Turkey ranks at about the same level as Thailand and Poland in terms of 'availability and quality of transport infrastructure', and ranks below Korea, Malaysia, and China, but above Poland and Greece.[4] In the overall ranking out of 138 countries Turkey ranks thirty-first in air transport infrastructure quality, fiftieth in railroad infrastructure quality, twentieth in the liner shipping

---

[2] TEU stands for '20-foot equivalent unit'.
[3] Due to data limitations, the growth rate for maritime freight is estimated only for the period 2001–11.
[4] The Enabling Trade Index assesses the extent to which economies have in place institutions, policies, infrastructures, and services facilitating the free flow of goods over borders and to their destinations. The set of trade-enabling factors is organized in four main categories: market access, border administration, infrastructure and operating environment. For infrastructure, the index assesses the availability and quality of a country's transport infrastructure, the associated services, and the communication infrastructure necessary to facilitate the movement of goods within the country and across the border.

connectivity index, fifty-eighth in port infrastructure quality, thirty-third in kilometres of paved roads, and fortieth in road quality. Although the Enabling Trade Index has been prepared since 2008 it is not possible to compare the index values over time as major methodological changes have been introduced to the calculations.

The World Bank's *Logistics Performance Index and its Indicators* (LPI) report ranks Turkey in 2014 as thirtieth out of 160 countries, with a score of 3.5.[5] In 2007 Turkey ranked thirty-fourth out of 150 countries, with a score of 3.15. Since LPI values range between 0 and 5, and a higher LPI value for a particular country indicates that the country's logistics sector is more developed, we can assert that the quality of Turkey's logistics sector improved between 2007 and 2014. But there is still more scope for improvement, as Turkey's LPI index lies below those of Taiwan, Korea, Malaysia, and China in both periods. According to the LPI, 51.6 (60) per cent of respondents believe that port (airport) charges were high/very high; 35.5 (24.1) per cent of respondents believe that the road (rail) transport rates were high/very high; and 37.9 (16.7) per cent of respondents believe that warehousing/transloading charges (agent fees) were high/very high during 2014.

The above considerations reveal that in Turkey there is a strong need to improve the transport infrastructure. Recognizing this need, in its 2010 transport strategy the Turkish government set ambitious targets for 2023, the one hundredth anniversary of the establishment of the Republic of Turkey.[6] The document announced plans to expand motorways threefold, from 2,250 km to 7,500 km, and to almost double the length of divided roads—from 19,700 km to 32,000 km. Similarly, the plan more than doubles the railway infrastructure capacity, from 11,005 km to 25,536 km. The government also aims to increase the share of railways from 5 per cent to 15 per cent in freight transportation and from 2 per cent to 10 per cent in passenger transportation. These targets require reducing the share of road transport to 60 per cent for freight and to 72 per cent for passengers. The government estimates a total cost of TL 379 (US$252.6) billion in 2010 prices for the new investments. Of that cost, the government is aiming to finance 21 per cent itself, which amounts to about TL 78 billion, and finance the rest through the private sector

---

[5] The logistics performance (LPI) is the weighted average of the country scores on six key dimensions: (i) efficiency of the clearance process (i.e. speed, simplicity, and predictability of formalities) by border control agencies, including customs; (ii) quality of trade- and transport-related infrastructure (e.g. ports, railroads, roads, information technology); (iii) ease of arranging competitively priced shipments; (iv) competence and quality of logistics services (e.g. transport operators, customs brokers); (v) ability to track and trace consignments; and (vi) timeliness of shipments in reaching their destinations within the scheduled or expected delivery times.
[6] See Ministry of Transport (2010). Note that the Ministry of Transport (MoT) was restructured in 2011 and MoT became the Ministry of Transportation, Maritime Affairs, and Communications (MoTMC).

by public–private partnership (PPP) projects. However, the need for additional annual fiscal resources at about 3 per cent of the GDP poses a major challenge. We now turn to a closer consideration of the developments in Turkey's road, rail, maritime, and air transportation sectors in some detail.

2.1.1 Road Transportation

Figure 2.1 shows the current road map of Turkey. Turkish public roads are classified into motorways, state highways, provincial roads, and rural roads.[7] As noted above, the General Directorate of Highways (KGM) is responsible for planning, designing, constructing, maintaining, and operating motorways, as well as state highways and provincial roads. It is a public entity with special budget financing under the auspices of the MoTMC, and its main financial resource is the government budget. The Special Provincial Administration is in charge of village and forest roads, and urban roads are under the administration of municipal authorities. Basic data on the road network provided by the KGM reveals that as of January 2015, the road network consists of 2,155 km of motorways, 31,280 km of state highways, and 32,474 km of provincial roads. The total length of roads with asphaltic concrete, that is, capable of handling heavy-axle loads, stands at 18,077 km, and roads with a surface treatment have a total length of 44,277 km.[8] The entire road network in Turkey, including village roads but excluding urban roads, is 386,500 km in length.

In 2003, the KGM began upgrading existing single carriageways into dual carriageways with the aim of reducing traffic fatalities and serious injuries from head-on collisions, and began improving the level of service that was due to inadequate capacity. Further benefits of dual carriageways include reduced emissions achieved through reduced stop-start traffic, reduced traffic congestion, reduced driver stress, improved journey time, and improved connectivity. The length of dual carriageway roads opened to traffic has increased from 5,821 km in 2001 to 22,460 km in 2014, including motorways.

Analysing the Turkish road network within an international context on the basis of length per 1,000 km^2 and length per 10,000 population reveals that Turkey's numbers are much lower than those of other countries. In the first

---

[7] Motorways are access-controlled, multi-lane, divided highways. On motorways tolls are collected at designated points. While state highways are highways of primary importance, connecting provincial centres, seaports, airports, and railway stations to each other, provincial roads are highways of secondary importance, linking districts within a province to each other, the provincial centres, the districts in neighboring provinces, state roads, railway stations, seaports, and airports.

[8] In Turkey, types of asphalt pavement are categorized as follows: bituminous surface treatment (some dating from the 1960s), cold-mix asphalt, and bituminous hot mix (BHM) asphalt. Although BHM costs more initially than bituminous surface treatment, it is more economical in the long term because it lasts longer and is easier to drive on.

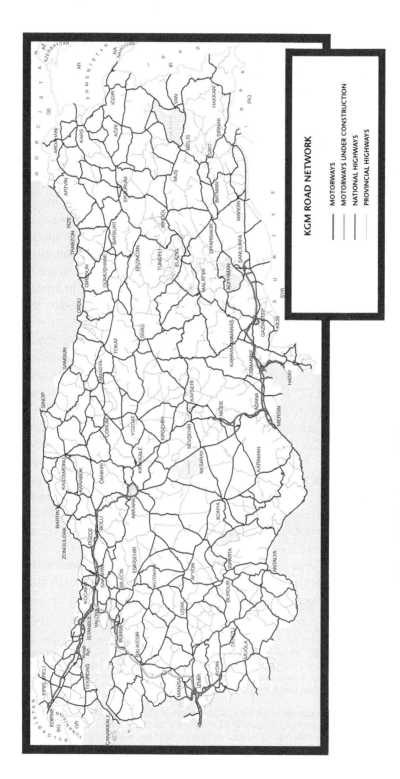

Figure 2.1 Road map of Turkey

Source: Directorate General of Highways (KGM). Reproduced with permission.

criterion, Turkey ranks lower than EU countries, the US, Japan, and India, and exceeds only Russia and China. In the second criterion, Turkey ranks lower than EU countries, the US, and Russia, ranking close to India.

In 2013, the total number of vehicles in Turkey amounted to 16.4 million, of which 9.3 million were passenger cars, 2.9 million small trucks, 756,000 trucks, and 219,900 buses. As modes of freight transport other than road are largely underdeveloped in Turkey, a great amount of pressure is put on the road infrastructure. The percentage of roads in good or fair condition in Turkey is low in comparison to the 95 per cent of roads in good or fair condition in Western European countries. Further, the heavy commercial vehicle traffic creates unsafe conditions. According to the Ministry of Transport (MoT, 2007), heavily loaded trucks make up 22 per cent of total trucks, and trucks with excessive axle loads form 20 per cent of heavy vehicles. The high density of heavy vehicle traffic leads to road deterioration. Insufficient maintenance due to inappropriate management procedures is also a serious road network problem. Thus, infrastructure development remains one of the key issues affecting Turkey's road transportation sector.

Examining basic data on traffic accidents in Turkey reveals that although road safety has improved over the last decade, accidents remain a serious socio-economic problem. While the fatality rate was 5.72 persons per 100 million vehicles per km during 2003, the rate has decreased to 2.17 persons per 100 million vehicles per km in 2014. Turkey intends to decrease the fatality rate to less than one person per 100 million vehicles per km by 2023. However, the current rate of eight fatalities per 10,000 vehicles is still about four times the average of that in the European Community (two fatalities per 10,000 vehicles). In 2014, a total of 1.2 million accidents took place in Turkey on urban and intercity roads, with total fatalities of 3,524 and total injured 285,100. According to the World Health Organization (2013), the number of deaths per 100,000 population was 12 in Turkey in 2013 while it was 5.4 in Spain and 4.7 in Germany. The reduction of fatalities over time in Turkey has mainly been a result of the introduction of air bags and seat belts in cars, and implementation of the divided road project.[9]

Recognizing that efficient road infrastructure is a key ingredient for national and regional development, Turkey plans to expand and improve its road network. Noting that road infrastructure investments amounted to $8.1 billion in 2011, forming 1.19 per cent of the GDP and $7 billion in 2012, forming 0.88 per cent of the GDP, investment must be increased substantially to expand the road network. Since financing the expansion of road network projects from the government budget alone is difficult, funds have been

---

[9] The use of seat belts in Turkey became mandatory only recently.

obtained from international financial organizations such as the World Bank and the European Investment Bank, and through PPP projects. Turkey considers PPPs one of the most effective alternatives to realizing the required investments without increasing public budget deficits.

Among ongoing PPP projects, the most important include the Istanbul-Izmir Motorway, the Northern Marmara Motorway, the Eurasia Tunnel Project, the Three Level Tunnel Project under the Bosphorus, and the Çanakkale bridge.[10] The Istanbul-Izmir Motorway Project, consisting of 384 km of motorways, 43 km of connecting roads and the 2,682-metre suspension bridge over Izmit Bay, will be partially completed in 2016 and the remainder in 2018. The project is estimated to cost $6.3 billion. The consortium constructing the motorway will collect tolls from road users for fifteen years and four months.[11]

The North Marmara Motorway project consists of 299 km of motorways, 115 km of connecting roads, and a 1,875-metre long bridge with a railway over the Bosphorus. The project, located north of Istanbul close to the Black Sea, will carry four lanes of traffic in either direction as well as dual rail lines. The aim is to reduce traffic and ease freight and passenger transportation time in Istanbul. The project will manage the transit cargo traffic passing through Istanbul so that truck traffic will not cross through the centre of the city. As a result, truck transport companies will save considerable time and money, and there will be a reduction in carbon emissions due to reduced fuel consumption achieved through less time in traffic. The bridge, 59 metres wide and 320 metres high, will be one of the biggest suspension bridges in the world with a railway as part of it. Trains crossing the bridge will continue to Bulgaria and on to Europe. The total investment of the bridge project is about $2.5 billion, and the project is expected to be completed in 2016. The Northern Marmara Motorway project is expected to cost $6.2 billion. The consortium constructing the motorway and the bridge will collect tolls from road users for seven years and six months.[12] While the bridge toll for a car will be $3, the motorway toll will be calculated at $0.08/km.

The Eurasia Tunnel Project is the construction of a 14.6-km road link between the Asian and European sides of Istanbul, with 5.4 km of the tunnel passing under the Bosphorus. Construction is expected to be completed by the end of 2017, and the cost of the project will amount to $1.25 billion. The approach roads on either side of the tunnel will carry four lanes of traffic in both directions. A Build-Operate-Transfer (BOT) model was chosen for the construction of the tunnel, and the Eurasian Tunnel Operation Construction

---

[10] See Investment Support Promotion Agency (2013).

[11] The consortium consists of the Turkish construction firms Nurol, Makyol, Yüksel, and Gökçay, together with the Italian construction group Astaldi.

[12] The consortium includes the Turkish construction firm İçtaş and the Italian construction group Astaldi.

and Investment Company is carrying it out, responsible for operating and maintaining it for twenty-five years and eleven months.[13] The Three Level Tunnel Project under the Bosphorus is another tunnel that will connect the Asian and European sides of Istanbul, with an estimated cost of $3.5 billion. The 6.5-km long tunnel includes two highways and a subway system, and is planned for completion by 2020. Finally, a three-lane 3,623-metre suspension bridge is being planned between Lapseki and Gelibolu in Turkey's northwestern Çanakkale region. The bridge will be part of the Çanakkale-Tekirdağ-Kınalı-Balıkesir highway project that aims to lessen the load and traffic on Istanbul's bridges.

Figure 2.2 shows the existing, ongoing, and planned BOT motorway projects slated for completion in 2023. The planned projects will have a total length of 5,748 km, and are expected to cost $38.2 billion. Among these projects, the following three are considered the most important: The Ankara-Niğde Motorway Project, consisting of 342 km with three lanes of motorways in both directions and 57 km of connecting roads, will be completed by 2016, and is expected to cost $1.7 billion. The Gerede-Merzifon-Gürbulak Project will have a length of 1,276 km and will be completed in two stages, with the Gerede-Merzifon section completed in 2018 and the Merzifon-Gürbulak section completed in 2023. The investment cost of the whole project is estimated to be $9.7 billion. Finally, the Ankara-Kırıkkale-Samsun Motorway Project, consisting of 472 km motorway, will be completed by 2018 and is expected to cost $2.6 billion.

According to the MoT (2010) transport strategy document, the government is planning to resurface some roads with BHM, so that the total length of such roads will increase to 70,000 km. In addition, the dual-carriageway road network will increase to 36,500 km, as shown in Figure 2.2. Furthermore, 5,748 km of new motorways will be built, bringing the total motorway network to 7,827 km by 2023. Turkey will also develop the North–South axis (Black Sea–Mediterranean) road network, which will increase to 11,749 km by 2023. As noted above, the government is aiming to involve the private sector mainly in toll motorway projects on arteries with high traffic. The government also aims to benefit from smart transport systems for supplementing road security, and to change road configurations where traffic accidents happen consistently and in regions with a high risk of accidents. As a result, traffic

---

[13] According to the PPP implementation agreement, the Turkish Government has the right to assume the financial obligations of the project company in the event that the implementation agreement is terminated prior to the expiry of the operating term. There is a demand guarantee stating that there will be a certain minimum traffic flow. If not, the government will cover the related costs. Furthermore, the project is exempt from value-added tax (VAT), stamp duty, and fees. Finally, the equity part of financing obtained by the project company should be at least 20 per cent of the expected fixed construction cost of the project.

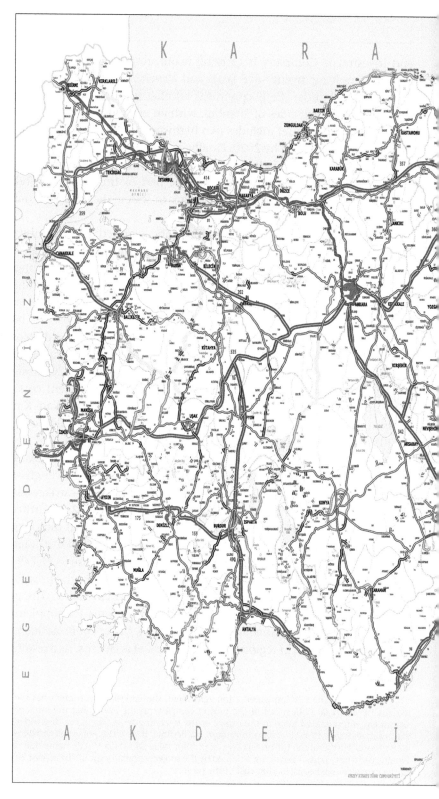

Figure 2.2 2023 targets for motorways and dual carriageways

Source: Directorate General of Highways (KGM). Reproduced with permission.

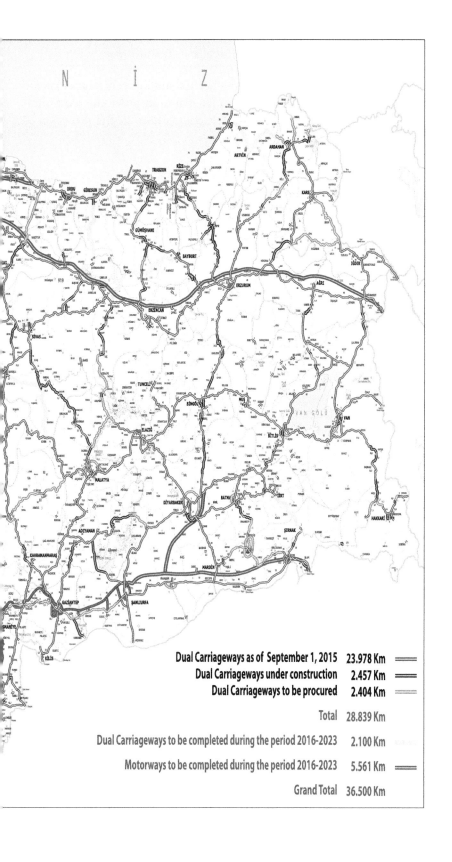

Dual Carriageways as of September 1, 2015	23.978 Km ═══
Dual Carriageways under construction	2.457 Km ═══
Dual Carriageways to be procured	2.404 Km ───
Total	28.839 Km
Dual Carriageways to be completed during the period 2016-2023	2.100 Km
Motorways to be completed during the period 2016-2023	5.561 Km ═══
Grand Total	36.500 Km

safety is expected to increase, and fatalities per 100 million vehicles per km are expected to decrease below unity. Within its goal to improve the road infrastructure, the government is aiming for fair competition in the provision of road services.

2.1.2 Rail Transportation

Until May 2013, Turkish State Railways (TCDD) had monopoly rights on all railway-related activities. The TCDD was until then a vertically integrated company that not only dealt with the supply of freight and passenger services but also with the provision of infrastructure. It was responsible for operating and maintaining railways, ports, and piers, guiding and coordinating affiliated companies, and carrying out complementary activities regarding rail transport, such as land transport that included ferry operations. Although the Liberalization of the Turkish Railway Transportation law was adopted by parliament in May 2013, we are still waiting for the implementing regulations to be published; until then and probably for some time thereafter, the TCDD will still be the main player in the Turkish railway sector.

The TCDD manufactures rolling stock and similar vehicles, sets up warehouses and passenger facilities, and undertakes railway construction work as a contractor in Turkey and abroad. Its companies include TÜLOMSAŞ (locomotive, motor, and freight wagons), TÜVASAŞ (passenger cars), and TÜDEMSAŞ (railway machines and freight wagons). The TCDD also operates a number of other manufacturing facilities, some of which involve joint ventures, including the Ankara Railroad Factory, the Ankara Long Rail Source and Road Maintenance Mechanical Tools Factory, the Sivas Sleeper Factory, and the Afyon Concrete Factory. In 2006, the TCDD established the Hyundai-Eurotem Adapazarı High-Speed Train Factory in cooperation with Hyundai-Rotem (Korea) and the Turkish private sector to manufacture electric trains, light rail vehicles, high-speed train sets, and high-speed passenger cars. Voestalpine Kardemir Railway Systems established the Çankırı Switch and Crossing Factory as a joint venture with the TCDD in 2010 to produce switches suitable for conventional and high-speed railways. In addition, the TCDD established Erzincan Rail Fastenings Factory as a joint venture with Germany, and began locomotive production at TÜLOMSAŞ with the US. Most recently, the TCDD has begun producing electric locomotives at TÜLOMSAŞ in cooperation with Hyundai-Rotem.

As of 2014, the total length of railways, shown in Figure 2.3, amounted to 12,485 km. Of this amount, 3,748 km are electrified and 4,412 km are signalled, comprising 30 per cent and 35.3 per cent of the total railway lines, respectively. Regarding rolling stock, we note that in 2013 there were 17,201 freight wagons, 820 passenger wagons, 378 active diesel mainline

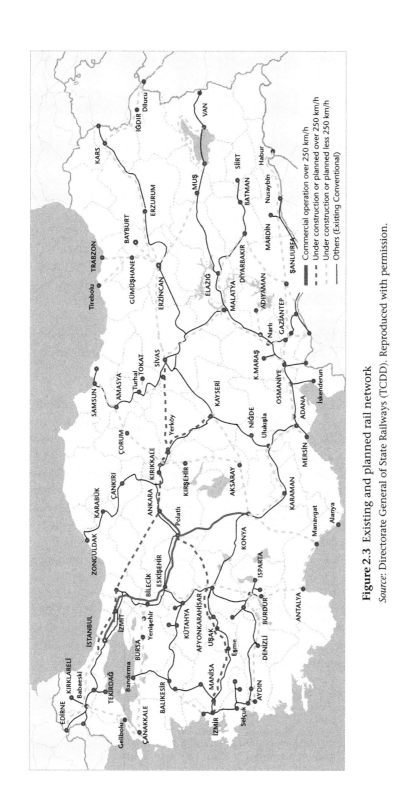

Figure 2.3 Existing and planned rail network

Source: Directorate General of State Railways (TCDD). Reproduced with permission.

Legend:
- Commercial operation over 250 km/h
- Under construction or planned over 250 km/h
- Under construction or planned less 250 km/h
- Others (Existing Conventional)

locomotives, 45 active electric locomotives, and ten active high-speed trains. The average age of Turkey's rail infrastructure is relatively high. In 2013, the share of rail more than 30 years old was 9.2 per cent; between 21 and 30 years old 19.2 per cent; and between 11 and 20 years old 20.3 per cent. On the other hand, the share of electric locomotives between 20 and 29 years old was 81 per cent, and the share of mainline diesel locomotives above the age of 29 was 48 per cent. In terms of the type of goods carried, we note that as of 2013, machine vehicles formed 43 per cent of the quantity of freight transported; ores and metal scrap 24 per cent, solid mineral fuels 11 per cent, and chemical products 5 per cent.[14]

Railway services offered by the TCDD include passenger transport, freight transport, and port handling. During 2013, 25.5 million passengers were carried on suburban lines, and 20.9 million passengers on mainlines. While passenger kilometres amounted to 755 million on suburban lines, passenger kilometres on mainlines amounted to 2,976 million. Similarly, the amount of freight carried amounted to 26.6 million tonnes and 11.2 tonne-km. The TCDD also owned a large number of ports. Recently, the management of several of its ports have been turned into concession agreements with private operators, and other ports are in the process of privatization. As of 2013, port handling amounted to 16.1 million tonnes.[15]

In Turkey, state-owned enterprises are divided into public economic institutions and state economic enterprises. The former consider public welfare and produce public goods and services with monopolistic characteristics, the latter operate in a free market, with a profit-making motive. The TCDD is a public economic institution, with the Treasury owning all of the capital. Although it is a legal entity, is financially autonomous and its liability is limited by its capital, the Treasury finances the TCDD's capital and operating deficits, and the MoTMC supervises it. The TCDD receives compensation for duty losses on certain trains operated and railway lines kept open for social purposes, as well as for railway infrastructure repair and maintenance costs. Together, these payments make up its operating subsidy. The Treasury also makes capital transfers to the TCDD each year, which cover capital investment and TCDD staff costs. From time to time, the Treasury also pays TCDD debts. As commercial revenues cover only a fraction of the total operating costs, subsidies have been increasing substantially over time. According to Monsalve (2011), the biggest source of losses is freight transport, followed by mainline

---

[14] See Turkish State Railways (2013).
[15] Currently, large logistics companies with their own rolling stock are providing services in domestic and international transport. Companies wanting to use railways for freight transport may apply to the TCDD and get discounted tariffs if they own freight cars. The TCDD evaluates applications based on operational and technical criteria.

passenger services. Ports were the only aspect of the TCDD that operated profitably, and they cross-subsidized rail operations.

In terms of passenger transport, the most significant problem faced by the railway sector has been the lack of railway lines capable of high-quality and high-speed transport to connect major centres. A longer duration of travel compared to road transport has been the major reason for low passenger railway demand. Regarding freight transport, Turkey's railway infrastructure was not sufficiently modernized for door-to-door transport services; this service is provided in a much better way by the road freight transport sector. In addition, the railway infrastructure did not provide sufficient hinterland connections with production centres and major ports. Further, because Turkey's railway infrastructure is rather old, maintenance was achieved at higher cost compared to international averages. According to R&H Consultants (2009), compared to international practices, the TCDD spends 18 per cent more for rolling stock, 58 per cent more for track, and 38 per cent more for electrification.

Lately, the government of Turkey has been prioritizing railway infrastructure, allocating a large amount of investment to the sector. In this context we note that the railway policies during the early years of the Republic, namely 1923 to 1950, differed considerably from the policies between 1950 and 2003. During the first period railway transportation experienced its golden age, but was neglected during the second period. Since 2003 railways have again become a priority. While public investment allocated to railways was a mere $470 million during 2003, annual appropriations increased from an average of $914 million between 2004 and 2006 to an annual average of $1.47 billion between 2007 and 2009, and further to $2.67 billion between 2010 and 2011. Between 2012 and 2014, the annual average was $3.64 billion (all measured at 2014 prices).

During the last decade the government has developed a new rail transport policy for passenger and freight transportation. Noting that high-speed rail has enjoyed a rapid expansion in other countries, the Turkish government decided to construct high-speed train (HST) lines between major centres in Turkey. It was recognized that HST lines have important safety, capacity, and sustainability characteristics, and that their potential for political integration of the country by linking territories is considerable. Furthermore, by improving accessibility to a broader geographic area, HST lines lead to increased mobility.

The first HST line, Ankara-Eskişehir, started operation in 2009, completing the first phase of the 511-km Ankara-Istanbul HST. The entire line was completed in July 2014. The Ankara-Konya HST, the second line, was commissioned in August 2011. Construction work for 393-km Ankara-Sivas HST and the Ankara-Bursa HST are ongoing. With the completion of the 105-km

Bursa-Bilecik line, the industrial city of Bursa will be connected by HST to Ankara and Istanbul. The construction of the 624-km Ankara-Izmir HST began in 2012. Turkey plans to connect Kayseri in Central Anatolia to Ankara with the construction of 142-km long Kayseri-Yerköy HST. Studies for a Sivas-Erzincan HST in Eastern Anatolia are ongoing. The Ankara-Bursa, Ankara-Sivas, and Ankara-Izmir HST projects are expected to be completed by 2020.

The TCDD has also been working on the Marmaray rail tube tunnel under the Bosphorus, connecting the Asian side with the European side of Istanbul. The project includes a 13.3-km underwater crossing, where immersed-tube tunnel technology was combined with bored-tunnel technology. The project includes a 63-km upgrade of suburban lines to create a 76.3- km high-capacity line between Gebze on the Asian side and Halkalı on the European side. Trains cross under the Bosphorus in an 1.8 km earthquake-proof tube, accessed from Yenikapı on the European side and Söğütlüçeşme on the Asian side. For Marmaray, 440 new rolling stocks (trains with five and ten cars) have been procured, and 300 of those have been assembled in the Eurotem factory in Adapazarı. The tunnel is used by suburban, long-distance, and freight services. Marmaray, built at a cost of $4.2 billion, started operation in October 2013. The Japanese International Cooperation Agency (JICA), the Council of Europe Development Bank, and the European Investment Bank have all invested in the project.

During the last decade a major achievement of the TCDD involved the modernization of Turkey's existing railway system. In this context, 8,706 km of conventional railway lines have been completely renewed, 1,568 km of lines have been electrified, and 1,570 km of lines have been signalled. During the same period 6,507 freight wagons and 155 passenger wagons were produced at TCDD factories in Eskişehir, Adapazarı, and Sivas. In addition, the TCDD has procured twelve HST sets, twenty-four diesel train sets, and eighty-nine mainline diesel locomotives. The diesel locomotives were produced by TÜLOMSAŞ with a General Electric license and the diesel train sets were produced by TÜVASAŞ. In the near future, Turkey plans to acquire twenty more diesel locomotives from TÜLOMSAŞ, eighty electric locomotives, and twenty-eight diesel train sets. Eight of the electric locomotives have already been imported from Korea, and the remaining seventy-two electric locomotives will be produced by TÜLOMSAŞ by the end of 2016. The twenty-eight diesel train sets will be produced by TÜVASAŞ.

The TCDD has also established logistic centres, integrating all transportation systems. While six of these centres are already operating, six other centres are under construction and Turkey is planning to build twenty more over the next few years across the country. Logistics villages are planned in areas with a high loading capacity that are close to organized industrial zones and in areas conducive to regional economic development. These hubs are integrated to all transportation systems and help lower costs and increase the efficiency of logistics networks. The private sector has also initiated similar centres/villages in Turkey, and these provide warehousing services, freight handling services, and accommodate many other related services.[16]

In 2004, the TCDD changed its freight transportation strategy, partially shifting to block train operations from piece-by-piece transportation. The former refers to trains where freight is transported uninterruptedly, from the loading to the unloading station without changing locomotives and wagons and without interval freight loading and unloading. With this change, freight trains, which used to move at an average speed of 5 km/hr, have increased to 25 km/hr. Goods such as automobiles, construction materials, and food products, which were not carried before 2002 by rail are now being transported by block trains. Within the framework of agreements signed with different countries, block trains pulled by TCDD locomotives travel to Europe (Germany, Hungary, the Netherlands, and Slovenia), Iran, and Central Asia (Turkmenistan and Kazakhstan). The large majority of block trains between Turkey and the EU and between Turkey and Central Asia carry containers. Currently, relatively large numbers of block trains per day are in operation both domestically and internationally. Most private companies using block trains own and operate warehouses for storing and handling freight. In 2010, 2.7 million tonnes of load transportation was transported through block train operations, representing a 107 per cent increase in load transportation compared to 2002.

According to its new strategy document, the MoTMC is planning to increase freight transportation from its 2011 level of 11.7 billion tonne-km to 95 billion tonne-km by 2023. Similarly, the government aims to increase the number of passengers from its 5.9 billion passenger-km in 2011 to 50 billion. The aim is to increase the share of railway transport in total transportation in Turkey by 10 per cent in passenger and by 15 per cent in freight transport. The HST goal is for 10,000 km by 2023, with all lines double tracked, electrified, and capable of running at 250 km/hr. The Ankara-Sivas-Erzincan, Ankara-Izmir, and Ankara-Bursa HST projects shown in Figure 2.4 are expected to be completed soon, and the government aims to integrate the Turkish rail network with the Pan-European/Trans-European Transport Network over time. Furthermore, Turkey intends to complete the renewal of the whole railway network by renewing an additional 4,400 km of lines by 2023. It will modernize the Halkalı-Kapıkule, Sivas-Erzincan-Erzurum-Kars, Ankara-Izmir, Kayseri-Şefaatlı, Bandırma-İzmir, Konya-Mersin, Bandırma-Bursa-Osmaneli, and Eskişehir-Antalya connections, as well as the Lake Van passage. The total length of fully electrified and signalled lines will increase to 22,504 km. Through branch lines, the country

---

[16] On logistic centres see International Transport Forum (2009b).

is also planning to connect logistics centres, factories, industries, organized industrial zones, and ports, all of which have great freight potential, and thus increase the combined and freight transport sectors. Turkey intends to complete the liberalization process of the railway sector by 2023. During this time period Turkey is also planning to manufacture all types of rolling stock within the country.

The (i) expansion of HSTs; (ii) the Marmaray project; (iii) the rehabilitation of existing railway lines; (iv) the modernization of rolling stock and infrastructure; (v) improved logistics and distribution, including multi-modal options; (vi) improved block train management; and (vii) establishing rail R&D facilities constitute key TCDD projects. To compete on a global scale, Turkey realizes it must improve the performance, competitiveness, and capacity of its rail sector. To improve the quality of rail transport and ensure it has sufficient capacity, Turkey aims to have fair competition in rail service provision by opening the railway transport market to the private sector, with the TCDD responsible for managing infrastructure and line operation. To provide good, reliable, and adequate paths for freight transport, Turkey knows it must give freight an appropriate level of priority by establishing 'freight corridors'.

2.1.3 Maritime Transportation

At the crossroads of Europe and Asia, Turkey is bordered by the Black Sea in the north, with 1,785 km of coastline, the Aegean Sea in the west, with 2,805 km of coastline, and the Mediterranean in the south, with 1,577 km of coastline. Including the Marmara coastline, (1,089 km) and the coastline of its islands (1,067 km), the country's total coastline is 8,323 km long. Turkey sits on important transport routes through the strategic waterways of the Istanbul (Bosphorus) and Çanakkale (Dardanelles) Straits, connecting the Black Sea and the countries bordering it to southern seas. Cargo coming from Europe and the Americas are handled in transit to the Commonwealth of Independent States (CIS), Iran, Iraq, and the Balkans, and vice versa. Turkey's major industrial centres are on or near the sea. It is thus not surprising that 54.76 per cent of the value of goods exported by Turkey, and 58.4 per cent of the value of goods imported were transported by sea in 2014. In 2013, 12.4 per cent of maritime exports were made to Italy, followed by Egypt and Spain, with 11.2 per cent and 6.3 per cent, respectively. The majority of Turkey's imports came from neighbouring Russia, followed by Ukraine, the US, and Egypt.

Total loading and unloading in the maritime sub-sector, including transit and cabotage cargo, rose from 189.9 million tonnes in 2003 to 384.9 million tonnes in 2013. Container handling amounted to 34.6 million tonnes in 2004 and reached 84.7 million tonnes in 2013 (7.9 million TEUs). While the total volume of exports by Turkish-owned ships amounted to 11.7 million tonnes in 2013, the total volume of imports by Turkish-owned ships amounted to 22.9 million tonnes. Thus, the share of Turkish-flagged vessels in the total volume of exports handled in Turkish ports decreased from 27.8 per cent in 2003 to 13 per cent in 2013, while the share of Turkish-flagged vessels in total volume of imports handled in Turkish ports decreased from 29.8 per cent in 2003 to 12.2 per cent in 2013.

The number of ships in the Turkish-owned shipping fleet (1,000 gross tonnage (GT) and above) excepting ships registered under different flags, rose from 569 in 2003 to 1,489 in 2014, indicating an increase of 161.7 per cent.[17] The total tonnage of the Turkish-owned fleet (1,000 GT and above) rose from 8.9 million deadweight tonnage (DWT) in 2003 to 30.4 million DWT in 2014, an increase of 241.4 per cent.[18] In 2014, 40.2 per cent of those ships were registered under the Turkish flag, but that percentage decreases to 28.2 per cent when measured in terms of DWT. Finally, we note that Turkish-owned merchant ships of 1,000 GT and over ranked thirteenth in the world in 2013.[19]

There have been important developments in Turkey's shipbuilding sector in recent years, most notably with it evolving into an internationally recognized industry. Turkey has modern, quality-certified shipyards that build yachts, mega-yachts, sailboats, and transport ships, and perform extensive repair and conversion works. As of 2013, there were seventy-two active shipyards, with another forty-nine reportedly under construction. Turkey's shipyards are mostly located in the Marmara region, namely in Tuzla, Yalova, and Izmit. Turkish shipyards are ranked fourth globally in the production of small- and medium-tonnage chemical/oil tankers, and also highly ranked in mega-yacht production.[20] Turkey is the world's fifth-largest ship recycler, and the largest outside South Asia and China. Most recycled ships are primarily from EU countries, which choose Turkey because it complies with the EU's ship recycling standards. Ship recycling and dismantling takes place mainly in Aliağa, located in the Aegean region.

In Turkey there are relatively large numbers of ports servicing domestic and foreign trade. These ports can be classified into three groups according to their operators: (i) those run by the TCDD; (ii) those run by the Turkish Maritime Administration (TDI); and (iii) private ports and those run by municipalities. During the second half of the twentieth century, the TCDD was entrusted with the task of operating, expanding, and renovating ports with railway connections. For most of the time since, the TCDD operated Turkey's seven

---

[17] Gross tonnage is a measure of total capacity, expressed in volumetric tons of 100 cubic feet, and is calculated by adding the underdeck tonnage and the internal volume of the tween-decks and deck space used for cargo.

[18] Deadweight tonnage is a measure of how much weight a ship is carrying or can safely carry. It is the sum of the weights of cargo, fuel, fresh water, ballast water, provisions, passengers, and crew.

[19] See Ministry of Transport, Maritime Affairs, and Communications (2013).

[20] See Organization for Economic Co-operation and Development (2011).

largest ports: Haydarpasa, Derince, Izmir, Samsun, Mersin, Bandırma, and Iskenderun. All of these ports are accessible by road and railway and are Turkey's most strategically important ports, handling the greatest cargo volume. Recently, Mersin, Iskenderun, Samsun, and Bandırma were privatized.[21]

Note that the Privatization Law No. 4046 of 1994, together with Constitutional Amendments of 1999, form the institutional basis for privatization in Turkey. While privatization decisions are made by the Privatization Higher Council, headed by the Prime Minister and five ministers, implementation is carried out by the Privatization Administration. In the case of ports, privatization is implemented through the transfer of operational rights, leases, or similar methods. As a result, privatization of ports in Turkey is only partial, in the sense that operation rights are either transferred to the private sector, or methods like Built-Operate-Transfer (BOT) and leasing are utilized, and ownership is held by the state. The private enterprise that will operate the port is determined by a bidding process and the result is then submitted to the Privatization Higher Council for approval. Then a contract for the transfer of operational rights is signed by between the Privatization Administration and the selected enterprise. The maximum operation period that may be offered to the private company is forty-nine years, depending on port conditions. During this period monitoring the performance of port operations is done by the TCDD, who will be responsible for post-privatization performance.

Ports run by the TDI are of lesser importance, serving local areas, such as Galataport in Istanbul which caters for cruise passenger traffic. The ports of Hopa, Giresun, Ordu, Rize, Sinop, and Tekirdag were originally owned by the TDI and privatized in 1997. The port of Antalya was privatized in 1998, followed by the ports of Alanya and Marmaris in 2000. The ports of Çeşme, Kuşadası, Trabzon, and Dikili were sold or offered under concession in 2003. The third group of ports primarily serves industrial plants, but may also be used by private parties. Some private ports are relatively large, such as BOTAŞ Haydar Aliyev, Mersin, Kocaeli TÜPRAŞ, Aliağa TÜPRAŞ, Ambarlı KUMPORT, İskenderun ISDEMİR, BOTAŞ Ceyhan, Erdemir, and Ambarli MARPORT ports. The most important container ports of the private sector are Ambarlı MARPORT, Mersin, Ambarlı KUMPORT, Kocaeli EVYAP, Ambarli MARDAŞ, Gemlik GEMPORT, Kocaeli YILPORT, Aliağa NEMPORT and Antalya ports.

---

[21] In 2005, the joint venture of Singapore-based PSA International and the Turkish construction company Akfen submitted the highest bids in response to the privatization tenders of Mersin and Iskenderun ports, but the competition board rejected the plan, arguing that securing both concessions would curtail competition. The concession contract for Mersin was signed in 2007 with the Turkish Privatization Authority. In October 2010, Limak Yatırım was awarded the tender for a concession to operate Iskenderun, and expects to do so for a 36-year period. Izmir port was tendered in 2007 to the highest bidder, a consortium of Hutchinson Port Holdings and some Turkish firms, but the deal fell through and the port will be re-tendered. A consortium under the leadership of Turkey's Turkeler Group has launched a bid for the port of Derince.

Figure 2.4 Turkish ports
Source: Turkish Naval Forces, Office of Navigation, Hydrography and Oceanography. Reproduced with permission.

Izmir's Alsancak Port is a large public sector port in Turkey. We also note that the Autoport in Izmit is expected to meet 25 to 30 per cent of total car handling, that Aliağa, Samsun, and Ceyhan ports will meet the traffic of oil and its derivatives, and Kusadasi, Istanbul, Izmir, and Marmaris ports will meet a large portion of cruise passenger traffic.

Turkish ports handle a variety of cargo, including bulk cargo, general cargo, container, and liquid bulk cargo. Data reveal that the Kocaeli ports in Izmit Bay are the leading ports in cargo handling due to their proximity to manufacturing and business centres in the Marmara region. In 2013, Ambarlı ports handled 3.3 million TEUs of containers. As a result, those ports came in as the top container handlers among Turkish ports, followed by Mersin with 1.4 million TEUs. Currently, the TCDD operates three ports: Haydarpaşa,

Derince, and Izmir. The Privatization Administration has recently added Izmir Port Enterprise and Derince Port Enterprise to its portfolio and the Haydarpaşa container port will be part of a tourism complex project.

Turkey is developing four major new container port projects: Filyos, Mersin, Çandarlı, and Derince. The Filyos port project is intended to decrease the number of vessel passages through the Bosphorus and Çanakkale straights. Cargo traffic from Black Sea countries will be connected via railway and motorways to Mersin on the Mediterranean and to Izmir on the Aegean. In addition, the Filyos port will support Kardemir's production of crude steel, and hence will facilitate its export. The project will create a capacity of 25 million tonnes per year within ten years at a cost of $0.87 billion. Mersin is planned to be a hub port and will provide a sufficient number of berths to accommodate postpanamax container vessels of 16 m depth, with a yearly capacity of 12 million tonnes. The cost is estimated to amount to $3.8 billion. This port will connect to railways, which will present a gateway not only between Euro-Med and Black Sea countries but also between landlocked Asian countries and the CIS. Çandarlı, on the North Aegean, will operate mainly as a container terminal, with a capacity of two million TEUs and 20 million tonnes per year, and will also be connected by railway. Preparatory infrastructural works includes a 900-metre-long breakwater, which has already been built. A dock of 2,000 metres will also be built. When completed, six 300-metre-long ships will be able to approach at the same time. The estimated cost of this superstructure will amount to $1.24 billion, and it will act as a new hub for the West Anatolian hinterland. Finally, the Derince project on the Marmara, with a capacity of 1.2 million TEUs and 11.5 million tonnes per year, will meet the future demands of that region, and will be connected by railway and motorway to Kocaeli Bay and the Central Anatolia hinterland. All four projects will be implemented as BOT models or through loan agreements. The Turkish private sector also expects to complete the Asyaport in Tekirdağ on the Marmara, with a capacity of 1 million TEUs and 10 million tonnes per year, as well as the DP World Yarımca port on the Marmara, with a capacity of 1.3 million. The terminal will be one of the biggest container terminals in Turkey.

During the 1990s, the Balkan conflict made road transport by Turkish operators to and from Western European markets increasingly difficult. As a result, traffic shifted to roll-on-roll-off (RO-RO) maritime operations, which refers to the transport by ship of trucks, containers, and semi-trailers on their own wheels or on wheels attached to them for this purpose. After the Balkan war, RO-RO operations intensified, as this mode allows transportation companies to avoid dealing with certificates and associated costs imposed by Balkan countries to pass through their territories. The Trieste port is favoured among Turkish logistics operators due to its ease of access to major locations in

Europe. According to the International Transport Forum (2009b), half of the truck operations between Turkey and Western Europe are carried out by this RO-RO shipping line. In addition, Turkey operates a RO-RO line as an alternative to the truck route through the Syrian border gate, and carries a large number of vehicles to the Middle East this way. RO-RO traffic is also used for the purpose of transporting TIR vehicles from Samsun and Trabzon to Russia and from Istanbul and Zonguldak to Ukraine via the Black Sea.[22]

The Turkish government has set rather ambitious targets for 2023. It aims to increase the GDP from $839 billion (2012 figures) to $2 trillion in 2023, increase exports from $152.6 billion in 2012 to $500 billion in 2023, and increase imports from $236.5 billion in 2012 to $750 billion in 2023. As a result, demand for freight transport, and hence demand for maritime transport, including containerized cargo demand, is expected to increase substantially over the next decade (currently, containerized cargo represents about 22 per cent of total cargo). Ports will be called on to accommodate very substantial increases in international trade, thus new port capacity must be brought on stream.

According to the MoT's new transport strategy, Turkey is planning to increase the total tonnage of the Turkish-owned fleet (1,000 GT and above) from its 2013 level of 30.3 million DWT to about 50 million DWT by 2023, increase the capacity of existing ports, and construct the new container ports. The extension of Derince and some of the Marmara Sea ports, amounting to a total of 20 million tonnes, is required to cope with the cargo growth of the Greater Istanbul area. Extending the Mersin port by 20 million tonnes would meet the traffic growth there. Finally, the development of Filyos meets the port requirements of the Zonguldak region and its hinterland and can support decongestion of the Istanbul area by attracting transport destined for Istanbul. The share of maritime transport in domestic freight transportation is expected to increase from its 2011 level of 3.7 per cent to 10 per cent in 2023, the share of maritime transport in domestic passenger transportation from 0.32 to four per cent, and the share of containerization in total domestic freight transport to 15 per cent.[23]

2.1.4 *Air Transportation*

Turkey has experienced tremendous development in the civil aviation sector since the start of air transport liberalization in 1983. Between 2002 and 2014, passenger traffic in total increased from 33.8 million to 166.5 million, with

---

[22] TIR vehicles are vehicles operating under the Convention on International Transport of Goods Under Cover of TIR Carnets (TIR Convention) discussed in Chapter 3.

[23] See MoT (2010).

domestic passenger traffic increasing from 8.7 million to 85.6 million and international passenger traffic from 25.1 million to 80.4 million. The average annual growth rates experienced between 2005 and 2014 amounted to 12.9 per cent for total passenger traffic, 17.2 per cent for domestic passenger traffic, and 9.7 per cent for international flights. During this period the total number of flights increased from 532,500 to 1.68 million, the number of domestic flights increased from 158,000 to 754,400, and the number of international flights from 218,600 to 589,900. The average annual growth rates experienced during this period amounted to 9.2 per cent for the total number of flights, 12.3 per cent for domestic flights, and 8.3 per cent for international flights. These increases are expected to continue. For Europe as a whole, the traffic growth rate is expected to amount to 2.1 per cent per year between 2012 and 2018, but a growth rate of 5.9 per cent is expected for Turkey. While total freight traffic increased from 896,900 thousand tonnes in 2002 to 2.87 million tonnes in 2014, domestic freight traffic increased from 181,300 tonnes in 2002 to 809,300 tonnes in 2014. International freight traffic increased from 715,600 tonnes in 2002 to 2.057 million tonnes in 2014. The average annual growth rates experienced between 2005 and 2014 amounted to 9.1 per cent for total freight traffic, 10.7 per cent for domestic freight traffic, and 8.6 per cent for international freight traffic.[24]

In 2003 there were 162 large aircraft in the Turkish fleet, and by 2013 the number had increased to 422. Simultaneously, the chair capacity of the Turkish fleet increased from 27,599 to 75,700. According to the 2013 Annual Report of Ecole Nationale de l'Aviation Civile (ENAC), Turkey is the eleventh-largest country (right after India) in the world ordering of passenger traffic, and in Europe it is the fifth-largest country. In 2013 the share of Turkey in total world passenger traffic was 2.4 per cent, and in European passenger traffic it was 8.7 per cent.

Turkey's spectacular air transport development in recent years has been due to the conjunction of various favourable factors, such as high GDP growth and stronger growth of the internal market relative to the growth of the inter-national air market. But as emphasized above, this evolution is largely due to regulatory reforms in Turkey's air transport sector, including liberalization of the internal market and new private operators for long- and short-distance services. The service supply increased considerably, with competitive prices and short travel times. At the same time, major airports' capacity increased.[25]

As of 2014, Turkey has fifty-three active airports. The major international airports are Atatürk, Antalya, Esenboğa, and Adnan Menderes. Forty-seven airports are operated by the Directorate General of State Airports Authority.

[24] See Directorate General of Civil Aviation (2013).
[25] See State Airport Authority (2013).

Sabiha Gökçen Airport in Istanbul is operated by Malaysia Airports Holdings Berhad. As of 2014, the company has operation rights for fourteen years of Istanbul Sabiha Gökçen International Airport, including the management of the terminal buildings, car park, ground handling, cargo and aircraft refuelling operations, the airport hotel, and commercially important persons' (CIP) facilities. Airport management is not limited to management companies, however; Eskişehir Anadolu Airport is operated by a university and a number of military airports are open to civil air traffic with permission from the military. There are also airports operated by private flight schools and the Turkish Aeronautical Association.

Recently, the government decided to construct a new international airport on the Black Sea coast some 35 km outside Istanbul, at a cost of €10.2 billion. The government awarded the concession to build and operate the airport to İGA Havalimanı İşletmesi A.Ş. consortium after it agreed to pay €22.2 billion plus the VAT over the course of the 25-year operating lease. The airport will have six runways and will be constructed in four phases. The first phase, to be completed in 2018, will serve 90 million passengers per year. This number will increase to over 150 million passengers once the project is fully complete. The airport will be connected to Istanbul via rail, metro, bus, and road. Following the opening of the new airport, Istanbul Atatürk Airport will close.

2.2 Inter-Industry Linkages

The transportation sector is crucial for Turkey. To show its importance quantitatively, we first examine the shares of transportation sub-sectors in GDP in Turkey in comparison with those of the EU. Next, we estimate the inter-industry linkage effects. Noting that each sub-sector uses inputs from other industries in its production process, we first estimate the transportation sub-sectors' backward linkage. The sub-sectors also supply inputs to other industries, which indicate forward linkages. Thus, the forward linkage in road transportation measures the relative importance of road transportation as a supplier to other industries in the economy, whereas the backward linkage measures the road transportation's relative importance as a demander.

Table 2.1 shows the transport sectors shares in the overall value added in Turkey as well as in the EU, derived from the latest available input-output tables from Eurostat.[26] In 2002, the Turkish transportation sector produced 9.8 per cent of the value added. Comparatively, in 2008, the transportation sector in the EU-27 produced 2.87 per cent of the total value added. Table 2.1

---

[26] The Turkish input-output table is from 2002 and the EU-27 input-output table is from 2008.

Table 2.1 Importance of transportation sub-sectors

	Turkey	EU-27
Share of transportation sub-sectors' value added in total value added (%)		
Land transport including transport via pipeline services	8.447	2.300
Water transport services	0.956	0.330
Air transport services	0.402	0.240
Total transport services	9.805	2.870
Backward linkages		
Land transport including transport via pipeline services	1.844	2.184
Water transport services	1.790	2.548
Air transport services	2.270	2.911
Forward linkages		
Land transport including transport via pipeline services	1.937	2.694
Water transport services	2.946	1.642
Air transport services	1.710	2.052

Source: Own calculations.

also reveals that in 2002, Turkish land transportation services (including pipelines) accounted for 8.44 per cent, water transportation services for 0.96 per cent, and air transportation services for 0.4 per cent of the total value added generated in Turkey. For the EU-27 in 2008, we note that land transportation services accounted for 2.3 per cent, water transportation for 0.33 per cent, and air transportation for 0.24 per cent of the total value added.

Although backward and forward linkages are widely used in the economics literature, discussion remains as how best to measure them.[27] In the current analysis, we follow Rasmussen's approach (1956) for determining backward linkages, and Ghosh's approach (1958) for determining forward linkages. Backward linkages, as they provide information about the sector's existing relationships with its upstream suppliers, measure the value of production the sector needs directly and indirectly from its upstream suppliers to generate one unit of sales. For example, to generate one TL of sales in road transportation, the sector must purchase inputs from its immediate supplier, the motor vehicles, trailers, and semi-trailers sector. In turn, the supplying firms may require inputs from their own suppliers. By tracking the web of inter-industry relationships round by round and calculating the total amount of production in the rest of the economy needed to support one TL of sales in road transportation, we can obtain Rasmussen's backward linkage indicator. By tracking all transactions round by round and computing the total amount of production in the rest of the economy that one TL of initial sales by the sector has helped to generate, we can determine Ghosh's forward linkage indicator.

---

[27] See, e.g. Hewing (1982) and Cella (1984).

Given the usual input-output system $X = AX + Y$, where X refers to the vector of gross output, $A = [a_{ij}]$ matrix of technical coefficients (where $a_{ij} = X_{ij}/X_j$ refers to the input of the i-th sector used to produce one unit of the j-th sector's output), X_{ij} denotes the input of the i-th sector used to produce the j-th sector's output X_j, and Y is the vector of final demands, the problem can be solved for the vector of gross output as $X = (I - A)^{-1} Y = K Y$, where I refers to the identity matrix and $K = [k_{ij}]$ is the Leontief inverse. Here, k_{ij} can be interpreted as the direct and indirect increase in the output of Industry i needed to supply a unit increase of final demand for the products of Industry j. Backward linkages following Rasmussen (1956) are then calculated as the column sum of matrix K, i.e., $B_j = \Sigma_{i=1}^{n} k_{ij}$, where n denotes the number of sectors in the economy and B_j the backward linkage for Industry j.

To determine forward linkages, we base our analysis on Ghosh (1958), whose core assumption is that output distribution patterns of inter-industry flows are proportionally fixed by sectoral origin. Let VA represent the row vector of sectoral value added, $G = [g_{ij}]$ the matrix of coefficients $g_{ij} = X_{ij}/X_i$, where g_{ij} is obtained by dividing each X_{ij} by the level of output of Industry i, and X^T the transpose of the output vector X. Hence, we have $X^T = X^T G + VA$. Solving for X^T we get $X^T = (I - G)^{-1} VA = L VA$, where L is the inverse of the matrix $(I - G)$. Each element of L denoted by l_{ij} represents the direct and indirect increase of the output of Industry i brought about by an increase of value added of Industry j. Forward linkages are calculated as the raw sum of matrix L, that is, $F_i = \Sigma_{j=1}^{n} l_{ij}$, where F_i denotes the forward linkage of Industry i.

Table 2.1, showing the backward and forward linkage indicators for the three sub-sectors in Turkey and the EU-27, reveals that in Turkey, a one-unit change in the final demand of the road transportation sector results in a 1.844-unit increase in the total output of all sectors; a one-unit increase in final demand for the maritime transportation sector results in a 1.79-unit increase in the total output of all sectors; and a one-unit increase in final demand for the air transportation sector results in a 2.27-unit increase in the total output of all sectors in the economy. By comparison, a one-unit increase in the value added of the road transportation sector results in a 1.94-unit increase in the output of that sector; a one-unit increase in the value added of the maritime transportation sector results in a 2.95-unit increase in the output of that sector; and a one-unit increase in the value added of the air transportation sector results in a 1.71-unit increase in the output of that sector. The results can also be interpreted for a particular sector, such as road transportation. Since for road transportation the backward linkage is 1.84 and the forward linkage is 1.94, we note that to produce a one-unit output for final consumption, the sector uses 0.84 TL of output produced directly and indirectly by other sectors, and sells 0.94 TL worth of output as intermediate inputs to other industries. There are fifty-eight sectors in the 2002 Turkish input-output table, and ranking the sectors from highest to lowest we find that in terms of backward linkages, air transportation is twenty-fifth, road transportation fortieth, and maritime transportation forty-third. In terms of forward linkages, maritime transportation is fifteenth, land transportation thirty-ninth, and air transportation forty-fourth.

In the case of the EU-27, we note that producing a one-unit output in land transportation for final consumption uses 1.18 units of output produced directly and indirectly by other sectors, and sells 1.69 units of output as intermediate inputs to other industries. To produce a one-unit output in water transportation for final consumption uses 1.55 units of output produced directly and indirectly by other sectors and sells 0.64 units of output as intermediate inputs to other industries. To produce a one-unit output in air transportation for final consumption uses 1.91 units of output produced directly and indirectly by other sectors and sells 1.05 units of output as intermediate inputs to other industries. There are sixty-four sectors in the 2008 EU-27 input-output table, and again ranking the sectors from highest to lowest, we determine that in terms of backward linkages, air transportation is fifth, water transportation nineteenth, and land transportation thirty-fourth. In terms of forward linkages, land transportation is twenty-fifth, air transportation thirty-ninth, and water transportation fifty-first.

The above considerations reveal that transport sectors are indeed important sectors in Turkey and the EU-27, with relatively high shares of sectoral value added in total value added generated in the economy, and with relatively strong backward and forward linkages.

2.3 Firms in Transport Sectors

The purpose of this section is to analyse several aspects of firms' economic performances in Turkish transport sectors using firm-level data. Our main data source is the Annual Industry and Service Statistics database, which comprises information from surveys conducted by the Turkish Statistical Institute (TURKSTAT) in the industry and service sectors. Our sample covers the period between 2003 and 2008. For the 2008 survey, TURKSTAT visited 100,152 firms, using the full enumeration method for enterprises with twenty employees or more and the sampling method for enterprises with one to nineteen employees. The database contains information on employment, wages, investment, value added, turnover, and foreign ownership.[28] Firms were also asked to report

---

[28] Note that previously, TURKSTAT periodically conducted its Census of Industry and Business Establishments (CIBE) of all firms and its Annual Surveys of Manufacturing Industries (ASMI) covered all firms with 10 or more employees. The set of addresses used for the ASMI was

whether or not they are engaged in services exporting and/or importing activities. We used the NACE Rev. 1.1 to classify economic activity.[29] Our analysis is based on the following transportation sectors: rail (60.10), road (60.24), maritime (61), air (62), and logistics (63.1 + 63.2 + 63.4).

Table 2.2 presents firm characteristics in different transport sectors for the period average between 2003 and 2008.[30] The summary data presented in the table cover all the firms.[31] Employment, turnover, production value, gross value added, and gross tangible investment in the tables are the aggregate figures for the sector. For the purpose of comparison, the nominal variables for the period 2003 to 2008 have been deflated by the GDP deflator, choosing 2011 as the base year. Thereafter, all nominal variables have been expressed in 2011 US dollars. Capital–labour ratio is capital per number of employees, where capital is calculated by dividing depreciation values at constant prices by sector-specific depreciation rates. Labour productivity is measured first as the ratio of production deflated by the GDP deflator to number of employees, and thereafter as the ratio of value added deflated by the GDP deflator to number of employees. Foreign participation is the percentage of foreign ownership of the total in the sector. Finally, percentages of services exporters and importers are the ratio of firms engaged in export and import activities, respectively, to all firms in the sector. In Table 2.2, rail enterprise characteristics could not be derived from the TURKSTAT database because the TCDD held a monopoly in the sector until very recently, and TURKSTAT does not give firm-level information when the number of firms in a sector is very small. To determine railway sector characteristics we use annual statistics prepared by the TCDD.

Table 2.2 shows that the road transportation sector has the highest number of firms among the transport sectors. Furthermore, the road transport sector generates most of the employment, production, and value added in the transport sector overall, followed by the logistics sector. The TCDD is the

---

obtained through the CIBE. In addition, every non-census year, addresses of newly opened private establishments with 10 or more employees are obtained from the chamber of industry. Since 2003, TURKSTAT has conducted its Annual Survey of Industry and Services. The questionnaires used in these surveys are available from http://www.tuik.gov.tr (accessed 9 February 2016). Until 2006, the surveys did not include any information on foreign ownership. Note that the analysis in the following is based largely on the approaches developed by Bernard et al. (2007), Mayer and Ottaviano (2007), and Breinlich and Criscuolo (2011).

[29] The acronym is derived from Nomenclature statistique des Activités économiques dans la Communauté Européenne (Statistical Classification of Economic Activities in the European Community).

[30] Although data are available from the Annual Industry and Service Statistics for the 2003 to 2009 period, we only consider surveys between 2003 and 2008, for two reasons: First, in 2009, TURKSTAT switched from NACE 1.1 to NACE 2, causing comparability problems. Second, 2009 was when the global financial crisis led to substantial decreases in economic activity in Turkey.

[31] Due to confidentiality protocols, the table was prepared from the summary statistics in the database on the TURKSTAT website rather than from the micro-data itself.

Table 2.2 Descriptive statistics

	Turkish State Railways	Road (60.24)	Maritime (61)	Air (62.1 + 62.2)	Logistics (63.1 + 63.2 + 63.4)
Number of firms	1	128,692	3,395	55	12,695
Employment	32,430	266,860	28,659	16,864	92,592
Production value (US$)	1,637,523,581	20,922,276,022	5,655,924,719	6,030,612,370	7,870,628,498
Gross value added (US$)	—	3,131,135,901	1,660,539,496	1,222,225,633	2,965,240,081
Average wage (US$)		3,784	16,463	40,589	9,852
Labour productivity					
production-to-employment	50,494	78,402	197,352	357,603	85,003
value added-to-employment		11,733	57,941	72,475	32,025
Employment per firm	32,430.00	2.07	8.44	306.62	7.29
Gross tangible Investment (US$)	—	2,389,904,572	777,472,344	330,733,824	887,265,892
Capital:Labour ratio (US$)	—	565,730	156,395	125,721	140,062
Foreign participation (%)	13.63	0.02	0.35	2.28	0.15

Note: The US$ values refer to 2003–8 averages. In case of foreign participation the value is 2006–8 average.

Source: Own calculations.

third-largest employer in the transport sector, followed by maritime and air transport employers. In terms of production value, the air transport sector is the third most important sector, followed by the maritime and rail transport sectors. In terms of value added, the third-largest sector is maritime transport, followed by air transport.[32]

Analysing the labour productivity figures (measured by a value of the production-to-employment ratio) reveals that the highest labour productivity is obtained in air transport, followed by maritime transport, logistics, road transport, and rail transport. Similar results are obtained when productivity is measured in terms of a value-added-to-employment ratio. Analysing the employment structure reveals that the number of employed persons per firm is very large in the rail transport sector, followed by the air transport, maritime transport, logistics, and road transport sectors. Examining the capital–labour ratio reveals that it is high in the road transport sector, and that the maritime transport, logistics, and air transport sectors have quite similar capital intensity structures. Finally, we note that foreign participation is rather low in all transport sectors; it is highest in air transport, followed by maritime transport, logistics, and road transport.

The figures on service exporters and service importers provided in Table 2.3 are based on responses to the question in the samples of whether or not firms exported or imported services in the years 2003 to 2008.[33] The figures for 2008 reveal that 58.27 per cent of maritime transport firms are engaged in exporting, while 50 per cent of air transport firms, 35.21 per cent of road transport firms, and 13.92 per cent of logistics firms, respectively, are engaged in exporting. The share of air transport enterprises engaged in importing is 7.81 per cent, which decreases to 3.96 per cent for maritime enterprises, 2.82 per cent for road transport enterprises, and 1.72 per cent in the case of logistics firms.

Table 2.3 Descriptive statistics on trade in transportation services in 2008

		Firms in sample		Share	
		Exp.	Imp.	Exp.	Imp.
1	Rail	2	0	40.00	0.00
2	Road	400	32	35.21	2.82
3	Maritime	162	11	58.27	3.96
4	Air	32	5	50.00	7.81
5	Logistics	97	12	13.92	1.72
	Total	693	60		

Source: Own calculations.

---

[32] In the TURKSTAT data there is no value-added data for railways.
[33] We do not use all the data in Table 2.2 due to consistency considerations. We use the cleaned sample of the data presented in Table 2.2.

Therefore, half the firms in the air transport and maritime transport sectors engage in exporting, whereas the number of firms engaged in exporting in the other transportation sectors is relatively low. We note that firms in transport sectors import less than they export.

Table 2.4 provides basic information on transportation service exporters and importers in Turkey for 2008. The table shows that these activities are

Table 2.4 Importers and exporters of transportation sectors in 2008

1) Share of firms

	Firms that do not trade	Firms that only export	Firms that only import	Firms that both export and import
Maritime	41.37	54.68	0.36	3.60
Rail	60.00	40.00	0.00	0.00
Air	50.00	42.19	0.00	7.81
Road	64.61	32.57	0.18	2.64
Logistic	85.51	12.77	0.57	1.15
Total	67.89	29.36	0.32	2.43

2) Share of sector in total

	Employment	Turnover
Maritime	6.87	14.74
Rail	14.13	3.97
Air	7.94	25.92
Road	40.50	36.19
Logistic	30.56	19.18
Total	100.00	100.00

3) Employment share

	Firms that do not trade	Firms that only export	Firms that only import	Firms that both export and import
Maritime	43.42	51.71	0.05	4.82
Rail	0.24	99.76	0.00	0.00
Air	6.10	26.16	0.00	67.75
Road	49.71	47.82	0.09	2.38
Logistic	65.05	20.48	0.36	14.11
Total	43.54	45.33	0.15	10.99

4) Turnover share

	Firms that do not trade	Firms that only export	Firms that only import	Firms that both export and import
Maritime	42.24	54.24	0.00	3.51
Rail	1.74	98.26	0.00	0.00
Air	5.24	26.37	0.00	68.39
Road	44.15	51.06	0.06	4.73
Logistic	57.96	24.36	0.58	17.10
Total	34.78	41.86	0.13	23.22

Source: Own calculations.

rare in the sector; only 32.11 per cent of firms are engaged in either exporting or importing. However, a decomposition of the transportation sector shows that the services trade tendency varies across sectors. In the maritime and air transportation sectors, half or more of the enterprises engage in services trade, with 58.63 per cent of maritime firms and 50 per cent of air firms. In rail transportation, 40 per cent of firms on average are engaged in trade, whereas only 35.39 per cent of road transport firms are engaged in exporting or importing. The transport sector with the lowest share (14.49 per cent) of traders is the logistics sector. Firms in the transport sectors mainly export; only 0.32 per cent of the enterprises in the sample engage in importing.

Table 2.4 reveals that the road transport sector generates the highest employment and turnover among the transportation sectors. The share of employment in road transportation is 40.5 per cent of the total employment generated in the sector as a whole and the turnover share is 36.19 per cent. The logistics sector generates 30.56 per cent of employment in the transportation sector and 19.18 per cent of turnover; the rail sector generates 14.13 per cent of employment and 3.97 per cent of turnover, the maritime sector generates 6.87 per cent of employment and 14.74 per cent of turnover, and the air transport sector generates 7.94 per cent of employment and 25.92 per cent of turnover.

Although firms engaged in trading transportation services form only 32.11 per cent of all firms in the transportation sector, these firms account for a large share of economic activity. Service traders in the sector account for 56.46 per cent of employment and 65.22 per cent of turnover. These figures provide the first signs of the large variations between services traders and non-traders in this sector. For example, in each of the years studied, although the *percentage* of firms engaged in services trade did not increase by much, firms that trade services grew in *size* at a significantly higher rate than non-trading firms.

The rail transportation sector is composed of the TCDD and the affiliates formed from this company. Therefore, it is natural that this monopoly (a service trader) accounts for almost all of the employment and turnover in the rail sector.

Although only half the firms in the air transportation sector engage in trade, the share of employment and turnover of these firms comprises more than 90 per cent of the overall employment and turnover in this sector. Services traders in the road transportation sector account for 50.29 per cent of employment and 55.85 per cent of turnover in that sector, and services traders in maritime transportation account for 56.58 per cent of employment and 57.76 per cent of turnover in that sector. The employment share of services traders in the logistics sector is 34.95 and the turnover is 42.04 per cent.

To further explain the characteristics of transport firms that export services, we turn to Table 2.5, which shows the export premia for transport sector

Table 2.5 Exporter premia in the transport sector

	Log turnover	Log employment	Log capital intensity	Log productivity	Log wage
Year fixed effects					
Exporter premia	0.0588***	0.0766***	0.482***	−0.0114	0.102***
	(0.0192)	(0.0138)	(0.129)	(0.0155)	(0.0291)
Year and industry fixed effects					
Exporter premia	0.0565***	0.0766***	0.479***	−0.0129	0.0999***
	(0.0191)	(0.0138)	(0.129)	(0.0155)	(0.0291)
Observations	12,303	11,815	11,815	11,815	12,303

Note: Standard errors are reported in brackets. ***, **, and * denotes significance at 1 per cent, 5 per cent, and 10 per cent respectively. The upper panel reports the coefficients from year fixed-effects regressions whereas the lower panel reports year and industry fixed-effects estimations. The dependent variables are the firm characteristics, whereas the explanatory variable is the export premia defined as a dummy variable that takes the value 1 if the firm exports services and takes the value 0 otherwise.

Source: Own calculations.

exporters between 2003 and 2008. Noting that these premia are derived from the results of a series of bivariate ordinary least square regressions, where the explanatory variable is a dummy variable that takes the value 1 if the firm is involved in services exports and takes the value 0 otherwise, and that the dependent variables are firm characteristics such as turnover, employment, capital intensity measured as capital–labour ratio, labour productivity, and wages, we report the results of the regression analysis in Table 2.5. All the dependent variables in the table are in real terms, except employment, and they are all measured in logarithms. The regressions are fixed-effects panel estimations.[34] The first part of the table presents the year fixed-effects regressions and the second part summarizes the year and industry fixed effects.

The coefficients in Table 2.5 can be interpreted as percentages because all the variables in the regressions are in their logarithmic forms. The highest export premia are in the capital-intensity variable. Services-exporting firms are 48 per cent more capital intensive than non-exporters. They pay 10 per cent higher wages. Moreover, exporting firms in the transport sector have 5.9 per cent more turnover and generate 7.7 per cent more employment compared to non-exporters. These simple observations do not indicate any differences in productivity between exporting firms and non-exporting firms in Turkey's transport sector for the period 2003 to 2008. The second part of the table repeats the same estimations by including industry and year fixed effects. Services-exporting firms remain different from non-exporting firms in this setting also. The fact that the coefficients are very similar with and without industry fixed

---

[34] We performed the Hausmann test for all regressions and the results were in favour of fixed effects. They are available upon request.

effects suggests that the characteristics of exporting firms are not different across transport sectors.[35] Studying the characteristics of importing firms, we now note that firms in the Turkish transportation sector are not services importers, as shown in Table 2.3. As services imports in the transport sector are almost zero in Turkey, we consider firms that export and import in the following: Considering a table similar to Table 2.4 but taking the period average for 2003–8, we note that in the air transport sector 10.34 per cent of firms both export and import transport services, and that this share is 1.65 per cent in the maritime transport sector, 0.11 per cent in logistics, and 0.07 per cent in road transport. We now ask whether there are differences between firms that export only and firms that both export and import.

In Table 2.6 we run fixed-effects regressions to compare the characteristics of exporting and importing firms in the transport sector. The dependent variables in Row 1 of the table are firm characteristics: turnover, employment, capital intensity measured as capital–labour ratio, labour productivity, and wages. All dependent variables are measured in real terms and shown in their logarithmic forms. The explanatory variables in these regressions are the dummy variables representing trade premia. The exporter premia variable takes the value 1 if the firm engages in services exports but not imports, and takes the value 0 otherwise; the importer premia variable takes the value 1 if the firm imports but not exports, and takes the value 0 otherwise; and finally the exporter and importer premia take the value 1 if the firm exports and imports, and take the value 0 otherwise.

We have already observed exporter premia. Firms that engage in services exports in the transport sector have higher turnover, higher employment, pay higher wages, and are more capital intensive compared to non-exporters, as before. However, we do not observe any significant difference between importers and non-exporters as the number of observations for importers is not enough to capture regularity. Finally, we observe that premia for firms that both export and import are larger in size compared to non-traders. On the other hand, these firms are not significantly different from non-exporters in capital intensity, productivity, or wages. Table 2.6 shows that firms that both export and import are larger in size, which is measured in terms of employment and turnover, compared to only exporters. While firms that only export are larger than non-exporters by 5.21 per cent, firms that both export and import are larger than non-exporters by 9.94 per cent

---

[35] The export premia that we observe in the Turkish transport sector is consistent with the results reported in the literature. Bernard et al. (2007) and Mayer and Ottaviano (2007) find export premia for goods exporters. Breinlich and Criscuolo (2011) determine export premia for service exporters for the UK.

Table 2.6 Trade premia in the transport sector

	Log turnover	Log employment	Log capital intensity	Log productivity	Log wage
Year fixed effects					
Exporter premia	0.0521***	0.0759***	0.614***	−0.0159	0.110***
	(0.0199)	(0.0142)	(0.1330)	(0.0161)	(0.0302)
Importer premia	0.00106	0.00151	0.0865	0.0156	−0.0389
	(0.1060)	(0.0742)	(0.6930)	(0.0838)	(0.1610)
Exporter and importer premia	0.0994***	0.0813***	-0.325	0.0178	0.0461
	(0.0358)	(0.0253)	(0.2370)	(0.0286)	(0.0544)
Year and industry fixed effects					
Exporter premia	0.0497**	0.0759***	0.6110***	−0.0174	0.109***
	(0.0198)	(0.0142)	(0.1330)	(0.0161)	(0.0302)
Importer premia	0.0012	0.0016	0.0828	0.0147	−0.0408
	(0.1050)	(0.0742)	(0.6940)	(0.0837)	(0.1610)
Exporter & Importer Premia	0.0974***	0.0813***	−0.330	0.0163	0.0438
	(0.0357)	(0.0357)	(0.2370)	(0.0286)	(0.0544)
Observations	12,303	11,815	11,815	11,815	12,303

Note: Standard errors are reported in brackets. ***, **, and * denotes significance at 1 per cent, 5 per cent, and 10 per cent respectively. The upper panel reports the coefficients from year fixed-effects regressions whereas the lower panel reports year and industry fixed-effects estimations. The dependent variables are the firm characteristics, whereas the explanatory variables are the exporter premia defined as a dummy variable that takes the value 1 if the firm exports services and takes the value 0 otherwise. The exporter and importer premia defined as dummy variable that takes the value 1 if the firm both exports and imports services and takes the value 0 otherwise.

Source: Own calculations.

in terms of turnover. Note that we observe a similar pattern when we include industry effects into the regressions, as presented in the bottom part of Table 2.6. Therefore, these characteristics of exporter premia and exporter and importer premia are not specific to the transport sub-sectors; the results suggest that whether firms export or import, firm characteristics are systematically related to participation in international trade.

2.4 State of Competition: Evidence of Mark-Ups

The state of competition in a particular market may be affected, as emphasized by Martins et al. (1996), by the number of firms in a market, the prevailing regulations, the openness of an economy to international competition, the existence of anti-competitive or collusive behaviour, and the strictness and enforcement of competition policies, government procurement policies, and trade policies. When trying to estimate empirically the degree of competition in a particular market, the so-called 'Lerner index' is used, defined as the mark-up of product price (p) over marginal cost (MC), that is, (p − MC)/p. With perfect competition, price equals marginal cost and the index will be zero. When prices exceed marginal cost, the Lerner index becomes positive and varies between zero and unity.

Direct empirical estimation of the Lerner index is quite difficult since marginal costs are not observable. In the 1980s, Hall (1988) proposed an indirect approach. Given the production function $Q = A\,F(K, L)$, where Q denotes output, K capital, L labour, and A the index of Hicks-neutral technical change, define marginal cost as:

$$MC = \frac{w\,\Delta L + r\,\Delta K}{\Delta Q - \theta Q},$$

where w and r are the wage rate and rental price of capital, and θ is the rate of technical progress. This relation can be written as $MC\,\Delta Q - MC\,\theta Q = w\,\Delta L + r\,\Delta K$. Dividing by MC, we get $\Delta Q - \theta Q = \frac{w \Delta L}{MC} + \frac{r \Delta K}{MC}$, which, by dividing by Q, can be written as:

$$\frac{\Delta Q}{Q} = \frac{wL}{MC\,Q}\frac{\Delta L}{L} + \frac{rK}{MC\,Q}\frac{\Delta K}{K} + \theta.$$

Subtracting $\frac{\Delta K}{K}$ from both sides, we get:

$$\frac{\Delta Q}{Q} - \frac{\Delta K}{K} = \frac{wL}{MC\,Q}\frac{\Delta L}{L} - \left(1 - \frac{rK}{MC\,Q}\right)\frac{\Delta K}{K} + \theta.$$

Under constant returns to scale, since $\frac{wL}{MC\,Q} + \frac{rk}{MC\,Q} = 1$, we have:

$$\frac{\Delta Q}{Q} - \frac{\Delta K}{K} = \frac{wL}{MC\,Q}\left\{\frac{\Delta L}{L} - \frac{\Delta K}{K}\right\} + \theta.$$

Defining mark-up as $\mu = \frac{p}{MC}$, where p denotes the output price, we get:

$$\frac{\Delta Q}{Q} - \frac{\Delta K}{K} = \mu\frac{wL}{pQ}\left\{\frac{\Delta L}{L} - \frac{\Delta K}{K}\right\} + \theta.$$

Letting q stand for the output-to-capital ratio $q = \frac{Q}{K}$, and l for the labour-to-capital ratio $l = \frac{L}{K}$, and assuming mark-up remains constant over time, Hall (1988) derives the fundamental equation:

$$\frac{\Delta q}{q} = \mu\,a_t\frac{\Delta l}{l} + \theta,$$

where $a = \frac{wL}{pQ}$ denotes the share of labour in value added. Hall's approach aims to estimate the mark-up ratio from this equation by assuming that the rate of technical progress can be described as a random deviation from the underlying constant rate:

$$\theta_t = \theta + u_t.$$

The equation to be estimated is written as:

$$\frac{\Delta q_t}{q_t} = \mu\,a_t\frac{\Delta l_t}{l_t} + \theta + u_t.$$

Thus, the observed labour share in value added is used as a benchmark for the coefficient associated with the growth of the labour–capital ratio. Since, in general, the labour–capital ratio is correlated with the productivity term, an ordinary

73

least squares estimate will not be consistent. Hence, Hall (1988) proposes to replace the labour–capital ratio with a set of instrumental variables.

Roger (1995) proposes an alternative way of computing mark-ups. Using the definition of the Lerner index $B = \frac{p - MC}{p} = 1 - \frac{1}{\mu}$, we get $\mu = \frac{1}{1-B}$ and hence:

$$\frac{\Delta q}{q} = \left(\frac{1}{1-B}\right) a_t \frac{\Delta l}{l} + \theta.$$

Multiplying this relation by (1–B), we get:

$$\frac{\Delta Q}{Q} - a\frac{\Delta L}{L} - (1-a)\frac{\Delta K}{K} = B\frac{\Delta Q}{Q} - B\frac{\Delta K}{K} + (1-B)\,\theta. \tag{1}$$

Next, Roger (1995) considers the cost function for a representative firm operating under constant returns to scale:

$$C(w, r, Q, A) = \frac{G(w, r)Q}{A},$$

where A is the index of the Hicks-neutral technical change. The marginal cost is defined as:

$$MC = \frac{\partial C}{\partial Q} = \frac{G(w, r)}{A}.$$

Taking the natural logarithm, the relation reduces to:

$$\ln MC = \ln G(w, r) - \ln A,$$

and taking the derivative, we get:

$$\frac{d\,MC}{MC} = \frac{\partial G}{\partial w}\frac{dw}{G} + \frac{\partial G}{\partial r}\frac{dr}{G} - \theta.$$

Making use of Shephard's Lemma, Roger (1995) reduces the above relation to:

$$\frac{\Delta\,MC}{MC} = \left[\frac{wL}{w}\right]\left(\frac{\Delta w}{w}\right) + \left(1 - \frac{wL}{C}\right)\frac{\Delta r}{r} - \theta$$

and further to:

$$a\left(\frac{\Delta w}{w}\right) + (1-a)\left(\frac{\Delta r}{r}\right) - \frac{\Delta p}{p} = -B\left(\frac{\Delta p}{p} - \frac{\Delta r}{r}\right) + (1-B)\theta. \tag{2}$$

Equations (2) and (3) contain the term (1–B) θ. By subtracting (2) from (1) and rearranging the terms, we obtain:

$$\left[\frac{\Delta Q}{Q} + \frac{\Delta p}{p}\right] - a\left[\frac{\Delta L}{L} + \frac{\Delta w}{w}\right] - (1-a)\left[\frac{\Delta K}{K} + \frac{\Delta r}{r}\right] = B\left[\frac{\Delta Q}{Q} + \frac{\Delta p}{p}\right] - B\left[\frac{\Delta K}{K} + \frac{\Delta r}{r}\right].$$

Next, Roger (1995) defines the dependent variable as:

$$\Delta y = \left[\frac{\Delta Q}{Q} + \frac{\Delta p}{p}\right] - a\left[\frac{\Delta L}{L} + \frac{\Delta w}{w}\right] - (1-a)\left[\frac{\Delta K}{K} + \frac{\Delta r}{r}\right].$$

and the independent variable as:

$$\Delta x = \left[\frac{\Delta Q}{Q} + \frac{\Delta p}{p}\right] - \left[\frac{\Delta K}{K} + \frac{\Delta r}{r}\right].$$

The equation to be estimated reduces then to:

$$\Delta y = B\,\Delta x. \tag{3}$$

Interpreting the dependent variable as the nominal Solow residual and the explanatory variable as the growth rate of nominal output/capital ratio, we end up with the estimation equation:

$$\Delta y_t = B\,\Delta x_t + \epsilon_t.$$

We estimate Equation (3) for mark-ups in Turkey's transport sector using the firm-level data from Section 2.3. Following Roger (1995), we obtain mark-ups as $1/(1-B)$ using the Lerner index. We use fixed-effects regressions with robust standard errors. We also use ordinary least square estimates and the results were similar. Although we provide the results of the estimation for the railway sector, one should consider that the number of observations for the sector is low for the estimation.

The mark-up estimation results shown in Table 2.7 suggest that imperfect competition prevails in the road transport sector. In other words, prices in road transport sector exceed marginal costs. The mark-up estimates for other

Table 2.7 Mark-up estimations for transport sectors in Turkey

	B	M	#obs
Maritime	0.158	1.188	1,067
	(0.219)		
Rail	0.023	1.024	13
	(0.277)		
Air	0.219	1.280	164
	(0.209)		
Road	0.274***	1.377	3,416
	(0.044)		
Logistics	0.080	1.087	2,132
	(0.342)		

Note: Standard errors are in parentheses. *** Denotes significance at 1 per cent. M denotes mark-up and is calculated as $M = 1/(1-B)$, following Roeger (1995).

Source: Own calculations.

transport sectors are not significant. Moreover, the lowest mark-up estimate we obtain is in the logistics sector, implying that the sector is competitive.

2.5 Conclusion

Developments at both the level and quality of transportation infrastructure in Turkey indicate considerable improvements over time. According to the WEF, Turkey ranks fortieth among 144 countries in the quality index for roads, and thirty-fourth according to the quality of air transport infrastructure. The World Bank's LPI ranks Turkey in the top thirty countries of the world. Today, Turkey's road network has reached 65,909 km and the length of dual- carriageway roads is 22,460 km. In addition, the government has begun a large motorway programme through PPPs. Turkey plans to increase the motorway network to 7,827 km by 2023, the one hundredth anniversary of the establishment of the Republic. The country is in the process of over-hauling its railway sector by promoting competition and private sector participation. The Law on Liberalization of Railway Transportation became effective in 2013 and over a period of five years, Turkey plans to put in place the regulations necessary to implement the law. Furthermore, during the last six or seven years, Turkey has upgraded its seaports substantially, and is planning further upgrades until 2023. Turkish Airlines is considered one of the fastest growing airlines in the world, and Istanbul's Atatürk Airport has turned into a major international transit hub.

Examining the strong forward and backward linkages of Turkey's transport sectors reveals that transport sectors in Turkey are very important. However, investigating Turkish enterprise characteristics in different transportation sub-sectors using firm-level data reveals that exporting and importing are rather rare activities in the sector. Services trading mainly takes the form of exporting, and firms rarely import. Although the percentage of firms that engage in trading transportation services is rather low, these firms account for a large share of economic activity. Finally, studying the mark-ups in different transport sectors reveals that imperfect competition appears in the road transport sector.

3

The Regulatory Framework in Road Freight Transportation

Road transport represents between 0.4 and 4.9 per cent of countries' gross domestic product (GDP) and between 0.3 and 3.9 per cent of countries' employment, depending on their geography and the structure of their transport networks.[1] Studies show that road is the main mode of freight transport for a large number of countries. According to Eurostat (2015), road haulage measured in tonne-kilometres represented 49.4 per cent of Europe's freight transport in 2013.

This chapter, studying the regulatory framework in road freight transportation, is structured as follows: Section 3.1 discusses the functioning of the road freight transportation sector. Section 3.2 considers international rules and regulations in the road freight transportation sector, Section 3.3 covers EU rules and regulations in the sector, and Section 3.4 discusses Turkish rules and regulations. Finally, Section 3.5 concludes.

3.1 Road Freight Transportation Services

The road freight industry is geared to distribution, logistics, and basic physical transport. As emphasized by Boylaud (2000), road freight is a key sector of the economy, playing a major role in market integration and having a direct impact on transaction costs for economic agents. The World Trade Organization (WTO) Secretariat (2001a) emphasizes that because of the downstream nature of road transport activity, steadily increasing complexity of production methods, and generalization of just-in-time production, road transport has a considerable impact on GDP and employment.

---

[1] See WTO (2010a). According to Grosso et al. (2014), in 2010 road transport together with rail transport accounted for 2.43 per cent of the GDP and 2.9 per cent of employment in countries that are part of the Organisation for Economic Co-operation and Development (OECD).

The road freight transportation industry is divided into two segments. The first segment consists of a large number of small firms providing basic transport services, and the second segment incorporates a limited number of major hauliers providing more sophisticated logistics services. Firms in the first segment compete mainly on price, and barriers to entry into the sector are low because, in general, little start-up capital is needed. This segment of the sector is competitive because of its small economies of scale with low entry and exit costs. Firms in the second segment, however, compete both in price and in the range and quality of services. Here, economies of scale are important, and information and communications technologies are increasingly used, such as electronic data transfers and tracking systems, because they enable hauliers to provide better-quality services to a much wider range of destinations. Studies reveal that the most important attributes for shippers of manufactured goods are freight rates and arrival time reliability.[2] Avoidance of damage and deterioration, communication with respect to problems, and frequency of service are also important, but to a lesser extent.

According to the Final Resolution of the twenty-sixth Congress of the International Road Transport Union held at Marrakesh on 20 March 1998, there are different types of barriers to cross-border trade in road freight transportation services. The first of these barriers is roads and motorway blockages as a result of political conflicts. For example, consider the border closure between Lebanon and Syria and between Israel and Syria; the border closure between Armenia and Azerbaijan; and the border closure between Morocco and Algeria. The issues causing these closures are very complex, and their resolution is important because they represent a prerequisite for enabling any kind of border crossing. The second type of barrier to border crossings includes document standardization for customs, customs declaration and clearance procedures, and poor infrastructure and equipment at border points. Finally, the third type of barrier to cross-border trade concerns access to the profession, vehicle standards, drivers' working conditions, and checks and sanctions.

To facilitate customs declarations and clearance procedures at the borders, a large number of countries use information technology (IT) packages. Often, however, these packages do not support modern risk-management techniques and are not linked to the EU's overall port management systems, thus they do not allow electronic data interchanges (EDI) with service providers and economic operators, such as freight forwarders and customs officials. As a result, the rate of inspections at customs in such countries continues to be much higher than the rate in EU countries (2 per cent).

---

[2] See Londono-Kent (2009).

When parties involved in the process of clearing cargo are connected through IT and EDI, then full automation of customs declarations, cargo manifests, illustrations of cargo distribution on ships, cargo invoices, certificates for tax and duty payments, and certificates issued by monitoring authorities can be achieved.

The infrastructure and equipment at the border points of non-EU countries is often insufficient or in need of upgrading. The main issues here are the lack or underdevelopment of laboratories, warehouses, road approaches to the border, border gates, vehicle parking areas, reliable electricity and power sources, reliable telecommunications services, and offices for inspection and control agents. Eliminating these shortfalls would improve the efficiency of customs services and procedures and decrease barriers to trade in road freight services. According to the WTO Secretariat (2001a), the annual cost of all barriers amounts to between 1 and 7 per cent of the total transport costs in Western Europe, and between 8 and 29 per cent of total transport costs in Central and Eastern Europe.

The use of the *single administrative document* (SAD) by customs authorities in different countries facilitates trade. The SAD is a standard form that can be shared by all involved border authorities, thereby enabling significant time-savings in crossing borders and clearing cargo. In the EU, the SAD is used within the framework of trade with third countries and for the movement of non-EU goods within the EU. It is aimed at ensuring openness in national administrative requirements, rationalizing, and reducing administrative documentation, reducing the amount of requested information, and standardizing and harmonizing data.

There are also regulatory barriers to trade, with two broad categories of regulations: those regarding traffic and vehicles, and those regarding market operations. The first category includes vehicle standards, highway codes, and traffic restrictions. The second category covers market access conditions, price regulations, fiscal conditions, social conditions, technical conditions, and road safety.

Vehicle regulations address how motor vehicles should be manufactured. They are numerous and apply to a great many technical points, such as fittings and roadworthiness tests and to specific vehicle characteristics. The United Nations Economic Commission for Europe (UNECE) set up a Working Party on the Construction of Vehicles (WP29) in 1953 and agreed upon its first regulation in 1958. The 1958 UNECE Agreement and the regulations under it set out the technical norms with which road vehicles must comply. The scheme was, as emphasized by Braithwaite and Drahos (2000), such that if, for example, a German factory was approved by the German government to manufacture vehicles of a certain design, other European states would grant mutual recognition to the type approval. The job of WP29 was to ensure that the grounds for type approvals in different states converged sufficiently to make mutual recognition acceptable. Recently, the European Commission helped develop new standards. Once the Commission decides on a standard that is agreed upon among experts in its member states, then a member state is delegated to take it to the WP29. In this way, the European Commission uses the WP29 to attempt to globalize a direction for standards.[3]

The rules and regulations pertaining to market access conditions, price regulations, fiscal conditions, social conditions, technical conditions, and road safety have been developed in two ways: through bilateral agreements concluded by the decisions of the European Conference of Ministers of Transport (ECMT), the UNECE, and WTO negotiations, and through the domestic regulations of sovereign nations as well as the regulations of regional political and economic partnerships such as the EU.

3.2 Bilateral and Multilateral Road Freight Transport Agreements

Market access regulations on road transport, as emphasized by Kunaka et al. (2013), have their roots in the 1930s, when governments sought to protect railways from competition by introducing a system of licenses, quotas, and tariffs for road transport. Tight regulations were introduced in North America and Europe on road transportation, and were implemented mainly at the national level. This system prevailed until the 1980s, when transport services across various modes were deregulated. Boylaud (2000) emphasizes that the main rationale for regulating the road freight business relates to road safety, the environment, and infrastructure congestion. In both cases, bilateral agreements were concluded to implement quantitative restrictions at an international level.

Bilateral road transport agreements typically restrict the number of vehicles allowed to provide services between two countries. The contracting states exchange blank licenses that each issues to its transporters on behalf of the other. Bilateral licenses cover the activities of own-account transport operations

---

[3] We shall not consider vehicle regulations in the rest of our study. During the Transatlantic Trade and Investment Partnership (TTIP) negotiations between the United States (US) and the EU, one of the major problems faced by negotiators was how to achieve regulatory coherence in the automobile industry. Since the US has its own safety vehicle standards, which deviate considerably from the EU standards, and both sides consider their own standards as superior to the other's, car manufacturers have to make separate models for US and EU markets. Since returns to scale are underutilized, consumers in both countries face higher average prices. With trade liberalization between the EU and the US, consumers would face lower prices and more variety. For a discussion of related issues see Freund and Oliver (2015) and Commission of the European Communities (2015).

and of public transport operations.[4] Bilateral licenses can be valid for a return journey undertaken within a given time (to a maximum of three months from the date of issue) or for a period of one year and an indeterminate number of journeys. Moreover, it may be that the foreign issuing country only makes a certain license valid for transit, whereas others make them valid for both the return journey and/or transit. Bilateral licenses, granted according to the principle of reciprocity, present the advantage for the issuing countries of enabling them to control the flow of commercial traffic and, in principle, of producing a certain balance of national operators.

According to the WTO (2010a), the international road transport regime is made up of thousands of bilateral agreements. Countries prefer these agreements in part because they are easy to negotiate and manage, but their sheer numbers require establishing institutions, procedures, documentation, conditions, and penalties. The most common implementing structures involve ministries in charge of transport, foreign affairs, or communications, as well as road regulators, road infrastructure administrations, border agencies, chambers of commerce, and associations of transport operators. Usually, the process of obtaining a permit is burdensome, discretionary, paper-based, and can require the physical presence of the transport operator, who may need to travel long distances from his or her home base to the place of permit distribution. However, this process can be straightforward, as pointed out by Kunaka et al. (2013), if countries are willing to reduce the burden on transport operators and computerize procedures.

Note that the full utilization of bilateral quotas in relations between two non-adjacent countries depends on the availability of transit quotas in the countries between the original two. In fact, the countries at the ends of the chain must negotiate their transit quotas individually with each of the intermediate countries. Thus, for a given transit route, the full utilization of the bilateral quota depends theoretically on the lowest transit quota, which may be less than the bilateral quota. There is also a visa issue because the driver must obtain visas for each country involved in a journey.

Lately, bilateral road transport agreements have contained clauses on qualitative market access criteria, such as the strict application and enforcement of driving and rest time rules for hauliers established in the country of the other

---

[4] According to the ECMT (1997), 'transport on own account' means transport in the following ways: (i) using vehicles owned by the operator or that the operator has hired under a long-term contract or leased and that are driven by employees of the enterprise; (ii) that is only an ancillary activity in the context of all the other activities of the enterprise or association; (iii) either of goods that are the property of the enterprise or association or have been sold, bought, let out on hire, or hired, produced, extracted, processed, or repaired by the undertaking, the purpose of the transport being to carry the goods to or from the enterprise or to move them for its own requirements; and (iv) of employees of the enterprise or members of a non-profit-making association for whom the transport is part of its social or welfare activities.

contracting party; the application for hauliers established in the country of the other contracting party of admission-to-the-occupation rules of a qualitative nature, similar to those of the EU; the extended use of more environmentally friendly vehicles (the higher on the environmentally friendly norm scale of engines, the better, and the more rewarded by additional permits); and adherence to various UNECE conventions (WTO, 2010a and UNECE, 2012).

In 1997, the ECMT developed a model for bilateral agreements to be conducted by countries mainly in Europe. Covering both own-account transport and transport on behalf of third parties, the agreement consists of the following conditions: it prohibits cabotage except with special authorization; vehicles of the home country are exempt from payment of all tax related to the ownership, registration, and running of the vehicle as well as special taxes on transport services; weights (permissible maximum weight, axle weight) and dimensions of vehicles may exceed the upper limits in force in the host country only with a special permit applied for in advance; vehicles have to comply with the provisions of the UNECE's international conventions as well as the EU's environmental standards.[5] Furthermore, there is a permit requirement for transport, except for transport by light vehicle, transport on own account, transport of perishable goods, transport of livestock, transport between neighbouring countries (in certain cases only), and combined transport. The quota requirements, specified in terms of the number of individual journeys or the number of permits valid for specified period, form the core of the bilateral capacity control system. Finally, note that the full utilization of bilateral quotas in the relationship between two non-adjacent countries depends, as indicated, on the availability of transit quotas in the intervening transit countries (ECMT, 1997).[6]

3.2.1 European Conference of Ministers of Transport and the International Transport Forum

The ECMT, an inter-governmental organization established by a protocol signed in 1953, is a forum in which ministers responsible for transport, and more specifically the transport sector, could co-operate on policy. The group is administratively linked to the OECD, whose geographical realm has progressively expanded to include the countries of Central and Eastern Europe and

---

[5] The related UNECE conventions are the 'European Agreement Concerning the International Carriage of Dangerous Goods by Road', the 'Agreement on the International Carriage of Perishable Foodstuffs and on the Special Equipment to Be Used for Such Carriage', and the 'European Agreement Concerning the Work of Crews of Vehicles Engaged in International Road Transport'. For a discussion of these agreements, see the following section on UNECE.

[6] For a discussion of the operation of bilateral agreements, including transit quotas, see WTO (2010a).

then the Caucasus. The ECMT's role primarily consists of (i) helping to create an integrated transport system throughout the enlarged Europe that is economically and technically efficient, meets the highest possible safety and environmental standards, and takes full account of the social dimension, and (ii) helping to build a bridge between the EU and the rest of the continent on a political level. Over the fifty years of its operation, the ECMT has developed a set of agreements and resolutions on general transport policy, market integration, trade facilitation, road freight transport, intermodal transport and logistics, infrastructure, and road safety, to which countries can subscribe. According to the rules accepted by the international community, individual transport operations may be undertaken without authorization in any ECMT member country.[7] However, the vast bulk of European international transport is subject to authorization. Transport operations (other than individual transport operations) to or from countries that do not belong to the EU require one of two types of international transport licenses: (i) the bilateral license discussed in the previous section, which may be used both for transport on own account and transport for hire or reward, and (ii) the ECMT multilateral license, only available for transport for hire or reward.[8]

The ECMT established a multilateral quota in 1973, to the benefit of undertakings engaged in regular carriage for hire or reward between ECMT member states. The ECMT licenses make it possible to carry a load from any ECMT state to any other ECMT state via any ECMT state. There are two types of licenses: annual licenses, known as 'green licenses', and short-term licenses, called 'yellow licenses'. Over time, changes have been made to the ECMT license system to accommodate environmental standards for eligible vehicles, and the number of licenses has increased, but only slightly. Finally, we note that the mechanism for allocating and increasing the quota is rather complicated.[9]

---

[7] The list of individual transport operations comprises (i) transport of vehicles that are damaged or have broken down; (ii) unladen runs by a vehicle sent to replace a vehicle that has broken down and also the return run, after repair, of the vehicle that had broken down; (iii) transport of goods by motor vehicle whose total permissible laden weight, including trailers, does not exceed six tonnes, or whose permitted payload, including that of trailers, does not exceed 3.5 tonnes; (iv) transport of supplies to meet medical and humanitarian needs; (v) transport of goods, on an occasional basis, to airports in the event of services being diverted; (vi) transport of works and objects of art for fairs and exhibitions or for non-commercial purposes; (vii) transport for non-commercial purposes of properties, accessories, and animals to or from theatrical or circus performances; (viii) transport of spare parts and provisions for ocean-going ships and for aircraft; (ix) funeral transport; (x) transport of livestock in special purpose-built or permanently converted vehicles for the transport of livestock, recognized as such by the member countries' authorities concerned; and (xi) transport of goods on own account.
[8] Freight transport 'for hire or reward' is the carriage for remuneration of freight on behalf of third parties.
[9] The mechanism is described in detail in WTO (2010a). See also International Transport Forum (2009a).

The quota's geographical area of application has evolved considerably since its introduction. Initially, it applied between EU member states, but was then replaced by an (intra-) European Community quota, which, in 1993, gave way to full liberalization of bilateral road transport relations between EU member states. Since then, the ECMT quota is only used in the EU for relations between member and non-member countries and for relations among the latter countries.

Bernadet (2009) notes that the basic quota for ECMT licenses in 2009 came to a total of 6,090, allocated to ECMT member countries to determine the number of licenses for different vehicle types and their duration. The percentage allocation by vehicle type in line with environmental standards was 49 per cent for Euro III vehicles, 40 per cent for Euro IV vehicles, and 11 per cent for Euro V vehicles; annual licenses account for 97 per cent of the total quota and thirty-day licenses for the remaining three per cent.[10] The share of transport performed by hauliers operating with ECMT licenses in total international transport between ECMT member countries has been estimated by the International Transport Forum (2009a) to amount to five per cent; the share of transport performed by hauliers operating with ECMT licenses from non-EU member countries in international transport between EU members 0.33 per cent; and the share of transport performed by hauliers operating with ECMT licenses from EU member countries in international transport between non-EU members 0.9 per cent. Since 1 January 2006, ECMT licenses can only be used for transport operations after a laden trip between the country of registration and another ECMT member country. Vehicles can only make three laden trips before they must return to the country of registration, either laden or unladen. The measure is aimed at preventing a vehicle roaming throughout Europe and exploiting the international haulage market. Other solutions in the same vein have been envisaged and indeed temporarily adopted, such as the obligation that a vehicle return to its country of registration within a period of six weeks.

In 2006, the ECMT was transformed into the International Transport Forum (ITF) as new members from non-European countries were invited 'to address

---

[10] Standards requiring the use of catalytic converters on gasoline cars in the EU first came into force in 1993 with EURO I, which was replaced by EURO II in 1997. Even stricter standards were implemented with EURO III and EURO IV, which came into force in 2001 and 2006, respectively, for passenger cars, and in 2002 and 2007 for light commercial cars. Catalytic converters result in marked reductions of carbon monoxide (CO), nitrous oxide (NO_x), and hydrocarbon (HC) emissions from gas-driven cars, and more-efficient catalytic converters will ensure compliance with future more-stringent standards. For heavy-duty vehicles, standards relate to emissions of CO, HC, NO_x, and particulate matter (PM). The first standards came into force in 1990 with EURO 0, which was replaced by EURO I in 1992 and EURO II in 1995. EURO III, IV, and V were adopted in 2000, 2005, and 2007, respectively. With EURO VI in 2013, the maximum permissible emissions compared to the 1990 levels have been reduced by 88 per cent for CO, 95 per cent for HC, 97 per cent for NO_x, and 98 per cent for PM.

transport issues on a global level and for all transport modes, and to create a public platform for a broad policy dialogue'.[11,12] As of 2014, the ITF had seventy members from thirty-five countries. The aim of the forum is to foster a deeper understanding of the essential role played by transport in the economy and society, and it took over ECMT responsibilities involving the management of the Multilateral Quota System (MQS) of freight transport licenses. The MQS is estimated to be used for 5 to 9 per cent of total international road freight in the EU, although some countries, such as Austria, Greece, Hungary, and Italy, impose restrictions on the use of multilateral permits. In such cases, bilateral permits must be used, or some other form of transport, such as truck-on-train. As in the case of the ECMT, quotas are determined every year by the Council of Ministers based on an agreement within the ITF. Finally, the ITF organizes an annual summit aimed at policy debate and also serves as a think-tank for policymakers and the global transport community.

3.2.2 United Nations Economic Commission for Europe

Since its creation in 1947, the UNECE's Inland Transport Committee has been working towards facilitating international transport while improving its safety and environmental performance. There are almost fifty-seven international agreements and conventions that provide an international legal and technical framework for developing international transport in the UNECE region. These legal instruments, some of which are also applied by countries outside the UNECE region, address a wide array of transport issues that fall under government responsibility and that have an impact on international transport. Such issues include coherent international infrastructure networks, uniform and simplified border-crossing procedures, and uniform rules and regulations aimed at ensuring a high level of efficiency, safety, and environmental protection.

Some of the important conventions with an impact on facilitating border crossings include the International Convention on the Harmonization of Frontier Controls of Goods, the Agreement Concerning the Adoption of Uniform Conditions for Periodical Technical Inspections of Wheeled Vehicles and the Reciprocal Recognition of Such Inspections, the European Agreement on Main International Traffic Arteries (AGR), the European Agreement

---

[11] The current (2014) ITF member countries are: Albania, Armenia, Australia, Austria, Azerbaijan, Belarus, Belgium, Bosnia-Herzegovina, Bulgaria, Canada, Chile, China, Croatia, Czech Republic, Denmark, Estonia, Finland, France, the former Yugoslav Republic of Macedonia, Georgia, Germany, Greece, Hungary, Iceland, India, Ireland, Italy, Japan, Korea, Latvia, Liechtenstein, Lithuania, Luxembourg, Malta, Mexico, Moldova, Montenegro, the Netherlands, New Zealand, Norway, Poland, Portugal, Romania, Russia, Serbia, Slovakia, Slovenia, Spain, Sweden, Switzerland, Turkey, Ukraine, the UK, and the US.

[12] http://www.internationaltransportforum.org/about/about.html (accessed 9 February 2016).

Concerning the Work of Crews of Vehicles Engaged in International Road Transport (AETR), the European Agreement Concerning the International Carriage of Dangerous Goods by Road (ADR), the Agreement on the International Carriage of Perishable Foodstuffs and on the Special Equipment to Be Used for Such Carriage (ATP), and the Customs Convention on the International Transport of Goods under Cover of TIR Carnets (TIR Convention).

The 1982 International Convention on the Harmonization of Frontier Controls of Goods aims to reduce the formalities and the number and duration of all types of controls, such as medico-sanitary, veterinary, or phytosanitary controls relating to compliance with technical standards or quality control. The 1997 Agreement concerning the Adoption of Uniform Conditions for Periodical Technical Inspections of Wheeled Vehicles and the Reciprocal Recognition of such Inspections defines the legal framework and procedures for adopting uniform rules for technical inspections and mutually recognizing the resulting certificates. The 1975 AGR defines a uniform legal framework for constructing and developing a coherent international road network in all UNECE member countries and territories, and the 1970 AETR establishes uniform working conditions for drivers of vehicles used in international road transport in accordance with the relevant provisions of the International Labour Organization.

The 1957 ADR requires that apart from some excessively dangerous goods, other dangerous goods may be carried internationally in road vehicles subject to compliance with the conditions laid down in Annex A, in particular as regards their packaging and labelling, and the conditions laid down in Annex B, in particular as regards the construction, equipment, and operation of the vehicle carrying the goods. Annexes A and B have been regularly amended and updated since the ADR's implementation. The 1970 ATP mandates that certain types of equipment be used to transport perishable food across borders and that such equipment be regularly inspected.

The most recent provisions of the TIR Convention entered into force on 17 February 1999. As of 2014, the Convention has sixty-eight contracting parties, including the EC, the rest of Europe, and countries in North Africa and the Near and Middle East. The US, Canada, Chile, and Uruguay are also contracting parties. The TIR customs transit procedure permits the international carriage of goods, as long as a road leg is involved, in international journeys from a customs office of departure to a customs office of arrival through as many countries as necessary, without any intermediate frontier control of the goods carried. This facilitation of international goods transport requires a number of measures to be fulfilled and applied by customs authorities and transport operators, which include the use of customs-approved vehicles and containers, the use of the TIR Carnet as an international customs document, the provision of an international TIR guarantee, and the mutual recognition of customs control measures in the countries involved.

3.2.3 International Road Transport Networks Supported by United Nations Programmes

Although not related directly to international rules and regulations in the road freight sector, we should also mention international transport networks supported by the UN system, such as the UNECE Trans-European Motorway (TEM) and the E-road network established through the European Agreement on Main International Traffic Arteries.[13]

The TEM project is a sub-regional cooperation framework established in 1977 by the governments of Central, Eastern, and South-Eastern European countries, under the aegis of the UNECE, for developing coherent road, rail, and combined transport infrastructure networks and for facilitating international traffic in Europe. At present, fifteen countries are members of TEM.[14] The project has been instrumental in developing international road links in the participating countries and is designed to harmonize the management, maintenance, and operational procedures of motorways in the region and their integration into the pan-European context. The projects are self-sustainable, supported by direct contributions from member countries to a trust fund established by the UNECE. The project network forms the backbone of the pan-European road corridors in the Central and Eastern European region, providing valuable contribution in the form of new European strategic transport plans and by extending the Trans-European Transport Network (TEN-T; see Section 3.6 for more details) in neighbouring countries and regions.

Finally, the AGR provides all member governments with an international legal framework to construct and develop a coherent international road network, aiming to streamline international road transport and traffic throughout the UNECE region.[15] It defines the E-road network, consisting of the arteries channelling major international road traffic flows in Europe, and the infrastructure parameters to which those arteries should conform. As

---

[13] The international E-road network is a numbering system for roads in Europe developed by the UNECE.

[14] The TEM members are Armenia, Austria, Bosnia and Herzegovina, Bulgaria, Croatia, the Czech Republic, Georgia, Greece, Hungary, Italy, Lithuania, Poland, Romania, the Russian Federation, Slovakia, and Turkey.

[15] The AGR's 36 member countries are Austria, Azerbaijan, Belarus, Belgium, Bosnia and Herzegovina, Bulgaria, Croatia, Czech Republic, Denmark, Finland, the former Yugoslav Republic of Macedonia, France, Georgia, Germany, Greece, Hungary, Italy, Kazakhstan, Latvia, Lithuania, Luxembourg, Montenegro, the Netherlands, Norway, Poland, Portugal, Romania, the Russian Federation, Serbia, Slovakia, Slovenia, Sweden, Switzerland, Turkey, Ukraine, and the UK.

emphasized by the Economic Commission for Europe and the Economic and Social Commission for Asia and Pacific (2008), the AGR was revised in the early 1990s to take into account new East–West traffic flows.

3.2.4 The World Trade Organization

With the 1995 creation of the General Agreement on Trade in Services (GATS), trade liberalization on a global scale covered not only trade in goods but also trade in services, although the results of the latter's negotiations were fairly limited.[16] Commitments were undertaken in the GATS' four modes of supply: (i) cross-border (mode 1), (ii) consumption abroad (mode 2), (iii) commercial presence (mode 3), and (iv) movement of natural persons (mode 4).[17] Under GATS, each WTO member decides for itself whether to make binding market access and national treatment commitments. When making these commitments, countries have to list all measures they wish to retain that would otherwise violate the specific commitments being made. Since the commitments each apply to the four modes of supply, trading conditions are ultimately defined in the form of eight entries per sector. Commitments may vary within a spectrum whose opposing ends are guaranteed market access and/or national treatment without limitations (full commitments) and the denial of any such guarantees (no commitments). While the relevant entry would be 'none' in the former case, the absence of commitments would be indicated as 'unbound'. The non-scheduling of a sector or a non-commitment on a particular mode do not imply that the relevant policies are beyond all GATS disciplines. The market access and national treatment commitments are inscribed in national 'Schedules of Specific Commitments', which are annexed to the GATS; the Schedules also specify any limitations on market access or national treatment commitments that a country chooses to maintain in one or more of the four modes of supply.

The WTO document W/120 identifies five subcategories under road services (passenger, freight, rental, maintenance, and supporting services). But many countries have given commitments using the UN's more-detailed Central Product Classification (CPC), which distinguishes between twenty-five types of road transportation services. Under CPC road freight transportation is itself distinguished into seven types: freight by refrigerator vehicles; freight by tank

---

[16] There is a large literature analysing the results of WTO negotiations in services. The most comprehensive overview is probably presented in the WTO Secretariat (2000).
[17] While mode 1 refers to services supplied from the territory of one member in the territory of another, mode 2 consists of services supplied in the territory of one member to the consumers of another. Mode 3 refers to services supplied through any type of business or professional establishment of one member in the territory of another (foreign direct investment (FDI)), and mode 4 includes independent service suppliers and employees of the services supplier of another member (consultants).

trucks or semi-trailers; containerized freight by trucks equipped with a container chassis; freight by human- or animal-drawn vehicles; moving services for household and office furniture and other goods; road transport services of letters and parcels; and other road transport services of freight.

In the case of freight transportation, twenty-five countries have made commitments within the context of WTO multilateral negotiations. According to WTO Secretariat (2001a) the most liberal mode in the case of freight transportation is mode 2 (consumption abroad), where full commitments have been given in four-fifths of cases. In the case of mode 4 (movement of natural persons), all countries preferred to remain unbound except as indicated in the horizontal commitments. In more than three-quarters of cases there are no commitments in the case of mode 1. Only five members have taken full commitments for mode 1 (cross-border trade) and there are two cases of partial commitments. Mode 3 (commercial presence) is evenly split between full commitments and partial commitments. Restrictions listed are typically an economic need test, foreign ownership restrictions, an incorporation requirement, nationality of the board of directors (being citizens of the member country), a citizenship requirement, an authorization requirement (but not extended to foreign-registered vehicles), emergency safeguards on the number of services suppliers, services operations, and services output, and limitations on the use of leased vehicles. Only two members have given no commitments for this mode.

In the case of national treatment for freight transportation, we note that there are a few specific restrictions: a requirement of establishment in the country concerned to provide cabotage services, prior approval, cargoes confined to containerized cargoes to be exported or imported, and a requirement on established entities to use vehicles with a national registration.[18] Finally, most-favoured nation (MFN) exemptions have an important bearing on the extent of the commitments undertaken.[19] Out of the twenty-five countries that have given commitments on freight transportation, ten also have one or more MFN exemptions regarding cargoes. Five members, including the EU, have felt it necessary to lodge separate exemptions for preferential fiscal treatment on the value-added tax (VAT), vehicle tax, and income tax. In other instances, preferential tax treatment has been combined with cargo-sharing provisions in a single derogation, either by mentioning preferential tax treatment specifically or by referring more generally to operating conditions. Cargo-sharing provisions are mainly bilateral, although there are cases

---

[18] 'National treatment' requires that once products have entered the market, they must be treated no less favourably than the equivalent domestically produced products.

[19] According to the MFN clause, members are bound to grant treatment to the products of one country no less favourably than that accorded to the products of any other country.

where they are regional or both bilateral and regional. In six cases they are unilateral and in five of those cases they are based on reciprocity. In nearly all cases they cover all countries and existing and future agreements, although sometimes accompanied by a detailed list of beneficiaries.

As far as auxiliary road transport activities are concerned, rental services of commercial freight vehicles with operators have been offered by only a few members, but with nearly no restrictions. Finally, supporting services for road transport covering bus station services/highways, bridges and tunnel operation services, and parking services have attracted very few commitments.

3.3 European Union Rules and Regulations

Although the Treaty of Rome, Title V, Article 71 provided for the freedom to supply international inland transport services by road by 1969 at the latest, this objective could not be achieved for a relatively long period. In 1969, the Council approved the creation of multilateral licenses, and these were to be phased in to replace the bilateral licenses that had regulated cabotage among member countries until 1969. When it came to increasing the number of licenses, the Council proved reluctant, and it took a ruling by the Court of Justice in 1985 to start the liberalization process. The Single European Act of 1986 intensified liberalization efforts, but liberalization was eventually only made possible through the single market reform in 1993, when quota restrictions were abandoned. The main objective in the EU is to create a single open market with freedom of establishment and freedom to provide services through liberalization, and the main concerns in doing so are market access, competition, and harmonizing legislation. Therefore, EU regulations aim to create a competitive, safe, and efficient transport system with minimal environmental effects.[20] Within the EU, non-EU firms in general do not have the same rights as EU firms. For example, cabotage in the EU was liberalized only in July 1998 and applies only to EU member states, excluding non-member countries. Finally, we note that although state ownership is becoming a relatively minor phenomenon, there are nevertheless several countries with state-controlled companies operating in the road freight haulage sector. These are often subsidiaries of state-owned companies in other sectors, such as railways or post offices, and they concentrate on only a few activities.

---

[20] The following discussion of EU rules and regulations on road transportation is based largely on 'Summaries of EU Legislation' available at the website http://eur-lex.europa.eu/browse/summaries.html (accessed 9 February 2016). See also European Conference of Ministers of Transport (2001).

The main international rules that regulate safety and commercial operations and practices have been transposed into Community law, ensuring that they have legal force and uniform application throughout member states. Union countries are the founding members of the UNECE and the ECMT, thus, the EU is party to most of the rules and regulations developed by the ECMT as well as to various UNECE conventions and agreements. In this context, it should be emphasized that the EU is party to the Convention on Harmonizing the Frontier Control of Goods, the Convention on Customs Pool Containers, the Convention on the International Carriage of Dangerous Goods by Road, the Agreement on the International Carriage of Perishable Foodstuffs, and the TIR Convention. As emphasized by the Commission of the European Communities (2007), the EU intends to replace thirty-eight Community directives with equivalent UNECE international regulations.

Turning to WTO road transportation service commitments made by the EU we note that for cross-border supply (mode 1) no commitments have been made in the case of passenger transportation, freight transportation, storage and warehouse services, and other transport services, and no limitations have been placed on maintaining and repairing road transport equipment, freight transport agency/freight forwarding services, and pre-shipment inspection. While there are no limitations for consumption abroad (mode 2), different restrictions have been placed on 'commercial presence' (mode 3) in 'market access' in the cases of passenger transportation and freight transportation. No limitations for 'commercial presence' (mode 3) have been placed on maintenance and repair of road transport equipment, services auxiliary to all modes of transport, and other transport services. Finally, mode 4 (movement of personnel) for all cases does not diverge from the pattern of 'unbound except as indicated in the horizontal commitments'.

3.3.1 Market Access and Competition

Historically, liberalization of the road transport sector in the EU started with the 1985 White Paper that stressed the importance of freedom to provide services and outlined the Community Common Transport Policy. Three important guidelines were accepted: having a free market by 1992, increasing bilateral as well as Community quotas, and eliminating distortions to competition. Infrastructure development, decreasing border controls and bureaucracy, and improving safety by the end of 1992 were also set as goals. As emphasized above, all quantitative restrictions and Community and bilateral quotas were abolished starting on 1 January 1993. The international transport of goods between member states was liberalized with Council Regulation 881/92. According to the regulation, a road transport operator that works between at least two member states must obtain a Community license that gives the operator the right to access the whole market with no quantitative restrictions. The conditions to obtain this license are set forth in the same regulation. It should be noted that own-account transport and vehicles of under 3.5 tonnes do not require such a license.

According to Regulation (EC) No 484/2002 (amending Council Regulation No. 881/92), every driver from a non-EU country driving an EU operator's vehicle while carrying out cross-border haulage activities within the Union must carry the correct driver attestation. This is a uniform document certifying that the driver of a vehicle carrying out road haulage operations between member states is lawfully employed by the Community transport operator concerned in the member state in which the operator is established, or lawfully placed at the disposal of that operator. This document enables inspecting officers in all member states to check the employment status of drivers carrying out transport operations between member states in Community vehicles and with a Community license, thereby helping authorities to effectively combat the use of irregularly employed drivers and the resulting distortions of competition.

The process of liberalization took longer for road cabotage where a non-resident carrier holding a Community License could transport goods, on 'a temporary basis' from two points within a member state. This situation was liberalized for freight transport in 1993 with Council Regulation 3118/93. Liberalization on 'a temporary basis' means that it is not continuously carried out. Council Regulation 3916/90 put forth measures that are to be taken in the event of a crisis in the market in the carriage of goods by road. With the implementation of deregulation measures, the road haulage market in the EU has become very competitive, integrated, and efficient. The cabotage regime was extended to EFTA countries on 1 July 1994, with the exception of Austria, which joined the EU on 1 January 1997, and Switzerland, which had a separate agreement with the EU. The EU/Switzerland land transport agreement entered into force in 2002. Following their accession to the EU on 1 May 2004, restrictions were lifted for hauliers from Cyprus, Malta, and Slovenia as well. Other new member states were to enjoy the right to cabotage services after a transitional period that expired in 2009, but running cabotage services in this manner provoked anxieties in the sector about possible adverse effects, such as potentially unfair competition from lower-wage countries that could undercut operators who have to bear greater costs in a more tightly regulated environment.

In May 2010, Regulation No. 1072/2009 on common rules for access to international road haulage, entered into force, repealing Regulations 881/92 and 3118/93. The aim of the new regulation is to improve the efficiency of road freight transport by reducing empty trips after the unloading of international transport operations. Article 8 provides that every haulier is entitled to perform up to three cabotage operations within a seven-day period, starting the day after unloading international transport. Any carrier performing the carriage of goods by road for hire or reward is entitled to carry out cabotage operations in the territory of EU member states if he/she holds a Community license. If the driver is a citizen of a third country, he/she must hold a driver attestation. Cabotage services can be delivered in any member state, but they are limited to one within three days following the unloaded entry to a given member state. It should be noted that carriers without a registered office or other establishment within a member state are permitted to carry out transport services in that state only on a temporary basis. Recently, Directive 2006/1/EC set out conditions for hiring vehicles for international road transport. Such vehicles must comply with the laws of the member state of origin and be driven by the personnel of the undertaking using them.

Harmonizing rules regarding access to the profession is outlined in Directive 96/26/EC, based on Article 75 of the Treaty on European Union (TEU).[21] According to the directive, being a road haulage operator requires good repute in the exercise of business, a minimum financial standing, and professional competence. These aspects involve a policy that replaces quantitative licensing with qualitative criteria for allowing access to the road transport market. Given that road haulage undertakings are subject to numerous rules that affect the safety of other road users, an operator who is certified as 'professionally competent' is one who follows all these rules and is also able to manage a company. 'Good repute' means that entrepreneurs who have few scruples about disregarding the law may be excluded from the occupation, while 'good financial standing' ensures that they have the capital required to continue managing the undertaking and maintaining the vehicles, so that any practice that might endanger safety is prevented. The directive requires that each member state must accept documents issued by another member state stating that these conditions are fulfilled. The scope of this directive excludes the operators of vehicles with a laden weight below 3.5 tonnes. Regular checks, at least every five years, ensure that undertakings continue to satisfy these three criteria, which are justified because they halt the proliferation of unscrupulous firms seeking to gain a market share by skimping on safety; they achieve greater harmonization of standards between member states, particularly regarding the levels of financial standing required and the standard of professional competence expected; they facilitate the establishment and mutual recognition of professional status in other member states; and improve the overall professional standing and quality of road transport.

---

[21] This corresponds to Article 95 of the 'Treaty on the Functioning of the European Union'.

Directive 96/26/EC was repealed in 2009 by Regulation 1071/2009, with the aim of promoting fair competition between road transport companies and increasing staff's professional qualifications. According to this regulation, every road transport undertaking shall designate a transport manager who shall be responsible for continuously managing the transport activities of the undertaking. Undertakings wishing to engage a road transport operator(s) are obliged to have an establishment with an operating centre where it can keep all of the documents required for the pursuit of business, and one or more vehicles registered in accordance with national legislation. In addition, the undertaking and the manager shall be deemed to be of good repute. The undertaking shall not have infringed Community rules in fields such as driving time and rest periods; the roadworthiness of commercial vehicles; safety in the carriage of dangerous goods by road; and driving licenses. Finally, the undertaking must be able to meet its financial obligations: it must have at its disposal, every year, capital and reserves totalling at least €9,000 when only one vehicle is used, increased by €5,000 for each additional vehicle, and the manager of the undertaking shall have passed a compulsory written examination that may be supplemented by an oral examination.

It should be noted that access to the transport market not only requires looking at services and access to infrastructure, but also involves developing traffic control systems such as road traffic control. Only by establishing non-discriminatory access to infrastructure can the goals of increasing efficiency and competition be met, and such access must be applicable to all current and potential service providers, as grandfather rights used by incumbents can be devastating to competition. Traffic control systems are not just an aspect of safety but are integral to properly allocating infrastructure capacity, and also play a crucial role in the relationship between operation and infrastructure.

3.3.2 Prices and Fiscal Conditions

Road transportation is projected to continue to increase, and there is universal recognition that it is not possible to increase road supply in relation with the forecasted increases in traffic unless financing issues are solved. Most countries with high-performance and access-controlled highway systems have financed their expressways by general tax revenues and toll receipts to varying degrees. Almost every country that uses tolls requires that a parallel untolled route be available to motorists, even though the alternative is usually not built to expressway standards.

The Common Transport Policy is based on the principle of 'sustainable mobility', which refers to maximizing efficiency in terms of energy, time, and distance while internalizing the external costs of infrastructure, environment, operation, upkeep, congestion, and accidents. Such a system, as well as internalizing average variable costs, requires developing a new approach to fiscal issues, and the EC's Green Paper of December 1995 put forth taxation as one of the important solutions to this problem.[22] The paper stated that internalizing costs would improve traffic flow and safety, mitigate environmental concerns, and remove distortions in competition. The White Paper of 1998 then emphasized a range of other issues, including the need to manage transport capacity more efficiently, finance transport infrastructure, and improve transport sector efficiency by institutional reform involving deregulation and privatization.[23]

According to the objective of 'sustainable mobility' outlined in the Common Transport Policy, the EU maintains that charges for infrastructure should reflect a marginal social cost. Hence, users should absorb the internal costs, such as fuel, driver time, and wear and tear, as well as a portion of the external costs, consisting of operating, infrastructure, congestion, environmental, and accident costs. According to Button (1990), the external environmental cost of road transport as a percentage of GDP is much higher than that of other modes. Charging vehicles for external costs should discourage them from making trips where the benefits do not exceed the total social cost. If successful, this method would decrease road demand and increase efficiency, thereby helping solve congestion problems.

Internalizing transport costs not only aids in improving traffic conditions, but is also environmentally sound, as it will reduce emissions overall.[24] When considering external costs we must also look at the combination of noise and air pollution, congestion delays, and aesthetic factors. According to Button (2002), estimates show that if the external costs of road transport were internalized, operating costs would increase by about 20 to 33 per cent. For that reason, the 1998 White Paper set out how to internalize externalized costs by a step-by-step approach, where the objective was to harmonize transport charges across all member states. Individuals would participate in funding road systems and cover some social costs. The main goal for the White Paper was to ensure that harmonization due to liberalization was also in accord with social aspects, safety measures, and environmental concerns. It should also be noted that the aim of internalizing costs is not to increase transport costs but to make sure that costs are apportioned properly, with external costs incurred across all transport modes to avoid competition distortions. It is also important to state that while internalization is based on a marginal social cost, a

---

[22] See Commission of the European Communities (1995).

[23] See Commission of the European Communities (1998).

[24] Consider the case of nitrous oxide (N_2O), which is a greenhouse gas with tremendous global warming effects. Studies reveal that about 40 per cent of total N_2O emissions come from human activities in agriculture, transportation, and industry. In transportation, N_2O is emitted when transportation fuels are burned, and motor vehicles, including passenger cars and trucks, are the primary source of such emissions. The amount of N_2O emitted from transportation depends on the type of fuel used, as well as vehicle technology, maintenance, and operating practices.

multi-tier charging system should be designed to incorporate taxes based on factors such as emissions. Given the projected continued dominance of road transport, in addition to pricing one should consider other options for increasing safety and reducing environmental impact, such as making transport modes more environmentally friendly through initiatives that will encourage using less-harmful fuels and adopting cleaner technologies.

Directive 1999/62/EC (Eurovignette Directive), based on Articles 71 and 93 of the Treaty establishing the European Community, sets forth rules for harmonizing requirements on heavy-goods vehicle taxes for their infrastructure use. The Directive covers vehicle taxes, tolls, and user charges imposed on vehicles intended for the carriage of goods by road and with a maximum permissible gross laden weight of no fewer than 12 tonnes. With the 2006 revision, this threshold dropped by the year 2012 to 3.5 tonnes. The directive states that tolls should be levied according to the distance travelled and the type of vehicle, and user charges should relate to the duration of infrastructure use. Tolls and user charges may vary according to congestion and vehicle emission class. As a general rule, distance-based tolls and time-based user charges shall not be applied on the same stretch of road. Tolls and user charges can only be imposed on motorway users, or on users of multi-lane roads similar to motorways, as well as on users of bridges, tunnels, and mountain passes. National tolls and charges should be non-discriminatory and easy for the motorist to understand, so as to avoid delays and problems at toll booths. Mandatory checks at the EU's internal borders should also be avoided. Directive 2006/38/EC (amending Directive 1999/62/EC) establishes a new Community framework for charging for road infrastructure use. It lays down rules for member state application of tolls or user charges on roads, including roads on TEN-T and roads in mountainous regions, and applies from 2012 onwards to vehicles weighing between 3.5 tonnes and 12 tonnes. According to the directive, member states are able to differentiate tolls according to a vehicle's emission category (its EURO classification) and the level of damage it causes to roads, as well as the place, time, and amount of congestion.[25] This system makes it possible to tackle the problems of traffic congestion, including damage to the environment, on the basis of 'user pays' and 'polluter pays' principles.[26]

3.3.3 Social Conditions

With liberalization and the creation of a free market, certain social, technical, and safety conditions must be harmonized in the EU to achieve the

---

[25] For the EURO classifications, see footnote 10 in Section 3.1 above.
[26] For recent developments on estimating external costs in the transport sector, see CE Delft, Infras, and Fraunhofer ISI (2011).

aforementioned sustainable mobility. Harmonizing social conditions includes harmonizing maximum working times, installing necessary technical components, and eliminating controls at frontiers.

Regulation 561/2006 concerns harmonizing certain social legislation with respect to road transport. It aims to improve road safety by limiting driving times, improve working conditions, and harmonize conditions across member countries[27] The regulation also stipulates that as of 1 May 2006, a digital tachograph be installed in all new vehicles that begin service for the first time. This regulation is wide-ranging, including national and international transport, long and short distances, own-account and for-hire transport, and it applies to employees' vehicles as well as the vehicles of those who are self-employed. Council Regulation 3821/85 concerned the recording equipment in road transport vehicles, primarily the analogue tachograph, which recorded driving time, breaks, and rests. Council Regulation (EC) 2135/98 amended that regulation to require the fully digital tachograph, which is more reliable and includes a printer for roadside inspections. Directive 2006/22/EC lays down the minimum conditions for implementing Regulation 3821/85 (now 2135/98) regarding the number of roadside inspections of driving time, rest periods, breaks, and checks at the premises of road transport undertakings. Finally, Directive 2002/15, regarding the working time of people performing road transport activities, sets forth the minimum requirements for working time to improve road safety and worker health, and it defines working time, place of work, night work, and the maximum working week.

3.3.4 Technical Conditions

Harmonizing technical conditions incorporates interoperability, safety, and environmental issues, and deals with matters such as tyre tread depth, installing speed limitation devices, maximum authorized weights and dimensions, roadworthiness tests, technical roadside inspections.

Council Directive 2002/85/EC (which amended 89/459), sets forth conditions with respect to tyre tread depth in certain categories of motor vehicles and their trailers, where the minimum tread depth in the main grooves must

---

[27] The maximum daily driving period is nine hours, with an exception of two days in the week where it can be ten hours if the driver is driving six days a week. Total weekly driving time must not be more than fifty-six hours, and total fortnightly driving time must not be more than ninety hours. The driver must rest for at least eleven hours a day, with an exception of nine hours three times a week. There is a stipulation for a split rest of three hours followed by another nine hours (totalling twelve hours) a day. Weekly rest is forty-five hours (continuous), which can be brought down to twenty-four hours, where one forty-five-hour rest must be taken every two weeks. Breaks are at least forty-five minutes (where that can be broken up into fifteen and thirty minutes) and should be taken every four-and-a-half hours.

be 1.6 mm in vehicle categories M1, N1, O1, and O2.[28] Council Directive 92/6, regarding heavy-goods vehicles and buses, and with environmental and safety concerns at the fore, sets out the necessary installation and use of speed limitation devices for M2, M3, N2, and N3 vehicle categories. The directive further stipulates that M2 and M3 vehicles can have a maximum speed of 100 km/h, and N2 and N3 vehicles can have a speed limit of 90 km/h.

Council Directive 96/53/EC puts forth the maximum dimensions authorized for M2, M3, N2, and N3 vehicles in national and international traffic, as well as the maximum authorized weights in international traffic.[29] According to the directive, any vehicle or vehicle combination exceeding the maximum dimensions may only be used if special authorization has been received, and member states must ensure that vehicles are provided with one of three proofs of permission: (i) a 'manufacturer's' plate supplemented by a plate concerning dimensions; (ii) a single plate containing the data from the two plates referred to above; or (iii) a single document issued by the competent authority in the member state in which the vehicle is registered or was placed in service, and which contains the same data as those on the abovementioned plates.

Council Directive 96/96/EC states that member states must conduct periodic roadworthiness tests for vehicles and trailers registered in the state, and the test will have mutual recognition by other member states. These inspections should be carried out once a year for heavy vehicles, and at least every other year for light vehicles and passenger cars. This directive was later amended by Directive 2009/40/EC, harmonizing the frequency of roadworthiness tests and detailing which parts of motor vehicles must be tested.[30]

---

[28] In Directive 70/156/EEC of 6 February1970, the categories are specified as follows: Category M1: Vehicles used for the carriage of passengers and comprising no more than eight seats in addition to the driver's seat; Category M2: Vehicles used for the carriage of passengers, comprising more than eight seats in addition to the driver's seat, and having a maximum weight not exceeding five metric tonnes; Category M3: Vehicles used for the carriage of passengers, comprising more than eight seats in addition to the driver's seat, and having a maximum weight exceeding five metric tonnes; Category N: Motor vehicles having at least four wheels, or having three wheels when the maximum weight exceeds one metric tonne, and used for the carriage of goods; Category N1: Vehicles used for the carriage of goods and having a maximum weight not exceeding 3.75 metric tonnes; Category N2: Vehicles used for the carriage of goods and having a maximum weight exceeding 3.75 but not exceeding 12 metric tonnes; Category N3: Vehicles used for the carriage of goods and having a maximum weight exceeding 12 metric tonnes; Category O: Trailers (including semi-trailers); Category O1: Trailers with a maximum weight not exceeding 0.775 metric tonnes; Category O2: Trailers with a maximum weight exceeding 0.775 metric tonnes but not exceeding 3.75 metric tonnes; Category O3: Trailers with a maximum weight exceeding 3.75 but not exceeding 10 metric tonnes; Category O4: Trailers with a maximum weight exceeding 10 metric tonnes.

[29] Maximum length of a motor vehicle is 12 metres, articulated vehicle 16.5 metres, road train 18.75 metres. Maximum width of a vehicle is 2.55 metres, while conditioned vehicles are 2.6 metres. Maximum weight is 40 tonnes for road train or articulated vehicle with five or six axles, 44 tonnes for a motor vehicle with three axles with a semi-trailer (two- or three-axle) that transports a 12.19-metre ISO container (combined transport).

[30] Annex I of Directive 2009/40/EC details the categories of motor vehicles that will be subject to roadworthiness tests, as well as the required frequency of tests for each category. Annex II sets out

Directive 2009/40/EC has been repealed by Directive 2014/45/EU on periodic roadworthiness tests for motor vehicles and trailers. Aiming to improve road safety by setting minimum requirements for periodic roadworthiness tests for motor vehicles and trailers in the EU, the directive applies to vehicles capable of more than 25 km/h in the following categories:

- M1 and N2 passenger cars and light commercial vehicles are to be tested four years after the date when first registered, and every two years thereafter;
- M1 vehicles used as taxis or ambulances, M2 and M3 buses or minibuses, N2 and N3 heavy goods vehicles and O3 and O4 heavy trailers are to be tested one year after first registration, and yearly thereafter;
- T5 fast tractors with a design speed above 40 km/h and used commercially are to be tested four years after registration, and every two years thereafter.

The tests are to be conducted by approved and compliant testing centres, and inspectors must meet competence criteria. Directive 2000/30/EC sets out the legal framework for roadside roadworthiness checks on commercial vehicles. These checks are unannounced on a commercial vehicle travelling within an EU country, and comprise a check of documents relating to the vehicle compliance with a technical roadside inspection and a check to detect any poor maintenance. In this instance, the inspector should take the most recent documents and any other safety certificate into consideration. If the results of a roadside check show that a commercial vehicle does not meet the standards set out in the directive, the use of that vehicle on the public highway will be immediately banned. Recently, Directive 2000/30/EC was repealed by Directive 2014/47/EU on the technical roadside inspection of the roadworthiness of commercial vehicles circulating in the EU. The Directive sets out the minimum requirements and harmonized rules for technical roadside inspection of M2 and M3 buses and coaches, N2 and N3 trucks and O3 and O4 trailers over 3.5 tonnes, as well as T5 tractors. The inspections focus on brakes, tyres, wheels, and chassis as well as noise and exhaust emissions. The Directive aims to inspect 5 per cent of all commercial vehicles annually registered in the EU.

which items must be compulsorily tested: vehicle identification; braking equipment; steering; visibility; lighting equipment and parts of the electrical system; axles, wheels, tyres and suspension; chassis and chassis attachments; other equipment such as safety belts, fire extinguishers, locks, anti-theft devices, warning triangles, first-aid kit, speedometer, etc.; nuisance factors such as noise, exhaust emissions, etc.; and supplementary tests for public transport vehicles, such as emergency exit(s), heating and ventilation systems, seat layout, and interior lighting. Vehicles passing the test will be certified, and all EU countries will mutually recognize the proof issued.

Directive 2005/55/EC, setting out limit values for emissions of gaseous and particulate pollutants and for opacity of exhaust fumes, was amended by Regulation 715/2007.[31] On the other hand, Regulation 715/2007 covers vehicle categories M1, M2, N1, and N2. The Euro V standard came into force on 1 September 2009 for vehicle approvals, and applied as of 1 January 2011 to new car registrations and sales. The Euro 6 standard came into force on 1 September 2014 for vehicle approvals, and applied as of 1 January 2015 to new car registrations and sales. Finally, Directive 2006/40/EC aims to cut back fluorinated greenhouse gas emissions (used in vehicle air conditioning systems), and Directive 70/157/EEC lays down similar limits for the noise level of the mechanical parts of vehicle exhaust systems with a design speed exceeding 25 km/h. Noise level limits range from 74 dB(A) for motor cars to 80 dB(A) for high-powered goods vehicles.

3.3.5 Road Safety

According to the Commission of the European Communities (2003a), each year more than 40,000 people die in the EU-15 as a result of road accidents and 1,700,000 are injured, with the total cost to society corresponding to about 2 per cent of the EU's GNP. Although there have been improvements in safety overall, the situation is considered socially unacceptable. As a result, the Commission proposed that the EU should set a target of halving the number of road deaths by 2010. Studies revealed that the main causes of accidents are excessive and improper speed, consumption of alcohol and drugs, fatigue, failure to wear seat belts, lack of sufficient protection provided by vehicles in the event of an impact, non-compliance with driving and rest times (for commercial drivers), poor visibility of other users, and poor road infrastructure. Since many road safety improvements could be achieved by complying with existing rules, the EU aims to encourage road users to improve their behaviour through better compliance. In 2010 the Commission proposed to

---

[31] According to Regulation 715/2007 the Euro V standards as specified in this regulation state that emissions from diesel vehicles should not exceed the following: CO, 500 mg/km; particulates, five mg/km (an 80 per cent reduction of emissions compared to the Euro IV standards); NO_x, 180 mg/km (a 20 per cent reduction of emissions compared to Euro IV); and combined emissions of HC and NO_x, 230 mg/km. On the other hand, emissions from gasoline, natural gas, or LPG vehicles should not exceed the following: CO, 1,000 mg/km; non-methane HC, 68 mg/km; total HC, 100 mg/km; NO_x, 60 mg/km (indicating a 25 per cent reduction of emissions compared to Euro IV); and particulates for lean-burn direct-injection gasoline vehicles, 5 mg/km. Finally, according to Regulation 715/2007 regarding the Euro VI standards, all vehicles equipped with a diesel engine are required to substantially reduce their emissions of NO_x. In this context, emissions from cars and other vehicles intended to be used for transport will be capped at 80 mg/km, indicating an additional reduction of more than 50 per cent compared to the Euro V standard. Combined emissions of HCs and NO_x from diesel vehicles are also to be reduced, and will be capped at 170 mg/km for cars and other vehicles intended to be used for transport.

maintain the target of halving the overall number of road deaths between 2010 and 2020 by improving driver education and training, increasing road rule enforcement, developing safer road infrastructure and safer vehicles, promoting modern technology to increase road safety, and improving emergency and post-injury services.

Turning to the EU's existing rules on road safety, we start with the issuance of national driver's licenses and their mutual recognition in the EU. Directive 91/439/EEC introduced mutual recognition along with the harmonization of many aspects of driver's licenses, including categories, issuing conditions, and requirements. A review in some member states showed that 30 per cent of commercial drivers did not undergo driver training. This situation was mitigated with Directive 2003/59/EC, regarding qualifications and periodic training of drivers of road vehicles carrying goods or passengers. As of the end of 2008, all new drivers must be trained in road safety, technical aspects of the vehicle, fuel consumption, loading, accidents and physical risk, criminality, emergencies, and the company's economic image. The goal is better driver skills, improved service and higher quality, improved road safety, reduced fuel consumption, and reduced costs.

Directive 2006/126/EC, recasting Directive 91/439/EEC and introducing into it amendments previously introduced by Directive 2003/59/EC, aims to reduce the scope of fraud, ensure free movement of citizens, and help improve road safety. According to this directive, all licenses have a given period of validity and will be unconditionally valid in all EU countries. Category A (motorcycles) and category B (cars) licenses are valid for ten years, and category C (lorries), and category D (buses/coaches) licenses are valid for five years. The directive harmonizes the frequency of medical checks for professional drivers and introduces minimum requirements for the initial qualification and training of driver examiners.

The Commission recommendation of 2001 concerning the maximum authorized level of alcohol in the blood, recommends that two different alcohol levels be applied. The standard alcohol level for all motor vehicle drivers (which should be adopted by all member states) is one not exceeding 0.5 mg/ml. A second alcohol level of 0.2 mg/ml is recommended for drivers of large vehicles, that is, trucks weighing more than 3.5 tonnes, and drivers of vehicles carrying dangerous goods. The recommendation suggests that, to dissuade drivers from drinking, all member states adopt a system of random detection that analyses expelled air.

Seatbelts are another important aspect of road transport safety. Directive 91/671/EEC, regarding 'the approximation of the laws of EU Member States having to do with the compulsory seat belt use in motorized vehicles weighing fewer than 3.5 tonnes', applied only to cars and vans and did not require parents to use child restraints for their children. The new Directive 2003/20/EC extends the application scope, requiring the use of seatbelts, where provided, by all those in motor vehicles. Furthermore, it states that children must be restrained by an appropriate child restraint system that conforms to the latest UNECE standard when travelling in M1 and N1 vehicles.

Directive 2004/54/EC concerns minimum safety requirements in dealing with various organizational, structural, technical, and operational aspects for tunnels that facilitate communication between various areas of the EU. Because many tunnels are aging, many lives have been lost in recent years from tunnel accidents. As the costs in closing a tunnel are great, the directive's objectives are, for all tunnels longer than 500 metres, to prevent situations that endanger lives and to protect the tunnels and the environment. According to the directive, each EU country must designate one or more administrative authority(ies) to be responsible for tunnels, ensuring testing and inspecting on a regular basis and drawing up related safety requirements; putting in place organizational and operational schemes for training and equipping emergency services; and establishing a procedure for immediate closure of a tunnel in case of an emergency. In addition, the authority will identify a tunnel manager who must prepare an incident report of any significant incident or accident occurring in a tunnel. For each tunnel, the tunnel manager, with the prior approval of the administrative authority, nominates a safety officer who coordinates all preventive and safeguarding measures to ensure the safety of users and operations staff. Finally, EU countries must ensure that inspections, evaluations, and tests are carried out by the inspection entities, and risk analysis is carried out by an independent body, taking into account all design factors and traffic conditions that affect the tunnel's safety, length, and geometry, as well as the projected number of heavy-goods vehicles per day.

Another issue of importance for safety is the transportation of dangerous goods, which has long been governed by established agreements. For example, the rules of Directive 94/55/EC are based on the European Agreement concerning the International Carriage of Dangerous Goods by Road. Council Directive 96/35/EC regards appointing safety advisers for the transportation of dangerous goods by road, rail, and inland waterway, and stipulates that all operations involved in the transportation, loading, or unloading of dangerous goods appoint a safety adviser who has undergone the necessary training, passed an examination, and received a certificate. The adviser must seek all appropriate means and promote all appropriate action to ensure that dangerous goods are transported in the safest possible way. Directive 2000/18/EC concerned examination requirements for safety advisers, and was repealed in 2008 by Directive 2008/68/EC, which states that EU countries have the right to regulate or prohibit, strictly for reasons of safety during transport, the transport of dangerous goods within their own territory, and they may set down specific safety requirements within their own territory. Directive 95/50/ EC sets out uniform procedures for random checks on the road transportation of dangerous goods. For example, consignments found to be in infringement may be immobilized, to be brought into conformity before continuing their journey, or may be subject to other measures, such as not permitted to enter the EU.

Directive 2010/35/EU, referred to as the Transportable Pressure Equipment Directive, repealed previous directives such as 1999/36/EC. The new directive aims to increase safety in relation to transportable pressure equipment by setting out technical requirements. For example, manufacturers must ensure that when placing their transportable pressure equipment on the market, the equipment has been designed, manufactured, and documented to be in compliance with the requirements in both this directive and in Directive 2008/68/ EC (on the inland transport of dangerous goods). Compliance must be demonstrated through a conformity assessment process by or under the surveillance of the notified body. In addition, importers and distributors may place on the EU market transportable pressure equipment that complies with Directive 2008/68/EC, under which no EU country may prohibit, restrict, or impede the free movement of, placement on the market of, or use of transportable pressure equipment on their territory when the above complies with this directive.

The Community Database on Accidents on the Roads in Europe (CARE) was set up in 1993 by Council Decision 93/704/EC. The objectives of CARE are to identify and quantify problems in road safety, study situations leading to accidents, examine the efficiency of measures taken for road safety, and play a role in disseminating and exchanging information to find appropriate solutions to accidents.

3.3.6 International Transport Networks

The Maastricht Treaty gave the Community powers and instruments to develop the Trans-European Transport Network (TEN-T), which was established by the European Commission in 1996. At that time, the first guidelines for its development were adopted, which incorporated fourteen projects of common interest. Its aim is to ensure that national networks for all modes of transport are accessible, interconnected, and interoperable. The TEN-T is considered fundamental for securing a single market with free movement of passengers and goods, as well as for reinforcing economic and social cohesion and promoting economic competitiveness and sustainable development. The enlargement of the EU in 2004 and 2007 led to the need for a thorough revision of TEN-T guidelines. In 2004, the number of priority projects increased from fourteen to thirty, all of which are expected to be completed by 2020. In 2007, the rules for granting Community aid were modified to allow for a higher maximum co-funding rate for priority projects and for providing greater incentives for setting up public–private partnerships (PPPs). The EU is supporting TEN-T implementation through the TEN-T program, the Cohesion Fund, the European Regional Development Fund, and loans and credit guarantees from the European Investment Bank.[32] Of the thirty priority projects, eighteen are railway projects, two are inland waterways and shipping projects, and four are road projects. The cost of all projects is estimated at €400 billion, of which €126 billion had been reached by the end of 2006. If one includes projects of common interest not identified as priority projects, the costs would be €900 billion, of which €408 billion had been reached by the end of 2006.

Pan-European Corridors (PEC) were developed during ministerial conferences in Crete (1994) and Helsinki (1997), with the aim of connecting the EU-15 with neighbouring countries. During the Crete conference, nine multimodal pan-European transport links were identified as being of interest and are considered a basis for future work on transport infrastructure development in Central and Eastern Europe. At the Helsinki meeting, the conference established a new corridor (Corridor X) that broadly follows the traditional transport route in South-Eastern Europe. The ten corridors are currently mainly within the EU and thus part of the TEN-T network. The EU supports corridor implementation through the TEN-T program, the Cohesion Fund, the European Regional Development Fund, and European Investment Bank loans and credit guarantees. According to Regulation 680/2007/EC, the EU will fund priority TEN-T projects for not more than 20 per cent of the cost of the work, and up to a maximum of 30 per cent of the eligible cost for cross-border sections, provided that the member states concerned have given the Commission all necessary guarantees regarding the financial viability of the project and the timetable for carrying it out. Projects other than priority projects will be funded to a maximum of 10 per cent of eligible costs. All these corridors are multi-modal, having a total length of about 48,000 km, of which 25,000 km are part of the rail network and 23,000 km part of the road network.

Over time it became apparent that the corridor concept, based on the development of links between major activity centres, did not adequately address transport infrastructure needs in certain areas, particularly those surrounding or linked to sea basins. The result was the adoption of the complementary concept of Pan-European Transport Areas (PETrA). It has been agreed that the countries concerned should work on infrastructure

---

[32] See Regulation (EC) No. 680/2007, laying down general rules for granting Community financial aid in the fields of trans-European transport and energy networks.

development plans for each area, and links with Pan-European Transport Corridors and TEN-T. This work should aim at ensuring PETrA's greatest possible integration with the former of the two networks.[33]

In October 2011, the European Commission published a proposal for a new regulation on Union guidelines for TEN-T development. According to the document, TEN-T can best be developed through a dual-layer approach, consisting of a comprehensive network and a core network. The former, constituting the basic layer of TEN-T, consists of all existing and planned infrastructure meeting the requirements of the guidelines, and is to be in place by 31 December 2050 at the latest. The latter, consisting of the strategically most important parts of the network, concentrates on those components with the highest European added value: cross-border missing links, key bottlenecks, and multi-modal nodes. That network is to be in place by 31 December 2030 at the latest.

The new legislative framework came into force with the adoption of Regulation (EU) No. 1315/2013 on Union Guidelines for the Development of Trans-European Transport Network, and Regulation (EU) No. 1315/2013 as regards Supplementing Annex III thereto with New Indicative Maps. The Connecting Europe Facility (CEF), governing EU funding in the transport, energy, and telecommunications sectors between 2014 and 2020, was established with Regulation (EU) No. 1316/2013. The new policy, concentrating on a much smaller and more tightly defined transport network for Europe, aims to focus spending on a smaller number of projects called Core Network Corridors. The core network of the Scandinavian-Mediterranean Corridor, the North Sea-Baltic Corridor, the North Sea-Mediterranean Corridor, the Baltic-Adriatic Corridor, the Orient/East-Med Corridor, the Atlantic Corridor, the Rhine-Danube Corridor, and the Mediterranean Corridor is planned to be completed by the end of 2030. The CEF will be the financing tool for investing in transport, energy, and information and communications technology infrastructure. The CEF's total budget is €50 billion, with €31.7 billion dedicated to the transport sector.

During a September 1995 dialogue between the Transport Council of the EU and transport ministers of EU-associated countries, it was recommended that a transport infrastructure needs assessment (TINA) for EU-accession candidates be prepared. The Commission launched the TINA process with the objective to define the future TEN-T in the enlarged Union, using the Decision on Guidelines criteria for its development. The cost of fulfilling TINA recommendations was estimated for the then-acceding countries as €91.6 billion. With the 2004 EU enlargement, TINA networks were incorporated into TEN-T networks. Finally, we note that the Transport Corridor Europe-Caucasus-Asia

---

[33] The PETrAs identified by the conference are the Barents Euro-Arctic Area, the Black Sea Basin Area, the Mediterranean Basin Area, and the Adriatic/Ionian Seas Area.

(TRACECA) Program was launched at a May 1993 conference in Brussels, which brought together trade and transport ministers from the original eight Caucasus and Central Asian countries. The aims of the project as proposed by the Intergovernmental Commission were to (i) support economic relations, trade and transport communication in Europe, Black Sea region and Asia; (ii) ensure access to the world market for road and rail transport and commercial navigation; ensure traffic security, cargo safety and environment protection; (iii) standardize transport policy and its legal structure in the field of transport; and (iv) provide a level playing field in terms of competition for transport operations. Thus, TRACECA aims to develop, with EU assistance, a transport corridor on a west–east axis from Europe to Central Asia, travelling across the Black Sea and through the Caucasus and the Caspian Sea.

3.4 The Regulatory Framework in the Turkish Road Transportation Sector

Turkey is a founding member of the ECMT and the UNECE. It has ratified various ECMT and UNECE resolutions, agreements, and conventions. Among others it has ratified the Convention on Customs Containers, Customs Convention on the International Transport of Goods under Cover of TIR Carnets (TIR Convention), Declaration on the Construction of Main International Traffic Arteries, European Agreement on Main International Traffic Arteries (AGR), Convention on Road Traffic, European Agreement on Road Markings, European Agreement concerning the Work of Crews of Vehicles engaged in International Road Transport (AETR), Convention on the Contract for the International Carriage of Goods by Road (CMR), European Agreement concerning the International Carriage of Dangerous Goods by Road, Convention on the Harmonization of Frontier Controls of Goods, and ILO Convention on Hours of Work and Rest Periods in Road Transport.

Examination of Turkey's WTO commitments reveals that for passenger transportation and freight transportation no commitments have been made for market access and national treatment in the case of cross border supply (mode 1) and no limitations have been placed on cases of consumption abroad (mode 2) or movement of personnel (mode 4) for market access and national treatment. For commercial presence (mode 3), limitations have been placed on market access and no limitations have been placed on national treatment. In addition, Turkey has signed thirty-two bilateral agreements with different countries to increase access to foreign markets. These agreements are co-operation agreements in the field of passenger and freight transport, and usually have capacity clauses imposed on foreign carriers, that is, constraints on the number allowed. Some agreements even have tariff clauses. However, according to the Accession Partnership with the EU, Turkey has started to align its legislation on road transport with EU standards (i.e. improving implementation and enforcement of, in particular, road transport standards) and is beginning to adapt the Turkish road transport fleet to EU standards.

3.4.1 Market Access

In Turkey the responsibilities of the Ministry of Transport, Maritime Affairs and Communications (MoTMC) include, among others, regulating access to the market and profession, regulating and issuing operating licenses, and inspecting and monitoring market conditions in the road transport sector.[34] In addition to the MoTMC, there is the Ministry of Interior, which is responsible for roadside inspections; the Ministry of Science, Industry, and Technology (MoSIT), which regulates technical standards including tachographs and speed limiters; and the Ministry of Labour and Social Security (MoLSS), which regulates social conditions such as driving times, working times, and rest periods. After the abolition of the General Directorate of Rural Affairs of the Ministry of Agriculture, the construction and maintenance of rural roads has been decentralized and given to rural authorities.[35]

The regulatory framework in Turkey's transport sector is comprised of one general law regarding the duties of the MoTMC and a number of other laws specific to the sub-sectors. The main legislation in the road transport sector is the Law on Road Transport No. 4925 of 2003, which gives the framework for access to the market and profession. The By-Law on Road Transport, which became effective in July 2004, was repealed by the June 2009 By-Law on Road Transport. This by-law puts forth secondary legislation for access to the market and profession. Other related laws are the By-Law on Training for Professional Competence in Road Transport Operations, the Foreign Direct Investment Law No. 4875, and the Turkish Commercial Code No. 6102.[36] These regulations put forth conditions for admission to the occupation and market access;

---

[34] The following discussion of Turkish rules and regulations on road transportation has benefitted from Republic of Turkey Ministry for EU Affairs (2007), various issues of 'Turkey Progress Reports' of the Commission of the European Communities, various issues of Trade Policy Review prepared by the Secretariat of the WTO, various issues of 'Pre-Accession Economic Programme' prepared by the State Planning Organization, which with the restructuring in 2011 became the Ministry of Development, Togan (2010), and World Bank (2014c).

[35] In 2011 the Ministry of Agriculture and Rural Affairs (MARA) was restructured and MARA became the Ministry of Food, Agriculture, and Livestock.

[36] For the Law on Road Transport No. 4925, see the *Official Gazette* of 19 July 2003, No. 25173; for the By-Law on Road Transport, see the *Official Gazette* of 11 June 2009, No. 27255; for the By-Law on Training for Professional Competence in Road Transport Operations, see the *Official Gazette* of 3 September 2004, No. 25572; for the Foreign Direct Investment Law No. 4875, see the *Official Gazette* of 17 June 2003, No. 25141; and for the Turkish Commercial Code No. 6102, see the *Official Gazette* of 17 July 2013. The By-Law on Road Transport has been amended six times, the latest on 23 October 2012, published in *Official Gazette* No. 28450.

a licensing system for transport operations as well as other auxiliary transport categories; the rights and responsibilities of the carriers, undertakings, and consumers; conditions for vehicles; competition in the sector; rules regarding inspections and the rights and responsibilities of personnel; and rules and procedures for training and obtaining a Certificate of Professional Competence (CoPC).

With the Law on Road Transport of 2003 and the By-Law on Road Transport of 2009, Turkey introduced a licensing system in line with EU conditions that has resulted in registering 90 per cent of commercial vehicles in domestic freight transport and almost all commercial vehicles in international freight transport. According to this system, natural and legal persons registered under the Turkish commercial registry can apply for a license as long as they meet the following conditions: (i) good repute, (ii) registration with relevant chambers of trade and industry or chambers of tradesmen and craftsmen, (iii) employ at least one mid- or high-level manager who has a CoPC, and (iv) sufficient financial resources as well as sound management and operation practices. 'Good repute' requires that the applicants should not have been convicted of any freedom-limiting penalty for crimes such as smuggling, fraud, false bankruptcy, falsification, narcotics or gun smuggling, human trafficking or trade, theft, or corruption. In addition, the applicant should not violate too often the rules on weights and dimensions, driving and resting times, or working and wage conditions during their operation. Finally, we note that according to the financial condition for obtaining a license, the applicant must have a minimum number of trucks or tonnage, respectively, and a minimum number of buses and seats. The operators must also have the necessary capacity or tonnage conditions and financial standing values indicated in the relevant article of the by-law. Depending on the type of license, a certain amount of capital is also required. Operators applying for an international freight transport license must have a commercial vehicle fleet consisting of minimum ten units specific for goods transport, corresponding to a total of 300 tonnes loading limit, registered and recorded in their own names, and capital of €50,000.

The By-Law on Road Transport is the main legislation governing market access for national and international road goods transport for resident operators, and the MoTMC is responsible for regulating the conditions of access to market and issuing licenses and permits. Natural and legal persons who are not Turkish nationals can obtain the license as long as the applications are in accordance with the requirements of FDI law and satisfy the conditions specified in the road transport law and the related by-law. However, it should be noted that foreign vehicles may not conduct transport operations between two points in Turkey, and that foreign vehicles transporting goods to, from, or through Turkey require a permit unless it is specified otherwise in bilateral agreements. Moreover, goods coming to Turkey by sea, rail, or air and carried to a third country can only be transported by Turkish hauliers, and special permission for registered foreign vehicles is required from the MoTMC. International freight transport licenses are valid for five years, are not transferable, and may be suspended in cases of loss of good repute or financial standing. Conditions for withdrawal are outlined in the law. According to Article 7, fire brigades, ambulances, funeral transports, transport of medicine/medical equipment, postal services, and transport related to accidents are exempt from permits. However, the MoTMC may implement further restrictions and make new arrangements in the event of a crisis.

The By-Law on Training for Professional Competence in Road Transport Operations lays down in detail the rules and procedures for training and examining professional competence, qualifications for institutions in charge of training, issuing authorizations to training institutions, and issuing CoPCs. Applicants prove such competence by passing a written examination that contains a variety of questions about the subjects indicated in the above-mentioned legislation. Ten institutions have been authorized by the MoTMC to provide professional competence education. Examinations are carried out by the MoTMC or the Ministry of Education Examination Centre, authorized by the MoTMC. There are three types of CoPCs specified in the By-Law on Training for Professional Competence in Road Transport Operations: CoPC for Medium Level Manager (MLM), CoPC for Top Level Manager (TLM) and CoPC for Professional Drivers. The by-law also specifies some categories that are exempt from professional competence training and/or examination, such as university graduates specialized in transport or certain high-level positions in the Ministry of Transport dealing with road transport issues.

Transport operators are subject to the Law on Protection of Competition No. 4054. Article 86 of the By-Law on Road Transport refers to this law, and when deemed necessary, the MoTMC may intervene in the transport market to prevent unfair competition. To prevent companies engaging in unfair competition via a steep discount of charges, the MoTMC allows operators to apply a maximum discount of 20 per cent on the determined price tariffs. All rules and procedures are enforced by the Competition Authority and the MoTMC.

The above considerations reveal that the new law and its series of by-laws helped to bring Turkish national legislation in line with international standards, and in particular, in line with the EU road freight transport *acquis*. These legal regulations allow the creation and development of strong and efficient enterprises that are financially and professionally competent.

3.4.2 Prices and Fiscal Conditions

There are a number of administrative units in Turkey in charge of road prices. The Ministry of Finance is responsible for vehicle tax. According to the Law on Motor Vehicle Tax No. 197, trucks, pick-up trucks, and other similar vehicles used for freight transportation are taxed based on their ages and maximum total weights. The MoTMC is responsible for transit passage fees, which are charged to foreign vehicles at borders, but vehicles can be exempted within the context of bilateral agreements. The fee in euros is calculated according to the following formula: 'gross weight of truck measured in terms of tonnes x kilometres x 0.01'. In some cases, exemptions are accorded through bilateral agreements and in other cases tolls have been implemented, for example, on some motorways and Istanbul Strait bridges. Tolls depend on axle count, axle distance, and distance travelled. Non-stop tolling and contactless smart cards are the toll payment modalities. Foreign vehicles and domestic vehicles pay the same tolls.

Tolling is the primary Intelligent Transport System (ITS) application of the General Directorate of Highways (KGM) on motorways in Turkey. Urban roads in some major cities and some parts of inter-city roads have been designated for ITS foci on traffic management systems and traveller information systems. Such installations are continuing on the motorway network. There is no centralized authority for implementing ITSs, and implementation and controls are carried out by the establishments that install them. To increase road safety, the KGM and the Turkish Radio Television Corporation (TRT) signed a protocol with regard to broadcasting traffic information. Variable message signs (VMSs) are used on a few road sections to disseminate traffic information, and users are encouraged to check the Internet for traffic updates as well. Road users can also receive information about winter road conditions, road construction, and lane closures by dialing '159' toll free. Finally, we note that the selection rules for road maintenance contractors are those of the public procurement law.

Turning to issues related to state aid, we note that according to Decree No. 2002/4367, investments in the transportation sector are encouraged where the objective is to support and orient investment in line with international commitments, create new employment opportunities, and add value to achieve international competitiveness.[37] The investment encouragement programme covers investments in trailer/truck renewal for international land transport, public transportation, heavy construction equipment, bus terminal construction, and combined container transport. In such cases, imports of machinery and equipment are exempt from customs duty and imported and

---

[37] See the *Official Gazette* of 9 June 2002, No. 24810.

domestically purchased equipment is exempt from the VAT. Foreign financing is provided for transport sector projects, including constructing highways and toll roads, where the project must be part of the Annual Investment Programme prepared by the Ministry of Development (formerly the State Planning Organization).[38] Finally, we note that road construction is the responsibility of the KGM.

Although Turkey has road and vehicle charges in place, it is doubtful whether these charges reflect the social costs of the road sector, as outlined by the Commission of the European Communities (1998). According to the Commission, users should bear internal and external costs, which include infrastructure damage, congestion, scarcity, environment, and accident costs. As emphasized by Goodwin (2002), the decision of one person to make a trip during a peak traffic period imposes delays on others, which results in more time spent on the trip than expected. It is clear that the increase of car ownership and road transport is partly due to the fact that road transport has not internalized its full cost. Internalizing these costs would prevent excessive use of road transport, and would be a way to equalize the conditions of competition across different modes of transport. Thus, the government must establish mechanisms to secure short-term road maintenance financing and tolling based on a willingness-to-pay principle. More differentiation could also be introduced into toll structures. Turkey realizes that there is need to rebalance its transport modes and to improve linkages for intermodal transport.

3.4.3 Social Conditions

Aspects of social conditions covering rules for working time, rest periods, and driving time are the responsibility of the MoLSS. The Ministry of Interior is responsible for enforcing these rules and MoSIT is responsible for determining the technical specifications for vehicle recording equipment. The related laws are Labour Law No. 4857, the By-Law on Working Time that Cannot Be Divided into Weekly Working Days, and the By-Law on Road Traffic.[39] The Ministry of Interior and the MoTMC are the responsible public institutions for implementing the provisions of the By-Law on Road Traffic, while the MoLSS is responsible for the By-Law on Working Time.

The objective of the Labour Law is to regulate the rights and obligations regarding working conditions as well as the work environment of employers and workers who have a labour contract; the law does not apply to those who

---

[38] See the Law on Public Finance and Regulation of Debt Management No. 4749, published in the *Official Gazette* of 12 April 2002, No. 24721.
[39] For Labour Law No. 4857, see the *Official Gazette* of 10 June 2003, No. 25134 and for the By-Law on Working Time, see the *Official Gazette* of 6 April 2004, No. 25425.

are self-employed. The purpose of the By-Law on Working Time is to lay down methods and principles to be applied to working time and periods of work that cannot always be done, due to its nature, during regular weekly working hours, such as transport work in highway, railway, sea, lake, and river vehicles that does not fall under the scope of the Maritime Labour Law. Turkish legislation on driving times, breaks, and rest periods for drivers has been harmonized with the provisions of the European Agreement concerning the Work of Crews of Vehicles Engaged in International Road Transport (AETR Agreement) and the ILO Convention No. 153 on Hours of Work and Rest Periods in Road Transport. The 2004 By-Law on Road Traffic applies to drivers of vehicles with weight limits exceeding 3.5 tonnes and carrying commercial goods, as well as to commercial passenger vehicles with a transport capacity of nine persons, including the driver.

Turkish national legislation concerning tachograph installation in trucks and buses includes the Law on Road Traffic of 1983, the By-Law on Road Traffic of 1997, and the By-Law on Manufacturing, Modification, and Assembly of Motor Vehicles of 2004. According to the By-Law on Road Traffic, (i) the operators of vehicles transporting goods and passengers are obliged to make tachographs available in buses, trucks, and towing vehicles and ensure the tachographs are in working order; (ii) they are obliged to keep tachograph records for one month in the vehicles and for five years in their offices; (iii) they are obliged to keep records regarding the types and license plates of their vehicles in operation, the identities of the drivers, and the start date and place of work and destination; (iv) the authorized persons of the establishments performing transport of goods and passengers are obliged to monitor the working hours of the drivers and check whether the drivers obey these rules, and to train drivers who are accustomed to violating the rules and take the necessary measures to resolve this matter; and (v) for the vehicles that conduct inter-city transport of goods and passengers, the driving and resting hours are taken into account, driver destination and route are taken into consideration, and if necessary, these vehicles have second drivers available in the provinces, districts, and roadside stations where the vehicle would stop. Again regarding tachographs, they may be mechanical, electronic, or electro-mechanical, but digital tachograph systems became obligatory for vehicles used in international transport registered after June 2010, with a mass of more than 3.5 tonnes for trucks and carrying more than nine persons for buses. Drivers are obliged to obtain a CoPC and, according to the By-Law on Road Traffic, Article 99/a, the Ministry of Interior affirms that a prerequisite for the various qualifications, functions, and technical features of tachographs is necessary, and that they are produced or imported in accordance with the technical specifications prepared by MoSIT.

Checks must be done annually for at least 1 per cent of the days worked by vehicle drivers, where at least 15 per cent of the checks are roadside and 25 per cent are at the undertakings level. Roadside checks of drivers' and vehicles' working and rest times are carried out by Ministry of Interior personnel, who examine the daily driving hours, breaks, weekly and daily resting hours, irregularity signs in the records, previous records, and tachograph functioning. Working and rest time checks on company premises are carried out by Ministry of Labour and Social Security inspectors, who are selected after a nationwide competitive exam from amongst graduates of certain branches of universities. During controls the inspectors examine weekly resting hours and the driving hours between these resting hours, two-week driving period limitations, whether drivers are compensated for reduced daily or weekly resting hours, whether certificates of entry are used, and whether driver working hours are organized. The Labour Inspection Board of the MoLSS is responsible for enforcing the rules at the undertakings. Labour inspectors conduct their duties on three grounds at the workplace: inspection, control, and investigation. According to the ILO Convention Concerning Labour Inspection in Industry and Commerce No. 81 and other relevant legislation, collecting statistical data is of prime importance. The data is published in the General Report of Labour Inspection and submitted to the ILO annually.

3.4.4 Technical Conditions

The MoTMC is responsible for conducting roadworthiness tests. In 2004 it issued the By-Law on the Establishment and Management of Vehicle Technical Inspection Stations, which states that technical inspections and roadworthiness tests will be carried out in vehicle technical inspection stations owned by real or legal persons authorized by the MoTMC. Recently, a consortium was authorized to build and operate technical inspection stations for twenty years. The consortium set up fixed and mobile stations that are to be supervised by the MoTMC. Freight weights and dimensions are regulated by the 1997 By-Law on Road Traffic and by its later amendments prepared in conformity with EU regulations. Freight weight controls are done effectively by implementing fixed and mobile control systems. Within the framework of the Renewal, Improvement, and Construction of Weight and Dimension Control Stations Project, preliminary studies on the renewal of existing stations and construction of additional stations have been completed.

The 2002 By-Law on Speed Limitation Devices or Similar Speed Limitation on Board Systems of Certain Categories of Motor Vehicles renders type approval of motor vehicles mandatory and is enforced by MoSIT. In 2003 the By-Law on Road Traffic was amended, and installation and use of speed limitation devices for N3 trucks and tractors and M3 buses having a maximum mass exceeding 10 tonnes became mandatory. Finally, it should be emphasized that a new circular was issued in November 2012 for scrapping commercial vehicles manufactured before 1990 till the end of 2013.

3.4.5 Road Safety

The General Directorate of Security of the Ministry of Interior is responsible for regulating road safety on all motorways, state and provincial roads, and the gendarmerie are responsible for the remaining roads. The MoTMC is responsible for regulating and monitoring the transport of dangerous goods by road, the Ministry of Education for training drivers, the Ministry of Health for assessing drivers' health, and MoSIT for type approvals of transportable pressure equipment.

According to Article 5 of the Law on Road Traffic, the duty on collecting and evaluating information and statistical data about causes of traffic accidents, taking precautions according to accident results, and submitting proposals to relevant institutions on how to reduce traffic accidents was given to the General Directorate of Security of the Ministry of Interior. The recent Traffic Accident Project aimed to compile detailed information on traffic accidents, including casualties and fatalities in areas under police jurisdiction. The data obtained through the project include detailed information required by the CARE database. However, in gendarmerie districts, only numerical information is obtained about deaths and injuries from traffic accidents; studies on other information in line with the CARE database formats are ongoing.

To secure road safety, Turkey must improve road quality, vehicle quality, and driver quality. In this context, Turkey aims to substantially improve road infrastructure over time and benefit more from smart transport systems. A safer road infrastructure also requires effective roadside controls and removing economically and technically outdated commercial vehicles from the road. Steps taken to improve the quality of technical inspection stations were summarized above in the sub-section on technical conditions, and a project began in 2008 to remove outdated vehicles. Within the context of this project, certain regulations were introduced (including payments) to ensure that owners of sub-standard commercial motor vehicles deliver their vehicles to recycling centres. As a result, a large number of older motor vehicles are no longer transporting freight. For effective roadside controls, Turkey aims to introduce effective control stations to conduct weight and dimension examinations and check vehicles' technical capacity, vehicle registration, insurance, and required documents by means of an online system. Authorities will also check for CoPCs, compliance at borders with international transport rules, compliance with national legislation, and compliance with fair market conditions.[40] These stations, if run effectively, will prevent unfair competition, secure road and environmental safety, maintain vehicles' technical specifications, and preserve the quality of goods.

Increasing the capabilities of all drivers is to be achieved through issuing appropriate driving licenses and ensuring all drivers have a CoPC. Regarding ways of earning a commercial driver's license, we note that persons first meeting the conditions indicated in Article 41 of the Law on Road Traffic must attend driving school and complete theoretical and practical final exams. The Ministry of Education develops driving school curricula and administers theoretical and practical exams to candidate drivers. Driver's licenses for those who pass these examinations are issued by the General Directorate of Security on behalf of the Ministry of Interior. In addition, there are age limitations for drivers engaged in the carriage of goods and/or passengers.[41] A draft law was recently prepared on what format to issue driver's licenses in. According to the Law on Road Traffic, health requirements of driver candidates will be defined in a by-law that will be prepared by the Ministry of Health in coordination with the Ministry of Interior. The draft law on driver's licenses states that they will be renewed every ten years for those under 60 years age, and every five years for those over 60 years age after a health exam; beginner driver's licenses, consisting of some limitations, will be issued for two years to those who have acquired the right to have a driver's license. If a beginning driver violates the red-light rule more than five times, drives under the influence of drugs or alcohol, or exceeds 75 penalty points, his/her license will be revoked. Furthermore, the draft law requires three years to pass after obtaining a B, C1, or D1 driving license in order to obtain a license for categories C and D. To obtain an authorized license to drive trailer vehicles it is compulsory to have a license belonging to that vehicle category. Thus, the process of harmonizing Turkish driving licenses with the EU is almost complete.

According to the By-Law on Road Transport, driving commercial vehicles requires a CoPC. The certificate can be obtained after attending a certain training programme and taking the appropriate examination. The Ministry of Interior, Ministry of National Education, and the MoTMC are the authorities responsible for enforcing the relevant legislation. The carriage of

---

[40] In 2003, Turkey established the Traffic Information System, a reliable and consistent relational database supported by state-of-the-art infrastructure. The system renders online and mobile services as well as stores all archival information relating to traffic and traffic safety in Turkey (motor vehicles, drivers, accidents, and roads). The main objective of this system is to improve the effectiveness of traffic law enforcement and to make personnel and equipment planning more effective through online inquiries and centrally collecting and storing all traffic-related data.

[41] To drive motorized bicycles, motorcycles, agrimotors, and specialized vehicles for disabled people, the minimum age is 17; for automobiles, minibuses, and light-duty trucks, the minimum age is 18; for trucks, tractors, and buses, the minimum age is 22; for buses with seat capacities of 15 or more, the minimum age is 26. For drivers engaged in the commercial carriage of goods and passengers, the maximum age is 63.

dangerous goods is regulated by the By-Law on Transport of Dangerous Goods by Road and the By-Law on Training for Professional Competence in Road Transport Operations.[42] In February 2010, Turkey became party to the European Agreement concerning the International Carriage of Dangerous Goods by Road, which became effective in October 2013.[43] With regard to administrative capacity, we note that new staff have been recruited, the new Department for Professional Competence has been set up within the MoTMC, and the new Department for Transport of Dangerous Goods was established. Furthermore, the institutional capacity of the Directorate General for Land Transport (DGLT) has been improved.

According to the Law on Road Traffic, motor vehicles are registered with the Directorate General of Turkish National Police on behalf of the Ministry of Interior. Exceptions include military vehicles, which are registered to the Turkish Armed Forces; vehicles operated by the rail system, which are registered to the owner institution of these vehicles; construction vehicles belonging to public bodies, which are registered to their own institutions; and construction vehicles belonging to natural and legal persons, which are registered to the chambers of agriculture, industry, or commerce, as appropriate. Finally, we note that the Turkish By-Law on Transportable Pressure Equipment transposes the relevant EU legislation (1999/36/EC).

Regarding the accreditation and certification of inspection bodies, we note that the Communiqué on the Basic Criteria for the Designation of Notified and Approved Bodies in accordance with the By-Law on Transportable Pressure Equipment does not require the accreditation of the aforementioned bodies. If the bodies are accredited, the evaluation should be made on a file-by-file basis by the Turkish Accreditation Agency (TURKAK).

From the information provided above it follows that legislative studies are in progress for harmonizing driver's licenses in Turkey with those in the EU. Installing speed-limit devices in all vehicle types, regulating drivers' working and rest hours, building a compatible database with EU standards on traffic accidents, and ensuring the equivalence of driver training in Turkey with that of EU member states consistent with EU regulations have already been achieved. All operations and transactions in the road transport sector are now conducted electronically in real time through the recently developed Land Transportation Automation System.

---

[42] For the By-Law on Transport of Dangerous Goods by Road, see the *Official Gazette* of 22 October 1976, No. 15742, and for the By-Law on Training for Professional Competence in Road Transport Operations, see the *Official Gazette* of 3 September 2004, No. 25572.
[43] Dangerous goods include explosives, gases, flammable liquids, flammable solids, oxidizing substances, toxic and infectious substances, radioactive material, corrosives, and miscellaneous dangerous goods.

3.4.6 International Transport Networks

Turkey is keenly interested in establishing transportation connections between Europe, Asia, and Africa. Realizing that its transport infrastructure could be developed by integrating itself with the TEN-T network, the Turkish government commissioned a TINA study for Turkey.[44] The aim was to authoritatively analyse the needs of the Turkish transport sector and bring forward realistic and systematic solutions. For this purpose the study attempted to identify Turkey's core transport network to ensure the integration of the Turkish transport infrastructure with TEN-T and to develop a multi-modal transport network within Turkey. The study began in December 2005 and was completed in May 2007.

Turkey's core road network includes almost 12,000 km. Within the TINA project, priority was placed on completing missing links, ensuring efficient use of existing infrastructure, and removing bottlenecks. Priority international road projects shown in Figure 3.1 aim to improve road transport infrastructure and connections with neighbouring countries. For example, upgrading the Kınalı Junction-Greek border area will improve connections with the TEN-T network there, where it will be linked to the EU PP7, and upgrading the Refahiye Junction-Erzurum-Gürbulak-Iranian border section will enhance connections with Iran. Despite their political relevance, links to Georgia, Syria, Armenia, Azerbaijan, and Iraq have not been included on the TINA priority project list.

From Turkey's perspective, Pan-European Transport Corridors IV and X and the TRACECA are very important. Corridor IV is a multi-modal northwest-southeast link running from Dresden/Nürnberg (Germany) via Vienna (Austria)/Bratislava (Slovakia), and Budapest (Hungary) to Romania, where the corridor divides into two. The northern branch runs from Arad via Bucharest to Constanta at the Black Sea, while the southern branch runs from Arad via Craiova to Sofia (Bulgaria) and divides again, with one branch running further to Thessaloniki (Greece) and the other to Istanbul (Turkey). Corridor X, also running from northwest to southeast, connects Salzburg (Austria) to Belgrade (FR Yugoslavia) and Thessaloniki (Greece). The main axis is connected along Corridor IV to Istanbul. For Corridors IV and X a memorandum of understanding (MoU) has been concluded among the participating countries at the level of ministers of transport and the European Commission. But note that the MoU is a voluntary commitment among the participants and has no legal binding character; it merely indicates the intention of the concluding partners to undertake joint efforts in developing the Pan-European Transport Network.

---

[44] See TINA Turkey Joint Venture (2008).

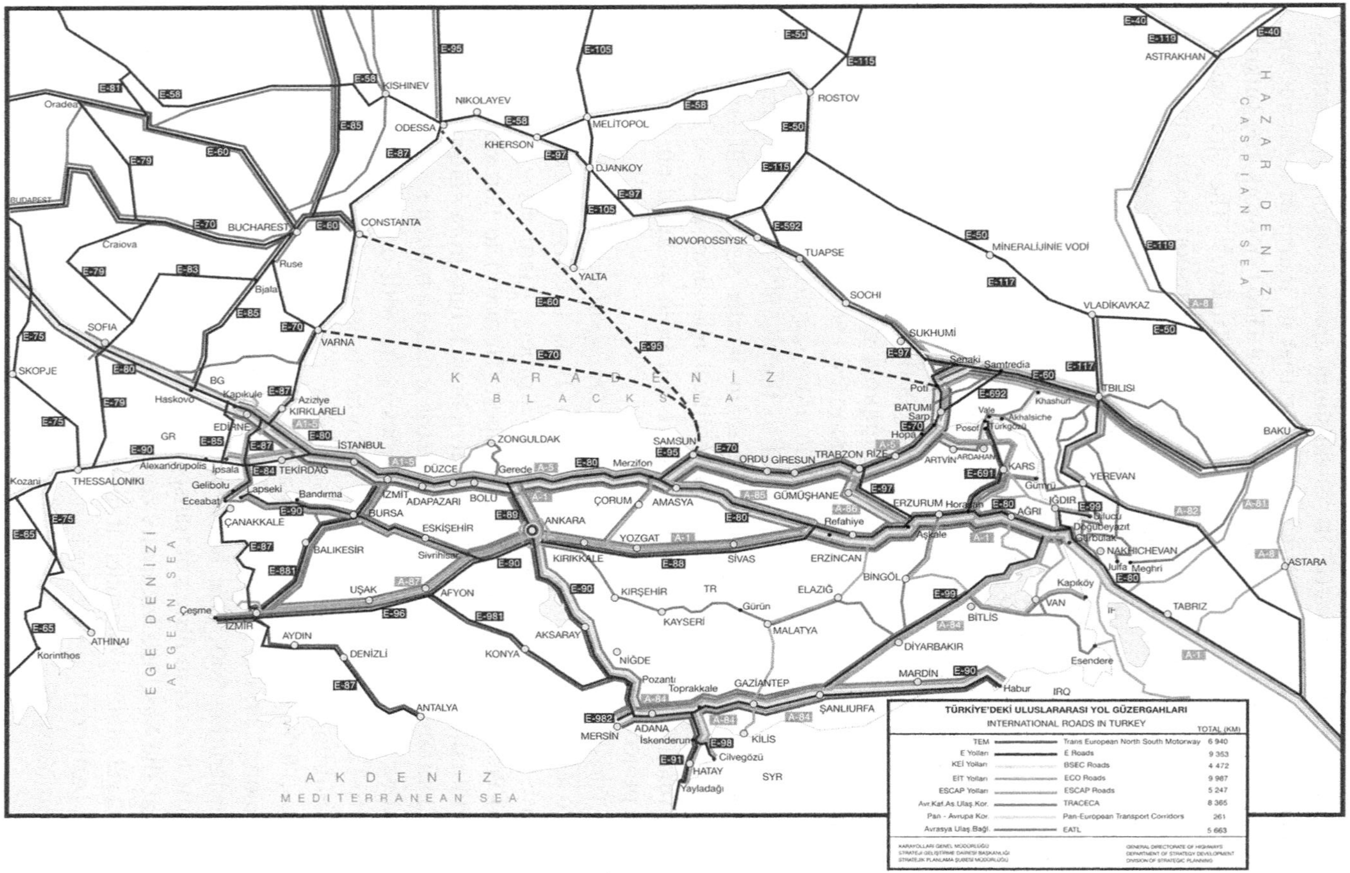

Figure 3.1 International routes

Regarding TRACECA, we note that Turkey's east-west TRACECA corridor (shown in Figure 3.2) provides efficient road connection between Europe and Asia. Total length of highways and roads that have been built under the scope of the project is 8,365 km. Within the context of the project ten different ports in Turkey connect TRACECA roads to Europe and Balkans with more than eleven maritime routes, and there are there are twelve airports in Turkey that have connection to TRACECA.

Examining the international transport networks supported by the UN system reveals that Turkey's road network is included in the TEM project, the regional transportation infrastructure project beginning in Poland, continuing through Southeastern Europe and Turkey, and stretching to Asia via the Middle East. The regional members are Austria, Bosnia-Herzegovina, Bulgaria, Croatia, Czech Republic, Georgia, Hungary, Italy, Lithuania, Poland, Romania, Slovakia, and Turkey. Sweden and Ukraine have observer status. In Turkey, the TEM starts at the Bulgarian border, passes through Istanbul and divides into one eastern and one southern branch in Ankara. The eastern branch divides into two at Aşkale, with one travelling to Trabzon in the Black Sea region, and the other ending in Gürbulak at the Iranian border. The southern branch connects Istanbul to İzmir and Antalya and ends at the Syrian and Iraqi border. The total length of TEM in Turkey is approximately 6,940 km.

Turkey is party to the AGR within the UNECE framework. According to AGR provisions, two arteries stretch into Turkey: the E-80, from the Bulgarian border at Kapıkule, and the E-90, from the Greek border at Ipsala. These two main routes meet the international road network from the Middle East and Asia at Turkey's southern and eastern borders via Anatolia. The total length of E-ways is 9,353 km. On the other hand, the Tran-Eurasia Highways (EATL) plans to connect Pan-Europe corridors with the main regions of Asia. Turkey's EATL roadway covers a distance of 5,663 km. Moreover, 208 km to the Filyos and Çandarlı port will connect to the EATL. Note that Turkey is involved in the construction of the Black Sea Ring Highway, which is planned to be 4,472 km and the highway will pass through twelve Black Sea Economic Co-operation countries. The secretariat for this highway, which will be connected to the EU core network, was established in 2007. As shown in Table 3.1, 5,247 km of road network have been designated as Economic and Social Commission for Asia and the Pacific (ESCAP) roads, 6,940 km of road network as Trans-European North-South Motorway (TEM) roads, 9,987 km of road network as Economic Cooperation Organization (ECO) roads, and 8,365 km of road network as Transport Corridor Europe–Caucasus–Asia (TRACECA) roads.

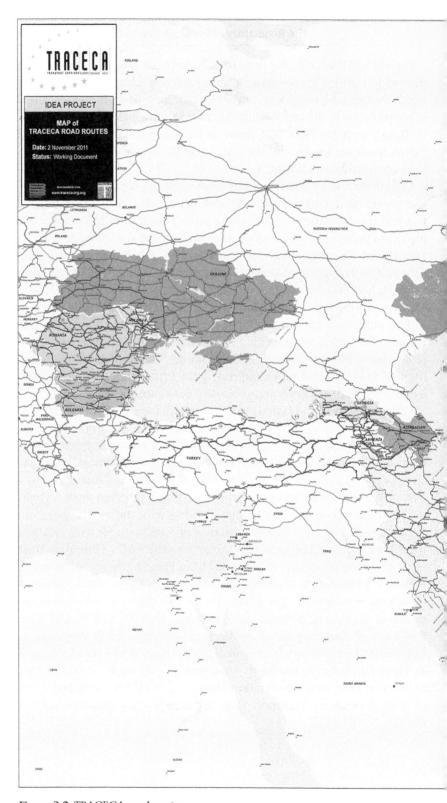

Figure 3.2 TRACECA road routes

Source: The Intergovernmental Commission (IGC) TRACECA. Reproduced with permission.

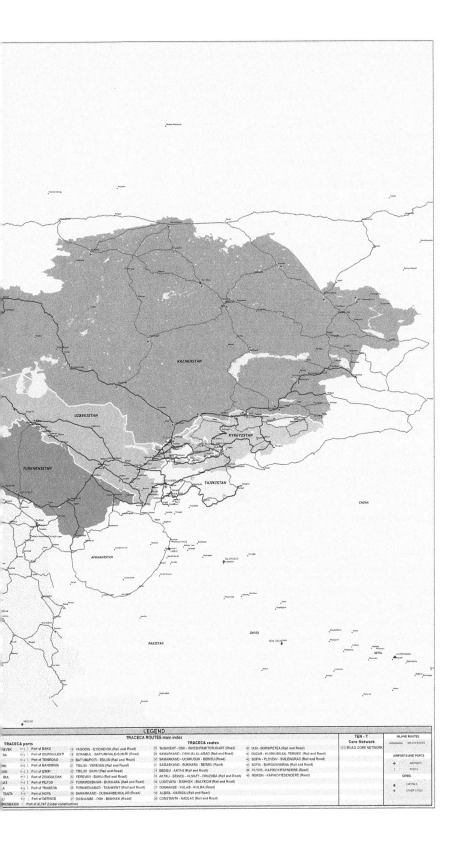

Table 3.1 The international road network in Turkey

	Length (km)
Trans European Motorway (TEM)	6,940
AGR E-Roads	9,353
Black Sea Economic Cooperation	4,472
TRACECA	8,365
Pan European Corridors (Corridor IV)	261
ECO roads	9,987
ESCAP roads	5,247
EATL	5,663

Source: Directorate General of Highways (KGM).

3.4.7 Epilogue

The above considerations show that Turkey aims to align its road transport legislation with the EU, including market access, road safety, and social, fiscal, and technical rules. Turkey will also ensure effective implementation and enforcement of transport legislation, particularly as regards road transport, and implement an adaptation programme for the Turkish transport fleet (particularly road transport) to Community technical norms. Besides adopting the legal framework, Turkey aims to recruit sufficient staff to strengthen the administrative capacity of the General Directorate of Road Transport to meet requirements for the minimum level of training for road transport drivers and implement professional competency conditions, train personnel to implement the related EU *acquis*, and strengthen the structures to implement legislation.

3.5 Conclusion

As revealed by the EU experience, liberalizing road freight transport services is a daunting task, requiring harmonizing and strictly implementing rules and regulations in the road transport sector among member countries. The legislation concerns market access and competition, pricing and fiscal conditions, social conditions, technical conditions, and road safety. In addition, road infrastructure should be accessible to all current and potential service providers on a non-discriminatory basis, and should, on the whole, be sufficient. Furthermore, border-crossing points should be modernized by increasing the efficiency of customs procedures and checks.

The EU has successfully harmonized its rules and regulations largely by adopting the road freight transportation *acquis*, and has taken major steps in strictly implementing the *acquis*. It has also resolved the issue of border crossings between member countries, although waiting times at borders between non-member states and the EU vary considerably. In addition, problems remain in the field of tax harmonization among member countries, and also due to different interpretations of the rules on vehicle standards and drivers' working conditions. Although the EU sets minimum and maximum taxation thresholds, fuel taxes and charges for infrastructure use vary considerably among member countries. As long as vehicle standards in Turkey for domestic haulage remain more generous than European standards, problems will remain because it is impossible to check all vehicles crossing borders. Similar considerations apply to drivers' working conditions. There may also be a lack of confidence in the ability or will of member states to enforce harmonized rules and regulations. To avoid problems in this area, harmonizing inspection practices among member countries is necessary.

One case where the EU has failed to create a single road freight transportation market is in road cabotage. As emphasized above, cabotage was liberalized in 1993, with the adoption of Council Regulation 3118/93. But it was not possible to overcome protectionist leanings within the Community, and the protectionist lobby made use of Article 1 of the Regulation, which specifies that any road haulage carrier for hire or reward who holds Community authorization shall be entitled, under the conditions laid down in the Regulation, to operate national road haulage services for hire and reward in another member state on a 'temporary basis'. The issue centred on how 'temporary basis' should be interpreted, and several countries tried to restrict cabotage by interpreting the phrase to their liking. In 2002, France restricted the duration of a foreign vehicle's stay to one week, but the Council of State annulled the decision. In 2004, a decree by France defined cabotage as transport operations that do not give rise to the presence on national territory of one and the same vehicle for more than ten consecutive days, nor more than fifteen days in any sixty-day period. This provision was also sanctioned by the Council of State. In 2005, the French government made another attempt to restrict cabotage by adopting a law restricting the stay of a foreign vehicle from another member country to a maximum of thirty consecutive days, or for not more than forty-five days in any twelve-month period. France also adopted a labour law requiring that drivers of firms carrying out cabotage in France are subject to the same rules on salary as drivers of French firms, whether these derive from legal provisions or collective bargaining arrangements, and to the same social security rules.[45] In the end, the Commission adopted Regulation 1072/2009, Article 8 of which states that every haulier is entitled to perform up to three cabotage operations within a seven-day period starting the day after unloading international transport.

Turkey has started the process of adopting and implementing the legislative, regulatory, and institutional framework of the EU's road freight

---

[45] See Bernadet (2009).

transport sector. By changing its regulatory regime, Turkey aims to increase competition in the sector, and increase access to the EU road freight transportation market.[46] But there are still major issues in implementing these rules as well as with improving infrastructure.

---

[46] For a discussion of issues related with increasing access to EU road freight transportation market see Chapter 7.

4

The Regulatory Framework in Rail Transport Services

During the eighteenth century, the industrial revolution generated unprecedented demand for high-capacity movement of raw materials, especially coal. At that time road conditions were poor and the canal system was inflexible. As a result, when freight wagons equipped with steel wheels and pulled by powered locomotives began riding on fixed steel rails, there was considerable demand for that type of transportation. By the end of the nineteenth century, developed countries had extensive national railway networks, built mainly by private companies. These networks provided rail connections between industrial and population centres and major ports, and for the most part, they monopolized long-distance freight transport, except where commercial waterways provided some competition.

The development of the internal combustion engine and its application to road haulage in the early twentieth century was followed by massive investments in national road systems. Railways lost their monopoly of the transportation sector, but a monopolistic market structure remained in the railway industry, leading to economic inefficiency. Railway companies were usually vertically integrated, with a single organization responsible for train infrastructure and operations.

Over time, as air, land, and sea transport options developed, passenger and freight traffic by railway declined due to competition from trucks, cars, buses, and aeroplanes; an extraordinary increase in the efficiency of road transport beginning in the 1950s; the flexibility of trucks, buses, and automobiles in the market; relatively low taxes and tolls for road transportation; and poor railway performance due to the economic inefficiencies. The large necessary investment in railway infrastructure became rarely profitable on a commercial basis. The post-World War II decline in the modal share of rail freight transportation led to rail company bankruptcies, but because railways were considered to create important positive social and economic externalities, railway networks were consolidated, and in many cases, nationalized. In England, railways were nationalized into British Railway through the Transport Act of 1947, and in Germany, Deutsche Reichsbahn was created in 1920. As a consequence, in the majority of developed countries, classic public monopolies began to operate railway infrastructures and trains, usually functioning as a department of a ministry or as a public entity with an administrative reporting relationship to a ministry. In addition to offering passenger and freight transport services, railways managed their own infrastructure and undertook a range of non-core railway activities, such as building and managing hotels, ferries, and ports, and creating haulage companies.

In developed countries, political pressure for deregulation, privatization, and opening up the railway sector to competition began in the 1980s. The concept of contestable markets provided intellectual support for deregulation processes. Many European countries sought to increase the efficiency of national railroad companies through a range of reforms, such as separating infrastructure and operations, creating independent regulatory institutions, and providing third-party access to the network. At the same time, the World Bank was encouraging countries in transition and developing countries to liberalize their railway transport systems. The aims were to make the railway sector financially sustainable, increase over time its transport market share by shifting traffic from roads, and create greener, lower-carbon economies.

This chapter explores the liberalization of railway services and is structured as follows: Section 4.1 introduces the basic characteristics of railway services and Section 4.2 considers the international regulatory regime in the rail sector. Section 4.3 covers European Union (EU) railway rules and regulations, Section 4.4 considers regulatory issues in the railway sector in Turkey, and Section 4.5 concludes.

4.1 Railway Services

The railway sector has several characteristics that, according to economists, make it a perfect case for a natural monopoly. These elements include the multi-product nature of the activity, the particular cost structure of railroad companies, the role played by infrastructures and networks, the existence of indivisibilities in inputs and outputs, the organization of rail transport as a public service, and the existence of externalities in the transport system as a whole.[1]

---

[1] See Campos and Cantos (1999).

Rail companies are usually multi-product firms. They provide different types of freight, such as cargo wagons, parcel and postal services, and different passenger transport services, such as long-distance and local traffic. In consequence, at the accounting level, it is often difficult to allocate total costs among different services because the majority of costs may not be attributable to a particular service. As emphasized by Amos (2009), rail freight costs can be divided into infrastructure, train operations, and corporate administration.

Basic railway infrastructure includes ballast, sleepers, rail, track fastenings, and sub-ballast. Because railways must have low gradients, railway designers use bridges and tunnels to traverse vertically challenging territory, cut through rolling hills, and fill in low spots to keep tracks as level as possible. In addition, railways require maintenance depots as well as switches and crossovers to allow trains to change from one track to another. Tracks may be single or double-track lines. Railways install signals to control train movements, and high-speed or busy railways are often electrified. Infrastructure costs are mainly fixed, and do not vary with infrastructure usage, although some components vary with traffic levels, at least in the long run. Rolling stock consists of locomotives, freight wagons, components such as bogies and couplers, and passenger rolling stock such as metros, trams, light rail systems, and commuter or suburban services.[2]

The main sources of costs in an existing railway infrastructure are related to track maintenance and renewal, structure maintenance and renewal, signalling systems, and electrification systems. Track maintenance consists of inspections, resurfacing, ballast cleaning, rail grinding, and track formation maintenance. Track renewal consists of re-sleepering and re-railing. Structure maintenance costs consist of maintaining tunnels, embankments, and bridges, inspecting and servicing signalling components, and maintaining and renewing electrification infrastructures.

Train operating costs consist of diesel fuel or electrical energy purchases, locomotive capital depreciation, locomotive maintenance, locomotive crew salaries and benefits, wagon capital depreciation, wagon maintenance, and other minor operation costs. These costs are mainly variable with traffic volume, and depend on the size of train, use of rolling stock, and ratio of net tonnes of a wagon to its empty weight wagon. Finally, corporate overhead includes the costs of executive management, finance, legal, security, and personnel functions. These costs are considered to vary with traffic levels in the long term.

---

[2] A bogie is a structure underneath a train to which axles (and hence, wheels) are attached through bearings, a coupler is a mechanism for connecting rolling stock to a train, and a railway sleeper is a rectangular support for the rails in railroad tracks.

Because of the heavy fixed costs associated with rail operations, Kessides and Willig (1995) emphasize that there are substantial economies of scale in providing some rail services, whether focusing on particular routes or types of freight. Because infrastructure costs do not rise with traffic volume, few additional fixed costs are incurred when more traffic uses a section of railway. In addition, a large firm may have lower average administrative costs than a smaller firm.

Because of the above considerations, fixed costs per tonne of freight transported by railways will fall as traffic volume increases. These economies are usually termed economies of density, and are attributed to declining average capital costs. In such cases, the cost-minimizing market structure for a route may be a natural monopoly. Another feature of the railroad industry, leading to economies of scope, is the multi-product nature of rail companies. A carrier that provides an array of services can do so at a lower total cost than a set of carriers providing each service separately.

The rail industry is considered to be capital intensive, with several indivisibilities within its productive process. Capital units such as rolling stock, track, and stations can be expanded only in indivisible increments, whereas demand may fluctuate in much smaller units, having implications for investment and pricing. Transportation costs of an additional unit of freight or passengers may be insignificant when there is excess capacity, but may be substantial when the infrastructure or rolling stock is at full capacity.

According to the World Bank (2011), rail transport competes fiercely with road transport for container shipments, as most time-sensitive freight moves by road transport from origin to destination. However, rail transport of containers for distances greater than 500 km costs about 20 per cent less than road transport, and the cost advantage increases as distances increase. Thus, efficiently run railways provide an inexpensive means of transporting high volumes of freight and passengers, and low transport costs improve the competitive positions of shippers and entire economies.

In a large number of countries, the rail industry is regarded as a public and social service. The industry is supposed to aid the economic development of underdeveloped regions and provide minimum transport services for particular segments of the population. These considerations have led to public service obligations (PSOs) being imposed on the rail industry. A further characteristic of the rail industry concerns its environmental impacts. A recent study by the European Commission revealed that road haulage in Europe has up to five times more external environmental costs per tonne-km than rail freight.[3] Amos (2009) reports similar results for the United States (US) and China.

---

[3] See Maibach et al. (2008).

An analysis of the total external costs of transportation provides a fuller picture of the externalities. External costs are the negative effects of transport that are not internalized into the price paid by the user and are therefore not taken into account by users when they make a transport decision. These costs have a real impact on society, and include global warming and health costs, and costs due to delays. Although the estimation of external costs must consider several uncertainties, there is consensus at the scientific level that they can be measured by best practices within reliable bandwidths. According to Delft, Infras, and Fraunhofer (2011) the average external cost for road freight transport for EU-27 including Norway and Switzerland expressed in euros per 1,000 tones-km amounts to €50.5 while the average external cost of freight for rail is €7.9. Thus, the average external cost for road is 6.4 times higher than for rail. These statistics provide a strong argument in favour of rail in a society that cares about environmentally friendly growth. Other studies show that railroad transportation is relatively fuel-efficient. The technology of steel wheels and steel rails causes very little friction, thus rail transport is estimated to be on average 63 per cent more fuel-efficient than road transport.[4]

Rail transport is considered to be an effective means of transporting bulk commodities such as coal, iron ore, phosphates, grains and cereals, and lumber and other construction materials for larger volumes over relatively longer distances. While rail transport is used extensively in transporting automobiles and heavy objects, rail container transport is also used in shipping manufactured goods. The rising role of containerization and the development of intermodal terminals that link roads with rails have improved the likelihood of rail transport remaining economically viable.

A final characteristic of the rail industry is its extensive regulation. Historically, the industry has precluded competitive organization. In different countries price, entry, exit, financial structure, accounting methods, vertical relations, and operating rules have been subject to different forms of governmental controls. It is emphasized that regulation has contributed substantially to railways' poor performance.[5] With the liberalization of the rail industry, a restructuring of railroad regulation is also occurring.

The World Bank (2011) emphasizes that the best regulator is the market, and that regulatory intervention is required if public interest is expected to differ from the commercial interests of service providers, a situation called *market failure*. Rail regulation usually includes economic regulation, railway safety regulation, environmental protection regulation, and harmonization of technical standards.

---

[4] See World Bank (2011).   [5] See Kessides and Willig (1995).

Economic regulation addresses problems with natural monopolies and managing industry interfaces. Because railways have monopoly power in infrastructure provisions, regulating the competitive environment may be required to protect the final consumer. If a regulated price is set below average cost, the consumer may benefit in the short run, but may suffer in the long run as this practice may discourage railway companies from making the longer-term investments required for preserving service quality. Hence, regulation should ensure that revenues adequately cover costs and that corresponding rates are best for public interest. Another important task for the regulator is to help establish competitive markets so the need to regulate tariffs will be eliminated. If there is third-party access to infrastructure, regulation should ensure that access rules and charges are not discriminatory. Finally, the regulator should create a framework that encourages the right amount and type of infrastructure investment.

Since cross-border railways are of growing economic importance, regulatory frameworks need to meet national requirements and should be sufficiently flexible to achieve compatibility across borders in operating or building new systems. Noting that railway companies for commercial reasons may neglect safety and environmental concerns, regulation is required to protect the public and the environment. Furthermore, the railway industry exhibits a need for common technical standards, for example, for track gauges, signalling and electrification systems, maximum axle loads, and safety systems, because railway companies appear to lack incentives to develop and apply common standards on their own. Since national railway systems with diverging technical standards may create troublesome operating constraints, inter-governmental agreements are essential to provide coherent frameworks for railway management co-operation, to streamline national border controls, to minimize delays, and to avoid unreliability. These regulations may require that tracks, wheels, and signalling systems be compatible with each other on all lines within a country as well as across borders.

4.2 International Rules and Regulations

Many countries have railway lines built to several different gauges. An early development making international railway traffic possible in Europe was the adoption of the 1,435 mm rail gauge by many countries. During the 1830s, British engineers built lines in several parts of Britain and much of Belgium using 1,435 mm gauge, and other British engineers had introduced this gauge to several parts of Germany and Italy by the early 1840s. These railways set the pattern for subsequent lines, as compatible gauges were adopted to facilitate through traffic. Through interconnection, national networks provided a basic material infrastructure on which international passenger and goods trains could run. In 1887, the Technical Unity on Rail Transport was signed among government representatives of Austria-Hungary, France, Germany, Italy, and Switzerland, securing uniformity in rolling-stock exchange in Europe. The protocol determined technical parameters such as loading gauge dimensions, maximum vehicle length, and maximum axle load, and it fixed the positions of couplings, continuous brakes, and steam-heating pumps. Although more protocols, conferences, and agreements followed, we concentrate next on international agreements undertaken within the context of the International Union of Railways (UIC), the Intergovernmental Organization for International Carriage by Rail (OTIF), and the World Trade Organization's (WTO) General Agreement on Trade in Services (GATS).[6]

4.2.1 *International Union of Railways*

The purpose of the UIC, founded in 1922, was to deal with all technical and operating matters relating to the development of international rail transport. To promote international railway traffic during the interwar period, the UIC formed different sub-committees to work on various aspects of this goal, such as revising international regulations for goods transport, promoting similar regulations for passenger traffic and luggage, revising technical standards for international traffic, and moderating financial disputes between different nations' railway administrations. During World War II, the UIC halted its activity, but resumed after the war. In the post-war period it became head of the various national railway organizations. It continued its work of standardizing railway material and tariffs and of promoting the unification of railway networks throughout Europe.

As of 2014, the UIC comprised 202 members across five continents, including integrated railway companies, rail passenger and freight operators, infrastructure managers, railway service providers, and rail research institutes from Europe, Russia, the Middle East, North Africa, South Africa, India, Pakistan, China, Japan, Korea, Kazakhstan, and companies operating worldwide. The latest changes in UIC statutes took place in March 2009. According to these new regulations, the UIC aims to promote rail transport at a global level with the objective of optimally meeting current and future challenges of mobility and sustainable development, promote interoperability, improve the overall coherence of the rail system, and create new world standards for railways.

The UIC has developed almost 700 'Leaflets' covering the main railway components, including passenger traffic, freight traffic, finance/statistics,

---

[6] UIC stands for Union Internationale des Chemins de Fer and OTIF is the abbreviation for L'Organisation Intergouvernementale pour les Transports Internationaux Ferroviaires.

operations, rolling stock, traction, infrastructure, and information technology, among others. These leaflets are professional-level documents, and aim at unifying or standardizing construction measures and railway operating procedures with a view to facilitating international traffic. They are applied, according to their content, by railway undertakings, infrastructure managers, industry, and public works undertakings. Their measures are often integrated in national norms, EC norms, and global invitations to tender for railway equipment. They contain technical requirements that must be respected to facilitate the exchange of equipment between networks, as well as cross-border transport. The Leaflets coexist with national and international laws, and often act as a reference and technical basis for drafting norms and regulations decreed by authorized organizations, such as the European Committee for Standardization (CEN).[7]

4.2.2 Intergovernmental Organization for International Carriage by Rail

The first International Convention concerning the Carriage of Goods by Rail occurred in 1890, and created an administrative union according to international law of that time. These unions were institutionalized continuations of international diplomatic conferences. In 1956, their supervisory functions were transferred to an administrative committee made up of representatives from some of the member states. In 1980, at the eighth revision conference, the institutional provisions of the original conventions were fundamentally reformed, creating an intergovernmental organization. With the entry into force in 1985 of the Convention Concerning International Carriage by Rail (COTIF), OTIF was born.[8] At the end of 2013, OTIF had forty-eight member states, including all the European states, Baltic States, and the Ukraine, as well as a number of Near Eastern and North African states.

The old rules of the convention reflected a traditional approach to railway systems, where national railways had a monopolistic position and were closely related with state administration. Railway infrastructure was usually managed by national (usually state-owned) railway companies. Challenges to traditional rail transport laws came both from European integration and from a general move towards liberalization in countries' transport policies and in railway companies themselves.[9] The separation of railways from state administration, as well as the separation of infrastructure management from the transport of passengers and goods, required a fundamental revision of the international rail transport law in force at the time.

---

[7] CEN stands for Comité Européen de Normalisation.
[8] COTIF is the abbreviation for Convention relative aux Transports Internationaux Ferroviaires.
[9] This process will be described in detail in Section 3, on EU legislation.

Aiming to promote, improve, and facilitate international traffic by rail, OTIF established a uniform system of law covering the contract of carriage of passengers and goods in international through traffic by rail between member states, the contract of using wagons as means of transport in international rail traffic, the contract of using infrastructure in international rail traffic, and the carriage of dangerous goods. In addition, OTIF aims to achieve interoperability and technical harmonization in the railway field, and to approve technical railway material intended for use for international traffic and to facilitate border crossings in international carriage by rail.

After preparatory work, a decision was made in 1999 at OTIF's fifth general assembly in Vilnius, Lithuania to adopt a new version of the convention (COTIF 1999), which allowed regional economic integration organizations to accede to COTIF. Previously, only individual member states were allowed to do so. At the beginning of 2002, the EC declared accession to COTIF as one of its aims. At present, all EU members except Italy have ratified COTIF 1999, which came into force in the majority of these countries in 2006.

The rules of OTIF's international carriage by rail are contained in Appendices A–G to COTIF 1999: (i) Rules concerning the Contract of International Carriage of Passengers by Rail (CIV); (ii) Rules concerning the Contract of International Carriage of Goods by Rail (CIM); (iii) Regulation concerning the International Carriage of Dangerous Goods by Rail (RID); (iv) Rules concerning Contracts of Use of Vehicles in International Rail Traffic (CUV); (v) Rules concerning the Contract of Use of Infrastructure in International Rail Traffic (CUI); (vi) Rules concerning the Validation of Technical Standards and the Adoption of Uniform Technical Prescriptions applicable to Railway Material intended to be used in International Traffic (APTU); and (vii) Rules concerning Technical Admission of Railway Material used in International Traffic (ATMF).

Developing regulations concerning the carriage of dangerous goods by rail is one of OTIF's main tasks. The RID annex has about 1,000 pages, is reissued every two years, and has become an independent appendix to COTIF. Another of OTIF's major tasks is to facilitate border crossing in international rail transport. The organization has made numerous proposals and recommendations for improving border crossing procedures for passengers and goods. Smooth border crossings require technical uniformity in the rail sector, technical approval, and supervision. The APTU appendix to COTIF 1999 deals with this issue, and its aim is to ensure the interoperability of technical systems in international rail transport. It lays down procedures by which technical standards and uniform technical provisions for railway equipment should be validated or adopted. These provisions contribute to achieving safe, reliable international transport, taking into account environmental and public health issues. The ATMF uniform rules delineate the procedure under which railway vehicles and other railway equipment are approved for use in international transport. *Technical admission* (technical approval) is the task of the competent national or international authority according to the laws and regulations of the respective state, and must be based on the validated standards and uniform technical provisions adopted in accordance with the APTU.

As emphasized by Intergovernmental Organization for International Carriage by Rail (2014), in 2013 the legal service of the organization was involved in the revision of CIV, CIM, CUV, and CUI. In addition, thirty-seven countries of the United Nations Economic Commission for Europe (UNECE) have signed a joint declaration with OTIF to promote rail transport between Europe and Asia, and cooperation between the two organizations are carried out along the lines set out in the declaration.

4.2.3 International Rail Transport Networks Supported by United Nations Programmes

The European Agreement on Main International Railway Lines (AGC) provides an international legal framework for developing a coherent international rail network in Europe, aiming to facilitate international rail traffic throughout the continent. It identifies rail lines of major international importance, the E-rail network (consisting of arteries channelling major international rail traffic flows in Europe), and defines infrastructure parameters and standards for tracks, railway crossings, and stations to which contracting parties should conform. Parties commit themselves to constructing or upgrading E-rail lines in their territories within the framework of their national programmes.[10] The Trans-European Railway (TER) project is, as emphasized by the United Nations Economic Commission for Europe and the United Nations Economic and Social Commission for Asia and the Pacific (2008), a sub-regional cooperation framework established in 1990 by the governments of the Central, Eastern, and South Eastern European countries under the aegis of the UNECE to develop coherent rail and combined transport infrastructure networks and facilitate international traffic in Europe. At present, seventeen countries are members of TER.[11] The project has been instrumental in developing international rail links in the participating countries and is designed to harmonize railway management, maintenance, and operational procedures in

---

[10] Parties to the AGC include Albania, Austria, Belarus, Belgium, Bosnia and Herzegovina, Bulgaria, Croatia, Czech Republic, the former Yugoslav Republic of Macedonia, France, Germany, Greece, Hungary, Italy, Latvia, Lithuania, Luxembourg, Moldova, Montenegro, Poland, Portugal, Romania, the Russian Federation, Serbia, Slovakia, Slovenia, Turkey, and Ukraine.

[11] Trans-European Railway member countries are Armenia, Austria, Bosnia and Herzegovina, Bulgaria, Croatia, Czech Republic, Georgia, Greece, Hungary, Italy, Lithuania, Poland, Romania, the Russian Federation, Slovakia, and Turkey.

the region and their integration in the pan-European context. The project has contributed to the interoperability of the European railway system, enabling the integration of respective national systems.

4.2.4 The GATS' Commitments in Railway Services

In the General Agreement on Trade in Services (GATS) the relative importance of different modes of supply is closely related to the structure of railway companies.[12] Traditionally, at times when national railway monopolies functioned in all countries, cross-border supply (mode 1) for international transportation meant cooperation between national railway companies in terms of fares and in technical responsibility for transport. But in general there was no competition, except in the rare cases of transit between two points using different routes.[13] The commercial concepts of competition emerged when high-speed international trains and rail freight-ways (freeways) started operating in some European countries. The number of technical problems involved in crossing a border is potentially very large, including different gauges and signalling systems, electric power, braking systems, and commercial speed limits, to name just a few. Some of these problems have already been resolved through the OTIF initiative. On the other hand, the second mode of supply, that is, consumption abroad, is almost never restricted, so there is no need to undertake any specific commitments in this field. Some European countries, in cooperation with others, introduced preferential systems, such as Euro-rail cards and youth rail passes, to encourage certain customers to use the international railway network.[14]

When railway companies were state-owned monopolies in almost every country, there was no third mode (foreign direct investment). In the late 1990s, when the railway services liberalization process started, companies from one country began to provide services in other countries or purchase shares of existing companies in those countries. But in the early 1990s, when the Uruguay Round was in its last phase, such activities on a global scale were almost non-existent. Finally, mode four (movement of natural persons) also had a very limited importance in the past. It covered a marginal flow of railway technicians, mainly towards developing countries. It is now becoming more important due to liberalized access to railway infrastructure in European countries. In the early 1990s, the railway sector was not a priority

---

[12] For a brief discussion of GATS see Section 3.2.4 of Chapter 3.
[13] WTO Secretariat (2000).
[14] The Euro-rail pass lets people travel on European trains in popular countries, including France, Spain, Italy, and Germany.

in negotiations regarding services liberalization, which is why liberalization in this area is fairly limited.

According to the WTO's sectoral services classification given by the WTO document W/120 railway services are divided in GATS into five subcategories: (i) passenger transportation (interurban, urban, and suburban), (ii) freight transportation, (iii) pushing and towing services, (iv) maintenance and repair of rail transport equipment, and (v) supporting services (terminal services, cargo handling, other support services).[15] Freight transportation is further divided into (a) transportation of frozen and refrigerated goods, (b) transportation of bulk liquids and gases, (c) transportation of containerized goods, (d) mail transportation, and (e) transportation of other freight.

In the Uruguay Round, only twenty-two countries (the EC counting as one) undertook any commitments in the railway sector. The majority of liberalization commitments were offered in the subsector of equipment maintenance and repair, which clearly is not the most important one. The only non-OECD non-European countries that offered some liberalization in the rail sector were Brazil, Nicaragua, Nigeria, Philippines, Sierra Leone, and Thailand. Full market access in consumption abroad was granted by sixteen countries, commercial presence by twelve countries, and full commitments regarding passenger transportation were made in ten cases. Similar patterns of commitments exist in the case of railway freight transportation. Thus, worldwide liberalization in the railway sector is limited, even among developed countries. There are no proposed general commitments in mode 1, with the exception of Hungary and Estonia. On the other hand, all EC members (with the exception of Austria, Cyprus, Malta, Latvia, and Poland) proposed liberalization of consumption abroad. There is also an offer to liberalize commercial presence for other WTO members (once again, excepting the four members above, as well as Slovakia and Sweden). There is an unbound proposal regarding movement of natural persons (mode four) and a limited offer regarding supporting services in the case of rail freight agency and forwarding services.[16] Here again, the offer is unbound, with the exception of Latvia. Thus, there will be no significant liberalization of EU external trade in railway services. The main liberalization of services trade took place only within the EU.

4.3 Rules and Regulations in the European Union

The main objectives of the rail reforms introduced in Europe in the early 1990s were to (i) improve competition; (ii) create more and better integrated

---

[15] See WTO (1991).   [16] 'Unbound' means no commitments.

international freight rail services; (iii) improve efficient use of infrastructure capacity; (iv) facilitate the creation of a single European rail space; (v) and to reduce the declining modal share of railways.[17] The reform started with directives issued in 1991, 1995, and 1996, and continued with four Railway Packages. In January 2013, the Commission adopted its proposal for the fourth Railway Package, and once it is adopted the liberalization of rail transport services will be complete in the EU.[18]

Directive 91/440/EEC, on the development of Community railways, required that railway undertakings be granted management independence, that they should behave as commercial enterprises, and that the management of railway infrastructure be separated from the provision of railway transport services. To achieve management independence, the directive maintained that railway undertakings should have independent status, in accordance with which they would hold assets, budgets, and accounts separate from those of the state. They should be managed according to the principles that apply to commercial companies, and they should set out their business plans, including their investment and financing programmes. Member states were required to ensure that the accounts for providing transport services and managing railway infrastructure be kept separate. The Directive did not require that the two activities be conducted in different institutions, nor even in distinct divisions within the same institution, but it did stress that this was possible. Thus, organizational or institutional separation was optional. Railways could assign a manager the railway infrastructure, who should charge a fee to railway undertakings and international groupings using that infrastructure. Also according to the directive, international groupings should be granted access to the railway infrastructure under equitable conditions and transit rights throughout member states for the purpose of operating international combined transport services.

The basic provisions of Directive 91/440 were supplemented by two directives issued in 1995 and two directives issued in 1996. Directive 95/18/EC set out the criteria for obtaining licenses for railway undertakings, requiring that they be granted on a uniform and non-discriminatory basis. A license is valid throughout the territory of the EC, but urban, suburban, or regional services can be provided without a license. The applicant for a license must have a management organization that possesses the knowledge and experience necessary to exercise safe and reliable operational control and supervision of the type of railway service to be provided. A railway undertaking should be

---

[17] See Monsalve (2011).
[18] The following discussion of EU rules and regulations on rail transportation is based largely on 'Summaries of EU Legislation' available at the website http://eur-lex.europa.eu/browse/summaries. html (accessed 10 December, 2015).

adequately insured or make equivalent arrangements to cover its liabilities in the event of accidents. If an applicant meets stated licence criteria covering financial standing, professional qualifications, and insurance and has a safety certificate, then, according to the directive, the applicant must be granted a licence.

Directive 95/19/EC regulated the allocation of railway infrastructure capacity and the charging of infrastructure fees. The directive developed a set of common principles for infrastructure charging, while leaving the level of charges to be determined by the infrastructure manager. Fees should not be set lower than the marginal costs of a line. According to the directive, companies should set up a user-fee scheme based on actual costs. The directive states that each country should designate an allocation body that should be informed of all train paths available. The body should ensure that railway infrastructure capacity is allocated on a fair and non-discriminatory basis and that the allocation procedure allows optimal and effective use of the infrastructure. According to the directive, member states should designate national independent bodies responsible for granting licenses and ensuring access to railway infrastructures.

Directive 96/48/EC, on the interoperability of the European high-speed train network, aimed to make it easier for train operators to use the systems in other member states by ensuring that infrastructures, equipment, and rolling stock were all compatible. In such a case, the EC railway manufacturing industry would be assisted by adopting common standards. The directive did not require interoperability from every point in the network to every other point in the network, but only where necessary for the operation of international services over the network. The allowance of safe and uninterrupted movement of high-speed trains rests on regulatory, technical, and operational conditions that must satisfy essential requirements, which take the form of Technical Specifications for Interoperability (TSIs). The main purpose of TSIs is to harmonize national laws that are based on differing ideas about safety, environmental protection, health and consumer protection, and operational requirements. Directive 96/49/EC concerns approximating the laws of the member states with regard to transporting dangerous goods by rail. This directive aims to establish national safety standards at the level of the international standards set out in COTIF.

Ideas regarding further liberalization were presented in the European Commission's (Commission) 1996 White Paper, 'A Strategy for Revitalizing the Community's Railways'. In it, the Commission emphasized that the railway sector was in decline and that its market share was falling, despite characteristics that could make it a more attractive form of transport. To exploit those opportunities, the paper suggested that the EC needed a genuine single market because rail systems based on national lines make it difficult to operate across frontiers. At that time, infrastructure planning was inadequate, markets were fragmented, and integration was far from being complete. The basic idea presented in the White Paper was to introduce market forces into rail, which would give firms incentives to reduce costs, improve service quality, and develop new products and markets. To reach these goals, the White Paper stressed that railways should be run on a commercial basis.

To increase the role of market forces, the Commission proposed to (i) extend access rights to railway infrastructure for all freight services and international passenger services; (ii) examine options for improving the institutional framework for developing domestic passenger transport in the future; (iii) modify European Community legislation to separate infrastructure management and transport operations into distinct business units; and (iv) promote the creation of a number of trans-European rail freeways for freight. The Commission also stressed the role of public services, proposing to improve the quality/price ratio in the transport sector and to generalize the use of public service contracts agreed upon between the state and transport operator. Finally, the Commission recognized that it was necessary to integrate national systems. For the above reasons, the Commission proposed to (i) examine the scope for improving interoperability on major international routes in cost-effective ways; (ii) study how to eliminate delays at frontiers for freight traffic; and (iii) assess what improvements had to be made to the infrastructure to develop freight transport.

In a follow up to the 1996 White Paper, the Commission put forward the idea of Trans-European Rail Freight Freeways (TERFFs).[19] The concept of TERFFs was to provide a framework for voluntary co-operation between member states, freight train operators, and infrastructure managers to make international freight services more attractive to customers. The Commission advocated introducing rail corridors to operate on the following principles: (i) access to freeways must be fair, equal, and non-discriminatory for all train operators licensed in the EC; (ii) granting licenses, allocating infrastructure capacity, and charging fees within the framework of these freeways should be in compliance with Directive 95/18/EC; (iii) freeways should be open to cabotage; and (iv) freight terminals should allow non-discriminatory access for all train, road haulage, and waterway operators.

4.3.1 First Railway Package

The first railway package of 2001, consisting of Directives 2001/12/EC, 2001/13/EC, and 2001/14/EC, required operational separation of the functions of

---

[19] Commission of the European Communities (1997).

managing infrastructure and providing transport services, and laid down rules governing the allocation of infrastructure capacity. Furthermore, international groupings of railway undertakings providing international services had to be granted access and transit rights in EU member states in which their constituent railway undertakings were established, and transit rights in other EU member states were granted.

The provisions of Directive 2001/12/EC, amending Directive 91/440/EEC, concerned separating the functions of managing infrastructure and providing transport services, as well as the progressive opening of national networks to non-national railway undertakings. According to the directive, the infrastructure manager has responsibility for its own management, administration, and internal control, and establishes a business plan that includes the investment programme designed to ensure financial equilibrium and the optimal use of the infrastructure. Each EU member state takes measures to ensure that separate profit-and-loss accounts and balance sheets are kept for business relating to the provision of services by railway undertakings and for business relating to the management of railway infrastructure. Member states are allowed to provide that this separation requires the establishment of distinct divisions within one undertaking or requires the infrastructure management function to be performed by a completely separate entity. Thus, capacity allocation, infrastructure licensing, and charging are undertaken by an organization that does not provide transport operations so as to create non-discriminatory access to infrastructure. Furthermore, the directive requires open access for international freight services on the TERFF.[20] Member states ensure that compliance with safety standards are verified, that rolling stock and rail undertaking are certified, and that accidents are investigated. The financial statements of rail undertaking revenues from PSOs are shown distinctively and not transferred to another item. No transfer of public funds provided for passenger services is allowed to be used to cross-subsidize freight operations.

Directive 2001/13/EC, on the licensing of railway undertakings and amending Directive 95/18/EC, establishes an EU-wide licensing regime for EU railway undertakings in order to prevent international operators from facing entry barriers. According to the directive, each EU member state designates an independent body responsible for issuing licences. Railway undertakings demonstrate that they meet the requirements specified in the directive relating to good repute, financial fitness, professional competence, and coverage for civil liability. Licences are valid only as long as these requirements are

---

[20] Initially, access only applied to the major lines in each member state shown on the map in the directive, plus feeder lines and access to track in ports and multi-user terminals; by 2008 open access was granted to the entire European rail network for all international freight.

satisfied, and licences granted by national licensing authorities under the directive are valid throughout the EU.

Directive 2001/14/EC, on allocating railway infrastructure capacity and levying charges for using railway infrastructure and amending Directive 95/19/EC, aims to ensure that member states adopt transparent processes in relation to access charging and capacity allocation. The key principles are contained in Article 30 of the directive, which require the creation of national regulatory bodies (RBs) independent from the infrastructure manager (IM), the allocation or charging body, or the railway undertaking seeking railway capacity. An applicant must have a right of appeal against unfair discrimination, and RBs must make decisions on any complaints, take remedial action, and ensure that the charges for access to infrastructure are non-discriminatory. Regulatory bodies must also ensure that IMs are able to balance income and expenditure and that member states will establish a charging framework with specified rules. The directive also lays down charging principles, requiring that the charge for using railway infrastructure is equal to the cost directly incurred as a result of operating trains. But the infrastructure charge can also include a sum reflecting the scarcity of capacity, and the charge can be adjusted to take into account the cost of the environmental impact of operating trains.[21] Charge calculation and collection must be performed by the IM, who is to receive the track access fees and use them to fund the business.

The right to use railway infrastructure is granted by the IM, who allocates the available capacity, which, once allocated, cannot be transferred to any other undertaking by the recipient. The rights and obligations of the IM and of the authorized applicants are laid down in a contract. The directive sets out a schedule for the capacity allocation process and describes how railway undertakings should apply to use the infrastructure. The IMs must make every effort to meet all requests for capacity and ensure the best possible matching of all requirements. Except for exceptional cases, no priority can be given to any service or undertaking within the scheduling and coordination process. If IMs are unable to meet all requests for capacity they must declare the section in question to be congested. They then must carry out a capacity analysis to determine restrictions on capacity and propose alternatives. Thus, the IM should ensure that infrastructure capacity is allocated on a fair and non-discriminatory basis and in accordance with EC law. Furthermore, railway undertakings must be granted access on non-discriminatory terms to a range of service facilities, such as refuelling facilities, stations, terminals, marshalling yards, and maintenance facilities.

---

[21] Pietrantonio and Pelkmans (2004) point out that Directive 2001/14/EC applies the marginal cost principle, and to secure cost recovery it proposes applying Ramsey (1927) pricing.

Directive 2001/16/EC, on the interoperability of the Trans-European conventional rail system, was designed on the basis of the structure and content of High-Speed Directive 96/48/EC.[22] It lays out a gradual approach to introducing new EC specifications, and recommends adopting a work programme and priorities for the joint representative body and the committee. The directive contains essential requirements to be met by the system, and provides technical specifications for interoperability (TSIs) and all other European specifications, including standards from the European Committee for Standardization (CEN), the European Committee for Electrotechnical Standardization (CENELEC) and the European Telecommunications Standards Institute (ETSI). The directive stipulates that work on common standards should focus first on control/command and signalling, telematic applications for freight services, traffic operation and management, freight wagons, and noise problems. The Commission adopted TSIs for maintenance, control command, signalling, infrastructure energy, operation, and rolling stock subsystems in 2002. The controlling and signalling subsystem for the high-speed Trans-European network required a unified control system, namely the European Rail Traffic Management System (ERTMS).[23]

In 2001, the Commission published the White Paper entitled 'European Transport Policy for 2010: Time to Decide', the prescriptions of which are based on an assessment of the ten years of transport policy pursued until then. The paper identifies rail as an important sector but lists weaknesses to be addressed: (i) infrastructure not suitable for modern transportation and interoperability; (ii) poor information systems; (iii) opaque costing; (iv) uneven productivity; and (v) mediocre reliability. The White Paper proposed many changes, which are classified under the objectives of creating an integrated rail transport market, using the infrastructure more efficiently, improving quality and safety for users, and reducing congestion. Specific measures proposed include opening national rail freight and passenger markets to cabotage and increasing members' allocations of train slots to freight rather than passengers, the latter of which would be more efficiently served by a high-speed rail network. The White Paper also proposed including some sections of TERFF into the Trans-European Network to make them eligible for European and national funding.

---

[22] The Trans-European conventional rail system defined by Council Directive 2001/16/EC, together with the Trans-European high-speed rail system defined by Directive 96/48/EC, make up the Trans-European Rail system, which in turn is one of a number of the EU's Trans-European transport networks (TEN-T).

[23] The rationale for proposing a uniform control system was the recognition that more than fifteen different signalling systems operated on the European network. The ERTMS, set up by European signalling suppliers, is intended to provide a common rail traffic management system across the entire European network.

4.3.2 Second Railway Package

The Second Railway Package, consisting of Directive 2004/49/EC, Directive 2004/50/EC, Directive 2004/51/EC, Regulation (EC) 881/2004, and a recommendation, provided a framework for further liberalizing the freight market and harmonizing the regulation on safety and technical standards across the EU, for EU accession to COTIF, and for establishing the European Railway Agency (ERA). It accelerated the liberalization of rail freight services by (i) bringing forward the date from which international freight service providers had to be granted access to the entire EU rail network by two years, to 1 January 2006 and (ii) providing that access had to be granted to the entire EU rail network by 1 January 2007 at the latest for all types of rail freight services.

Railway Safety Directive 2004/49/EC, later amended by Directive 2008/110/EC, established a common regulatory framework for railway safety and harmonized the content of safety rules, the safety certification of railway undertakings, and the tasks and roles of national safety authorities. According to the directive, before a railway company can run trains on the European network, it must obtain a safety certificate providing evidence that the railway undertaking has established its safety management system and can meet the requirements laid down in the TSIs and other relevant EC legislation. The directive requires that each EU member state must establish a national safety authority; ensure that safety rules are laid down, applied, and enforced in an open and non-discriminatory manner; collect information on common safety indicators set out in an annex to the directive; and introduce progressively common safety methods and common safety targets as drafted by the ERA. In addition, member states must establish an investigating body independent from any rail undertaking, infrastructure manager, or charging or allocating body, which must investigate any serious accident and publish an annual report.

Directive 2004/50/EC, on the interoperability of the trans-European high-speed and conventional rail systems,harmonized Directives 96/48/EC and 2001/16/EC, taking into account the new legislation of the second rail package. It clarified interoperability requirements regarding design, construction, placing in service, upgrading, renewal, operation, and maintaining parts of the system placed in service after 30 April 2004. The directive was updated in 2008 by Directive 2008/57/EC. Directive 2004/51/EC, on the development of the EU's railways and amending Directive 91/440, accelerates the liberalization of rail freight services. In that regard, railway undertakings had to have been granted access to the entire EU rail network at the latest by 1 January 2006 for providing international freight services, and to the entire EU rail network for providing all types of rail freight services at the latest by 1 January 2007.

Regulation (EC) 881/2004, later amended by Regulation (EC) 1335/2008, set up the ERA to co-ordinate groups of technical experts seeking common solutions to safety and interoperability. The agency's tasks include: (i) recommending to the European Commission common safety methods and common safety targets; (ii) defining the content of common safety indicators; and (iii) contributing to the development and implementation of rail interoperability though the drafting of TSIs and reporting on progress with interoperability. Thus, the main objectives of the ERA are to increase the safety of the European railway system and improve the level of its interoperability. By providing the necessary technical assistance to implement Directive 2004/49/EC regarding safety on Europe's railways, the ERA has been a driving force in modernizing the European railway sector. Because mutually incompatible technical and security regulations among member states are a major handicap to railway sector development, the ERA aims to align these regulations and establish common safety objectives for all European railways.

In 2005, the Commission published a 'Communication' noting that the coexistence of more than fifteen different signalling and speed control systems for rail transport in Europe on a national level is a barrier to the development of international rail traffic because not all locomotives can read signals from different networks. Systems are very different in terms of performance and safety, and the publication shows that a more effective signalling system, with automatic train speed control, could improve railway safety. The Commission called for a gradual transition to a system common to member states—the ERTMS—using components of the Global System for Mobile Communications–Railway (GSM-R).[24]

In 2006, the Commission published a Communication on facilitating the movement of locomotives across the EU, noting that one of the main obstacles to developing an EC railway system is that rolling stock approved for operational service in one member state, particularly locomotives, is not automatically accepted in another member state. The cross-acceptance of locomotives is, in fact, subject to very different national requirements, and international operators must repeatedly undergo approval procedures in each state in which they intend to operate, which often requires supporting evidence that is not mutually recognized by other states, resulting in delays and additional expenses for railway companies and manufacturers. The Commission therefore proposed to amend the legislation on the procedure for authorizing entry into service of new and existing rolling stock, making it

---

[24] The GSM-R is a radio communication system based on the standard Global System for Mobile Communications (GSM), but using frequencies specific to rail. The Commission also recommended implementing the European Train Control System (ETCS), which allows permitted speed information to be transmitted to the engineer and monitors his/her compliance with these instructions.

possible to create a precise framework procedure to assist the newly created national safety authorities.

4.3.3 Third Railway Package

The Third Railway Package, composed of Directive 2007/58/EC, Directive 2007/59/EC, Regulation (EC) 1370/2007, and Regulation (EC) 1371/2007, provided for the liberalization of international passenger services. According to the package, railway undertakings providing such services had to have been granted access to infrastructure in all EU member states as of 1 January 2010, and cabotage must be allowed.

According to Directive 2007/58/EC on the development of the EU's railways and amending Directive 91/440/EEC and Directive 2001/14/EC, railway undertakings have rights of access to infrastructure in all EU member states as of 1 January 2010 for the purpose of operating international passenger services, and such railway undertakings have the right to pick up passengers at any station located on an international route and set them down at any other station located on that route, including stations located in the same member state.

Directive 2007/59/EC, on the certification of train crews, provided for the phased establishment of a common regulatory framework for certifying train drivers and certain other crew members. According to the directive, train drivers must hold a 'Community model' train driving licence issued by the national safety authority of the EU member state concerned and that is mutually recognised throughout the EU; train drivers must hold a 'harmonised complementary certificate' issued by the railway employing the train driver and specifying the type of rolling stock that the holder is authorized to drive and the infrastructure on which he/she is authorized to drive. Thus, the directive introduced a European driver's license, allowing train drivers to circulate on the entire European network. Certification of cross-border drivers was planned for 2009, and of within-state drivers for 2011. According to the directive, drivers must meet basic requirements concerning their education level, age, physical and mental health, and specific knowledge and practical training of driving skills. The directive also specifies tasks for which the competent authorities of member states, train drivers, and other stakeholders in the sector, as well as the rail undertaking, infrastructure managers, and training centres, are responsible.

Regulation (EC) 1371/2007, on rail passengers' rights and obligations, applies to international journeys undertaken within the EU with a particular concern being to improve the quality and attractiveness of international rail services relative to other modes of transport. It ensures basic rights for passengers in such areas as insurance, ticketing, and reduced-mobility access. While long-distance travellers enjoy a wider range of rights, minimum-quality standards must be guaranteed to passengers on all lines. According to Regulation 1370/2007, on public passenger transport services by rail and road, public service contracts related to the franchising and other contracting by public authorities of rail services and bus services must be awarded by competitive tender.

According to the Commission of the European Communities (2010), the European railway industry, following a long period of decline, has managed since 2000 to increase passengers and freight volumes transported and to stabilize its modal share. This recovery has been largely due to liberalization measures introduced since the early 1990s. But, the Single European Railway Area, requiring an integrated infrastructure network and interoperable equipment enabling seamless transport services throughout Europe, had still not been established. The EU Commission stresses that the aim of EU rail policy is to promote the development of an effective EU rail infrastructure, establish an open rail market, remove administrative and technical barriers, and ensure a level playing field with other transport modes.

Sustainable rail transport is one of the EU's long-term strategic priorities. In 2009 Commission of the European Communities (2009) proposed the Greening Transport Package, which includes measures to internalize the external costs of transport in a coordinated manner across modes so that charges reflect the level of external cost imposed on society as a whole. This method ensures that pricing systems more accurately reflect the true costs borne by transport modes. Today, there is still no fair inter-modal competition; the charging principles applicable to rail, road, and air transport differ vastly among member countries. Infrastructure costs and the instruments for internalizing or modulating external costs such as air pollution, noise, climate change, and congestion are still very diverse. The Commission's 2008 proposal to revise the first railway package and the measures set out in the Greening Transport Package in the field of road freight transport already contain new provisions aimed at ensuring convergence between the charging principles applying to rail and road transport and enabling a genuine level playing field among transport modes. The revised Eurovignette Directive 1999/62/EC will allow the internalization of external environmental and congestion costs.[25]

According to the Commission of the European Communities (2010), the insufficient level of investment in rail infrastructure in many EU member states is a key reason contributing to the decline of the rail share in transport services. Poor maintenance and slow modernization have a direct negative

---

[25] Directive 1999/62/EC, modified by Directives 2006/38/EC and 2011/76/EU, sets common rules on distance-related tolls and time-based user charges for heavy goods vehicles for the use of certain infrastructure.

effect on the low level of competitiveness in the whole sector. The Commission aims at mobilizing EU national and private funds to develop new rail transport projects and to ensure that existing infrastructure is adequately maintained. The majority of financial support will be provided from TEN-T projects to create a rail network for competitive freight. The main goal of a single European railway area is to create a genuinely open market through enforcing and improving existing rules. According to the Commission, market opening will be incomplete as long as European railway undertakings do not have the right to provide domestic passenger transport services throughout the EU. Much has been achieved with the Commission's adoption of a set of TSIs for high-speed and conventional rail, but at this stage all TSIs remain applicable only to TEN-T projects. However, a mandate has been given to the ERA to extend the scope of TSIs so that the whole railway system would be covered in the near future by harmonized specifications. However, because of the long lifespan of rail equipment and the need to keep investment costs at levels the sector can bear, moving towards interoperability is a slow process.

Despite the progress reached through the three railway packages, competition between railway undertakings as of the early 2010s was still limited by various factors, from the protectionist behaviors of historical incumbent operators to the collusive management of rail infrastructure, which, being a natural monopoly, should in principle be accessible to all applicants in a fair and non-discriminatory manner. In many countries, there is insufficient market transparency and ineffective functioning of the institutional framework. Operators entering a new market continue to face discrimination in obtaining access to infrastructure and rail-related services, which are often owned and operated by the incumbent rail undertaking. In addition, safety requirements still impose significant barriers to entry, stemming mainly from the cost and duration of the safety procedures necessary at a national level and their disparity across Europe.

Finally, note that in 2008, the EU set out uniform regulations for the transport of dangerous goods by rail. Directives 94/55/EC and 96/49/EC were repealed and replaced by Directive 2008/68/EC, which states that EU countries have the right to regulate or prohibit the transport of dangerous goods within their own territories. They may also set down specific safety requirements for the international transport of dangerous goods within their own territory with regards to (i) the transport of dangerous goods by wagons and waterway vessels not covered by this directive; (ii) the use of prescribed routes, where justified, including the use of prescribed modes of transport; and (iii) special rules for the transport of dangerous goods in passenger trains. Thus, in addition to efforts to harmonize safety processes, the EU is allowing some level of national autonomy in this area. In 2012, Directive 2012/34/EC was published, recasting the First Railway Package. As a result, Directive 91/440/EEC, Directive 95/18/EC, and Directive 2001/14/EC were amended.

4.3.4 The Commission Proposal for a Fourth Railway Package

On 30 January 2013, the European Commission adopted the proposal for a Fourth Railway Package consisting of a set of draft directives and regulations, amending much of the legislation described above. The proposed legislation, which still needs approval by the European Parliament focuses on three key areas: (i) opening the market for domestic passenger transport services by rail, (ii) infrastructure governance, and (iii) interoperability and safety.

First, the Commission is proposing that domestic passenger railways should be opened up to new entrants and services as of December 2019. As a result, member states would have to allow railway undertakings access to rail infrastructure for all purposes, namely to all types of freight operations (international and domestic), international passenger services, and domestic passenger services. In addition, public service contracts would no longer be protected from the obligation to be competitively tendered, and this will apply to all new public service contracts as of December 2019, and all existing public service contracts as of the end of 2022. Second, the Commission is proposing greater separation between infrastructure management and railway undertaking businesses through complete institutional separation or through strong 'Chinese walls' to achieve full functional separation within a single corporate group.[26] In addition, the Commission proposes to increase the responsibilities of infrastructure managers so that in addition to overseeing day-to-day operations and maintenance, they will control infrastructure investment planning. Third, the Commission is proposing an enhanced role for the ERA so that it has the legal power to issue vehicle authorizations for market placement as well as the power to issue safety certifications for railway undertakings. The ERA will also be authorized to monitor national safety authorities and supervise their national rules.

4.3.5 Trans-European Rail Transport Networks and Rail Freight Corridors

Although a freight market on a European scale was established through the first and second railway packages, rail transport for a long time remained the least-integrated transport mode of that market, leading to delays, extra costs, and insufficient use of potential rail options, especially for time-sensitive cargo. With these considerations in mind, in 1994, the Commission proposed

---

[26] Chinese wall is defined as an insurmountable barrier, especially to the passage of information.

that competitive freight on a European rail network be based on nine international rail freight corridors, linking Europe's main industrial regions. In fact, in 1997 a ministerial conference adopted to establish a new corridor that broadly follows the traditional transport route in South Eastern Europe. The ten corridors are currently mainly within the EU and thus part of the TEN-T network, and they have a total length of about 48,000 km.[27]

Regulation 913/2010 recognizes that strengthening the competitiveness of rail freight requires a corridor approach that crosses national borders, and it aims to improve operations on international freight corridors through improved cooperation among rail infrastructure managers on issues such as coordinating investments and works, capacity allocation, and traffic management, with guarantees in terms of performance, reinforced cooperation with terminals, centralized publication of conditions of access, and enhanced power for regulatory bodies to monitor non-discriminatory access. For each freight corridor, EU countries must establish a management board made up of representatives of the infrastructure managers. This board shall draw up an implementation plan that includes an investment plan, the measures foreseen to implement the corridor, and the main elements of a market study. The management board will designate a joint body to provide authorized applicants with a single place to provide answers relating to infrastructure capacity for freight trains crossing at least one border along the freight corridor. The regulation also promotes harmonizing infrastructure, with the specific objectives of removing bottlenecks and harmonizing relevant parameters such as train lengths, train gross weights, axle loads, and loading gauges. Reference is made to the ERTMS and TEN-T corridors, emphasizing that interoperability is an essential feature of rail freight corridors.

With the revision of the TEN-T guidelines through Regulation No. 1315/2013, the EU is concentrating on a much smaller and more tightly defined transport network for Europe, focusing spending on a smaller number of projects, called Core Network Corridors. The core network consists of the strategically most important parts of the TEN-T network and constitutes the backbone of the development of a multimodal transport network. The Rail Freight Corridors mentioned above will be adopted over time to fit with the core network corridors. The construction of these corridors will be aided considerably by using the Connecting Europe Facility.[28] Finally, we note that ERTMS corridors will be integrated into the new policy framework.

---

[27] For a discussion of TEN-T see Section 3.3.6 of Chapter 3.
[28] As pointed out in Chapter 3 the Connecting Europe Facility is the financing tool of the EU for investing in transport, energy and ICT infrastructure with a total budget of €50 billion of which €31.7 billion is dedicated to the transport sector.

4.3.6 Concluding Remarks

The above considerations reveal that liberalization of the EU rail system has been achieved through four Rail Packages.[29] The First Railway Package, of 2001, requiring operational separation of the functions of managing infrastructure and providing transport services, laid down rules governing the allocation of infrastructure capacity and allowed granting to international freight service providers access to the Trans-European Rail Freight Network as of March 2003 and to the entire EU rail network as of March 2008, which was later changed to January 2006. The Second Railway Package (2004) provided for EU accession to COTIF, established the ERA and set a common regulatory framework for rail safety. In addition, it required that access had to be granted to the entire EU rail network by January 2007 at the latest for all types of rail freight services. Noting that rail liberalization across borders can only be achieved if there is interoperability between the railway infrastructure, rolling stock, and systems of different member states, the ERA was established to facilitate this, producing common technical standards and safety indicators and targets. The Third Railway Package (2007) provided for the liberalization of international passenger services, and cabotage also had to be allowed. Finally, the European Commission's proposals for a Fourth Railway Package (2013) took the rail liberalization process to its logical final conclusion.

4.4 The Regulatory Framework in the Turkish Rail Transportation Sector

The rail industry in Turkey is dominated by Turkish State Railways (TCDD), a state-owned, vertically integrated company that provides freight and passenger services as well as infrastructure. The TCDD, which has monopoly rights to provide rail services in Turkey, operates and renews railways and ports; guides and coordinates affiliated companies; carries out complementary activities regarding rail transport, such as maritime and land transport, including ferry operations; manufactures rolling stock and similar vehicles; and constructs warehouses, depots, and passenger facilities.

4.4.1 Regulatory Framework

Until November 2011, the Turkish railway legislation included Law No. 3348 of 1987, regulating the tasks and duties of the Ministry of Transport (MoT); Decree Law No. 233 of 1984, defining the legal status of state-owned

---

[29] See Norton Rose Fulbright (2013).

enterprises (SOEs); and the TCDD's Incorporation Statue of 1984, defining its responsibilities and competencies.[30,31] The Ministry of Transport was restructured in November 2011 to become the Ministry of Transport, Maritime Affairs, and Communications (MoTMC) by Governmental Decree No. 655, concerning the organization and duties of the MoTMC, and the TCDD was restructured in May 2013 through Law No. 6461, on the Liberalization of Turkish Railway Transportation.[32]

As of 2015, the TCDD is comprised of twenty specialized departments at its headquarters, such as Permanent Way, Traction, Passenger, Freight, Railway Construction, and Ports. In addition there are six units, such as the Safety Management and Systems Directorate and the Protection and Security Directorate. The Permanent Way Department is responsible for track maintenance and repair.[33] The Traction Department deals with standards and compliance regarding rolling stock, and includes the Office of Train Operators, which is specifically responsible for stock safety. Traction Inspectors perform internal inspections. The Freight Department defines the principles for loading, labelling, and sealing freight, as well as planning demand and allocating,

---

[30] The MoT, which included the General Directorate (DG) of the Construction of Railways, Ports, and Airports (DLH), the DG of Land Transport (DGLT), and the TCDD were the authorities responsible for railways. The MoT was responsible for determining and planning shipping according to transport needs, defining the basic principles regarding the arrangement of rail transport systems, and regulating relations with international railway organizations. The DLH was responsible for constructing new railway lines, and for railway plans, programmes, facilities, and equipment. The DGLT was responsible for ensuring that railway transport was carried out in accordance with national security, economic, technical, and social needs; that rail transport was in harmony with other modes; and for coordinating international activities in the railway sector. Regarding rail transport of dangerous goods, the DGLT was responsible for setting rules and for supervision, while the TCDD was responsible for the actual carriage of goods.

[31] Construction, operation, and infrastructure administration expenditures in Turkey are in line with the EU *acquis*. With respect to financial transfers to the TCDD, the responsible authorities are the DG of SOEs in the Undersecretariat of the Treasury, and the Privatization Administration. The responsibilities of the former include overseeing SOE ownership, providing financing to SOEs, and planning and monitoring SOEs' annual budgets. The TCDD receives capital from the Undersecretariat of the Treasury and the Privatization Administration. Legislation on this front are Article 37 of the Decree Law on State Owned Enterprises No. 233 (*Official Gazette*, 18 June 1984; No. 18435), which states that the Treasury will transfer capital for investment and operational deficits of SOEs, and Article 10 of the Law on Privatization No. 4046, which states that capital obligations of the Privatization Administration can be met by sources from the Privatization fund. Other financial transfers include subsidies for track maintenance/repair from the MoT (Decree Law No. 233 and the TCDD's Incorporation Statute).

[32] The following discussion of Turkish rules and regulations on rail transportation has benefitted from Republic of Turkey Ministry for EU Affairs (2007), various issues of 'Turkey Progress Reports' of the Commission of the European Communities, various issues of Trade Policy Review prepared by Secretariat of the WTO, various issues of 'Pre-Accession Economic Program' prepared by the State Planning Organization which with the restructuring in 2011 became the Ministry of Development, and the information provided on the website of TCDD http://www.tcdd.gov.tr (accessed 10 December 2015).

[33] Technical specifications and regulations are set out according to UIC standards for track gauge, axle load, speed, etc. Bridges and culverts are built according to BE German Railways Steel Bridge Calculation Basics and EUROCODE standards. Tracking infrastructure, projects, and applications are the responsibility of the Permanent Way Department.

distributing, and transporting freight wagons, and defining principles of loading, unloading, transferring, and labelling dangerous goods. Finally, the Passenger Department is concerned with passenger transportation and the Ports Department is responsible for ports owned by the TCDD and for the Van Lake Ferry Operations.

The TCDD has a single set of accounts, thus there is no accounting separation between infrastructure and rail transport operations, nor between freight and passenger transportation. Certain rail services are provided under a PSO. Because of the lack of accounts separation, there is no information available on the true costs of rail transportation in Turkey. Consequently, corporate customers have no understanding of whether or not TCDD prices actually reflect costs. Currently, TCDD tariffs for carrying goods are determined based on information about distance and on type and weight of load. Prices are published on the TCDD website and apply equally to all customers.[34] A protocol may be drawn between the customer and the TCDD for regular transportation of goods by TCDD rail cars, or rail cars can be arranged upon request. From the above discussion, we see that the TCDD is not unbundled vertically, does not have separation of accounts, does not have a proper accounting scheme to calculate unit costs with respect to infrastructure, nor a charging or performance scheme. Regarding safety, we note that the TCDD sets and enforces safety rules and standards for constructing, maintaining, and managing rail infrastructure, as well as for providing rail transport services. Finally, we note that TCDD legislation on the transportation of dangerous goods by rail includes the Internal Operational Instruction on the Carriage of Dangerous Goods by Rail (No. 505 28 April 2005).

Until recently, the TCDD did not operate on commercial principles, it had a monopoly on both rail infrastructure management and on rail transport services, and there was no independent regulatory body in the rail transport sector. For those reasons, the Turkish government decided to change the TCDD structure and update its technology to make it a more competitive player in the market and to increase the modal share of railways in the transport sector over time. Both the eighth Five-Year Development Plan prepared by the State Planning Organization in 2000 for the period 2001–5 and the ninth Seven-Year Development Plan prepared for 2007–13 clearly put forward the goals of separating infrastructure management from transport services and restructuring the TCDD with a commercial mindset to increase its performance and to allow for private sector enterprises to compete in providing transport services. The TCDD Business Plan for 2005–10 states that the TCDD aims to improve its financial situation, establish a client-oriented

---

[34] See the website http://www.tcdd.gov.tr (accessed 10 December 2015).

structure, increase competitiveness and market share, integrate the network into the European and Asian networks, and provide a more secure and economical service.

In 2005, the TCDD launched a €4.2 million restructuring project funded by the EU. The project had three parts: a twinning project with Germany, a service project, and a financial management information system project. Its objectives were to (i) establish a legislative and institutional framework for the rail sector in accordance with the EU *acquis*; (ii) define a stable financial relationship between the TCDD and the Turkish government that satisfies the requirements of the *acquis*; and (iii) develop/customize a financial management information system, providing the necessary information technology platform, measuring financial performance (profit and loss), and monitoring actual performance. The project also entailed (a) increasing TCDD managers' levels of knowledge and gaining new capabilities for commercial conditions; (b) preparing proposals for capacity improvements of employees, training programmes, and budgets; (c) defining employees and sources to be transferred to new business units and programming the mobility of such personnel; (d) defining the targets and aims of business units and management; (e) defining business unit budgets and five-year activity plans; (f) defining public service contracts between the government and the TCDD and preparing draft contracts; and (h) defining separate accounting for infrastructure, operations, and PSOs with the principle of non-transferability of funds between services.

Governmental Decree No. 655, concerning the organization and duties of the MoTMC, was adopted in November 2011. The decree envisions the creation of a new DG for railroad regulation, however this will not come into effect legally until the state monopoly in the railway sector is removed. The new DG's duties will include, among others, providing an environment of free, fair, and sustainable competition, where activities of railway transport can be provided in a fast, economical, convenient, secure, and qualified way depending on commercial, economic, and social needs, as well as technical developments, by promoting public benefit and in a way to cause the least harm to the environment. These activities should be provided with other types of transport and be mutually complementary; specifying the service principles, financial capacity, and professional respectability conditions of railway infrastructure managers, railway undertakings and organizers, agents, commissioners, railway terminal and station operators in the railway transport business, and those who deal with similar activities; authorizing these people and supervising them; and defining the rights, liabilities, and responsibilities of those who produce services in the railway transport business and those who use such services; specifying the professional competency conditions of railway infrastructure managers and railway undertakings and organizers, agents, commissioners, railway terminal and station operators, and those who deal with similar businesses, especially train drivers in the railway transport business; providing necessary education or having others provide it; testing them or having others test them; authorizing these people and supervising them; specifying minimum safety limits and conditions for the use of railway infrastructure and rolling stock, and supervising these; granting relevant safety certificates to railway infrastructure managers and railway undertakings, or authorizing and supervising those who are capable of doing this; and settling disputes between railway infrastructure managers and railway undertakings that may arise from using railway infrastructure, its allocation, access to it, and charges for it.

In addition, Governmental Decree 655 of 2011 established the Accident Investigation Board under the MoTMC, whose duties include, among others, carrying out investigations on and examinations of severe accidents that happen in the transport sector, preparing proposals to improve transport infrastructure and safety according to the examinations when required, and submitting these proposals to the minister. Until the establishment of the independent Accident Investigation Board, accidents were investigated by ad hoc committees within the TCDD, where the investigation included a technical and an administrative component. The technical component defined the causes of the accident and determined measures to prevent future accidents, and the administrative component tried to determine who was responsible for the accident. There was also a judicial investigation by legal authorities independent from the TCDD.

For the twinning project, two draft laws were prepared (Railway Law and TCDD Law). The former provides a new legal framework for rail activity and the latter supports reorganization through separating and eventually privatizing affiliated companies and port operations. Regulations on railway safety, interoperability, licensing, and access to railway infrastructure were also drafted. In 2008, a commission was formed within the TCDD to complete the technical work necessary to draft the General Railroad Framework Law and the TCDD Law. After several revisions, at the beginning of 2013 the Draft Law on the Liberalization of Turkish Rail Transportation was presented.

Law No. 6461, on the Liberalization of Turkish Railway Transportation was adopted in May 2013, and makes the TCDD the new infrastructure manager, continuing to operate as a public economic institution (PEI), but discharged it from its train-operation–related duties. Rolling stock, tracks, track components, and signalling will now be under the supervision of the TCDD and its affiliated companies; TÜLOMSAŞ (locomotive, motor and freight wagons), TÜVASAŞ (passenger cars), and TÜDEMSAŞ (railway machines and freight wagons) will remain part of the TCDD. A new joint stock company, the TCDD Transportation Company (TCDD-TC), was created as the rail undertaking, providing passenger and freight rail services as a state economic enterprise (SEE) entirely owned by the TCDD.[35] According to the Law 6461, independent private rail undertakings can provide passenger and freight rail services similar to the TCDD-TC's operations. Thus, the TCDD's monopoly rights on train operations will end; domestic and international passenger transportation as well as domestic and international freight transportation will open up to competition, and infrastructure management will be opened up to third-party access. According to Temporary Article 1 of Law No. 6461, certain assets of the TCDD, which include all the relevant vehicles and trains, along with personnel employed in the train operation service unit, will be transferred to the TCDD-TC through a spin-off process. All relevant transfers are required to be completed within one year of the TCDD-TC's incorporation date. To maintain the provision of railway passenger transportation services on a specific line on which any railway train operator cannot provide services on commercial terms, the ministry would assign an operator to provide such services by authorizing it under an agreement. Finally, we note that all TCDD infrastructure investments will be financed from the central government budget, and deficits on any other TCDD investments will be covered for five years by the Turkish Treasury. All investments and operating deficits of the TCDD-TC will also be covered for five years by the Treasury. Personnel of the current TCDD will be employed on similar terms by the restructured TCDD and TCDD-TC.

Law No. 6461 seeks to rapidly improve and expand the Turkish railway network by giving the lead to private and public investors for infrastructure projects. In the forthcoming structure, the TCDD will be able to undertake construction of new railway lines. However, because infrastructure investments demand excessively high funding, the law acknowledges that there will be allocations deriving from the ministry budget. Such state funding may finance programmed projects, including constructing high-speed train lines and converting existing lines into double-track or multiple-track lines; track repair and maintenance; and constructing other complementary facilities for signalization, electrification, and communication services. The law facilitates private sector involvement in infrastructure investment by allowing expropriation of the necessary property at market values by the ministry for a project realization on the condition that the private investor agrees to pay for the expropriation costs. In such a case, the private company would be entitled to a leasement right over the expropriated lands for up to forty-nine years and would be authorized to operate the relevant lines during that period. When

---

[35] Note that PEIs and SEEs are both SOEs, subject to Decree Law No. 233 of 1984. Whereas PEIs produce public goods and services carrying monopolistic characteristics by taking into account public welfare, SEEs operate in a free market with a profit-making motive.

the operation period elapses, the ministry would acquire full title to the relevant lands and the facilities constructed on them.[36]

On 15 January 2015, the TCDD held a dialogue meeting with related non-governmental organization trade unions in the railway sector and informed them about the re-organization plans in the sector.[37] According to the information provided, in the future the TCDD will consist of infrastructure construction, infrastructure maintenance, network administration, administrative services, and financial services units, and the TCDD-TC will consist of passenger, freight, vehicle maintenance, administrative services, and financial services units. The TCDD and TCDD-TC statutes that have already been adopted by the TCDD board of directors will become effective once they are adopted by the High Planning Council. The Draft Law on Allocating Railway Infrastructure Capacity and Levying Charges for Using Railway Infrastructure, prepared in accordance with Directive 2012/34/EC and recasting the First Railway Package and RailNetEurope's (RNE) related guidelines, will become effective after publication in the *Official Gazette*. Work is ongoing regarding the determination immovables, vehicles, and personnel that will be transferred to the TCDD-TC.

To successfully implement the reform process, the TCDD must publish in the *Official Gazette* the by-laws on safety, license, and interoperability. The safety by-law will regulate safety requirements for railway undertakings and infrastructure managers and set out rules for establishing a safety management system, safety certificate, and safety authorization; the licensing by-law will set out the provisions necessary for obtaining licenses; and the interoperability by-law will set out processes to be observed to obtain an authorization of technical interoperability. In addition, the successful implementation of the reform process requires strengthening administrative capacity in regard to free and non-discriminatory access to the rail network; independent allocation of capacity and charging; fully commercial operation of transport activities; providing for the long-term financial viability of the infrastructure manager; examining TSIs with an aim to preparing national safety rules; training staff about interoperability; establishing a safety unit and preparing a safety management system; separating infrastructure and transport services (passenger and goods) accounts; and PSOs.

4.4.2 International Rail Networks

Currently, international freight transportation by railway in Turkey is carried out through the following border points: (i) to Bulgaria and other European

---

[36] See Çakmak Avukatlık Bürosu (2013).   [37] See Turkish State Railways (2015).

countries through Kapıkule; (ii) to Greece and other European countries through Uzunköprü; (iii) to Iran and Central Asian countries through Kapıköy; (iv) to Syria and Iraq through Islahiye; and (v) to Syria and Iraq through Nusaybin. Noting that an uninterrupted and efficient transport network between Europe and Asia is essential for developing trade between the two continents, Turkey realizes that it can play a central role in providing opportunities to Europe for accessing the Middle East, the Caucasus, and Asia. Detailed analysis and a needs assessment of the infrastructure for the main corridors was done first within the framework of Turkey's Transport Master Plan Study, completed in 2005, also by the Transport Infrastructure Needs Assessment (TINA) study in 2008, and by the Transport and Communications Strategy–Target for 2023 in 2010. The objective of TINA was to develop a multi-modal transport network within Turkey and to extend the EU TEN-T to Turkey. The TINA study defined thirty-two priority projects, thirteen of which concerned railways. Prominent among the thirteen are the Istanbul Strait tube tunnel (Marmaray); high-speed lines; the Kars (Turkey)-Tblisi (Georgia)-Baku (Azerbaijan) Railway; and the international Iron Silk Railway, connecting Kapıkule at the Bulgarian border with Kars at the Georgian border.

The Baku-Tbilisi-Kars Railway project connects China to the Middle East, and links Turkey to other countries in the region such as Russia, Ukraine and Georgia, and emphasizes Turkey's position as a major logistics hub. As emphasized by Investment Support and Promotion Agency (2013) the line will be a part of the 2,000-km Trans-Asia Railway after completion of the project. This project is included in the TRACECA. It is expected that 17 million tonnes of cargo will be transported per year via the route. However, this capacity will gradually increase. The route will become a direct route to the European rail network, and the project will be connected to the major sea ports of Turkey, including Mersin, Samsun, Haydarpaşa and Iskenderun ports. On the other hand, Turkey is confident that the Silk Road, the historic trade route between Asia and Europe, can be revived and expanded using Turkish rail via this last project.[38] Once completed, these projects will provide uninterrupted railway service between London and China. The high-speed rail project is also very ambitious, and aims to extend Turkish high-speed lines to 10,000 km by 2023, the centenary of the Republic. In addition, there is the Pakistan-Iran-Turkey Railway Project connecting China to Turkey via the Pakistan-Iran-Turkey rail corridor. Investment Support and Promotion Agency (2013) points out that for the development of this project, several agreements between countries were signed including the Economic Cooperation Organization Trade Agreement (ECOTA), and the Istanbul-Teheran-Islamabad Container

---

[38] On the history of Silk Road see Section 1.1 of Chapter 1, and for a discussion of the modern Silk Road see Togan (2015).

Train Collaboration Agreement. The total distance of the railway is 6,566 km, and the train travel time is thirteen days.

Turkey is also working on developing the·Kurtalan-Nusaybin-Iraq, Kars-Nahcevan-Iran, Istanbul-Aleppo-Makkah, and Istanbul-Aleppo-North Africa transport corridors. Turkey's intention is to improve the rail network in the Middle East and North Africa to allow for rail transport from countries in that region into the heart of European markets.[39] Finally, we note that access to Russian-gauge rail (1,520 cm) is provided by means of gauge conversion facilities where bogies can be changed.

Regarding rail transportation between Turkey and Europe, two TEN-T rail corridors are important: Corridor IV, connecting Dresden/Nürnberg to Istanbul, and Corridor X, connecting Salzburg/Graz/Budapest to Sofia, and hence to Istanbul. According to Monsalve (2011), delays in rail transport on these corridors caused by border-crossing times are one of the main factors affecting the competitiveness of rail transport vis-à-vis other transport modes, increasing logistical costs and creating a negative perception of rail in terms of reliability, predictability, and punctuality. Another factor working against diverting traffic to rail corridors is the absence of full interoperability in the rail sector. As a result, the market share of Corridors IV and X between Central Europe and Turkey is estimated at 1 to 2 per cent. To pursue the aim of providing opportunities to Europe for accessing the Middle East, the Caucasus, and Asia via the Turkish rail network, these problems must be resolved, and the solutions lie in furthering integration. It is crucial that Turkey and the Balkan countries approach rail freight investments and performance from a corridor perspective, with enhanced cross-border coordination. Monsalve (2011) maintains that to reduce border-crossing time, countries need to improve (among other aspects) border-crossing arrangements by applying the single-window principle for freight customs, a one-stop shop for using infrastructure in the joint border zone, and by having passenger controls such as passport checks on moving trains, all of which are requirements set out in the EU's railway *acquis*.

4.5 Conclusion

Over the last two decades, the EU has managed to build a good basis for a genuine single market for railway transportation. It started in 1993 when access rights for international groupings providing international services and for international combined transport goods service providers were granted,

---

[39] Because of the civil war in Syria, the implementation of the project has been postponed.

and access to the Trans-European Rail Freight Network for international freight services was granted in 2003. Access to the entire EU rail network for international freight services was extended in 2006. In 2010, access rights were granted to infrastructure in all EU member states for the purpose of operating international passenger services, including cabotage; access to infrastructure in all EU member states for all rail services, including domestic passenger services, will be granted in 2019.

The EU experience has been beneficial not only to the EU but also to the neighbouring countries of the EU including Turkey. The EU liberalization shows that for the neighbouring countries, the first step would be to separate the accounts of infrastructure managers and transport services, as set out in Directive 91/440/EEC. On the other hand, the First Railway Package requires (i) developing multi-annual contracts between the state and infrastructure manager; (ii) introducing track access charges; (iii) developing public service contracts; and (iv) implementing mechanisms to reduce indebtedness of rail incumbents. The EU directives also require establishing a regulatory authority (Directive 2001/12/EC and Directive 2001/14/EC), licensing body (Directive 2001/13/EC, amending Council Directive 95/18/EC), safety authority (Directive 2004/49/EC), and an accident investigation body (Directive 2004/ 49/EC). To act in a fair and non-discriminatory fashion, these institutions must be independent, where independence is understood in terms of financing and organizational independence from transport ministries, with boards of directors and managers hired through an open process and not appointed by the transport ministry or government, and with decision-making independent from transport ministries.[40]

Despite its desire to increase trade with Europe, Turkey did not pass its Law on the Liberalization of the Turkish Railway Transportation until May 2013. The next stage of Turkey's reform process is to publish the by-laws on Allocating Railway Infrastructure Capacity and Levying Charges for Using Railway Infrastructure, as well as by-laws on safety, licensing, and interoperability. In addition, Turkey has to establish an independent regulatory authority, licensing body, safety authority, and an accident investigation body. In the EU the whole process of the railway liberalization has taken more than twenty years. But Turkish authorities hope to complete the process in less than twenty years by making use of the EU experience.

---

[40] See Monsalve (2011).

5

The Regulatory Framework
in Maritime Transportation

Maritime transport is inherently international in character, and vessels on most voyages must operate under the regulatory regimes of many jurisdictions. Thus, there is an intrinsic need for harmonization across countries. To liberalize the sector, countries, especially developing countries, must adopt not only international norms, but in the case of regional integrations concluded with industrialized countries, also stricter rules and regulations of those countries. Furthermore, liberalization requires removing all legal and administrative provisions restricting market access and commercial presence in maritime transport services.

This chapter considers the regulatory framework in maritime transportation and is structured as follows: Section 5.1 discusses the basic characteristics of maritime transportation services. Section 5.2 considers the sector's international regulatory regime. Section 5.3 covers European Union (EU) rules and regulations in maritime transportation, and Section 5.4 the Turkish rules and regulations in the sector. Section 5.5 concludes.

5.1 Maritime Freight Transportation Services

Maritime transport services consist of three types of activities: (i) international maritime transport, that is, the actual transportation service performed from the time the commodity is on board a ship in one country until the moment the vessel reaches the destination port of a different country; (ii) maritime auxiliary services, that is, any activities related to cargo manipulation in ports and on ships; and (iii) port services, that is, activities related solely to ship management in ports.[1]

---

[1] See Fink et al. (2002).

Maritime transport constitutes over 80 per cent of total world trade transported, expressed in tonnes. According to the United Nations Conference on Trade and Development (UNCTAD, 2014), world seaborne trade amounted to 9,548 million tonnes in 2013. During the same year, oil products (commodities such as crude oil, kerosene, diesel, and liquefied gas) formed 29.8 per cent, main bulks (iron ore, grain, coal, bauxite/alumina, and phosphate rock) formed 30.6 per cent, and other dry cargo 39.6 per cent of total seaborne trade.

Historically, all merchant vessels belonged to the general cargo type, but today a variety of vessels exists, such as crude oil carriers, liquefied gas carriers, dry bulk carriers, container ships, refrigerated vessels (reefers), roll-on/roll-off (RO-RO) vessels (equipped with a ramp that allows cargo to be driven on and off), and multipurpose vessels. Of all vessel types, container ships are of paramount importance because their role in global seaborne trade has increased rapidly over the last fifty years. In fact, containers have led to a revolution in cargo handling in terms of vessel capacity and dimensions, new types of terminals, and changes in hinterland connection modalities.

Containers are usually expressed in 20-foot equivalent units (TEUs), meaning a container is 20 feet long, 8 feet wide, and 8 feet, 6 inches high. The maximum cargo load for one TEU container used to be about 22 tonnes, with the capacity of container vessels from between 800 to approximately 1,700 TEUs, and with limited width. These dimensions were required because the Panama Canal could only accommodate a maximum beam dimension of 32.2 m, and these ships were called Panamax container vessels. Eventually, however, vessels were built with capacities of more than 3,000 TEUs, and soon reached capacities of 8,000 TEUs. Currently, the largest container vessel has a capacity of 14,000 TEUs. With the increase in container dimensions, the ratio of 20ft/40ft containers has decreased from 2.16 in 1986 to 0.94 in 2007.[2] Currently, containers are carried mostly by container vessels.

International maritime freight transport has developed specialized branches mainly due to differences in commodity types and technological improvements in the shipping industry. For instance, a clear distinction is made between liner shipping and non-liner shipping. Liner shipping is regular shipping, with set schedules in different harbours published in advance. The capital-intensive character of liner shipping, particularly container shipping, has led to a substantial degree of concentration. As emphasized by the World Trade Organization (WTO, 2010b), the top twenty liner operators, eleven of which are based in Asia, accounted for around 70 per cent of total liner traffic in 2008–9. Non-liner shipping, on the other hand, is performed irregularly: on a demand basis predominantly by specialized bulk carriers. Such vessels carry

---

[2] See Levinson (2006) and Kruk and Donner (2009).

unpacked dry carriages or liquid cargoes, and bulk-shipping operations are carried out for individual shippers. Compared to liner shipping, bulk shipping is less concentrated, and there are many small owners, with fleets of one or two vessels. While non-liner tankers and bulk carriers dominate in terms of trade volume, liner vessels are far more significant in value terms, since they tend to carry relatively high-value and low-volume cargoes.[3]

A principal organizational feature of the liner sector is the operator's ability to enter into co-operative arrangements and agreements through *conferences*. As one of the oldest arrangements in the world, shipping conferences/cartels commonly involve collusion to set prices and limit competition among members. Closed conferences not only set freight rates, which apply to all members, but also allocate cargo quotas and restrict membership, while open conferences merely set freight rates on a specific route.[4] A recent development in the sector has been to supplement conferences with verbal agreements and similar arrangements. Compared to independent shipping operations, conferences are expected to determine fleet capacity, create scale economies, prevent unexpected fluctuations in freight rates, limit competition between members, and generate higher profits. However, even if conferences create cost savings, these savings are not always passed on to consumers or producers of shipped commodities. Conferences usually cause increased shipping rates and only establish market power for their members, thereby restricting newcomer entry and delaying improvement in shipping service quality. According to the Organisation for Economic Co-operation and Development, in 2000 there were over 300 liner conferences worldwide.[5]

The prevalence of conferences flows directly from the exemption they enjoy under the anti-trust laws of the United States (US) and many other countries. Under these systems, shipping conferences are considered necessary to ensure stability and certainty in freight movement. In 2008, however, the European Community prohibited conferences, and at that time it was the only jurisdiction to do so.[6] In recent years, containerization has also eroded the power of conferences; outsiders can now supply the same services at a lower cost to consumers. In 2010, the WTO reported that conferences in the world liner shipping market controlled less than 60 per cent of the traffic. Non-conference lines offering independent, partial, or full container services at a frequency varying between weekly and fortnightly have emerged, based mainly in the newly industrializing economies of East Asia. Other methods, such as

---

[3] See WTO (1998) and WTO Secretariat (2001b).
[4] Closed conference regimes mean that the right of admission and withdrawal is prescribed and that specific and varying conditions must be met. In open conferences, however, newcomers cannot be denied entry.
[5] See OECD (2001).
[6] See Section 5.3 for further discussion of exemptions in the EU.

discussion/stabilization agreements, consortia, vessel-sharing agreements, alliances, and tramp pools have also gradually gained importance. Under these agreements, players can coordinate routes and co-operate technically and commercially through the joint use of vessels and marketing organizations, as well as by exchanging slots on certain routes.

Bulk traffic, on the other hand, is organized as a spot market, and contracts are allocated on an extremely competitive basis. The WTO Secretariat (2001b) notes that business is won on the basis of freight rates only a few cents per tonne lower than a competitor. Hence, bulk shipping services and related freight rates respond to market developments and to supply and demand pressures. Bulk-shipping pools are occasionally created, but fail to survive over long periods.[7] In addition, these pools are not generally exempt from competition policy laws and are therefore dealt with by competition agencies in the same way other commercial activities are handled.

Classification societies are another organizational feature of the maritime transport sector. These societies set out rules for ship construction and maintenance and issue a *class certificate* to reflect compliance. These groups arose from the efforts of insurers to establish that the vessels for which they were writing insurance were sound.[8] Although they have no legal authority, they aim to enhance the safety of life and property at sea by securing high technical standards for the design, manufacture, construction, and maintenance of mercantile and non-mercantile ships. More than fifty organizations worldwide (claim to) provide marine classification, and twelve of them form the International Association of Classification Societies (IACS).[9] It is estimated that these twelve societies collectively class ships dealing with more than 90 per cent of all commercial tonnage involved in international trade worldwide.[10] The voluntary nature of classification implies that classification societies compete with each other to offer attractive classification services to shipowners. In general, these services fall into two major categories: developing rules and implementing rules. The societies continuously update the rules to reflect changes in maritime technology and then apply them, including

---

[7] Some bulk companies do enter into pooling arrangements, whereby they share the profits and losses made by their respective fleets.

[8] Although a shipowner must class a vessel to obtain insurance, and in some instances a government may require a ship to be classed, the importance of the classification certificate extends beyond insurance. It is, as stated by Stopford (1997), the industry standard for establishing that a vessel is properly constructed and in good condition.

[9] The twelve member societies that form the IACS are the American Bureau of Shipping (US), Bureau Veritas (France), China Classification Society (China), Croatian Register of Shipping (Croatia), Det Norske Veritas (Norway), Germanischer Lloyd (Germany), Indian Register of Shipping (India), Korean Register of Shipping (South Korea), Lloyd's Register (UK), Nippon Kaiji Kyokai (Japan), Polish Register of Shipping (Poland), Registro Italiano Navale (Italy), and the Russian Maritime Register of Shipping (Russian Federation).

[10] See the IACS website (http://www.iacs.org.uk, accessed 9 February 2016).

technically inspecting ship plans, performing surveys during construction, and performing periodic surveys to ensure ships maintain their class.

Regarding maritime auxiliary and port services, we note that seaports offer many different services. According to Trujillo and Nombela (1999), seaport activities can be divided into: (i) infrastructure; (ii) services provided by ports that require the use of infrastructure; and (iii) coordinating among different port activities. *Infrastructure* consists of the infrastructure within ports (berths, quays, docks, and storage yards) as well as the superstructure (sheds, fuel tanks, office buildings, cranes, van carriers, and transtainers). In addition to providing the basic infrastructure for transferring goods between sea and land, ports provide numerous other services, such as pilotage, towing, tying, cargo handling, freezing, administrative paperwork, permits, cleaning, refuse collection, and repair facilities. Since many different activities are performed simultaneously within the limited space of port areas, there is a need for an agent to act as coordinator to ensure the proper use of common facilities and to oversee safety. In most seaports, these functions are performed by the port authority, which is usually a public organization.

A major characteristic of ports today is that most are competing with one another on a global scale, as emphasized by the World Bank (2007). The tremendous gains in ocean transport productivity achieved over the past several decades have forced countries to improve port efficiency, lower cargo-handling costs, and integrate port services with other components of the global distribution network. Because of the capital intensity of such efficiency improvements, the private sector increasingly operates a wide range of port-related activities.

Today, there are three main organizational modes for seaports. Under the so-called *landlord ports* system, the port authority owns and manages port infrastructure, and private firms provide the rest of the port and maritime auxiliary services. Private firms are able to own superstructures and operate assets pertaining to infrastructure by concession or licensing. Under a *tool ports* system, the port authority owns both the infrastructure and superstructure, but private firms provide services by renting port assets through concessions or licenses. Finally, under the *service ports* regime, the port authority owns assets and supplies services by directly hiring employees.

Port reform processes refer in general to the movement from the public service port management model towards the landlord port management model, since the tool port management model is no longer applied in many countries. The landlord port model is considered to be the optimum public–private partnership (PPP) model. However, when the public port sector in a particular country decides to enter into a PPP with a private operator, it is essential that regulation is introduced, as emphasized by Kruk and Donner (2009). Through properly managed regulation, the public sector can ensure that ports operate efficiently and safely, and that fair and competitive services are provided. Container terminal efficiency is usually measured by *dwell time*, defined as the period of time that a container stays at a container terminal before it is moved to a hinterland destination or loaded on a vessel.[11] In addition, ports are expected to expand the use of information technology to support port user requirements. Such systems electronically link port administration with terminal operators, truckers, customs, freight forwarders, and ship agents, and thus reduce cargo delivery time and the manpower needed for paperwork involving port use and operation. Finally, ports are expected to have good connections to the hinterland. Thus, their rail and road infrastructures should be sufficient.

Currently, the number of sizable ports in the world has been estimated to be around 3,000, where *sizeable* means that these ports handle a number of cargo types in considerable quantities. Of the top ten container ports, all are located in Asia. In the case of dry bulk ports, the majority are located in Australia, while the largest port is in China. Of the top ten cargo ports, seven are located in China, one in Korea, one in Singapore, and one in the United Arab Emirates. As containerization has spread in freight shipping, distribution patterns have evolved into hub-and-spoke networks, which are intended to maximize utilization of large container ships while providing market coverage to a maximum number of ports. While ships with 4,000 and greater TEU capacity provide service between regional hubs, smaller ships pick up and distribute containers within a region. One such region is the Eastern Mediterranean, where Damietta, Limassol, Piraeus, and Port Said serve as hubs, and all other ports are for distribution.

5.2 International Rules and Regulations

International maritime laws are developed with the participation of flag and port states in treaties or conventions.[12] International conventions set out agreed objectives for legislation on particular issues, such as maritime safety, pollution control, and the conditions of seafarers' employment. They provide internationally accepted templates from which individual flag states can develop their own national maritime legislations. By so doing, it is hoped that most countries will have the same law on key maritime transport issues to avoid major inconsistencies between national maritime legislations.

---

[11] At a typical container terminal today, the average container dwell time amounts to five or six days.

[12] The *flag state* of a commercial vessel is the state under whose laws the vessel is registered or licensed, and the *port state* is the state where the port is located.

Consultation, drafting, adopting drafts, opening drafts for government signature, and country ratification were the major steps in creating a maritime convention where several UN agencies and the OECD were involved. At the global level, the maritime industry is principally regulated by the International Maritime Organization (IMO), a small UN agency responsible for the safety of life at sea and the protection of the marine environment.[13] The International Labour Organization (ILO), also part of the UN, is responsible for developing labour standards applicable to seafarers worldwide.[14] The third UN agency dealing with international shipping conventions is UNCTAD's Shipping Committee. Finally, the WTO's General Agreement Trade in Services (GATS) commitments, ongoing services negotiations at the WTO, and the OECD's Maritime Transport Committee (MTC) provide important forums for liberalizing maritime services.[15]

The shipping industry is controlled by a web of national and international regulations and practices. Overall, they can be classified, following the OECD (2001), under two broad headings: (i) regulations related to commercial operations and practices and (ii) regulations related to states' rights and obligations to safety and environment.

5.2.1 Regulations Related to Commercial Operations and Practices

Regulations related to commercial operations and practices include shipping-specific economic policy regulations, ship registration conditions, cargo reservation/cargo sharing provisions, cabotage laws, cargo liability regimes, national security measures, and competition legislation. These regulations are aimed at implementing government policies, achieving economic or national objectives, ensuring national participation, or regulating commercial activities. While some of these regulations such as competition or anti-trust laws are intended to free up the market, the majority probably distort or interfere with the market to some degree.

In the case of liner shipping, the basic regulatory framework among OECD countries consists of the Code of Liberalisation of Current Invisible Operations and the Common Shipping Principles. The code was formally adopted

---

[13] The Inter-governmental Maritime Consultative Organization (IMCO) was founded in 1958. In 1982, the IMCO changed its name to the IMO. As of 2015, the IMO has 171 member states.

[14] Regarding maritime transport, the ILO's major interest is in working conditions on ships, such as provisions for manning, hours of work, pensions, vacation, sick pay, and minimum wages. Between 1923 and 2005, forty-one maritime labour conventions concerning seafarers and dockworkers were adopted, in addition to thirty-three maritime labour recommendations.

[15] The MTC is the only international forum that looks at the sector from both the policy and economic perspective. The committee's key activities include developing common shipping policies and exchanging information on shipping policy developments with organizations outside the OECD, combatting substandard shipping to achieve better ship safety, and protecting the environment by involving the entire maritime industry.

by the OECD Council in 1961 and under it, members are obliged to eliminate restrictions on current invisible transactions and transfers relating to maritime transport operations, such as harbour services, repair, and chartering. According to Note 1 of the code's Annex A, the provisions of maritime freight policy are intended to give member state residents the unrestricted opportunity to avail themselves of and pay for all services in connection with international maritime transport offered by the residents of any other member state. These provisions include chartering, harbour expenses, disbursements for fishing vessels, all means of maritime transport, including harbour services (bunkering and provisioning, maintenance, repairs, expenses for crews), and other items that have a direct or indirect bearing on international maritime transport. As member states' shipping policies are based on the principle of free circulation of shipping in international trade under free and fair competition, it follows that the freedom of transactions and transfers in connection with maritime transport should not be hampered by exchange control, legislative provisions in favour of the national flag, arrangements made by governmental or semi-governmental organizations giving preferential treatment to national flag ships, preferential shipping clauses in trade agreements, import and export licensing systems to influence the flag of the carrying ship, or discriminatory port regulations or taxation measures. These policies aim to ensure that liberal and competitive commercial and shipping practices and procedures are followed in international trade and that normal commercial considerations alone determine the method and flag of shipment. Thus, the code generally obliges OECD members to refrain from introducing and maintaining legislation or other measures in favour of national flag vessels within the OECD, and having subscribed to the Code, OECD member states are generally obliged to eliminate barriers to free trade in maritime transport services.

The Common Shipping Principles, adopted in 1987, lay down a common approach to international shipping policies and practices among OECD members based on the following main principles: (i) open trade and free competitive access to international shipping operations; (ii) a coordinated response to external pressure based on full consultations among member countries; (iii) the role and recognition of government involvement by member countries to preserve free competitive access and the provision of choice to shippers; and (iv) a common approach to applying a competition policy to the liner shipping sector. All principles were reviewed in the late 1990s (there were thirteen at the time), and extensions and additions were formally adopted in September 2000.[16] Principle 14 deals with maritime auxiliary services and provides that access to and use of these services shall be non-discriminatory. Principle

---

[16] See OECD (2000a).

15 acknowledges the importance of international multimodal transport services involving a sea leg and stipulates non-discriminatory treatment in access to and use of those services as well as a free and fair competitive environment with regard to their provision. Finally, Principle 16 deals with measures related to safety, the environment, and the prevention of substandard shipping.

The OECD is also involved in liberalizing maritime services on a regional basis. Members signed an Understanding on Common Shipping Principles in 1993 with the republics of the former Soviet Union and Central and Eastern Europe, largely modelled on the common principles discussed above. The OECD has begun a dialogue with the Dynamic Non-Member Economies (DNME): Argentina, Brazil, Chile, Hong Kong, the Republic of Korea, Malaysia, Singapore, and Chinese Taipei. This dialogue aims to promote free access to international maritime trade, being respectful of the principle of free and fair competition on a commercial basis; promote maritime safety; protect the marine environment; prevent the operation of substandard vessels and improve the training of sea-going personnel; and promote modern business technologies such as electronic data interchange.

An important category of barriers applied to international maritime transport is the various cargo reservation schemes. These schemes require that part of the cargo carried in trade with other states must be transported only by ships carrying a national flag or a flag interpreted as national by other criteria. These policies have typically been justified by either security or economic concerns. Cargo reservation can be imposed in two ways: (i) unilaterally, if ships flying national flags are given the exclusive right to transport a specified share of the cargo passing through the country's ports through cargo sharing with trade partner countries on the basis of bilateral or multilateral agreements, or (ii) through a specific cargo reservation scheme. In the latter case, the governments of two or more countries may decide to distribute cargo arising from their common trade, so that each national-flag fleet is granted a significant share. Ships belonging to other countries are allowed access to a small share or, in some cases, no share at all.

We noted above that a principal feature of the liner sector is operator ability to enter into co-operative arrangements and agreements. To counteract the anti-competitive actions of liner conferences at the multilateral level, the UN Convention on a Code of Conduct for Liner Conferences was adopted in 1974. The so-called UN Liner Code, which entered into force in 1983 with its ratification by more than seventy countries, applies only to liner conferences in trades between contracting states, and embraces a self-regulatory philosophy for 'closed' conference shipping operations. The Code establishes a framework within which conferences should operate in trades between contracting states and grants certain rights to those conferences, but it also imposes certain obligations, thereby protecting shipper interests. The Liner

Code is best known for its cargo-sharing formula of 40:40:20, which suggests that cargo between member countries be divided, with 40 per cent of cargo being carried by vessels of the country of origin, 40 per cent by vessels of the country of destination and 20 per cent by cross-trading vessels. It should be noted that the 20 per cent figure, and therefore the 40:40, is only *recommended*, and two important qualifications must be made about this provision. First, it concerns conference trades only, not the totality of the liner trade. Second, it is for conferences themselves, not governments, to determine cargo share allocation between conference members. Countries opposing the Liner Code do so for a variety of reasons. Some countries state that cargo sharing leads to inefficiencies, reduced competition, reduction in shipper choice, and ultimately, higher freight rates. Some contend that shipper protection could be provided more efficiently through national legislation and that ratifying this code would be inconsistent with OECD obligations and would run counter to existing competition legislation. Despite having been in force for more than fifteen years, the code is of limited economic relevance, as numerous countries have not complied with it.

The primary legal authority governing merchant ship activity is the state in which the ship is registered, that is, the flag state. That country is responsible for regulating all aspects of the ship's commercial and operational performance. By registering in a particular country, the ship and its owner become subject to the laws of that state. That is, registration makes the ship an extension of national territory while it is at sea. Therefore, for shipowners, the choice of registry is a major issue that may have important consequences in terms of: (i) taxes, that is, applicable company law and financial law; (ii) compliance with maritime safety conventions; (iii) crewing and terms of employment; and (iv) naval protection. As well as national registries, there are also open, or international, registries, which aim to offer terms favourable to a shipowner.[17] Furthermore, in some cases it is possible for a shipowner to register a ship under two different flags. These alternatives force shipowners to carefully weigh the relative advantages and disadvantages of each possibility. In general, the restrictions that apply to ship registration set maximum allowable stakes for foreign nationals/corporate bodies or minimum levels that must be owned by domestic interest. Many countries also require that the person or organization owning the ship should have his/her/its principal place of business in the flag country or that certain senior management posts within the owning company be filled by nationals.

In an effort to reserve the largest possible share of a country's seaborne trade, states sometimes restrict foreign firms from entering or operating in the

---

[17] Panamanian and Liberian registries have been among the most popular open registries since the early 1920s.

domestic market. Ships engaged in cabotage, that is, transporting commodities between ports of the same country, may be required to be manned by the country's own citizens, be either wholly or majority owned by domestic nationals, be built at domestic shipyards, or registered under the national flag. In return, owners operating ships on cabotage routes may not have to compete with foreign flag vessels.

Finally, it should be noted that trade negotiations at the WTO in Geneva during the Uruguay Round (1986–94) with respect to opening maritime transport service markets were, as emphasized by the WTO Secretariat (2001b), of significant relevance to the fortunes of shipping. These negotiations proved difficult because of the sector's complex and diverse nature. The first issue negotiators had to deal with was to decide which sub-sectors and activities could be covered in the schedule for maritime transport services. It was decided that negotiations should cover the sector's three pillars: (i) international maritime transport, (ii) maritime auxiliary services, and (iii) access to and use of port services. The first pillar, international maritime transport, was recognized as being relatively liberal, although important aspects still needed to be addressed, such as national cargo reservation and unilateral retaliatory measures. During the Uruguay Round, considerable attention was given to the second pillar, maritime auxiliary services, including cargo handling, storage services, and providing services to ships while in berths. It was recognized that this pillar had considerable scope for liberalization. The third pillar, access to and use of port services, covered all other services provided to ships while accessing and berthing in ports. The negotiations aimed to improve commitments in international shipping, auxiliary services, and access to and use of port facilities through eliminating restrictions within a fixed time scale. Although they were scheduled to end in 1996, little progress was achieved because participants failed to agree on a package of commitments. Recently, talks have resumed, with some countries committing to certain parts of the three pillars.[18]

In the case of seaports, public budgets have been used until recently to finance the construction of most large infrastructure. Generally, public port authorities financed the costs of maintenance and repairs for infrastructure, and the port authority itself was financed with a combination of public funds and tariffs and fees exacted from private firms operating in the port. With the increase in private participation in seaport operation, the landlord port, as emphasized above, has become the most desirable from an efficiency standpoint, since it allows private enterprises and market forces to play a role in services supply while preventing private firms from monopolizing essential

---

[18] For an extensive discussion of maritime transport services in the WTO, see B. Parameswaran (2004). See also WTO (2010b).

assets. Trujillo and Nombela (1999) and Clark et al. (2001) maintain that the type of economic regulation changes with the size of seaport. For relatively small local ports that do not require more than a general cargo terminal, it is possible to consider some form of competition among firms willing to operate in the port. Once a single operator is chosen, it is necessary to have some regulation (such as price-cap systems or rate-of-return) over the charges that the firm imposes on port users; otherwise it would enjoy a monopoly position. For larger seaports, one could introduce competition within the port. If a large port is divided into several independent terminals, it is possible to induce competition between operators for the traffic that calls at the port. In such a case, price regulation is less of an issue, but some form of supervision would still be needed as parties could collude due to their small numbers.[19]

5.2.2 Regulations Related to Safety and the Environment

The regulations on safety and environmental protection are generally based on UN conventions such as the 1982 Law of the Sea (UNCLOS). According to this convention, the flag state has primary legal responsibility for the ship in terms of regulating safety and the environment, while the coastal state also has limited legal rights over any ship sailing in its waters. The limits of coastal states' rights to enforce their own laws are defined by dividing the sea into four *zones*, each of which is treated differently from a legal point of view: (i) the territorial sea, which is the strip of water closest to the shore not exceeding 12 nautical miles (ii) the contiguous zone, which is the strip of water not exceeding 24 nautical miles from the baselines from which the breadth of territorial sea is measured; (iii) the exclusive economic zone, which is the belt of sea extending up to 200 nautical miles from the baselines from which the breadth of the territorial sea is measured; and (iv) the high sea, which nobody owns.[20] On the high seas, all vessels enjoy, in principle, freedom of navigation under the exclusive jurisdiction of their flag state (UNCLOS Articles 87, 89, and 92). Thus, while the high seas are free from sovereignty claims by individual nations, the intensity of state control over the waters increases landwards. In the exclusive economic zone, the coastal state enjoys considerable sovereign exploration, exploitation, conservation, and management rights, as stipulated in UNCLOS Articles 56 and 60. Despite these rights, freedom of navigation under Article 58 applies in this zone, albeit with a number of explicit and implicit restrictions. Article 3 stipulates that coastal states have the right to enforce international and their own laws on safe navigation and pollution in a territorial area. Coastal states have limited powers to enforce customs, fiscal, or

---

[19] On the Argentinean experience of privatizing ports and waterways, see Estache et al. (1999).
[20] One nautical mile is equivalent to 1,852 metres.

immigration laws in the contiguous zone, and in the exclusive economic zone, they only have the power to enforce oil pollution regulations.

Since an international maritime transport service involves the movement of goods by vessel from the port of one country to the port of another, access to ports is an indispensable element of any international shipping service. Access includes loading and unloading cargo, embarking and disembarking passengers, taking on fuel and supplies, and even the possibility of conducting trade. As emphasized by Parameswaran (2004), it is a basic condition for the smooth operation of the international maritime transport industry that merchant vessels from all nations are permitted unhampered access to and the efficient use of ports. The 1923 Geneva Ports Convention and the statute annexed thereto secures freedom of communication by guaranteeing in maritime ports, under the sovereignty and authority of the parties and for purposes of international trade, equal treatment among the ships, cargoes, and passengers of all contracting states.

The 1982 Paris Memorandum of Understanding (MOU) on Port State Control (PSC) aims to eliminate the operation of substandard ships through a harmonized system. Ships are selected for inspection according to the PSC targeting system. Only internationally accepted conventions are enforced during PSC inspections. When serious deficiencies are found, the ship is detained and the captain is instructed to rectify the deficiencies before departure. Regardless of whether flag states are party to conventions or not, they receive no favourable treatment. The results of each inspection are recorded in a central database located in Saint-Malo, France. These periodically updated black-grey-white lists, which show the degree of riskiness of individual ships from different flag states, has become one of the major indicators of the safety and environmental friendliness of national shipping fleets in the last decade. Furthermore, an informal data exchange system provides MOU members with the results of inspections conducted in their ports to ensure compliance with IMO safety standards and ILO social standards, discussed in detail later.

The IMO adopted a comprehensive framework of detailed technical regulations in the form of international conventions, which govern ship safety and marine protection. National governments, which form the IMO membership, are required to implement and enforce these international rules and ensure that the ships registered under their national flags comply. The majority of IMO conventions fall into three main categories: (i) maritime safety, (ii) marine pollution prevention, and (iii) liability and compensation, especially in relation to damage caused by pollution. Outside these major groupings are a number of other conventions, dealing with facilitation, tonnage measurement, and unlawful acts against shipping and salvage.

Among the IMO conventions, the International Convention for the Safety of Life at Sea (SOLAS), which entered into force in 1980, covers a wide range of measures to improve shipping safety. The convention provisions cover the design and stability of passenger and cargo ships, machinery and electrical installations, life protection, life-saving appliances, navigational safety, and the carriage of dangerous goods. In 1990, the International Safety Management Code was incorporated into SOLAS regulations. The code requires shipping companies to develop, implement, and maintain a safety management system, which includes company safety, environmental policy, and written procedures to ensure the safe operation of ships and environmental protection. The code is effectively enforced and its violation could result in fines, vessel detainment, and/or denial of permission to enter an intended port of call.[21]

In 2002, the IMO adopted comprehensive maritime security measures at the Conference of Contracting Governments to SOLAS. Of a number of amendments to the 1974 SOLAS, the most far-reaching enshrines the new International Ship and Port Facility Security (ISPS) Code, which contains detailed security-related requirements for governments, port authorities, and shipping companies in a mandatory section, together with a series of guidelines about how to meet these requirements in a second, non-mandatory section. The conference also adopted a series of resolutions designed to add weight to the amendments, to encourage applying the measures to ships and port facilities not covered by the code, and to pave the way for future work on the subject.

The International Convention for the Prevention of Pollution from Ships (MARPOL), adopted in 1973 and amended in 1978 and 2008, deals with all forms of marine pollution except the disposal of land-generated waste.[22] It

---

[21] The SOLAS convention is regarded as the most important of all international treaties concerning merchant ship safety. The first version, in response to the *Titanic* disaster, was adopted in 1914. It was modified in 1929, 1948, and 1960. The 1960 modification was the IMO's first major task. In 1974, a completely new convention was adopted, which contained a new amendment procedure (tacit acceptance). The current convention includes articles setting out general obligations, an amendment procedure, and an annex divided into the following twelve chapters: Chapter I: General provisions, Chapter II.1: Construction—Subdivision and stability, machinery, and electrical installations, Chapter II.2: Fire protection, fire detection, and fire extinction, Chapter III: Life-saving appliances and arrangements, Chapter IV: Radio communications, Chapter V: Safety of navigation, Chapter VI: Carriage of cargoes, Chapter VII: Carriage of dangerous goods, Chapter VIII: Nuclear ships, Chapter IX: Management for the safe operation of ships, Chapter X: Safety measures for high-speed craft, Chapter XI.1: Special measures to enhance maritime safety, Chapter XI.2: Special measures to enhance maritime security, Chapter XII: Additional safety measures for bulk carriers.

[22] The body of MARPOL 73/78 and its amendments are divided into six thematic annexes covering different pollution sources from maritime transport: Annex I: Prevention of Pollution by Oil, Annex II: Control of Pollution by Noxious Liquid Substances, Annex III: Prevention of Pollution by Harmful Substances in Packaged Form, Annex IV: Prevention of Pollution by Sewage from Ships, Annex V: Prevention of Pollution by Garbage from Ships, Annex VI: Prevention of Air Pollution from Ships.

The annexes detail technical requirements and standards to which ship operators must adhere in order to comply with the convention. While all IMO members must accept and comply with the first two annexes, Annexes III through VI are voluntary. For more details on MARPOL 73/78, see OECD (2003).

defines violations, sets out special rules on ship inspections and enforcement, and reports on incidents involving harmful substances. It should be noted that most oil tankers built previously were a *single-hull* design. In such vessels, oil in the cargo tanks is separated from the sea only by a bottom and a side plate. Should this plate be damaged as a result of collision or stranding, the contents risk spilling into the sea and causing serious pollution. An effective way to avoid this risk is to surround the cargo tanks with a second internal plate at a sufficient distance from the external plate. This design, known as a *double hull*, protects cargo tanks against damage and thus reduces the risk of pollution. Following the *Exxon Valdez* accident in 1989, the US unilaterally imposed double-hull requirements on new and existing oil tankers according to vessel age, as well as deadlines for phasing out single-hull oil tankers. The IMO then established double-hull standards in 1992 through MARPOL, which requires all oil tankers with a deadweight tonnage (DWT) of 600 tonnes or more, as delivered from July 1996, to be constructed with a double hull or equivalent design. Therefore, no single-hull tankers of that size have been constructed since. The convention also requires that single-hull tankers with a deadweight tonnage of 20,000 tonnes or more delivered before 6 July 1996, comply with the double-hull standards by the time they are twenty-five or thirty years old at the latest, depending on whether they have segregated ballast tanks. Finally, note that the amendment to Annex VI of the 2008 MARPOL Convention seeks to reduce ships' sulphur oxide (SOx) and nitrogen oxide (NOx) emissions.[23]

The 1969 International Convention on Civil Liability for Oil Pollution Damage (CLC Convention) places the liability for damage resulting from maritime casualties involving oil-carrying ships on the owner of the ship from which the polluting oil escaped or was discharged. The owners of ships carrying more than 2,000 tonnes of oil are required to maintain insurance for oil pollution damage. In 2000, the compensation limits were amended as follows: (i) for a ship not exceeding 5,000 gross tonnage, liability is limited to 4.51 million special drawing rights (SDR); (ii) for a ship 5,000 to 140,000 gross tonnage, liability is limited to 4.51 million SDR plus 631 SDR for each additional gross tonne over 5,000; and (iii) for a ship over 140,000 gross tonnage, liability is limited to 89.77 million SDR.

It has long been recognized that limitations on the draught to which a ship may be loaded significantly contribute to its safety. These limits are set in the form of freeboards. In the 1966 International Convention on Load Lines, adopted by the IMO in 1996, provisions determine the freeboard of tankers

---

[23] While SOx refers to all sulphur oxides such as sulphur dioxide (SO2) and sulphur trioxide (SO3), Nitrogen oxides (NOx) consist of nitric oxide (NO), nitrogen dioxide (NO2), and nitrous oxide (N2O).

by subdivision and damage stability calculations. The regulations account for the potential hazards present in different zones and different seasons. The technical annex contains several additional safety measures concerning doors, freeing ports, hatchways, and other items, whose main purpose is to ensure the watertight integrity of a ship's hull below the freeboard deck. All assigned load lines must be marked midship on each side, together with the deck line.

The 1978 International Convention on Standards of Training, Certification and Watchkeeping for Seafarers (STCW) was the first to establish basic requirements for shipworkers at an international level. This convention prescribes minimum standards that countries are obliged to meet or exceed. The Convention on the International Regulation for the Preventing Collisions at Sea (COLREG) adopted in 1972 was designed to update and replace the Collision Regulation of 1960.[24] It concerns navigation rules to be followed by ships and other vessels at sea in order to prevent collisions between two or more vessels. On the other hand, the International Convention on Tonnage Measurement of Ships adopted by the IMO in 1969 introduces a universal tonnage measurement system providing for gross and net tonnages, both of which are calculated independently, and the rules apply to all ships built on or after July 1982. Ships built before that date were allowed to retain their existing tonnage for twelve years after the convention entered into force, or until July 1994.

The International Convention on Civil Liability for Bunker Oil Pollution Damage (BUNKER Convention) adopted in 2001 ensures that adequate, prompt, and effective compensation is available to persons who suffer damage caused by oil spills, when oil is carried as fuel in ships' bunkers. The convention requires that ships over 1,000 gross tonnage have insurance or other financial security to cover the liability of the registered owner for pollution damage in an amount equal to the limits of liability under the applicable national or international limitation regime.

Note that the levels of ratification and enforcement of IMO conventions are generally high. The principal responsibility for enforcement rests with flag states, which usually delegate ship inspections to a network of international surveyors via the classification societies. Flag state enforcement is supplemented by port state control, whereby officials in any country can inspect foreign-flag ships to ensure they comply with international requirements.

---

[24] COLREG includes thirty-eight rules divided into five sections: Part A: General, Part B: Steering and Sailing, Part C: Lights and Shapes, Part D: Sound and Light Signals, Part E: Exemptions. There are also four annexes containing technical requirements concerning lights and shapes and their positioning; sound signalling appliances; additional signals for fishing vessels when operating in close proximity; and international distress signals.

Because of seafaring's unique character, most maritime countries have special laws and regulations for seafarers. The ILO itself has adopted over sixty maritime labour standards during the past seventy-five years. Standards adopted specifically for seafarers are wide-ranging: a minimum age of entry to employment, recruitment, and replacement; a medical examination; articles of agreement, repatriation, holidays with pay, social security, hours of work; and rest periods, crew accommodation, identity documents, occupational health and safety, welfare at sea and in ports, employment continuity, vocational training, and competency certificates. Among the ILO conventions, one of the most important international labour agreements is ILO Convention No. 147, where conditions on board ships must be similar to those required by the ILO standards regarding safety and health, social security, and seafarers' living and working conditions. The 1996 ILO Convention No. 180 also aims to promote worker health and safety, improve maritime safety, and protect the marine environment. This convention establishes limits on seafarers' hours of work and rest on board ship, stipulating a maximum of fourteen hours of work per day and seventy-two hours per week, with minimum rest periods of ten hours daily and seventy-seven hours weekly. Finally, note that in 2006, the Maritime Labour Convention (MLC 2006) was adopted, which consolidates the maritime social standards agreed upon over a period of more than fifty years.

MLC 2006 establishes minimum working and living standards for all seafarers working on ships flying the flags of ratifying countries. The existing ILO labour conventions will be gradually phased out as countries that have ratified them ratify the MLC 2006. Article X of the MLC 2006 lists the consolidated thirty-six conventions and one protocol adopted since 1920.[25] According to the convention, all commercially operated ships of 500 gross tonnage or over operating on international voyages that fly the flag of member countries of the MLC 2006 will be required to carry, among other things, two specific documents: the Maritime Labor Certificate (MLC) and the Declaration of Maritime Labor Compliance (DMLC). These documents will provide evidence that the ships are in compliance with the requirements of the convention. The MLC and DMLC will be subject to inspection when ships enter the ports of other countries that have ratified the MLC 2006. Ships flying the flag of countries that have not ratified the MLC 2006 are also subject to inspection with respect to working and living conditions for seafarers when those ships enter ports of countries where the MLC 2006 is in force.

---

[25] The exceptions apply to the 2003 convention addressing seafarer's identity documents (Convention No. 185) and the 1958 Convention that it revises (Convention No. 108), as well the Seafarer's Pension Convention, 1946 (Convention No. 71) and the Minimum Age Convention, 1921 (Convention No. 15).

5.3 European Union Rules and Regulations

Europe, with thousands of kilometres of mainland coastline, is surrounded by a number of islands, including island-states. The EU, surrounded by five seas and one ocean, has the world's largest maritime territory, and Europe's maritime regions account for nearly half the EU's population and GDP. Twenty-three out of twenty-eight EU members are coastal states. After Romania and Bulgaria joined the EU, the region's borders extended to the Black Sea. Within the enlarged EU there are now more than 1,000 ports situated near industrial and population centres, representing the largest concentration of ports in the world. Since almost 90 per cent of EU external freight trade is seaborne, and the total gross weight of goods handled in EU ports was estimated in 2013 at 3.7 billion tonnes, maritime transport is of fundamental importance to Europe. Shipping is the most important mode of transport in terms of volume.

The EU's maritime transport legislation aims to apply the EC Treaty's principle of free movement of services to the EU's sea transport industry and its compliance with competition rules.[26] Thus, it aims to improve the functioning of the internal market in maritime services by promoting safe, efficient, environmentally sound, and user-friendly operations. The maritime transport *acquis* relates to market liberalization, technical and safety standards, security, social standards, and state aid control in the internal maritime transport market.

The main international rules that regulate commercial operations and practices and safety at sea have been transposed into Community Law, which ensures they have legal force and uniform application throughout member states.[27] In this context, we note that almost all EU member states subscribe to the OECD's Code of Liberalisation of Current Invisible Operations and Common Shipping Principles.[28] Regarding the UN Convention on the Code of Conduct for Liner Conferences, we note that the EC is not a party to it, since by providing for the allotment of freight on the basis of national shares, that code was held to be contrary to the Treaty of Rome. In 1979, Regulation 954/79 was adopted, requiring member states to enter a reservation while ratifying that code, according to which they had to open the national share granted under the code to all shipowners established in the EC. On 25 September 2006,

---

[26] The following discussion of EU rules and regulations on maritime transport is based largely on 'Summaries of EU Legislation' available at the website http://eur-lex.europa.eu/browse/summaries.html (accessed 9 February 2016).

[27] See Commission of the European Communities (2006).

[28] France has lodged a reservation to the OECD's Invisible Operations code regarding liberalization of maritime freights, including chartering, harbour expenses, and disbursements for fishing vessels. Regarding Common Shipping Principles, we note that Greece did not commit itself to accepting Principles 14 and 15, regarding auxiliary services and international multimodal transport, respectively.

the Council adopted Regulation 1419/2006, repealing Regulation 4056/86, which detailed rules for applying Articles 85 and 86 of the EC Treaty to maritime transport. By this regulation, shipping conferences became unlawful on trades to/from EC ports at the end of a transitional period that expired on 18 October 2008. As a result, member states party to the Code of Conduct were no longer be able to fulfil their obligations thereto, namely to ensure that their national shipping lines have the right to be members of conferences serving their foreign trade. Those member states therefore had to withdraw from it, and member states not party to it were no longer able to ratify or accede to it. Furthermore, we note that EU countries have ratified the UN Convention on the Law of the Sea, and subscribed to the Paris MOU on Port State Control. Most of the EU countries have ratified the Maritime Labour Convention 2006 and most of the IMO Conventions, such as SOLAS, MARPOL, Load Lines, COLREG, TONNAGE, STCW, and BUNKERS.

5.3.1 *Internal Market*

Studying EU rules and regulations on maritime transport services, we note that real progress towards realizing a common maritime transport services market free of restrictions was achieved in the EU during the 1980s and 1990s. The 1986 maritime package, consisting of a bundle of four EC regulations, enabled the EU economic units the freedom to provide services to the maritime transport sector. These four regulations are basic to EU commercial operations and practices. Council Regulation 4055/86 gives member state nationals (and non-EC shipping companies using ships registered in a member state and controlled by member state nationals) the right to carry passengers or goods by sea between any port of a member state and any port or off-shore installation of another member state or of a non-EC country. Regulation 4056/86 (repealed by Regulation 1419/2006), implements EC competition rules between one or more EC ports. Tramp vessel services are excluded, where *tramp vessel services* refer to transporting goods without a regular timetable and where freight rates are negotiated freely case by case in accordance with supply and demand. Council Regulation 4057/86, which entered into force on 1 June 1987, enables the EC to apply compensatory duties to protect shipowners in member states from unfair pricing practices on the part of non-EC shipowners. Concerned with anti-dumping in maritime transport, the EU adopted Regulation 4057/86 to respond to unfair pricing practices by non-member state shipowners engaged in international cargo liner shipping. Finally, we note that where a non-member state seeks to impose cargo-sharing arrangements on member states in liquid or dry bulk trades, the Council shall take appropriate action, in accordance with Regulation 4058/86, to safeguard free access to cargoes in ocean trades for shipping companies of member states or by ships registered in a member state.

It has been common practice in most nations to reserve a major part of goods and passenger transport between national ports to domestic fleets. In the EC, the southern member states have been reluctant to open up this sector to service suppliers from other EC member states. On the other hand, northern member states have insisted on easing national cabotage laws. A milestone in the process of liberalizing cabotage trades within EC member states has been achieved through Council Regulation 3577/92, which implements the freedom to provide services to national maritime transport operations, and provides for the progressive liberalization of cabotage restrictions. Accordingly, freedom to operate between two ports in the same member state is offered to all EC shipowners, not only nationals.

Council Regulation 3094/95, concerning state aid for shipbuilding, restricts that aid to social assistance, research and development, and indirect aid given in the form of state loans and guarantees. Member states are obliged to give the European Commission advance notice of any aid scheme or amendment of an existing scheme. Directive 2009/20/EC, on shipowner insurance for maritime claims, requires that ships flying the flag of a member state shall be insured by their owners, and that ships not flying the flag of a member state are to be insured when they enter ports under member states' jurisdictions. Insurance shall cover claims subject to limitation pursuant to the 1996 convention, and shall provide coverage up to the liability limitation thresholds laid down in that convention.[29] Directive 2010/65/EU applies to the reporting formalities set out in the annex, applicable to maritime transport for ships arriving at and departing from EU ports. According to the directive, every EU country must ensure that the reporting formalities at their ports are requested in a harmonized and coordinated manner. EU countries are also asked to accept electronic reports via a single window as soon as possible and at the latest by June 2015. Member states must ensure that the received information be made available nationally and to other EU countries via the SafeSeaNet system.[30]

In 2011, the European Commission published the White Paper 'Roadmap to a Single European Transport Area: Towards a Competitive and Resource Efficient Transport System', advocating a genuine Single European Transport Area in which all residual barriers between modes and borders will be eliminated. It is emphasized that barriers to trade arise mainly from formalities for

---

[29] The 1996 convention refers to the consolidated text of the 1976 Convention on Limitation of Liability for Maritime Claims adopted by the IMO, as amended by the 1996 Protocol.

[30] SafeSeaNet is a vessel traffic monitoring and information system, established in order to enhance maritime safety, port and maritime security, marine environment protection, and efficiency of maritime traffic and maritime transport.

vessels arriving in or departing from ports; veterinary and plant-protection regulations; and EU regulations on customs. To eliminate these barriers, the White Paper calls for a belt in the seas around Europe that will simplify processes for ships travelling between EU ports. In addition, the paper emphasizes that SafeSeaNet should become the core of all relevant maritime information tools supporting maritime transport safety, security, and environmental protection from ship-source pollution. In 2013, the European Commission published the Communication 'Blue Belt, a Single Transport Area for Shipping', which notes that ships leaving a member state's territorial waters are considered to have left EU customs territory, so that after departing from EU ports and arriving at other EU ports goods must go through customs formalities, leading to costs and delays. The Communication advocates the establishment of a Blue Belt, an area where vessels can operate freely within the EU internal market with a minimum administrative burden while safety, security, environmental protection as well as customs policies are enhanced by the use of maritime transport monitoring and reporting capabilities. It thus made a distinction among shipping EU goods between EU ports, shipping EU and non-EU goods between EU ports, and goods passing through non-EU ports. In the first case, goods should retain EU status even when leaving EU territorial waters on their journey between member state ports, and this status would be restricted to ships operating solely between member state ports. In the second case, since most containerized traffic has mixed cargo, a standardized eManifest (electronic cargo declaration) is to be introduced to distinguish between EU and non-EU goods, resulting in more efficient checks so that EU goods would be swiftly discharged while non-EU goods would be subject to customs procedures. The communication resulted in the adoption of Regulation (EU) No. 1099/2013 on the revision of the customs code required for the creation of a European maritime transport space without barriers.

Regarding ship registration conditions we note that Regulation 789/2004 concerns the transfer of cargo ships between registries within the EU, and states that EU countries will not withhold from registration, for technical reasons arising from the conventions, a ship registered in another EU country that complies with the requirements and carries valid certificates and marine equipment in accordance with Council Directive 96/98/EC. Before registering a ship, the country will subject the ship to an inspection to confirm that the actual condition of the ship and her equipment correspond to the certificates.

5.3.2 Safety, Environment, and Security

In 1993, the Commission published the Communication 'A Common Policy on Safe Seas', which proposed that ambitious measures be introduced at the

EC level to improve ship and crew safety and to more effectively prevent marine pollution. As a result, the EC adopted Directive 95/21/EC on port state control, providing for inspections on all vessels, and including specific requirements relating to oil tankers. It also adopted Directive 94/57/EC, laying down common rules and standards for ship inspection and survey organizations and for the relevant activities of maritime administrations, and Regulation 2978/94, governing the implementation of IMO Resolution A.747(18) on the application of tonnage measurement of ballast spaces in segregated ballast oil tankers.

Directive 95/21/EC of June 1995 aims to improve maritime safety in EC waters by banning substandard shipping. The directive applies to all merchant ships and crews using a member state seaport, an offshore terminal, or a ship and crew that are anchored off such a port or installation. Member states are obliged to establish and maintain national maritime administrations for ship inspection in their ports and in the waters under their jurisdiction. Each member state is obliged to inspect at least 25 per cent of ships flying other countries' flags that enter its ports. Vessels inspected within the previous six months are exempt. Additionally, enhanced controls must be carried out on all oil tankers scheduled for phase out within five years, all bulk carriers older than twelve years, and all passenger ships and gas and chemical tankers over ten years old. An obligation is placed on member states to ensure that any deficiencies revealed in the course of the inspection are rectified and that conditions warranting ship detention are properly documented. On the other hand, Directive 94/57/EC establishes common measures concerning ship inspections, surveys, and certification for compliance with international conventions on maritime safety and marine pollution prevention. The Directive requires that member states follow IMO Resolution A.847(20) on guidelines to assist flag states in implementing IMO instruments. State administrations must appropriately enforce international provisions on inspecting and surveying ships and issuing certificates. When such tasks are delegated to classification societies, these must be recognized organizations, as summarized in Section 5.1 of this chapter. Finally, note that Regulation 2978/94 aimsto encourage the use of oil tankers with segregated ballast capacity by requiring the EC's port and pilotage authorities either to apply the recommendations of Resolution A.747 (18) or to permit a system of rebates on dues. In that case governments would be invited to advise port authorities to deduct the segregated ballast tank tonnage from the gross tonnage wherever dues are based on the latter, and to advise pilotage authorities to act in accordance with the same recommendation to all tankers with segregated ballast tanks.

Council Directive 93/75, signed on 13 September 1993, establishes minimum requirements for vessels bound for or leaving EC ports and carrying dangerous or polluting goods. Carriers must declare the loading of such goods in accordance with international regulations. This directive defines the information that the operator must supply to the relevant authorities of the member state for which the vessel is bound or from which it is leaving, as well as the action to be taken in the event of an accident. That directive was repealed by Directive 2002/59/EC, which establishes an EC vessel traffic monitoring and information system (VTMIS). The aim of the Directive is to establish in the Community a VTMIS with a view to enhancing the safety and efficiency of maritime traffic, improving the response of authorities to incidents, accidents, or potentially dangerous situations at sea, including search-and-rescue operations, and contributing to better prevention and detection of pollution by ships. The directive covers all ships of 300 gross tonnage and upwards, and stipulates that ships built after July 2002 calling at an EU port must be fitted with an automatic identification system and a voyage data recorder. The directive sets out rules for notifying port authorities of dangerous or polluting goods on board ships, for monitoring hazardous ships, and for intervening in incidents and accidents at sea. When conducting any marine casualty or incident investigation, member states are required to comply with the provisions of the relevant IMO code.

Directive 96/98/EC, on marine equipment, has been amended several times, and the latest occurred with Directive 2013/52/EU, which applies to equipment for use on board a new European ship, even if it was constructed outside of the EU; and on an existing European ship in order to replace equipment or to install additional equipment. The directive requires that member states appoint bodies responsible for assessing conformity of marine equipment; and if a piece of equipment may compromise the health/safety of the crew or passengers or damage marine environment, the state will withdraw it from the market, and prohibit or restrict its use.

In December 1999, the oil tanker *Erika* broke in two 40 nautical miles off the coast of Brittany, spilling more than 10,000 tons of heavy fuel oil and creating an ecological disaster. The pressure of public opinion prompted the Commission to propose action on such tragedies at the EC level. In March 2000, the Commission published the Communication 'Safety of the Seaborne Oil Trade' and proposed the accelerated phasing-in of double-hull or equivalent design requirements for single-hull oil tankers. In December 2000, the Communication 'Second Set of Community Measures on Maritime Safety following the Sinking of the Oil Tanker *Erika*' was published by the European Commission. It proposed a regulation on establishing a fund for the compensation of oil pollution damage in European waters and related measures, as well as a regulation to establish the European Maritime Safety Agency, which would provide technical and scientific assistance to the European Commission and member states with the proper development and implementation of EU legislation on maritime safety, ship pollution, and security on board ships.

As a result, the EC adopted Directive 2000/59/EC on port reception facilities; Directive 2001/96/EC, establishing harmonized requirements and procedures for the safe loading and unloading of bulk carriers; Regulation 2099/2002, establishing the Committee on Safe Seas and the Prevention of Pollution from Ships (COSS) and amending the previous regulations; Regulation 417/2002, aiming to reduce the risk of accidental oil pollution in European waters by speeding up the phasing-in of double hulls; Directive 2002/59/EC, establishing the VTMIS; and Regulation 1406/2002, establishing the European Maritime Safety Agency to guarantee safe, secure, and clean maritime goods transport.[31]

Directive 2005/35/EC, related to Directive 2000/59, aims to ensure that persons responsible for ship discharges are subject to adequate penalties. Any person found to have caused or contributed to illegal pollution intentionally, recklessly, or by serious negligence will be subject to effective, proportionate, and dissuasive sanctions, which may include criminal or administrative sanctions. Directive 2001/96/EC follows up on the IMO's 1997 Code of Practice for the Safe Loading and Unloading of Bulk Carriers, and its aim is to reduce the number of shipping accidents involving bulk carriers during loading and unloading. The directive recognizes the principle of intervention by the competent authorities in the member state if cargo-handling operations give rise to situations which are likely to pose a threat to ship safety.

The Regulation 2099/2002 establishing COSS aims to simplify procedures by consolidating various committees set up by EC legislation, and to accelerate and simplify incorporating international rules into Community/EU legislation by allowing amendments to international rules to apply directly or semi-automatically. Regulation 417/2002, on double hulls, applies to all tankers of 5,000 tonnes deadweight or more entering or leaving a port or offshore terminal or anchoring in an area under the jurisdiction of a member state, irrespective of its flag. The regulation and all its amendments were merged in 2012 into Regulation No. 530/2012, which retains the essence of the previous regulation. It prohibits the transport to and from EU ports of heavy grades of oil in single-hull oil tankers, and lays down an accelerated phasing-in scheme for the application of the double-hull or equivalent design requirements of IMO's MARPOL to single-hull oil tankers with 2015 as the final deadline. Finally, note that the European Maritime Safety Agency (EMSA) set up by Regulation 1406/2002 aims to ensure a high, uniform, and effective level of maritime safety and maritime security in the EU, and works to prevent pollution and respond to pollution caused by ships or by oil and gas installations. EMSA

---

[31] For a discussion of Directive 2000/59/EC see Section 5.3.4 of this chapter. On the other hand Directive 2002/59/EC has already been discussed.

also operates the EU's Maritime Information and Exchange System (SafeSeaNet) discussed in Section 5.3.1.

Regulation 2244/2003 established the satellite-based Vessel Monitoring System (VMS) for fishing vessels of a certain size and above. The system's basic function is to provide reports of vessel locations at regular intervals. Electronic devices on board vessels automatically send data to a satellite system that transmits them to a ground station, which in turn sends them to a fisheries monitoring system. On the other hand, in 2006, the EC published Regulation 336/2006, on implementing the International Safety Management (ISM) Code within the EC. Based on the IMO's International Management Code for the Safe Operation of Ships and for Pollution Prevention and reproduced in SOLAS, the ISM code aims to ensure that the IMO's code is implemented correctly, strictly, and uniformly in all member states, which must comply with the provisions in Part B of the ISM Code and Title II of the annex to the regulation.

On 11 March 2009, the European Parliament adopted the third maritime safety package, emphasizing that substandard shipping would no longer be tolerated. Regulation 391/2009 establishes a harmonized framework of regulations and procedures applicable to organizations carrying out ship inspection and surveys. Directive 2009/15/EC creates a harmonized *legal* framework for organizations inspecting and certifying ships, as well as for their relationships with member states' competent authorities. Finally, Directive 2009/16/EC, on state port control, aims at increasing maritime transport safety by reducing the number of ships in EU waters that do not comply with existing safety standards.

Directive 2009/16/EC on port state control, recently amended by Directive 2013/38/EU, requires that Member states take all necessary measures to carry out the inspection of ships, particularly by making qualified inspectors available to the competent authorities. All member states shall inspect all Priority I ships, for which inspection is mandatory. Ships that very rarely call at Community ports and anchorages shall be considered a priority for inspection. On the other hand, member states shall inspect a given percentage of the total number of Priority II ships visiting Community ports, for which inspection is optional. The Directive requires that the risk profile allocated to a ship calling at a port is determined by parameters such as the type and age of the ship, the flag state, and the number of deficiencies or recent detentions. On the basis of the ship's risk profile, the competent authority decides whether the ship should be inspected or not. According to the Directive member states shall refuse port access to ships flying flags on the black or grey lists adopted pursuant to the Paris MOU. Finally, ships must also provide inspectors with copies of the maritime labour certificate and the declaration of maritime labour compliance according to the 2006 MLC.

Regarding environmental regulations, the 2002 Communication 'A European Union Strategy to reduce Atmospheric Emissions from Seagoing Ships' notes that sulphur dioxide (SO2) and nitrogen oxide (NOx) emissions from ships are responsible for acid deposition, which can be harmful to the environment as well as to health. Since ship emissions are higher than land-based transport emissions, and the bulk of EU legislation on atmospheric emissions does not apply to ships, the Communication proposes a number of actions, such as coordinating the position of EU member states within the IMO to press for tougher measures to reduce ship emissions, amending Directive 1999/32/EC to limit the sulphur content of marine fuels, and amending Directive 97/68/EC on NOx emission standards from non-road engines. On the other hand, Regulation 782/2003, amended by Regulation No. 219/2009, prohibits organotin compounds on ships flying the flag or operating under the authority of a member state and on ships sailing to or from member state ports.[32] The regulation aims to reduce or eliminate the adverse effects of these compounds on the marine environment and on human health in general. Council Decision 2002/762/EC aims to authorize member states to become contracting parties to the IMO's 2001 International Convention on Civil Liability for Bunker Oil Pollution Damage, described earlier in this chapter.

Finally, note that Regulation (EC) No. 725/2004, on enhancing ship and port facility security, requires that the EU countries rigorously monitor compliance with security rules by ships intending to enter an EU port, whatever their origin, and that security checks be carried out by the countries' competent maritime security authorities. Directive 2005/65/EC, also on enhancing port security, requires that each EU member state designate a port security authority that will be responsible for identifying and taking necessary port security measures in line with port security assessments and plans.

5.3.3 Social Conditions

Becoming a carrier of goods by waterway in the EU is governed by member states within a framework of common rules laid down in Directive 87/540/EEC. This directive is based on the principle of mutually recognizing diplomas, certificates, and other evidence of formal qualifications. Natural persons and undertakings must meet the condition of professional competence by possessing competences recognized by the authority or body appointed to this end by each member state in the areas listed in the annex to the directive. Once competency has been verified, the authority will issue a certificate, but if the carrier no longer meets the conditions at a later date, the

---

[32] Organotin compounds are chemical compounds based on tin with hydrocarbon substituents.

certificate may be withdrawn. Directive 2008/106/EC sets out training rules and competency standards to be met by seafarers who are candidates for the issue or revalidation of certificates that allow them to perform as masters, chief mates, deck officers and engineer officers, chief engineer officers and second engineer officers, and as personnel responsible for radio communications. For certain categories of vessels, such as tankers and RO-RO passenger ships, the directive lays down special training provisions and sets out the mandatory minimum requirements concerning their training and qualifications. According to the directive, certificates will be issued by the competent authorities of the member states to authorize the holder to serve as stated in the document or as authorized by national regulations. Certificate holders are required to prove, at regular intervals, that they meet the standards for skills and professional competence.

The June 1999 Council Directive 1999/63/EC, concerning the agreement on seafarer working time, was largely inspired by ILO Convention 180. The Directive is intended to enforce the 1998 European Agreement between the maritime transport sector's trade union and employers' organizations. Comprised in an annex to the directive, the agreement applies to seafarers on board every seagoing ship, whether publicly or privately owned, which is registered in a member state and is ordinarily engaged in commercial maritime operations. In addition to the explanations of maximum work and minimum rest hours noted earlier, hours of rest may not be divided into more than two periods, one of which must be at least six hours in length, and the interval between consecutive periods of rest must not exceed fourteen hours. Musters, fire-fighting and lifeboat drills, and drills prescribed by national laws and international instruments must be conducted in a manner that minimizes the disturbance of rest periods. Provision is to be made for a compensatory rest period if a seafarer's normal period of rest is disturbed by call-outs. Seafarers are entitled to paid annual leave of at least four weeks, or a proportion thereof for periods of employment of less than one year. The minimum period of paid leave may not be replaced by an allowance in lieu. Seafarers under the age of 18 are not permitted to work at night. In addition, no person under sixteen years of age is allowed to work on a ship. All seafarers must possess a certificate attesting to their fitness for the work for which they are employed and have regular health assessments.

Directive 1999/95/EC aims to protect seafarer health and safety of on-board third-country ships using Community ports. A member state that has received a complaint or obtained evidence that a ship does not conform to existing international standards must forward a report to the government of the country where the ship is registered, and take all necessary measures to ensure that any conditions on board ship hazardous to seafarer safety or health are rectified. The measures may include a ban on leaving port until such time as the irregularities have been resolved. Finally, note that with Decision 2007/431/EC, the EU has ratified the ILO's 2006 Maritime Labour Convention, which consolidates and updates a large number of international labour standards related to seafarers adopted over a period of fifty years. The convention, as emphasized in Section 5.2.2, sets out seafarers' rights to decent conditions of work on a wide range of subjects and aims to be globally applicable, easily understandable, readily updatable, and uniformly enforced.

5.3.4 Port Infrastructure

In 1997, the Commission published a Green Paper to launch a debate on port and maritime infrastructure efficiency, integrating them into the multimodal Trans-European Network for Transport (TEN-T), and applying competition rules to this sector. The paper notes that ports have a role to play in the TEN-T and that intermodal transport is an essential component of the common transport policy for sustainable mobility. Improved port efficiency will help integrate different modes into a single system on the conditions that interoperability and interconnection exist between systems through a common information system, that administrative procedures are reduced, and that loading units are standardized. The Green Paper also stresses the importance of maritime safety, suggesting ways to better integrate environmental considerations in port development.

Noting that financing ports and maritime infrastructure and that policies on charging users vary from one country to another, the Commission advocated a general framework requiring charges to be linked to costs. The most frequent port charges are for providing services and facilities to enable a ship to safely enter and use the port; charges for specific services or supplies rendered; and rents or charges for using land or equipment owned by the port. Noting that different approaches are possible with regard to infrastructure costs, such as average cost pricing, charging for operating costs only, and marginal cost pricing, the Green Paper advocated the last option, including capital, operating, environmental, and congestion costs. Outside the port area, however, the Commission advocated a user-pay policy, which would make for fair competition and affect the distribution of cargo flows among European ports. These services include navigational aids such as lighthouses, buoys, radio-navigation systems, and maritime traffic organization systems. Finally, services such as towing, mooring, and cargo-handling could be provided by either the public or private sector in competition with other operators. Since services such as pilotage need to be provided on a monopoly basis, a regulatory framework for them should be developed at the EU level.

Directive 2000/59/EC on port reception facilities for ship-generated waste and cargo residues seeks to reduce discharges (especially illegal discharges) from ships using Community ports. By improving the availability and use of port reception facilities for ship-generated waste and cargo residues, the Community hopes to enhance the protection of the marine environment. Member states must ensure the availability of port reception facilities adequate to meet ships' needs. Costs will be borne by ships, and the system must provide no incentive for ships to discharge at sea. Directive 2005/35/EC, on ship-source pollution and penalties for infringements, incorporates international standards into Community Law to ensure that persons responsible for discharges are subject to adequate penalties.

In 2001, the Commission adopted the Communication entitled 'Reinforcing Quality Service in Sea Ports: A Key for European Transport', proposing the adoption of a directive on market access through competition in port services, which was supposed to establish comprehensive rules for market access, taking safety and environmental protection requirements into account. But after almost three years of inter-institutional legislative process, at the end of the conciliation procedure, the European Parliament rejected the compromise text. In 2007, the European Commission published the 'Communication on a European Ports Policy', establishing a framework on market access to port services and financial transparency of ports. The Communication discussed the challenges faced by the sector under the headings of port performance and hinterland connections, the need to modernize ports while respecting the environment, the lack of transparency in the use of public funding, and market access restrictions. But the measures proposed had little or no impact.

According to the Communication 'Ports: An Engine for Growth', published in 2013, cargo volumes handled in EU ports are expected to rise by 50 per cent by 2030, there is growing trend towards larger ships carrying up to 18,000 containers, and there is concentration of activity in the EU's most efficient ports—Rotterdam, Antwerp, and Hamburg—resulting in congestion and longer journeys both on land and at sea, and thus leading to higher emissions. Although the biggest ports are efficient, the same is not true for many other ports. These ports face bottlenecks such as mismatches in storage and un/loading capacity; unsatisfactory terminal layout; inefficient routings and access from sea to land; long waiting times; insufficient security for trucks, trains, and barges; and excessive administrative requirements that prove to be costly in terms of time and money.[33] To remedy the situation, the Communication proposes to connect ports to the TEN-T to attract investment in the ports sector and modernize services.

The new guidelines for the development of the TEN-T have identified 329 key seaports that would become part of a unified network. The Communication

---

[33] See also PricewaterhouseCoopers (2013).

aims to improve port operations and onward transport connections at these seaports through legislative and non-legislative measures. While the legislative measures take the form of a regulation introducing common rules on the transparency of public funding and market access of port services, the non-legislative measures involve, among others, the integration of ports in the corridor, work plans set out in the TEN-T guidelines, and providing financial support to port infrastructure projects by using the Connecting Europe Facility (CEF).[34]

5.3.5 Motorway of the Sea

Noting that traffic on the heavily loaded road network generates negative consequences such as congestion, economic cost, and environmental impact, the Commission since the early 1990s has made short sea shipping (SSS) one of the major priorities for European transport.[35] By emphasizing the role of maritime transport, the EU aims to reduce the saturation of road networks and to encourage more environmentally friendly modes of transport. The 2001 White Paper, 'European Transport Policy for 2010: Time to Decide', pointed to the need to develop environmental objectives for a sustainable transport system. It considered that one of the TEN-T's primary missions was to relieve congestion on major road routes. Aware of the limitations to the spontaneous creation of SSS services, the paper proposed to support start-ups through European funding, and encourage the 'Motorway of the Sea' (MoS) as an innovative initiative to promote intermodality.[36] In 2001, the Marco Polo programme was set up to continue start-up support for intermodal initiatives and solutions allowing a reduction in road traffic. National and European aid can thus be an incentive for maritime operators in reducing their industrial risk and/or in creating a direct price incentive.

In June 2002, EU transport ministers held an informal meeting in Gijón, Spain dedicated to SSS. Following this meeting, the Commission prepared a programme for SSS promotion, setting out fourteen actions that could remove

---

[34] As emphasized in Chapter 3 the TEN-T's CEF established through Regulation No. 1316/2013 will govern EU funding in the transport, energy, and telecommunications sectors between 2014 and 2020.

[35] Short sea shipping is the waterborne transport of cargo and passengers by sea or inland waterways as part of the logistic transport chain in Europe and the regions connected to Europe. Thus, SSS refers to maritime transport that does not involve ocean crossings. The main aim in SSS promotion is to support a modal shift from Europe's congested roads.

[36] The concept of MoS aims at introducing new, integrated, intermodal maritime-based logistics chains with high-quality maritime links to connect the limited number of selected ports located on strategic points on European coastlines. It is thought that these chains will be more sustainable, and should be commercially more efficient, than road-only transport, providing regular and high-quality alternatives to road transport and permitting a massive modal shift of freight traffic from congested roads to key routes.

obstacles to its development. In 2004, the Commission published a Communication on SSS, emphasizing the roles of customs procedures and port services causing bottlenecks in SSS implementation. Article 12 of the TEN-T Guidelines of 29 April 2004 gave the legal framework for funding the MoS with four specific areas proposed: (i) the Motorway of the Baltic Sea, linking Baltic Sea states with member states in Central and Western Europe, including the route through the North Sea/Baltic Sea Canal; (ii) the Motorway of the Sea of Western Europe, leading from Portugal and Spain via the Atlantic Arc to the North Sea and the Irish Sea; (iii) the Motorway of the Sea of South Eastern Europe, connecting the Adriatic Sea to the Ionian Sea and the Eastern Mediterranean to include Cyprus; and (iv) the Motorway of the Sea of South Western Europe, namely the Western Mediterranean connecting Spain, France, Italy, including Malta, and linking with the Motorway of the Sea of South Eastern Europe.

In 2007, the Commission published the 'Communication on European Ports Policy', in which it was announced that port hinterland connections were key to improving capacity and which stated the need to explore alternative transport routes for SSS and feedering services, highlighting MoS as a sustainable modal alternative to road transport. The Commission of the European Communities (2009b) proposed the simplification of customs formalities for vessels sailing only between EU ports, guidelines for speeding up documentary checks related to animal and plant products carried between EU ports, the rationalization of documents requested under different bodies of legislation, and giving exemptions from mandatory pilotage to help reduce costs and make maritime transport more attractive. Furthermore, it was stated that implementation of modern technology with enhanced electronic data transmission supported by modern regulation at the European and national levels will be the key to the success of SSS and the MoS.

Regarding financing SSS and the MoS, we note that aid from European sources can be provided through the TEN-T and through financial aid for transport. According to 1996 TEN-T guidelines, a priority was the optimum combination of various modes of transport supporting the principle of sustainable mobility. In 2001, when the guidelines were amended, reference was made to the infrastructures for promotion of SSS services and the infrastructures inside port areas to increase intermodal efficiency for projects that were deemed to be of common interest. The guidelines were amended again in 2004 to include the MoS, which involved introducing a network of MoS linkages as one of the thirty priority TEN-T projects. That decision gave the MoS some importance within the TEN-T and opened up new possibilities for funding MoS projects, such as through The TEN-T and Marco Polo funds.[37]

---

[37] Launched in 2003, the Marco Polo programme aims to ease road congestion and its attendant pollution by promoting a switch to greener transport modes for European freight traffic.

As emphasized by Aperte and Baird (2013), TEN-T funding for MoS projects is mainly paid for improving port infrastructure and equipment. Marco Polo funding helps with costs incurred in the initial provision of the MoS service. In the case of financial aid, the Commission published the 2008 'Communication from the Commission Providing Guidance on State Aid Complementary to Community Funding for the Launching of the Motorways of the Sea'.[38] According to that document, MoS projects under Marco Polo can receive a maximum of 35 per cent of operating costs for a period of up to five years, and MoS projects under the TEN-T a maximum of 30 per cent of capital costs.

5.4 Turkish Maritime Rules and Regulations

In Turkey, all maritime-related decisions and policymaking activities, including signing international maritime conventions, are carried out by the Ministry of Transportation, Maritime Affairs, and Communications.[39] Maritime activities in Turkey are mainly subject to Turkish Commercial Law No. 6102, Cabotage Law No. 815, the Law on the Turkish International Ship Registry No. 4490, and Ports Law No. 618.[40]

According to the Law on Turkish International Flag Registration enacted in 2000, there are two different types of ships registries: the National Ship Registry (NSR) and the Turkish International Ship Registry (TISR). To be registered with the NSR, a shipowner must be a Turkish citizen; shipping companies must be 51 per cent owned by Turkish nationals, with the majority of partners Turkish citizens; first mates and shipmasters must be of Turkish nationality, and at least 60 per cent of ship officers engaged in international seaborne transportation must be Turkish. Ships that belong to legal persons, such as bodies, institutions, associations, and foundations set up in accordance with Turkish law, the majority of whose boards of directors are of Turkish nationality; and ships that belong to trading companies, the majority of whose managerial staff and representatives are of Turkish nationality and are registered in the Turkish Trade Registry, are considered Turkish. The TISR, established in 1999, is open to ships and yachts owned by foreign persons resident in Turkey and foreign-owned companies incorporated pursuant to

---

[38] See Commission of the European Communities (2008a).
[39] Previously, these tasks were performed by the Undersecretariat for Maritime Affairs.
[40] The following discussion of Turkish rules and regulations on maritime transportation has benefitted from Republic of Turkey Ministry for EU Affairs (2007), various issues of 'Turkey Progress Reports' of the Commission of the European Communities, various issues of Trade Policy Review prepared by the Secretariat of the WTO, various issues of 'Pre-Accession Economic Program' prepared by the State Planning Organization which with the restructuring in 2011 became the Ministry of Development, and Togan (2010).

Turkish legislation. On Turkish-flagged ships registered in the TISR, 49 per cent of the crew can be foreign seafarers, provided that the first captain is a Turkish citizen. In addition to special tax incentives offered through the international registry, flying the Turkish flag allows vessels to benefit from the 10 per cent preference in bidding for transporting public cargoes or strategic raw materials.[41]

Turkish regulations used to require that all public enterprise and public entity imports be transported by Turkish-flagged vessels. This restrictive policy was liberalized in 1983 by Decree 152, which stipulates that all imports for the account of public entities are to be carried on board Turkish-flagged vessels if the freight rate is not more than 10 per cent higher than that quoted by foreign operators. According to the Cabotage Act, however, cabotage is reserved to national flag carriers, and maritime transport among Turkish ports is assigned to Turkish ships only. Thus, ships registered in the NSR benefit from cabotage rights, while ships registered in the TISR can benefit from cabotage rights if the shipowner is a Turkish citizen, the majority of shares belong to Turkish citizens, and the majority of partners are Turkish citizens. Furthermore, according to Turkish regulations, certain sea-related professions in Turkey can only be pursued by Turkish citizens.

Regarding WTO commitments, we note that Turkey is one of the few countries that made substantial commitments to the negotiations on maritime transport services. Those commitments cover passenger transportation, freight transportation, renting vessels with crew, maintaining and repairing vessels, providing maritime auxiliary services, and other commitments. For passenger and freight transportation there are no limits on cross-border trade (mode 1) or consumption abroad (mode 2), except for cabotage transportation. With respect to commercial presence (mode 3), and the presence of natural persons (mode 4), the limitations and conditions specified in the discussion on the NSR and TISR apply. Additionally, the national treatment column states that the then-Undersecretariat of Foreign Trade was authorized to permit public entities to have their imported goods transported by foreign-flagged vessels (this authorization is now with the Ministry of the Economy). When renting vessels with crew, no limitations apply for mode 1 and mode 2 under market access; however, with respect to national treatment, vessels

---

[41] According to Article 12 of the Law on the TISR, earnings to be acquired from operating and transferring vessels and yachts registered in the TISR shall be exempt from income and institutional taxation and funds. Purchase, sales, mortgaging, registration, credit, and freight contracts related to vessels and yachts to be registered in the TISR shall not be subject to stamp tax, fees, or taxation on banking and insurance transactions and funds. But a registry fee and an annual tonnage fee must be separately collected from ship and yacht owners registered in the TISR. The article further states that if vessels and yachts registered in the TISR are registered directly or as a dual class to Turkish Lloyd, a discount of 50 per cent shall be given on the registry and tonnage fees. Furthermore, the wages of staff working on vessels and yachts registered in the TISR shall be exempt from income tax and funds.

rented by foreigners cannot operate inside Turkish coastal waters. On the other hand, there are no limitations for repairing vessels. In the case of maritime auxiliary services' cross-border trade, the mode is inscribed as unbound for 'maritime agency services', 'maritime freight forwarding services', and 'custom clearance services' in the market access column. Regarding commercial presence, we note that only agencies established in Turkey can provide these services. There is no limitation inscribed for the national treatment column. Finally, we note that Turkey scheduled additional commitments for maritime transport services, including pilotage; towing and tug; provisioning, fuelling, and watering; garbage collecting and ballast waste disposal; port captain's services; navigation aids; shore-based operational services essential to ship operations, including communications, water, and electrical supplies; emergency repair facilities; anchorage, berth, and berthing services; and container handling, storage and warehousing, and freight transport.

Regarding regulations on safety and the environment, we note that Turkey is one of thirty-eight states that have not signed UNCLOS. Until 2009, the Turkish flag was on the Paris MOU's grey list for PSC. Since then, Turkey has been on the MOU's white list. In accordance with Directive 95/21/EC, in 2006 Turkey published the By-Law on Port State Control, which is enforced in twenty-three major ports, including Istanbul, Tekirdağ, Ambarlı, and Tuzla. In accordance with Resolution A.739 of IMO and Directive 94/57/EC, Turkey also published the 'Regulation on Selection and Authorization of Classification Societies Acting on Behalf of the Flag State for Turkish-Flagged Ships' in October 2003. The regulation covers Turkish and foreign corporate persons that have applied to the administration to undertake the testing, inspection, approval, and certification of Turkish-flagged ships. Following the specified procedures, Turkey has authorized ten classification societies (nine IACS members together with Turkish Lloyd).[42] Turkish Lloyd, however, is not recognized by the EC, and as a result, ships classed by them are subject to further inspection in Paris MOU ports due to targeting factors.[43]

In December 2003, Turkey adopted the ambitious five-year Maritime Transport Action Plan to enhance maritime safety. This plan set out steps for aligning legislation with the EU *acquis* on maritime safety, measures aimed at strengthening administrative structures (in the area of flag state and port state

---

[42] The Authority Assignment Protocol was signed with the following classification societies: Turkish Lloyd, Bureau Veritas, Germanischer Lloyd, American Bureau of Shipping, Nippon Kaiji Kyokai, Lloyd's Register, Registro Italiano Navale, and Det Norske Veritas.

[43] The *target factor* is in use within the Paris MOU on PSC as a tool for selecting ships eligible for an inspection only. Calculating the target factor is divided into two parts, generic and history. While the generic factor is based on elements of the ship's profile, the history factor is based on the ship's inspection history in the Paris MOU. The former is updated when the ship's particulars change or its existing flag or class changes. The history factor is updated at the end of each day.

control), and training and equipment needs. Since January 2004, the Turkish Undersecretariat of Maritime Affairs has been conducting a broad legal and institutional harmonization project with Spain's participation as an EU partner country (the *twinning project*) to strengthen Turkish institutional infrastructure in maritime transport in advance of Turkey's accession into the EU.

Currently, Turkey is a signatory to many IMO rules and regulations. It is a contracting state to the 1948 IMO conventions establishing the IMO, and to the IMO 1991 and 1993 amendments. It has ratified the MARPOL (Mandatory Annexes I and II, and also Annex III, Annex IV, Annex V, and Annex VI) and SOLAS conventions (SOLAS Convention 74, SOLAS Protocol 74, and SOLAS Convention 78), and acceded to the Load Lines Convention 66, Load Lines Protocol 88, TONNAGE Convention 69 (International Convention on Tonnage Measurement of Ships), COLREG Convention 72 (Convention on the International Regulations for Preventing Collisions at Sea), STCW Convention 78 (International Convention on Standards of Training, Certification and Watchkeeping for Seafarers), Convention on Limitation of Liability for Maritime Claims (LLMC), International Convention on Civil Liability for Oil Pollution Damage (CLC), and BUNKERS Convention 01 (International Convention on Civil Liability for Bunker Oil Pollution Damage).[44] It has not ratified SOLAS Protocol 88, SOLAS Agreement 96, or STCW-F Convention 95 (International Convention on Standards of Training, Certification and Watchkeeping for Fishing Vessel Personnel).[45] In 2011, Turkey volunteered for the IMO's member audit scheme (VIMSAS), which requires IMO member states to sign up to all relevant maritime conventions. Turkey also adopted a VIMSAS strategy, which is reinforced by a board of directors set up through ministerial decision to establish a mechanism for monitoring and adopting all maritime conventions.

According to Turkish Environment Law No. 2872, discharging pollutants from ships, ports, and other coastal installations are prohibited, and fines for discharging from ships depend on the kind of pollutant. The law regulates obligations to establish port reception facilities and imposes penalties for violating these obligations. Part A and some of Part B of the ISPS Code are applicable in Turkey, with the Decree on Implementation of the ISPS Code covering a large majority of the relevant EU *acquis*. Technical studies for

---

[44] Turkey has also ratified the Convention for the Suppression of Unlawful Acts against the Safety of Maritime Navigation, 1988 the International Convention on Oil Pollution Preparedness, Response and Co-operation, and the International Convention for the Control and Management of Ships' Ballast Water and Sediments.

[45] Turkey is also not party (among others) to the International Convention for Safe Containers (CSC), the Convention on the Prevention of Marine Pollution by Dumping of Wastes and Other Matter, the International Convention Relating to Intervention on the High Seas in Cases of Oil Pollution Casualties, 1969, nor The Hong Kong International Convention for the Safe and Environmentally Sound Recycling of Ships.

preparing the by-law on implementing the code are underway; the by-law will include all principles and procedures of the *acquis* to align Turkish legislation with Regulation (EC) No. 725/2004, on enhancing ship and port facility security, and with Directive 2005/65/CE, on enhancing port security. It should be emphasized that Turkey has fulfilled its international obligations under SOLAS Convention/Chapter XI/2. Finally, we note that according to the Commission of the European Communities (2011a), ship-source emissions, maritime emergency response, waste reception, and dangerous goods handling in Turkey are still areas that need closer scrutiny.

Turkey has acquired considerable experience with the Istanbul Straits Vessel Traffic Services (VTS) and the EC's VTMIS. Izmit has been operating the VTMIS since 2012, and Turkey is planning to implement it at the Gulf of Izmir, Iskenderun, Mersin, and Aliağa, where maritime traffic is dense and risky. In addition, the Long Range Identification and Tracking (LRIT) system monitors Turkish-flagged vessels globally and foreign-flagged vessels within 1,000 nautical miles of the Turkish coastline. Finally, we note that the Automatic Identification System (AIS) has been operational since 2007.

Turkey is party to twelve ILO conventions concerning seafarers and dockworkers: the 1936 Shipowners' Liability (Sick and Injured Seamen) Convention; the 1946 Food and Catering (Ships' Crews) Convention; the 1946 Medical Examination (Seafarers) Convention; the 1936 Officers' Competency Certificates Convention; the 1949 Accommodation of Crews Convention (Revised); the 1970 Accommodation of Crews (Supplementary Provisions) Convention; the 1958 Seafarers' Identity Documents Convention; and the 1970 Prevention of Accidents (Seafarers) Convention. However, the country has not signed yet the ILO's Maritime Labour Convention 2006.

Regarding ports, we note that according to Turkish Ports Law No. 618 of 20 April 1925, only Turkish citizens and companies that are majority owned, managed, and controlled by Turkish citizens may exercise rights related to Turkish ports. Again, foreign ownership in companies involved in port undertakings is restricted to 49 per cent. Currently, the vast majority of ports are owned and operated by private enterprises as there is still no public port authority in Turkey. All port services such as port access, pilotage, towing, tug assistance, provisioning, fuelling, watering, and navigation aids are available to all users, however, they can be provided only by Turkish-flagged ships or Turkish companies.

5.5 Conclusion

Since maritime transport is inherently international in character, and vessels on most voyages must operate under the regulatory requirements of many jurisdictions, harmonization is necessary across countries. International rules and regulations are divided into: (i) regulations related to commercial operations and practices and (ii) regulations related to safety and environmental regulations. Compared to international rules and regulations, EU rules and regulations in the maritime sector are generally much stricter. Turkey is in the process of adopting and implementing the legislative, regulatory, and institutional framework of the EU maritime freight transport sector. By changing its regulatory regime, Turkey aims in the long run to increase competition in the sector and gain access to the large EU market.

6

The Regulatory Framework
in Air Transportation

Over the last few decades the airline industries in the European Union (EU) and Turkey have evolved from a system of state-owned carriers operating in a heavily regulated and protected markets to relatively free-market industries. With the adoption of three EU liberalization packages, the air transportation services market in Europe has been completely reshaped, resulting, as in the US, in tighter competition, more efficient use of infrastructure, and more consumer benefits.

This chapter, on regulatory policies in the air transport industry, is organized as follows. Section 6.1 provides a brief introduction to how the air transportation sector functions. Section 6.2 discusses international rules and regulations in the air freight transport industry, Section 6.3 focuses on EU rules and regulations, and Section 6.4 studies the regulatory framework in the Turkish air freight transportation sector. Finally, Section 6.5 concludes.

6.1 Air Transport Services

Providing air transport services involves transporting passengers and freight from one point to another by aircraft, as well as providing ancillary services such as air traffic services, airport services, computer reservation services and freight forwarders, ground handling, catering, and aircraft repair and maintenance.

6.1.1 Air Freight

The air cargo industry, although forming only about one per cent of the overall global freight industry measured by weight, is a crucial component of the supply chain, as revealed by the fact that in value terms, the share of air transport is 33 per cent of the total value of global trade. It fills a niche mostly in time-sensitive, high-value, low-density deliveries. Shippers demand that shipments arrive at their destination on time, undamaged, and at a reasonable price, regardless of the transportation mode. In the case of intercontinental freight, there is a choice between air and maritime transportation. Maritime transport offers the primary benefit of low cost, and air transport offers the benefits of speed and reliability. Thus, for goods to be transported by air, the value of timing the delivery must be larger than the savings in shipping costs by alternative modes.

Air cargo is essential to global sourcing, manufacturing, assembling, and distributing goods. As a result, the principal commodities shipped by air consist of perishables and refrigerated goods; computers, telecommunications equipment, and other technology products; capital and transport equipment; apparel and textiles; and intermediate goods for distributed manufacturing.

In 2013, according to the World Bank's World Development Indicators, the global air freight industry was estimated at 175.58 billion tonne-km. Over the period 1980 to 2013, the annual average growth rate of global air freight amounted to 6.1 per cent, compared to a 3.07 per cent growth in world GDP. Thus, over the long run, industry growth is closely linked to global GDP growth, with an estimated 1 per cent growth in GDP resulting in a roughly 2 per cent growth in freight traffic. Most air trade involves movements among North America, the EU, and Asia (primarily China); routes with origins or destinations in Asia account for 70 per cent of the total volume of air cargo. The principal growth has been in shipments of intermediate goods *to* China and in manufactured goods *from* China. Although its percentage is declining, North America still accounts for a large share of cargo handled in its airports. Both in revenue tonne-km (RTK) and in actual tonnage, Asian, North American, and EU markets dominate globally, with the US domestic market being a close runner-up in RTKs.[1] While the world market during 2013 amounted to 207.8 billion RTKs, Asia and Pacific region formed 34.6 per cent, North America 24.7 per cent, and Europe 21.2 per cent of the world market.

According to Boeing (2014), world air cargo traffic will expand at an average annual rate of 4.8 per cent over the next two decades, while world GDP through 2033 is forecasted to grow at an annual rate of 3.2 per cent. Asia's air cargo markets will continue to lead the industry. While the domestic Chinese market is expected to grow at the annual rate of 6.7 per cent, the Asia-North America market will expand by 5.4 per cent, and the Asia-Europe market by 5.3 per cent. The North American and intra-European markets will grow more slowly, with 2.1 per cent and 2.0 per cent per year over the next two decades.

---

[1] RTK is defined as one tonne of load (passengers and/or cargo) carried for one kilometre.

The airline industry is strongly influenced by economic developments. During the recent recession, world air cargo traffic dropped 13 per cent over the two years ending in 2009, but recovered in 2010, when traffic jumped 19.4 per cent. The growth rate in air cargo since 2008 has been only 1.7 per cent. Containership traffic slowed to a similar pace during this period.

World air cargo comprises three main service sectors: scheduled freight, charter freight, and mail. According to Boeing (2014), scheduled freight, comprised of general and express freight, is the largest component, accounting for 88 per cent of all world air cargo traffic. Express freight refers to cargo with a guaranteed or time-definite service component. Companies such as FedEx, UPS, and DHL offer an integrated transportation chain with door-to-door service. Regularly scheduled cargo services provide the least expensive way to ship by air. Charter air freight accounts for eight per cent of world air cargo traffic, and captures traffic with urgent and/or special handling requirements, which is carried on freighter aeroplanes.

The infrastructure and technology required for air cargo is, except for highly specialized cargo operations and hubs, very similar to air passenger services, sharing the same navigation, air traffic control, and runway needs. Dedicated apron areas for cargo are a minimum requirement for cargo-only operations. Most airports handle passengers and cargo and there exist relatively few airports solely for cargo. In international operations, the hub-and-spoke system is the main operating model for scheduled flights. While larger aircraft are used in international flights, smaller aircraft serve domestic origins and destinations.

Air freight transport (as with air passenger transport) is by necessity highly dependent on road access to the departing and arriving airport, and is thus multi-modal. Commodities shipped by air are brought to the originating airport by truck, and at the destination airport they are loaded onto a truck for delivery.

In the airline industry there are *asset-based operators*, who own and operate their own equipment, and *non-asset-based operators*, who rely exclusively on other operators' equipment. The basic types of asset-based operators include combination carriers, all cargo airlines, integrated carriers, and leasing companies. While combination carriers are mainly passenger airlines offering cargo services, all cargo airlines offer chartered and/or scheduled services, and integrated carriers offer door-to-door services by combining air and land transport. Finally, leasing companies provide aircraft on dry or wet leases.[2] Freight forwarders, who arrange all transportation segments (air, road, sea, or rail) by processing and preparing the necessary documents to ensure compliance

---

[2] A wet lease is defined as a lease in which the lessor provides both the aircraft and the crew. Leasing of an aircraft without crew is considered to be a dry lease.

with all legal and customs requirements and arranging the packaging of transported goods, are typically non-asset based operators.

A further characteristic of the airline industry is that it is the least efficient mode of transportation in terms of energy consumption per tonne-km, as emphasized by the International Energy Agency (2008). The air sector is the second most intense emitter of CO_2 in the transport sector (after roads), and environmental pressures are mounting.

6.1.2 Ancillary Services

Ancillary services consist, as mentioned, of air traffic services, computer reservation services and freight forwarders, airport services, ground handling, and slot allocation, and aircraft repair and maintenance.[3]

6.1.2.1 AIR TRAFFIC SERVICES

The objectives of air traffic services are to provide advice and information useful for the safe and efficient conduct of flights; to prevent collusion between aircraft companies; to prevent collusions between aircraft on the manoeuvering area and obstructions on that area; and to expedite and maintain an orderly flow of air traffic. To achieve these objectives, air traffic services are divided into four sub-services:

- Services consisting of navigation, including landing;
- Flight planning and in-flight advisory information, necessary for the safe and efficient conduct of flights;
- Air traffic control (ATC) services, aiming to prevent all collisions between aircraft and expediting and maintaining an orderly flow of air traffic;
- Alerting services, notifying appropriate organizations regarding aircraft in need of search and rescue.

As noted by the Office of Technology Assessment (1982), the low-frequency radio navigation aids allowing pilots to navigate during the 1930s were replaced in the 1950s by high-frequency omnirange (VOR) transmitters, which are part of a ground radio navigational system assisting the pilot in plotting his exact position. During the 1960s, the VOR system was supplemented by distance measuring equipment (DME) that permitted range measurement and plotting directions to a station. Currently, communication between controller and pilot is carried out by high-frequency, very high-frequency, and ultra-high frequency radio transmissions. As emphasized by Commission of the European Communities (1996), the present VOR/DME

---

[3] See World Trade Organization (2006a, 2006b).

navigation regime is considered satisfactory. The modern navigation and airborne computers enable an aircraft to determine its position by measuring its distance from two DME ground stations. Today, most commercial air carriers have *area navigation* (RNAV) capability, whereby the pilot can fly directly between any two points without restriction to a VOR airway. A *landing aid* refers to a low-altitude form of navigation aid with the accuracy and reliability needed for landing aircraft in conditions of reduced visibility. The standard system is the Instrument Landing System (ILS), providing guidance for approach and landing by two radio beams transmitted from equipment located near the runway. The two beams define a sloping approach path with which the pilot aligns the aircraft, starting at a point between 6 and 11 km from the runway.

Flight planning and information services provide up-to-date information on weather and flight conditions. The information includes current meteorological reports and forecasts, special air reports with emphasis on the occurrence or expected occurrence of weather deterioration, current surface wind, and current pressure data for setting altimeters and for locations specified by the flight information centre or concerned area control centre. Furthermore, the relevant institutions disseminate information on airport conditions, flight hazards, and air traffic conditions. All these services are provided under two basic sets of rules, Visual Flight Rules (VFR) or Instrument Flight Rules (IFR). If the pilot intends to fly at altitudes below 5,500 metres, he/she does not have to file a flight plan or follow prescribed VOR airways. The pilot is responsible for avoiding other aircraft by relying mainly on visual observation, and is thus under VFR. On the other hand, pilots in conditions of poor visibility or at altitudes above 5,500 metres but below 18,000 metres must fly under IFR. In such cases, the pilot navigates the aircraft by referring to cockpit instruments and by following instructions from air traffic controllers on the ground. Under IFR, the ATC system provides separation assurance from other IFR aircraft and also alerts the pilot to VFR aircraft. The IFR/VFR distinction also governs avionics qualifications. Aircraft flying under IFR are required to have radio and avionics equipment allowing them to communicate with all ATC facilities that will handle the flight from origin to destination. On the other hand, aircraft flying under VFR needs little or no avionic equipment. In addition, the IFR/VFR distinction determines the conditions regarding the filing of flight plans. While pilots flying under VFR are not required to file a flight plan or obtain clearance to use airspace, IFR flights must file a flight plan and obtain clearance.

Airspace is divided into *controlled airspace* and *uncontrolled airspace*. Controlled airspace has defined dimensions specified by altitude ranges or vertical boundaries, and an applicable surface area or horizontal boundaries. Within controlled airspace, ATC services are provided to all pilots operating under IFR. The services are provided also to some pilots operating under VFR even though they are using points on the ground to navigate. In uncontrolled airspace, which consists of all airspace not classified as controlled airspace, no ATC services are provided, and the only requirement for flight is certain visibility and cloud clearance minimums. In addition, a distinction is made between special use airspace and other airspace areas. In special use airspace, including prohibited areas, restricted areas, warning areas, military operations areas, alert areas, and controlled firing areas, aeronautical activity is limited, usually because of military use or national security concerns. Finally, other airspace areas include airport advisory areas, military training routes, and areas where temporary flight restrictions (TFRs) or limitations/prohibitions apply.

At the operating level, the air traffic services infrastructure is managed by area control centres, each of which is responsible for supervising the use of airspace within a territorial area called the Flight Information Region (FIR). The airspace within each FIR is divided into sectors in ways that best suit the process of controlling the aircraft within it. In addition to this horizontal separation, airspace is divided vertically into upper and lower airspace at a specified altitude level. Below this level is the FIR, where flights are controlled in the climb and descent phases, and above this level is the Upper Information Region (UIR), where flights are controlled at their cruising altitude.

The techniques used for allocating airspace are called airspace management and the aforementioned ATC. While the former refers to segregating traffic by allocating it to different pieces of airspace on a more-or-less permanent basis, the latter refers to real-time monitoring done by an air traffic controller, who detects potential conflicts and gives pilots appropriate instructions to avoid them. Thus, the role of airspace management is to allocate airspace to users so all get a reasonable share, allowing them to fulfil their tasks. Since ATC relies heavily on the individual performances of air traffic controllers, it introduces limits to the number of aircraft that can fly at the same time in a given area. Thus, the capacity of airspace for air traffic purposes is finite. When airspace users' demands to fly exceed that capacity, this generates delays. Queuing or holding in the air creates not only additional pollution, but also additional congestion in neighbouring areas, and could thus become dangerous. As much as possible, virtual queues should be organized on the ground by air traffic flow management.

In the 1930s, pilots relied solely on radio and telephone communication to be aware of other aircraft in the surrounding airspace, a service called *providing separation*. In the 1950s, airport surveillance radar was introduced at major airports to provide data on arriving and departing aircraft within 80 km and later within 320 km. During the 1960s radar systems began providing information on the altitude and identity of an aircraft by means of an on-board transponder. All commercial air carriers are now equipped with transponders.

Radar stations are connected by telephone to radar data processing systems in the ATC centre, converting radar data to appear on controllers' screens, tracking each aircraft's current, previous, and predicted position, as well as its altitude, course, and speed. Radar systems can warn controllers of potential hazards, such as when an aircraft's altitude or proximity to others seems likely to breach separation minima. With these improvements, the acquisition of information needed to provide the separation service has been simplified, but the decision-making process itself has depended for a long time upon the controller's skill and judgement in directing aircraft to avoid conflicts. With increasing traffic and improvements in computer technology, it became necessary to manage airspace and assist pilots in safely choosing and keeping to their routes to reduce the risk of colliding with other aircraft and terrain. Therefore, countries put air traffic management (ATM) systems in place, with the main objective of assisting airspace users in ensuring appropriate delays between aircraft, as well as appropriate distances between them and the ground.

Finally, regarding alert services, we note that they notify appropriate organizations regarding aircraft in need of search-and-rescue aid. Alerting services are to be provided for all aircraft using the air traffic control service, and insofar as practicable, to all other aircraft that have filed a flight plan or are otherwise known to air traffic services. Flight information centres or area control centres serve as a central point for collecting all information relevant to the state of emergency of an aircraft operating within the area concerned and for forwarding such information to the appropriate rescue coordination centre.

6.1.2.2 COMPUTER RESERVATION SERVICES AND FREIGHT FORWARDERS

Computer reservation services (CRS) related mainly to passenger traffic are defined as services provided by computerized systems that contain information about carrier schedules, availability, fares, and fare rules, through which reservations can be made and tickets issued. In the past, booking a ticket by hand or via a simple mechanism sufficed. Currently, CRSs involve much more.

The first real-time informatics system was SABRE (Semi-Automated Business Research Environment), established by American Airlines in 1959. Thereafter, other large players entered the CRS market such as TRAVELPORT and AMADEUS. Thus, the market is characterized by a high level of concentration.

In the past, CRS companies founded by airlines prepared incomplete or deliberately incorrect offers. Although they were, in principle, supposed to include a full range of competitors' flights in their databases, they mainly promoted their own services. Currently, each CRS provider must display all competitors' flights on their platforms. This regulatory regime was developed to ensure consumer protection and maintain airline companies' property rights, as market access is a major concern in this field. But because there are several systems available, in some markets a certain CRS dominates. From the consumer rights point of view, the first concern is the proper and convenient presentation of data. Passengers want to receive timely and detailed data closest to their flight needs. The second concern is obviously data privacy. With the growing popularity of online booking and the electronic data interchange in general, hackers also harvest the market. The CRS presence is thus an important factor in the air traffic trend.

Freight forwarders are another part of the transportation industry network. Most transport starts with shippers. When a shipper contracts with a freight forwarder, the forwarder arranges the entire transportation chain, from shipper to consignee. The freight-forwarding company arranges all transportation segments, including air, road, sea, or rail, prepares the necessary documents in compliance with all legal and customs requirements, and processes all these documents. In addition, the company advises shippers on arranging and packaging the goods to be transported. Most scheduled non-express air transporters have freight forwarders as direct clients, who purchase freight capacity ahead of time and schedule space for their clients' shipments. This arrangement can sometimes cause delays for smaller packages. Some companies, sometimes called logistics corporations, also offer full logistical services, providing freight forwarding as part of a total package that may include the carriage of goods by air.

6.1.2.3 AIRPORT SERVICES, GROUND HANDLING, AND SLOT ALLOCATION

Airport services consist of landing and take-off services, as well as other services provided for aircraft operators, such as hangars, space for aircraft parking, towing, and other aircraft handling; accommodation for airline offices; providing aircraft fuels and other technical supplies; security measures, including inspection and screening; accommodation for shops, hotels, and restaurants; accommodation for car parking and customs; and services for noise alleviation and prevention. Although public provision of airport facilities and services remains dominant, the prospects are strong for growth in private participation. The World Trade Organization (2006a) emphasizes that steady expansion in air transport combined with revenue security and limited competition in the sector will cause an increase in private involvement in the sector.

Ground handling, which applies only to passengers, is a link between the airports' entrances and exits, that is, the passenger is handled right after crossing the threshold of the take-off airport and then again before leaving the arrival airport. These services can be divided into two groups. *Landside services* are passenger related and include ticketing and baggage handling at check-in desks. *Airside services* comprise ramp handling, aircraft maintenance, fuelling and de-fuelling operations, and catering. These services all contribute to value creation for airlines and are crucial elements of competition.

Historically, providers of ground handling services held a monopoly in many airports. They often offered a standard package of services with no possibility of splitting them or using only the necessary amount, resulting in considerable waste. There was also a quality problem. Passengers complaining about inadequate services filed complaints about ground handling monopolies to several major airlines during the early 1990s. Since then, competition rules have been introduced in that aspect of air transport, and airlines and passengers seem to be more satisfied.

Slot allocation is usually defined as permission given by a coordinator to use the full range of airport infrastructure necessary to operate an air service at a coordinated airport on a specific date and time for the purpose of landing or take-off. Market access to slots has been historically frozen by so-called grandfather rights, but with ever-increasing air traffic, the problem of congestion is becoming more serious. Still, to be compliant with the spirit of liberalization, access to slots should be free by default and based on market conditions.

6.1.2.4 AIRCRAFT REPAIR AND MAINTENANCE SERVICES

Aircraft repair and maintenance services aim to keep aircraft fully functional. Doing so is a complex matter because the market structure for such services is diversified. In the industry, this aspect of air transport is called the maintenance, repair, and overhaul (MRO) market, and its segments include line maintenance, component upkeep, engine upkeep, and heavy maintenance of airframes. Each of these sub-divisions can be operated by different agents. For example, airlines can maintain their own equipment, and they can also provide such services to other airlines. The original equipment manufacturers usually offer after-sale MRO services, but there is a growing market for independent operators with MRO as their core activities.

It is important to note that market entry cost, especially to the engine sector, is very high and therefore there is a tendency for market operators to consolidate. Airlines seek alliances with their counterparts or with other operators, usually following three main types of strategies: (i) outsourcing MRO activities entirely (usually done by new-equipment and leasing companies); (ii) establishing subsidiaries devoted to such services and providing them to others (usually done by well-funded airlines); or (iii) deciding on a case-by-case basis which of the first two strategies to use—handle MRO on site or outsource it.

The main reason for regulating the field of aircraft repair and maintenance is concern about aircraft quality and flight safety. Security regulations are thus imposed at an international level by the International Civil Aviation

Organization (ICAO).[4] National civil aviation authorities define additional standards and require their fulfilment through certification programmes.

6.1.3 Competition in the Air Transport Services Industry

For better comprehension of all aspects of the vast range of air transport services, this section briefly explains the nature of competition in the industry.[5] Economists usually associate increasing returns to scale (IRS) with differentiated products and oligopolistic competition, and they note that the airline business is oligopolistically competitive.

Empirical studies have shown that the airline industry exhibits constant returns to scale.[6] Long-run average costs are constant with the increase of production beyond a certain traffic level, and IRSs are limited, with unit costs decreasing as the size of aircraft increases (the so-called economies of density, reflecting the diminishing costs of additional seats, passengers, freight, and flights on individual routes). These economies are exhausted at relatively low levels of output.[7] For example, it may sometimes be difficult to fill a large plane if the demand on certain routes is low. This situation has led to the emergence of the so-called hub-and-spoke system, where service can be provided to airports for which the volume of traffic to any other single destination would otherwise be insufficient to justify service.

The above-mentioned cost-side economies of scope have profound effects on airline behaviour in the market. Since the demand for airline services increases with the range and frequency of the offer, there are strong incentives for air carriers to enter into an alliance with other carriers that operate on the same hubs or on a complementary route network. Thus, airlines are driven towards holding a dominant position on a hub. On spoke routes, however, competition may be sustainable if the competitor has lower costs than the incumbent or differentiates itself in some way; for instance, in terms of the product offered. Also, if both ends of the route are hubs for different carriers (i.e. it is a hub-hub route), competition will be sustainable.

6.2 International Rules and Regulations

Since its inception, air transportation has been heavily regulated. Government control extends not only to technical and operational standards in the interests

---

[4] The ICAO is a specialized organization of the United Nations. It codifies the principles and techniques of international air navigation and fosters the planning and development of international air transport to ensure safe and orderly growth.

[5] See the Organisation for Economic Co-operation and Development (2000b).

[6] See Liu and Lynk (1999). [7] See Gönenç and Nicoletti (2000).

of safety, but also to the economic and commercial aspects of airline operations.

6.2.1 *International Airline Markets*

Civil aviation, dating back to the 1920s, grew rapidly during the two world wars. World War II, while interrupting civilian flying, significantly advanced the technical and operational possibilities of air transport. By 1942, it was apparent that civil air transport would play an important role in freight and passenger transportation after the war. In September 1944, the US extended an invitation to fifty-three governments and two US government ministers to an international aviation conference to be convened on 1 November 1944 to discuss the principles and methods to be followed in the adoption of aviation conventions. The conference was opened on 1 November 1994 in Chicago and lasted for thirty-seven days. An important result of the Chicago Conference was the drawing up of the Convention on International Civil Aviation. After ratification by twenty-six states, the Chicago Convention came into effect on 4 April 1947. The Convention consisted of forty-three articles dealing with all technical, operational, and organizational aspects of civil aviation, and foresaw the creation of the International Commission for Air Navigation (ICAN) to monitor developments in civil aviation and propose measures to keep states abreast of developments. Article 1 of the Convention recognizes that each state enjoys complete and exclusive sovereignty over the airspace above its territory and Article 6 holds that no scheduled flight may operate over or into the territory of a state without its permission, and pursuant to any terms or conditions thereon. Article 5 gives-scheduled flights the First and Second Freedom rights (see next paragraph), but restricts carriage for compensation on the Third and Fourth Freedoms to regulations, conditions, or limitations as the underlying state deems desirable. Let us now consider the different freedoms of the air specified by the Chicago Convention.

There are nine Freedoms of the Air. The First Freedom specifies that the civil aircraft of one country has the right to fly over the territory of another country without landing, provided the overflown country is notified in advance and approval is given. The Second Freedom states that a civil aircraft of one country has the right to land in another country for technical reasons, such as refuelling or maintenance, without offering any commercial service to or from that point.[8] According to the Third Freedom, an airline has the right to carry traffic from its country of registry to another country, and the Fourth Freedom states that an airline has the right to carry traffic from another

---

[8] See Dempsey (2008).

country to its own country of registry. The Fifth Freedom refers to the right or privilege, in respect of scheduled international air services, granted by one state to another state to put down and to take on, in the territory of the first State, traffic coming from or destined to a third State. Thus, it specifies that an airline has the right to carry traffic between two countries outside its own country of registry as long as the flight originates or terminates in its own country of registry. The Sixth Freedom states that an airline has the right to carry traffic between two foreign countries via its own flag state of registry, and the Seventh Freedom specifies that an airline operating entirely outside the territory of its state of registry has the right to fly into another state and there discharge or take on, traffic coming from or destined to a third state. According to the Eighth Freedom, an airline has the right to carry traffic from one point in the territory of one country to another point in the same country on a flight that originates in the airline's home country. Last, the Ninth Freedom specifies that an airline has the right to carry traffic from one point in a country to another point in the same country.[9]

Among the first five Freedoms, the most important one is the Fifth, which is closely related to cabotage, that is, the right of an airline company of one country to board or load passengers, mail, and/or goods in another country and carry them to another point in the third country for a fee. In the Chicago Convention declaration, cabotage refers to the right of each contracting state to reserve to its own aircraft the exclusive right to carry traffic between two points in its own territory. Since the five Freedoms did not cover cabotage, four additional Freedoms (Six, Seven, Eight, and Nine) were created later on. Of the additional four Freedoms, the most important are the Seventh, Eighth, and Ninth. The Seventh Freedom allows carriers to carry freight and passengers from one country to another without going through its home country, and the Eighth and Ninth Freedoms concern cabotage.

At the Chicago Conference, delegates set up the ICAO (now a specialized agency of the United Nations), and conferred to it advisory powers over economic issues. Delegates also signed the International Air Services Transit Agreement and

---

[9] One could state that the First Freedom refers to the right of a Turkish air carrier to transit Bulgarian airspace en route to Germany. The Second Freedom could refer to the right of a Turkish carrier to refuel in Bulgaria as part of an onward journey, and the Third Freedom to the right of a Turkish carrier to transport passengers from Turkey to Bulgaria. The Fourth Freedom could refer to the right of a Turkish carrier to transport passengers from Bulgaria to Turkey, while the Fifth Freedom to the case where a Turkish carrier flies from Turkey to Bulgaria, boards passengers at a Bulgarian airport, and flies those passengers to Germany. The Sixth Freedom could refer to the right of a Turkish carrier transporting passengers from Germany to Doha via Turkey and the Seventh Freedom to the right of a Turkish carrier to transport passengers from Bulgaria to Germany as a stand-alone flight. The Eighth Freedom could refer to the right of a Turkish carrier to transport passengers from Munich to Frankfurt as part of a service that originated in Istanbul and the Ninth Freedom to a Turkish carrier operating a service between Frankfurt and Hamburg in Germany as a stand-alone service.

the International Air Transport Agreement. The First and Second Freedoms of the Air were multilaterally exchanged in the Transit Agreement, which was ratified by 126 states, excluding the Russian Federation, Canada, China, Brazil, and Indonesia. The first five Freedoms were included in the Transport Agreement, but only eleven states are party to it. The ICAO characterizes all freedoms beyond the Fifth Freedom as 'so-called' because only the first five have been officially recognized by international treaty.

The failure at the Chicago Conference to agree on granting the Freedoms of the Air except for the first two led to bilateral negotiations of traffic rights. Consider the Bermuda I Agreement, signed in 1946 between the US and the UK. According to that agreement, each nation grants to the air carriers of the other nation transit privileges (the first two Freedoms). Each nation also grants to the other commercial privileges (Freedoms Three, Four, and Five), but these privileges are valid, as emphasized by Cooper (1946), only at airports named in the agreement on routes indicated, and in accord with certain traffic principles and limitations. Thus, states exchanged traffic rights on a *quid-pro-quo* basis, identified the routes to be served, and each state usually designated its flag carriers per city-pair route. Regarding capacity, it was understood that each nation or its designated air carrier is free at the outset to determine for itself the traffic offered to the public on designated commercial routes, but operations must be related to traffic demands, and there should be fair and equal opportunity for the air carriers of the two nations to operate over the designated routes. Regarding rates, it was agreed that rates set by the airlines subject to the approval by each government involved must be fair and economic. Finally, the dispute resolution clauses called for consultations between governments. In a case of dispute not settled by consultation, each nation has the right to insist on an advisory opinion from the ICAO, and in the case of rates, each nation will use its best efforts within its powers to make the rate recommended by the ICAO effective.

The Bermuda I Agreement served as a model for other such bilateral accords and led to the adoption of a large number of bilateral agreements between states. As a result, bilateral air transport agreements became the principal vehicle with which to authorize international scheduled air services to, from, and though the territory of different states. Bilateral air transport agreements typically addressed the issues of entry, capacity, rates, discrimination, and dispute resolution. With such issues, the rules were in general similar to those of Bermuda I. In the case of rates, tariffs were set by the International Air Transport Association (IATA) and then approved by national governments.[10]

---

[10] The IATA was founded in Havana, Cuba in April 1945, and is the prime vehicle for inter-airline cooperation in promoting safe, reliable, secure, and economical air services for the benefit of the world's consumers.

Finally, regarding discrimination, we note most bilateral agreements had clauses specifying that airport charges could be no higher than those imposed upon domestic airlines. In addition, in the cases of taxes, customs duties, and inspection fees, imported fuel, and spare parts, no discrimination can be applied to foreign or domestic airlines.

These considerations reveal, as emphasized by Borenstein and Rose (2007), that government policy rather than market forces shaped the development and operation of scheduled air service. While the US airline industry was characterized by privately owned firms subject to government regulation, the norm in the rest of the world was one or two scheduled air carriers, called flag carriers, operating as entirely or majority state-owned enterprises. State-owned flag carriers were protected from competition, and thus had no incentives to operate efficiently. Although the service quality offered to passengers was high, operating costs were also high, capacity utilization rates low, wages generous, and output growth restricted. Thus, agreements encouraging collusive behaviour led to high fares on most international routes.

Liberalization of international agreements began in the late 1970s, with open-market agreements modelled after the 1978 US–Netherlands agreement. After that time, agreements were signed by the US with Australia, Belgium, Fiji, Finland, West Germany, Iceland, Israel, Jamaica, Papua New Guinea, and Singapore. These agreements, as emphasized by Hanaappel (1980), had clauses on unlimited multiple designation of airlines; a liberal route structure; free determination by the designated airlines of capacity, frequencies and types of aircraft; no limitation on the carriage of Sixth Freedom traffic; encouragement of low tariffs, set by individual airlines on the basis of forces of the marketplace without reference to the rate-making machinery of the IATA; minimal government interference in tariff matters; and inclusion of liberal provisions on charter flights.

In 1992, the US began negotiating even more liberal open-skies bilaterals. As of April 2015, the US has a total of 114 Open Skies Agreements. The substances of these agreements are alike, apply to passenger, all-cargo, and combination air transportation, and encompass both scheduled and charter services. Key provisions of these agreements include: (i) free-market competition, implying that there are no restrictions on international route rights, number of designated airlines, capacity, frequencies, or types of aircrafts; (ii) pricing determined by market forces, implying that a fare can be disallowed only if both governments concur and only for certain, specified reasons intended to ensure competition; (iii) fair and equal opportunity to compete, implying that all carriers of both countries may establish sales offices in the other country and can convert and remit earnings in hard currencies at any time. Further, designated airlines are free to provide their own ground handling services, and airlines and cargo consolidators may arrange ground transport of air cargo and are guaranteed access to customs services. The agreements require that user charges cannot be discriminatory and should be based on costs, and airlines must establish procedures for resolving differences that arise under the agreement; and (iv) most Open Skies Agreements signed by the US include the Seventh Freedom for all-cargo services.

Thus, the bilateral regulatory system was undergoing a profound change because of the policy of reduced government involvement in businesses' commercial affairs. This policy can be pursued bilaterally, regionally, or multi-laterally. But in each case, economic liberalization means not only liberalizing passenger and freight transportation from one point to another by aircraft, but also liberalizing ancillary services and harmonizing economic policies on licensing rules, limits on foreign ownership, pricing policies, designation and capacity, and policies regarding public service obligations (PSOs) subject to minimal safety, security, and environmental considerations.

The degree of liberalization in the sector is determined by the stringency of regulations. Licensing can be granted on the basis of various criteria. Under more liberal systems, licensing is granted to firms satisfying economic fitness conditions of financial sustainability and liability coverage through insurance in regard to passengers, cargo, mail, and third parties. There may also be regulations restricting foreign ownership. Pricing policies concern whether carriers can set their own prices. Rules on designating authorized carriers, their entry on specific routes, and their freedom to establish capacity affect industry organization. Finally, under certain conditions, government(s) may impose PSOs on carriers. At present, safety and security rules are set by the ICAO and regional organizations. Currently, the ICAO has strategic objectives to enhance global civil aviation safety and security, minimize aviation's adverse effects on the environment, enhance the efficiency and maintain the continu-ity of air transport operations, and strengthen the law governing international civil aviation. Therefore, first and foremost, the ICAO sets international stand-ards in the following areas: (i) standards and recommended practices concern-ing aircraft materials and technology; (ii) aviation personnel and procedures; (iii) procedures for air navigation services; (iv) regional supplementary proced-ures; and (v) guidance material in several formats. To ensure the proper imple-mentation of these safety prerequisites, the ICAO runs its Universal Safety Oversight Audit Program, which determines the implementation status of relevant standards and recommended practices.

6.2.2 General Agreement on Trade in Services Attempts at Liberalizing Air Transport Services

On the multilateral level there have been attempts to liberalize air transport services through a trading mechanism under the WTO, which, among other mandates, had the mandate to liberalize and expand all service sectors through the General Agreement on Trade in Services (GATS). The GATS focuses on promoting trade by setting credible, non-discriminating, and liberalizing international trade rules, but for a variety of reasons governments were not willing to see their air transport sector covered by the GATS. Instead they decided to cover the sector via the GATS Annex on Air Transport Services (WTO, 2002, p. 309–10), which states in its first five articles:

1. This Annex applies to measures affecting trade in air transport services, whether scheduled or non-scheduled, and ancillary services. It is confirmed that any specific commitment or obligation assumed under this Agreement shall not reduce or affect a Member's obligations under bilateral or multilateral agreements that are in effect on the date of entry into force of the WTO Agreement.

2. The Agreement, including its dispute settlement procedures, shall not apply to measures affecting:
   • traffic rights, however granted; or
   • services directly related to the exercise of traffic rights, except as provided in paragraph 3 of this Annex.

3. The Agreement shall apply to measures affecting:
   • aircraft repair and maintenance services;
   • the selling and marketing of air transport services;
   • CRS.

4. The dispute settlement procedures of the Agreement may be invoked only where obligations or specific commitments have been assumed by the concerned Members and where dispute settlement procedures in bilateral and other multilateral agreements or arrangements have been exhausted.

5. The Council for Trade in Services shall review periodically, and at least every five years, developments in the air transport sector and the operation of this Annex with a view to considering the possible further application of the Agreement in this sector.

Thus, the annex states that the GATS shall not apply to traffic rights or services directly related to the exercise of traffic rights. Its coverage is limited to the provision of complementary services, such as aircraft repair and maintenance, selling and marketing air transport, and CRS services. The annex is indeed modest, applying to operations that are essentially basic to the industry. The first sub-sector was crucial in the liberalization process, as emergencies often happen abroad and must be handled accordingly. Selling and marketing air transport services including all aspects of marketing, such as market research and advertising and distribution, but not pricing. Marketing air transport services is an activity rarely banned anyway. By their nature, CRSs are a global undertaking. In total, forty countries made commitments in at least one of the three air transport services covered in the annex. Twenty-three countries made commitments in maintenance, twenty-six in sales and marketing, twenty-three in CRSs, and twenty-eight countries took most-favoured-nation (MFN) exemptions with respect to at least one of the three activities.

What are the reasons for such a modest development? The negotiators saw a clash between the MFN/national treatment disciplines and the bilateral, reciprocal relationships in the exchange of traffic rights.[11] Under bilateral air transport agreements, the MFN principle of the WTO is not satisfied because there is discrimination between foreign suppliers. Furthermore, the national treatment principle is not satisfied because foreigners in terms of access to the domestic market operate on different terms depending on the carrier. Finally, market access is restricted because the negotiators wanted to have the aviation sector liberalized between like-minded states but decided to leave this process in hands of the ICAO. If traffic rights were included into the GATS schedules of commitments and some members applied them while others maintained existing bilateral arrangements, it would create a kind of dual regulatory regime. In such a scenario, those unwilling to open their markets would still enjoy the benefits of liberalization due to the history of bilateral dealing. And this is exactly what neither states nor airlines wished to agree to.

Pursuant to a ministerial decision in 2000, the WTO launched the first mandatory review of the annex, covering developments in the air transport sector between 1995 and 2000.[12] In 2003, the WTO ended the first review process by concluding that the annex remain unchanged. In 2005, the second mandatory review commenced with assessing developments in the air transport sector and annex operation between 2000 and 2005.[13] The second review was concluded in 2006. In 2006, a group of WTO members prepared a plurilateral request calling for commitments in aircraft repair and maintenance, selling and marketing, CRSs, ground handling services, and airport services. No decision has been reached yet.

As emphasized by Hubner and Sauve (2001), a radical deviation from the existing regime, governed by about 3,000 bilateral air transport agreements among the 180 countries, could bring the sector under the disciplines of the GATS. Such a move would increase access and non-discriminatory treatment, promote a more predictable business environment, and would give the industry the advantages of the WTO's dispute settlement procedure. In addition, it would

---

[11] According to the Annex on Air Transport Services to GATS, traffic rights mean 'the right for scheduled and non-scheduled services to operate and/or to carry passengers, cargo, and mail for remuneration or hire from, to, within, or over the territory of a Member'.
[12] See International Civil Aviation Organization (2009).
[13] See World Trade Organization (2006a).

provide a vehicle for future liberalization. But despite these advantages, governments still seem reluctant to bring air services fully within the ambit of GATS.

6.3 Rules and Regulations in the European Union

Although the 1957 Treaty of Rome envisaged free competition in services and provided for a Common Transport Policy (CTP), competition could not be achieved in air transport services for a very long time and the CTP was not applied to air transport.[14] Member states preferred to protect their airlines, and protection was achieved through the system of bilateral air service agreements discussed in Section 6.2. The typical features of those agreements can be summarized following Button (2001) as follows: (i) in general, one airline from each country was allowed to fly on a particular route; (ii) the Fifth Freedom of the Air was in general not granted; (iii) 50:50 revenue pooling among member states was common; (iv) there was no competition on price; (v) airlines designated by each country were substantially owned and controlled by the country designating them; and (vi) many wholly or partially government-owned airlines enjoyed competition-distorting state aid.

In 1983, the European Parliament took the European Council to court for its inactivity in the area of transport policy.[15] In 1985, the Court of Justice ruled partly in favour of the European Parliament. As a result of that decision, as well as the signing of the Single European Act in 1986, the Council, under the influence of domestic air transport deregulation in the US in 1978, changed its policy towards the air transport sector. The Single European Act came into operation on 1 July 1987, and regulatory reform of the European air transport market was also introduced in that year. At that time, the situation of the air transport sector in Europe was rather grim. The regulatory regime protected inefficient operators, resulting in high costs for airlines, and thus in high prices for consumers as the international system worked in such a way as to set the fare level in relation to the cost of the least efficient operator on a route.

The reform was introduced over the period 1987–93 in three stages, called packages. The first package of measures, adopted in December 1987, contained regulations laying down the procedure for applying competition rules to the air transport sector. A system was introduced for approving airfares by member states that allowed for flexible pricing. The package gave some flexibility to airlines concerning seat capacity sharing and opened the way for freer

---

[14] In the Treaty of Rome, air and maritime transport were excluded from the general transport policy provisions.

[15] The European Council defines the EU's overall political direction and priorities. The members of the Council are the heads of state or government of the twenty-eight EU member states, the European Council President and the President of the European Commission.

market entry. The second package, adopted on 1 November 1990, opened up the market further, allowing greater flexibility over the setting of fares and capacity sharing, and providing access to Third, Fourth and Fifth Freedom traffic rights on scheduled flights within the Community. A major step toward liberalizing the sector was taken on 23 June 1992, when the Council adopted the third package, introducing the freedom to provide services within the EU, and, in 1997, the freedom to provide cabotage.

Since liberalizing air transport services involves not only market access but also liberalizing auxiliary services, as well as requiring common rules on economic policy, air traffic management, safety, security, environmental affairs, social matters, passenger protection, and external relations, we consider these policies in Sections 6.3.1–6.3.4.[16]

6.3.1 *Economic Policy*

In the context of economic policy, the main issue in the EU has been creating a single European air transport market. Within such a market, a company originating in any member state would have the right to create and operate an air carrier anywhere in the single market. The most significant liberalizing aspect of that policy has been that there is no need for a government to designate a certified and licensed air carrier.

Until 2008, the legal instruments guaranteeing the single air transport market within the context of the third aviation package consisted of Regulation 2407/92, on Licensing of Air Carriers, Regulation 2408/92, on Access to Air Routes and Regulation, and Regulation 2409/92, on Fares and Rates for Air Services. In 2008, those regulations were repealed and replaced by Regulation 1008/2008, establishing common rules for operating air services in the Community.

Regulation 2407/92 deals with the issue of operating licenses, which are to be granted under certain conditions regarding the candidate's economic and technical fitness. To make normal commercial decisions, a carrier must be financially fit; otherwise, it would have to use state aid, which would lead to non-market-based behaviour. Article 5 summarizes the specific requirements for financial fitness: the air carrier must produce a realistic business plan for two years and prove that it would be able to operate for three months with no income. Moreover, according to Article 7, the carrier must be insured to cover liability in regard to passengers, luggage, mail, cargo, and third parties. Regulation 785/2004, on insurance requirements for air carriers and aircraft

---

[16] The discussion of EU rules and regulations on air transportation is based largely on 'Summaries of EU Legislation' available at the website http://eur-lex.europa.eu/browse/summaries.html.

operators, contains further details regarding the interpretation of Article 7. As for technical fitness, Articles 9 and 10 of Regulation 2407/92 oblige authorities to conduct regular and thorough monitoring of an air carrier's safety equipment, staff, and operational methods to prevent the company from cutting costs by adopting cheaper but possibly more dangerous solutions. One more condition is set out in Article 8, and regards the registration of at least one aircraft owned or dry leased by the company. This condition is to avoid creating a simple sales-and-marketing organization. In addition, air carriers must hold an air operator's certificate confirming that the operator has the professional ability and organization to ensure the safety of the operations specified in the certificate, as provided in the relevant provisions of Community or national law, as applicable. Fulfilment of these conditions means that the state has no right to refuse a license if the candidate complies with all requirements (Article 3). Conversely, no air carrier without an appropriate operating license may carry out commercial operations within the single EU market or elsewhere. Finally, Article 4 of Regulation 2407/92 contains a provision liberalizing the ownership and control of Community air carriers, which enabled the switch from national ownership to the principle of non-discrimination, but still mostly within the EU's single market. Community air carriers must be majority owned and controlled by EU nationals unless the Community has entered into agreement with one or more third countries.

The second crucial legal instrument in the field of economic policy in the air services industry is Regulation 2408/92, on access to air routes. This rule liberalizes market access and ensures that access to air routes within the EU stays open for any Community air carrier under all circumstances. This condition applies equally to scheduled and non-scheduled services. The regulation also contains important provisions for PSOs within and between states, applying to routes which, under free-market conditions, are not financially attractive but provide a socially desirable advantage. If a route cannot be served appropriately and without interruptions by any other means of transport or can only serve a maximum of 30,000 passengers a year, it is given PSO status and the member state can limit access to the route for one carrier for up to three years. The allocation of PSO routes is based on a tender process, to which any Community carrier can submit offers. As of 2015, there exist 224 routes in the EU on which PSOs have been imposed.[17] Another exception to protecting domestic routes concern those routes served only by small aircraft, that is, routes of up to eighty seats. Such a route is still open for access by any Community carrier but cannot be served by a larger plane. Article 8 of Regulation 2408/92 states that while a Community air carrier is given operational freedom, traffic distribution within

---

[17] See http://ec.europa.eu/transport/modes/air/internal_market/doc/pso_routes_dec_2014.pdf.

the airport network remains under the member state's control, but without discrimination on grounds of nationality. The published Community, national, regional, or local operational rules relating to safety, environmental protection, and slot allocation must be respected.

With market liberalization and route access taken care of, the next field was fares. Regulation 2409/92, on Fares and Rates for Air Services, was the third legal instrument that created the single air transport market. Its most significant provision was the statement that carriers are free to set their own prices for passengers and freight. Airfares must, however, be filed, but only for informational purposes. The regulation also recognizes the need for certain limitations on fares, with the aim to safeguard the market against abuse from a dominant carrier. What may seem controversial is Article 6, which allows states to stop air fares from dropping persistently. Such an intervention might seem like protection for traditional airlines, but this is not the case: prices can only be limited if they leave a company in the red. The article does not apply to low prices resulting in prosperity, which is usually what most new entrants experience.

Regulation 1008/2008, repealing and replacing three regulations from the third aviation package, defines granting airline operating licenses, monitoring airlines, and airline access to the market. It guarantees a competitive air transport market, quality services, and more transparent fares. The undertaking must, in particular, hold an Air Operator Certificate, comply with insurance and ownership requirements, and provide financial guarantees. In addition, management is requested to provide proof that the undertaking is of good repute. The regulation also lays down general principles for PSOs. Further, exercising traffic rights shall be subject to Community, national, regional, and local operational rules relating to safety, security, environmental protection, and slot allocation. Finally, Community air carriers shall freely set fares for passengers and cargo, except in the case of a PSO.

The above-mentioned regulations give the basic framework for the economic policy of a unified air transport market in the EU. The remaining legal instruments in the field of economic policy regulate airports, slot allocation, ground handling services, and CRSs.

An EU objective is that there is sufficient airport capacity and that it is used efficiently. But many of EU's most important airports are facing capacity problems, and the situation will get worse over time unless appropriate measures are taken. As emphasized by the Commission of the European Communities (2011b) some two million flights, despite a predicted 40 per cent airport capacity increase between 2007 and 2030 amounting to 10 per cent of predicted demand, will not be accommodated because of capacity shortfalls. To remedy the situation, the Commission proposes that the use of existing capacity be optimized, airport capacity be increased, and that airport accessibility and efficiency be promoted through rail links. Charges for the use of airport infrastructure are another issue, and represented a significant expense for airlines in 2009, when the EU adopted Directive 2009/12/EC. The directive aimed at creating a common framework for the regulation of airport charges at EU airports with the highest number of passengers in each EU country. It advocates transparency on costs that charges are to cover, and requires that airport charges must not discriminate between airport users, implying that airlines receiving the same service should pay the same charges.

In the EU, slot allocation is regulated by Council Regulation (EEC) 95/93, on common rules for the allocation of slots at Community airports. The rules are based on the principles of neutrality, transparency, and non-discrimination, and slots are allocated by independent coordinators. In the allocation process, the concept of grandfather rights are fundamental, where an airline using a slot in one traffic season for at least 80 per cent is entitled to its use in the same traffic season the following year. Slots that are not sufficiently used by air carriers are reallocated. The slot allocation system of Regulation 95/93 has been criticized on a number of grounds, such as the distinction between new entrants and incumbents being arbitrary and the rules being inefficient in allocating scarce capacity to the highest value use. On 21 April 2004, Regulation (EC) 793/2004 was adopted, amending Regulation 95/93. The new regulation made the slot system more flexible and strengthened the coordinator's role and the monitoring of compliance. The latest proposal on slot regulation was adopted by the European Commission on 1 December 2011, and allows airlines to trade slots with each other at airports anywhere in the EU in a transparent way. The reforms are designed to help new entrants access the market at congested airports, tighten (among others) the rules on coordinator independence, and increase the level of transparency on slot transactions.

As one of the links in the chain of air transport services, ground handling has also attracted much attention from the Commission. With Directive 96/67/EC, the ground-handling market has gradually opened up. This change was needed because many airlines complained about high prices coupled with low quality, mainly as a result of a monopoly of services at most airports. The main objective of the directive was to ensure that no air carrier was given advantage over any of its competitors. The allocation and management of ground-handling services should be transparent, objective, and non-discriminatory. Article 4 of the directive states that the accounts of ground-handling activities must be rigorously separated from the accounts of any other of the provider's activities. But there are still complaints about the insufficiency of the current legal framework stating that ground-handling services have not kept up with evolving needs in terms of reliability, resilience, and safety performance. A new proposal on ground handling was adopted by the Commission on 1 December 2011. The proposal ensures that airlines have an increased choice of ground-handling solutions at EU airports, gives airports more control over coordination of ground-handling services, and introduces greater transparency on how airlines are charged for centralized airport infrastructure such as baggage-processing systems.

The remaining regulated elements are CRSs. Regulation (EC) No. 80/2009 aims to establish a harmonized code of conduct regarding the use of CRSs in order to ensure fair competition and protect consumer rights. According to the regulation, the system vendor, defined as any entity and its affiliate(s) which is or are responsible for the operation or marketing of a CRS, may not impose unfair or discriminatory conditions in contracts concluded with participating carriers or their subscribers, and may not prevent a participating carrier from using other reservation systems.

6.3.2 *Air Safety*

Europe has long traditions in rule-making cooperation for aviation safety. The latest legislation consists of Regulation 216/2008, detailing common rules in the field of civil aviation and establishing the European Aviation Safety Agency (EASA). The regulation aims to guarantee a high level of passenger security; ensure a level playing field for all stakeholders in the internal aviation market and facilitate the free movement of goods, persons, and services through recognizing certificates issued by competent authorities; and simplify and enhance the efficiency of the certification process by centralizing activities at the European level where possible. To achieve these objectives, the regulation provides for the EASA's creation. The agency's main tasks are to assist the Commission to develop common rules in the field of civil aviation and to provide it with technical, scientific, and administrative support to carry out its tasks; conduct standardization inspections to ensure that these rules are correctly applied within the member states; and issue certificates to European companies involved in aircraft design, certify aircraft used in Europe, and certify air carriers, maintenance organizations, and training organizations located in third countries.

The rules of Regulation 216/2008 are fully compliant with the ICAO's international standards and recommended practices. They cover all issues related to initial airworthiness, including the design and the production of aircraft and other aeronautical products; their continuing airworthiness and maintenance; as well as the training and licensing of aeronautical mechanics, technicians, and engineers, where *airworthiness* refers to the capability of an aircraft to fly safely. According to the regulation, aircraft must have valid airworthiness certificates before they can be used. The EU also extended the EASA's responsibilities to licensing and training aircraft crew. Thus, pilots must hold a license and a medical certificate appropriate to the operations to be performed. Training organizations and flight simulator operators must also hold appropriate certificates. Furthermore, cabin crew members must be certified for their work and periodically assessed for medical fitness to safely exercise their assigned duties. In addition, aerodromes determining the structures to be used for the departure and arrival of aircraft must have certificates guaranteeing their safety and the capability of the bodies responsible for using the aerodromes. Furthermore, enforcement actions can be taken if safety deficiencies are detected. In the EU, any European and non-European aircraft may be subject to safety inspections at European airports. If such checks (randomly conducted) reveal safety deficiencies, the breaches may lead to restricting or, at worst, banning the operation of the non-compliant air carriers from flying to and/or in Europe.

As accidents, especially with ever-growing traffic, may happen from time to time, the European policy is to do everything possible to increase the safety of air transport. According to Regulation 996/2010, on the investigation and prevention of accidents and incidents in civil aviation, each EU country must ensure that safety investigations are conducted or supervised by a permanent national civil aviation safety investigation authority, which must be independent from any entity whose interests could conflict with or influence the safety investigation authority's task or objectivity. It is necessary for each EU country to launch investigations into the cause(s) whenever incidents or accidents happen to learn safety lessons and prevent such dramatic occurrences from happening again. The regulation established the European Network of Civil Aviation Safety Investigation Authorities, comprised of all the national safety investigation authorities. The network is responsible for improving the quality of investigations conducted by safety investigation authorities and strengthening their independence, notably by encouraging high standards in investigation methods and investigator training. The regulation also clarifies EASA's role in accident investigations.

A new element to aviation safety is now being added to those described above, which introduces a pro-active and evidence-based component to aviation safety activities at the EU level. This component seeks to improve the EU-wide safety performance by identifying the main risks to aviation safety and taking action to address those risks in a coordinated fashion. The means of achieving this goal, together with the associated problems to be overcome, are spelled out in the October 2011 Communication from the Commission, setting up an Aviation Safety Management System for Europe.[18] Directive 2004/36/EC aims to improve air safety by ensuring that third-country aircraft using Community airports comply with international safety standards.

---

[18] See Commission of the European Communities (2011c).

Checks will be carried out in compliance with the international safety standards listed in the annexes to the 1944 Chicago Convention, to which all the member states of the EU are party.

6.3.3 Air Traffic Management and the Single European Sky

In the past, the national interests of EU member countries have discouraged them from giving up sovereignty over their airspace and operational network. Each country had its own rules and regulations, resulting in inefficiencies across the continent, and the hardware and software used for navigation and controls varied between countries. Since national ATC systems are heavily interdependent, there was need for harmonization at the EU level.

In 1960, the European Organization for the Safety of Air Navigation (Eurocontrol) was founded.[19] Although the first European plan for a harmonized European ATC system was proposed in 1962, it could not be implemented because of the objections of France and the UK for reasons linked to national military airspace control. The other four members of the then European Economic Community (EEC), namely Germany, Belgium, the Netherlands, and Luxembourg, agreed in 1964 to set up a single international air traffic control centre to manage their upper airspace. The centre was set up in Maastricht. The revised Convention of Eurocontrol was signed in 1997. The target was the establishment of a uniform, performance-based, air traffic management system. But unfortunately, this target could not be achieved until the adoption of the Single European Sky (SES) regulatory framework. At that time, the greatest problem in ATM was air congestion and subsequent delays, together with safety.

In December 1999, the European Commission published the Communication 'Creation of a Single European Sky'.[20] This document states that airspace is a common asset that should be managed collectively as a continuum, regardless of borders, with a view to satisfying all its users (civilian and military). To that effect, it suggests that a central organization should be given full responsibility for managing European airspace at both the strategic and tactical levels. The Commission then suggested that air traffic services be regulated to ensure they meet the necessary level of safety and interoperability.

---

[19] Eurocontrol is an intergovernmental organization. The current members are Albania, Armenia, Austria, Belgium, Bosnia and Herzegovina, Bulgaria, Croatia, Cyprus, Czech Republic, Denmark, Estonia, Finland, the former Yugoslav Republic of Macedonia, France, Georgia, Germany, Greece, Hungary, Ireland, Italy, Latvia, Lithuania, Luxembourg, Malta, Moldova, Monaco, Montenegro, the Netherlands, Norway, Poland, Portugal, Romania, Serbia, Slovakia, Slovenia, Spain, Sweden, Switzerland, Turkey, Ukraine, and the UK.
[20] See Commission of the European Communities (1999).

Transposing the working group's suggestions into EC legislation was a long process. In 2004, the Commission decided to launch the Single European Sky (SES), to modernize and restructure air traffic management in Europe. The rules governing the SES are covered in four pieces of legislation, all passed in March 2004: Regulation 549/2004, laying down the framework for the SES's creation; Regulation 550/2004, on providing air navigation services in the SES; Regulation 551/2004, on the organization and use of airspace in the SES; and Regulation 552/2004, on the interoperability of the European Air Traffic Management network.

Regulation 549/2004 lays down the framework for the creation of the SES. Its objective is to enhance safety standards for and overall efficiency of general air traffic in Europe, to optimize capacity to meet the requirements of all airspace users, and to minimize delays. The regulation sets out the framework for associated organs such as national supervisory bodies (NSBs), which must be independent from air navigation service providers (ANSP); the Single Sky Committee, on which every member state is represented and which is the vehicle for change under the Single Sky legislation; and an industry consultation body, advising the Commission on implementing the SES. Eurocontrol is also involved in implementing rules that fall within its remit, on the basis of mandates agreed by the Single Sky committee.

Regulation 550/2004, harmonizing the organization of air navigation services in the Single Sky, defines the principal responsibilities that will be assumed by NSBs, to ensure they operate on the same framework. NSBs ensure appropriate supervision in applying the regulation with regard to the safe and efficient operation of ANSPs, which are public and private entities providing air navigation services. Each NSB organizes inspection and surveys to check compliance with the regulation's requirements, and ANSPs facilitate this work. The regulation contains a non-exhaustive list of areas in which common requirements must be established, including technical and operational competence and suitability; systems and processes for safety and quality management; human resources; insurance; and quality of service. All provision of air navigation services within the Community is subject to certification by EU countries under common principles. Furthermore, EU countries must ensure the implementation of functional airspace blocks to reach the necessary capacity and efficiency of the ATM network within the SES, maintaining a high level of safety and reduced environmental impact. The regulation also provides the principles of a common charging system, which include a way to recuperate fully allocated costs, including investments in equipment and the cost of the supervisory body, non-discriminatory pricing, with an exception for cross-subsidization where it is objectively justified and identified, and pricing transparency.

The objective of Regulation 551/2004 is to make journeys in an SES without frontiers, while maintaining the highest level of safety. The aim of the regulation governing the organization and use of airspace in the Single Sky is to support the concept of a progressively more integrated operating airspace within the context of the common transport policy and to establish common procedures for design, planning, and management, ensuring efficient and safe performance of ATM. The regulation develops the European Upper Flight Information Region (EUFIR), where upper airspace refers to the space above a specific flight level, dedicated to overflight, and lower airspace is the space below that flight level, dedicated to airport approaches. Under the regulation, the division level between the upper and lower airspace is set at flight level of 8,700 metres. Creating this region in upper airspace has enabled this space to be reconfigured into delimited control areas without regard to national frontiers, thereby ensuring more efficient use of airspace systems and personnel. Regulation 551/2004 was supplemented later by Regulation 255/2010, which aims to optimize the available capacity of the European ATM network and enhance air traffic flow management (ATFM) processes through applying specific rules and procedures within the SES airspace.[21] According to the regulation, air traffic services (ATS) units must inform the central unit for ATFM of all events that may affect air traffic control capacity or air traffic demand.

The aim of Regulation 552/2004 is to ensure the interoperability of the European ATM network and introduce common requirements for the different ATM systems. According to this legislation, European standards are developed by standardization bodies assisted by the European Organization for Civil Aviation Equipment (EUROCAE) or by Eurocontrol, and member states are required to create or nominate agencies to verify manufacturers' compliance with these norms. Products must carry a declaration of conformity to be published in the EC *Official Journal*. Thus, compatible systems are expected to facilitate extended cooperation in the future.

On the technology side, SES is supported by the Single European Sky Air Traffic Management Research (SESAR) Program, established in 2007 via Regulation 219/2007. When completed, SESAR will provide advanced technologies and procedures with a view to modernizing and optimizing the future European Air Traffic Management network. The programme is composed of three phases: (i) a definition phase (2005–7), in which an air traffic modernization plan (Air Traffic Management Master Plan) was developed to define the different technological stages, priorities, and a timetable; (ii) a development phase (2007–16), consisting of research, development, and

---

[21] The role of ATFM is to ensure safety by preventing overloads and to regulate demand according to available capacity.

validation activities relating to new technologies and procedures that will underpin the new generation of systems; and (iii) a deployment phase (2014–20), which will see the large-scale production and implementation of the new technologies and procedures. Eurocontrol is assisting the EU with this programme, contributing to both the regulatory and the technology elements of the SES by drafting and implementing rules, guidance, and technical regulatory material for implementing the regulations; assisting member states in exercising their regulatory functions; and identifying needs for new regulations for the complex new ATM technologies and procedures delivered by SESAR.

In 2008, the European Commission published the Communication 'The Single European Sky II: Towards More Sustainable and Better Performing Aviation'.[22] The main issues considered were issues related to safety, capacity, the environment, and cost efficiency. As a result of these considerations, the Commission adopted the SES II package, consisting of Regulation 691/2010, Regulation 677/2011, and Regulation 1191/2010.

The SES II package is performance oriented, and its ultimate objective is to increase the economic, financial, and environmental performance of the provisions of air navigation services in Europe. On 22 February 2011, the Commission adopted EU-wide performance targets in areas of the environment, cost efficiency, and capacity. Regulation 691/2010 requires that National Supervisory Authorities (NSA) elaborate national performance plans that contribute to the EU-wide performance targets. Regulation 1070/2009, amending Regulation 549/2004, defined a Functional Airspace Block (FAB) as an airspace block based on operational requirements and established regardless of state boundaries, where the provision of air navigation services and related functions is performance-driven and optimized through enhanced cooperation among air navigation service providers or, when appropriate, an integrated provider. The FABs aim at enhanced cooperation between ANSPs and NSAs to de-fragment the airspace, and obtain operational efficiency gains through strategies such as common procurement, training, and optimizing air traffic controllers' resources. Regulation 677/2011 assigns a network manager at the EU level to manage ATM network functions such as airspace design and flow management, as well as to manage scarce resources such as transponder code allocations and radio frequencies. Finally, Regulation 1191/2010 lays down a legal framework of transparent reporting of en-route charges, and defines a legal basis for financing, through the charging system, of common projects in the context of deploying SESAR.

[22] See Commission of the European Communities (2008b).

6.3.4 The EU's External Policy

The EU's external aviation policy rests on three pillars. First and foremost, all bilateral agreements signed separately by individual member states must be amended and new agreements must take the form of horizontal ones. Such agreements are to be negotiated by the Commission on behalf of the member states to bring all existing bilateral air services agreements (ASA) in line with Community law. Second, the achievement of a Common Aviation Area with neighbouring countries was set as a target. Third, the European Commission sought (and continues to seek) agreements with its partners who most greatly impact the global economy.

A horizontal agreement is a result of negotiations between a third country and the European Commission acting on behalf of the member state(s) for which it has been authorized by the relevant government. Acting autonomously would be contrary to the principles of the single aviation market, which is clearly stated in the 'Communication from the Commission on Relations between the Community and Third Countries in the Field on Air Transport'.[23] This rule has a crucial consequence for any new EU member. Not only must such a country harmonize its aviation law to be compatible with the Community Air Carrier model, but it must also amend its existing bilateral agreements, which are surely numerous. The main reasons for these requirements are to ensure the legal certainty of aviation relations based on such agreements and to guarantee the same rights to all Community operators by virtue of the principles of non-discrimination and freedom of establishment. Amending air services agreements can be done in two ways: i) a country might come to the negotiation table with each of its partners and set the agreement in line with Community law; or ii) the Commission can negotiate a single horizontal agreement. The first method is regulated by Regulation EC No. 847/ 2004, which says that any member state can conduct negotiations with a third country if the relevant standard clauses jointly developed within the Community are included and proper notification procedures are fulfilled. Negotiations at the Community level regarding the so-called 'horizontal mandate' do not have to be formally regulated, as this is the common rule and not a deviation from such. These negotiations allow the third country to avoid individual negotiations with each member state with which air transport agreements are in place.

As a sector, aviation contributes also to the Community neighbourhood policy. It is one of the factors promoting cooperation between countries whose markets are essentially turned towards each other. The ultimate goal

---

[23] See Commission of the European Communities (2003b).

in the second pillar was to create a Common Aviation Area by the end of 2010 between EU members and their eastern and southern partners. As of the beginning of 2015, agreements have been concluded with Iceland, Norway, the Western Balkans, Morocco, Georgia, Moldova, and Jordan. An aviation agreement with Israel has been negotiated and is expected to be finalized in the near future. Negotiations are ongoing with Ukraine and Lebanon, and negotiations with Tunisia and Azerbaijan are to be initiated.

And last, but definitely not least, the third pillar of the Community Air Transport Policy covers horizontal agreements with global partners, which, even if remote, influence the European economy significantly. Countries with whom agreements have been reached include the US, Canada, and Brazil. Negotiations on similar agreements are ongoing with Australia and New Zealand. The most important development regarding global partners is the EU–US (Open Sky) Air Transport Agreement, which was signed on 30 April 2007 and came into force on 30 March 2008. Negotiations for a second phase were opened in May 2008 and concluded with the signature of a second-stage agreement in June 2010.

Previous to the EU–US 2007 agreement, Germany, France, and fourteen other EU members had bilateral open-skies agreements with the US, which gave EU airlines the right to fly without restrictions on capacity or pricing to any point in the US, but only from their home country; for example, French airlines from France, Polish airlines from Poland, and so on. These agreements included the Fifth Freedom and thereby also gave US airlines the rights to operate flights within the Community.

The main elements of the new EU–US agreement concern traffic rights, ownership and control issues, and regulatory cooperation. In particular, the agreement permits EU and US airlines to operate to any point in the US from any point in the EU; permits US airlines to fly between countries within the EU; removes all restrictions on pricing on all routes, except for US carriers which cannot price-lead on intra-EU routes; grants rights to enter into franchising and branding arrangements with other airlines or companies; and provides unlimited code sharing between US, EU, and third-country airlines. Conditions concerning matters related to ownership, investment, and control are specified in Annex 4 of the agreement. Finally, regarding regulatory cooperation, we note that cooperation will be achieved in developing common rules in the fields of security, safety, competition, and the environment; the ability to raise concerns about government subsidies and support; mutual commitment to enhance cooperation in the areas of climate science research and technology development that would enhance safety, improve fuel efficiency, and reduce emissions in air transport; and around the establishment of a joint committee responsible for resolving questions in relation to the interpretation or application of the agreement. The agreement also incorporates the possibility to operate all-cargo flights between the US and any third country without a requirement that the service start or end in the EU (the Seventh Freedom). The EU–US Air Transport Agreement of 2007 was amended by a protocol, signed, and provisionally applied on 24 June 2010. The protocol provides for considerable further advances, including additional investment and market access opportunities, as well as strengthening the framework of cooperation in regulatory areas such as safety, security, and, in particular, the environment.

6.4 The Regulation of Air Transport Services in Turkey

Turkey's General Directorate of Civil Aviation (DGCA), under the umbrella of the Ministry of Transportation, Maritime Affairs and Communications (MoTMC), is responsible for developing and supervising the country's civil aviation sector in accordance with international safety and security requirements, and it ensures equal opportunities for the provision of civil aviation services. Within the framework of these responsibilities, the DGCA develops civil aviation rules, supervises the implementation of international agreements, and ensures airworthiness, flight operations, licensing, and effective air traffic management. The MoTMC's General Directorate of State Airports Authority (DHMI) is in charge of airport operations, providing airport services, air traffic control, and setting up and operating navigation systems and the associated facilities. Turkey's main legislation regulating the air transport sector consists of Law No. 2920 of October 1983 on Turkish Civil Aviation and Law No. 5431 of November 2005 on the Duties and Organization of the DGCA.[24]

6.4.1 *Privatization in the Air Transport Sector*

Liberalization of air transport services in Turkey started in 1983, with the adoption of Law No. 2920 on Turkish Civil Aviation, which allowed the private sector to participate in air transport sector activities. Prior to 1983, only public companies were allowed to operate in the civil aviation industry. As emphasized by Gerede (2010), Turkey's state-owned flag carrier, Turkish Airlines (THY), was the predominant provider of passenger and freight services in Turkey's air transport sector, with monopoly rights in the domestic market. In addition, all airports were state owned and used to be operated by public

---

[24] The discussion of Turkish rules and regulations on air transportation has benefitted from Republic of Turkey Ministry for EU Affairs (2007), various issues of 'Turkey Progress Reports' of the Commission of the European Communities, various issues of Trade Policy Review prepared by the Secretariat of the WTO, and various issues of 'Pre-Accession Economic Programme' prepared by the State Planning Organization which with the restructuring in 2011 became the Ministry of Development.

companies. Ground-handling and catering services were also handled by a state-owned company, Plane Services Inc. (USAŞ).

In 1987, all USAŞ shares were transferred to the Privatization Administration. The ground-handling services were transferred to a new public enterprise, Airports Ground Handling Services Inc. (HAVAŞ), and USAŞ only offered catering services. With the privatization of 70 per cent of USAŞ in 1989 and the privatization of the remaining shares in 1993, USAŞ became the first privatized enterprise in the air transport industry. HAVAŞ was privatized by block selling the shares, with 60 per cent sold in 1995 and the remaining 40 per cent in 1998.

In 1984, THY was classified as a state economic enterprise (SEE), and its operating capital was raised, but it came under the jurisdiction of the Privatization Administration only in 1994. In 1996, the DGCA allowed private airlines to enter markets in which THY had no scheduled flights, and in markets in which THY did operate, private airlines were allowed to arrange flights on days that THY had no scheduled flights. If the private airline wanted to fly on the same day THY was flying to the same destination, it would be allowed to fly only if THY was not able to meet demand. Thus, the DGCA established barriers to entry into the market. In 2003, the Ministry of Transportation made a radical change in its policy, abolished the 1996 decision, allowed competition in domestic flights, and removed the barriers that inhibited private airline companies from entering into the market. In 2006, 51 per cent of THY shares were offered to the public. The privatization of THY was a real success, and led to substantial cuts in costs. Over time, domestic and international passenger numbers almost doubled. With the deregulation and liberalization in the sector, several private airline companies have entered the market in recent years. Currently, the largest private airlines are Onur Air, Atlas Jet, Pegasus, and Güneş Express. Today, in the Turkish civil aviation sector, there are thirteen airline companies, including three cargo operators.

Liberalization of air transport services continued with the restructuring of the airport sector through build-operate-transfer (BOT) projects. The tender for Antalya Terminal 1 was the DHMI's first public–private partnership (PPP) that took place in 1994. The tender of Antalya Terminal 1 was followed by the tender of Atatürk Terminal in 1997. In those projects, the private partners are responsible for financing. To attract investors to airport PPPs, the Turkish government under BOT scheme provided demand guarantees, shifting the business risk to the public sector and protecting bidders from the risk of losses. In the cases of Antalya's Terminal 1 and Istanbul's Atatürk Terminal, actual traffic has exceeded the minimum traffic levels guaranteed by the government since their construction. Dalaman New International Terminal, İzmir Adnan Menderes International Terminal, and Ankara Esenboğa Airport were also developed with the BOT model.

In line with these changes, the Turkish position in international air transport has improved. Turkish airports are becoming international hubs, not only for Central Asia, but also for Europe and the rest of Asia. Turkey's low share of air freight transport is increasing as well. New strategies are being applied for high-value goods, express transport, and perishable goods for export, and logistics equipment is developing in major airports to adapt to the expected high demand for these specialized air market segments.

6.4.2 Economic Policy

Authority for approval of new carriers is vested in the MoTMC. The By-Law on Commercial Air Transport Operators No. 28823 of 16 November 2013, regulates the rules and procedures in respect of granting, suspending, and cancelling the license of commercial air transport operators and sets forth the liability, duties, and required qualifications of air transport operators and crew. According to by-law articles 15–17, air carriers for domestic or international scheduled flights are authorized to schedule services if they are registered in Turkey and operate a minimum of five registered aircraft with at least 100 seats. Aircraft can be leased, as there is no requirement of ownership. In the case of non-scheduled domestic and international flights, at least three registered aircraft are required, and each aircraft must have at least 100 seats. However, for regional air transport, a carrier should own or lease at least two aircraft registered in the Turkish Civil Aircraft Registry, with a capacity of between twenty and ninety-nine seats. For cargo operations, the aircraft requirement is dropped to one. The regulation further requires that aeroplanes with more than fifty seats and airline companies that offer scheduled or unscheduled flights should have a minimum paid-in-capital of US $1 million per aeroplane, and that the minimum paid-in-capital requirement of the company, irrespective of the number of aeroplanes it operates, is US $15 million. Provided that these requirements are fulfilled, a market entry license can be obtained. Turkish regulations also require that the majority of the company's executive and authorized representatives must be of Turkish nationality, and that Turkish shareholders must have voting majority; the equity participation ratio of foreign shareholders is restricted to 49 per cent.[25] Airlines with a majority of shares controlled by foreigners are not permitted to carry passengers from one national point to another within Turkey. According to Article 31 of the Law on Turkish Civil Aviation, carriage of passengers, cargo, and mail for commercial purposes between two points in Turkey must be performed by registered Turkish air carriers. Technical and financial

---

[25] See Article 9 of the Regulation on Commercial Air Transport Operators No. 28823 of 16 November 2013, and Article 18 of the Law No. 2920 on Turkish Civil Aviation.

supervision of existing carriers, as well as rule enforcement, is carried out by the DGCA. Thus, the domestic air transport market is fully liberal in Turkey, and the Turkish licensing system is on the whole compatible with EU legislation.

In 2001, as the Turkish aviation sector was undergoing liberalization, an amendment to the Turkish Civil Aviation Code was adopted, allowing air carriers to set air fares without MoTMC approval. Thus, the government since 2001 no longer intervenes in pricing non-scheduled or air taxi services. In 2004, private Turkish air carriers began scheduled domestic flights, signalling the end of state-owned operators' de facto monopoly of domestic scheduled flights twenty years after the adoption of Law No. 2920, on air transport liberalization.

According to the Law on Turkish Civil Aviation, the minimum level of liability insurance required for passengers, baggage, and cargo is subject to the Warsaw Convention. Turkey signed the Montreal Convention for the Unification of Certain Rules Relating to International Carriage by Air of 28 May 1999, and the ratification process has been completed. Article 138 of the Law on Turkish Civil Aviation requires air carriers to be insured for third-party liability, and the insurance level is determined by the November 2005 Regulation on Insurance Requirements for Aircrafts Operating in Turkish Airspace, regulating the minimum level of insurance following EU rules.

A critically important factor in enabling equal competition in air transport relates to flight permits and slot allocations. For a flight to be realized, the air carrier must have a flight permit for that route and a slot allocation for the airport. An appropriate allocation mechanism for flight permits and landing slots, especially at busier airports, is instrumental in preventing market closure by traditionally dominant players and thus creating room for new entrants. In Turkey, flight permits are awarded by the MoTMC. Because slots are finite, the objective should be to set conditions for creating a contestable market on specific routes. In Turkey, landing and take-off rights are allocated on a slot-time basis, and slot allocation is applied at Atatürk, Antalya, Adnan Menderes, Dalaman, Bodrum, and Esenboga airports, and at Kayseri during the summer months.

Prior to 2010, slot coordination responsibility in Turkey was placed under the authority of the Commission for the Evaluation of Slot Allocation (CESA), established under the presidency of the DGCA. Since May 2010, however, slot allocation has been the responsibility of the DHMI. Currently, CESA is a consultative body comprised of national and international air carriers, DHMI, and ground-handling companies. A slot coordinator post, an evaluation committee, and a technical committee, in line with the EU *acquis*, have also been established. Given the importance of maintaining a contestable market, the current slot allocation procedures allow for new market entry by defining and protecting the rights of *new entrants*, meaning an air carrier requesting slots at an airport on any day and holding or having been allocated fewer than four slots at that airport on that day. After slots have been allocated to the historic slot holders, 50 per cent of the remaining capacity is allocated to new entrants. Finally, in order to increase slot allocation efficiency, fines have been introduced to prevent operators from changing their arrival and departure schedules. The new regulations thus aim to prevent unrealistic slot requests. Operators also face the risk of losing their slots if they fail to comply with the allocated slot schedules.

In Turkey, PSOs used to be fulfilled by the national flag carrier, THY. Since market liberalization, however, PSOs have been imposed on other carriers in a less-than-transparent way. More often than not, these obligations were enacted by linking the permit to fly requested routes to the obligation to fly to government-imposed destinations. Thus, actual practice is not compatible with EU rules. Harmonization will require that state authorities determine the routes that fall under the PSO regime, allocate and disclose the planned amount of state aid, and launch competitive tenders for servicing these routes.

Air carriers operating international scheduled services to Turkey are authorized on the basis of reciprocity within the framework of bilateral agreements, of which Turkey, as of 2014, has signed with 162 countries. Currently, Turkish carriers are servicing 236 destinations in 107 countries. Charter services are authorized on the basis of reciprocity under the rules of the European Civil Aviation Conference (ECAC).[26] Cargo transport is under the provisions of Law No. 2920 and the relevant articles of the Regulation on Commercial Air Transport Operations, as well as the applicable provisions of bilateral air transport agreements. Regarding membership to international organizations, we note that Turkey is a member of the ICAO, the ECAC, Eurocontrol, and the Joint Aviation Authorities Training Organization, and is party to a large number of international conventions such as the Chicago Convention.

Domestic and international air carriers apply to the DGCA at the beginning of each summer and winter schedule season for flight permission in the framework of the Turkish Airport Improvement Programme provisions. The applications are evaluated and authorizations are granted in accordance with existing bilateral air transport agreements, national, and international rules and regulations. No exclusive rights to specific air routes are granted to any air transport undertaking. Finally, note that an open-skies agreement

---

[26] The ECAC is an intergovernmental organization that was founded in 1955. Its objective is to promote the continued development of a safe, efficient, and sustainable European air transport system by harmonizing civil aviation policies and practices amongst its member states and promote understanding on policy matters between its member states and other parts of the world. Currently, it is composed of forty-four states consisting of all the countries in Europe and including Armenia, Azerbaijan, Georgia, Turkey, and Ukraine, but excluding Belarus and the Russian Federation.

was concluded between Turkey and the US in 2000. Turkey initialized a civil aviation agreement with the EU on 25 March 2010.

6.4.3 Airports

According to Article 34 of the Law on Turkish Civil Aviation, and Article 5 of the By-Law on the Construction, Operation, and Certification of Airports (SHY-14A), airports are operated by the state, public legal persons, natural persons, or private legal persons. The DHMI is in charge of airport operations, providing airport services.

Airport operation by natural persons or private legal persons is subject to MoTMC permission after affirmation from the Turkish General Staff, which is the governing body of the Turkish Armed Forces. The Commission for the Evaluation of Airport Operation Applications decides whether the applicant meets the standards indicated in SHY-14A. If so, an airport operation license is granted. Airport charges are set on a cost basis, as well as by considering the views of IATA and IACA members and charges in neighbouring countries and other European and African countries. The charges are endorsed by the MoTMC.

Airport management is not separate from airport ownership except at Istanbul's Sabiha Gökçen Airport. Airport charges are the same for domestic and foreign air carriers. Airport development is evaluated by the MoTMC with the coordination of the Turkish General Staff, according to SHY-14A, Article 5. The development of airports operated by the DHMI is based on an annually prepared investment programme approved by Cabinet and published in the *Official Gazette*. The same rules apply to international/domestic and main/ regional airports, but some congested airports' terminal buildings are constructed by the private sector under a BOT model.

The July 2005 By-Law on the Evaluation and Management of Environmental Noise was prepared by the Ministry of Environment and Forestry in accordance with EU Directive 2002/49/EC. Noise monitoring systems at three busy airports were installed in 2007. The regulation requires preparing a strategic noise map, to be accomplished by 2018.

Given the importance of ground-handling services for efficient and cost-effective air transport services, access to the ground-handling market remains a critical issue. In Turkey, three private-sector ground-handling companies provide services at all airports open to international civil air traffic. At Sabiha Gökçen Airport, ground services are provided by the airport operator. Although the presence of three ground-handling operators at other airports complies with EU requirements, ground handling at Sabiha Gökçen does not. Turkish legislation, unlike EU legislation, does not stipulate a minimum number of service providers; it sets forth a maximum number depending on the number of passengers, and thus the scope for competition remains limited. Catering services at international airports, however, are provided by five catering firms. Airlines may also use their own ground-handling services at all airports, and as of 2011, thirteen companies do so. The prices for these services are market determined.

6.4.4 Air Traffic Management

The Air Navigation Department of the DHMI is the provider of civil air navigation services for Turkey, by means of its approach control units and aerodrome control towers at forty-four Turkish airports, and en-route air navigation services throughout Turkish airspace from two separate area control centres, located in Ankara and Istanbul. The Izmir Approach Control Unit provides area control services for the southern part of the Istanbul FIR. The Air Navigation Department is responsible among others for air traffic management, aeronautical information management, flight inspection services, Eurocontrol management, and system project development and assessment.

In 2013, traffic amounted to 1,574,973 flights, a 9.3 per cent increase from 2012. The largest growth rate was achieved in international traffic, with 13.6 per cent, while domestic flights achieved a growth rate of 9.9 per cent. The total number of overflights through Turkish airspace amounted to 281,178.

Responsible for certifying ATM personnel, the DGCA's air navigation department has the regulatory responsibility for ATM. These responsibilities are mandated through Article 10 of the 2005 Law on the Organization and the Duties of the Directorate General of Civil Aviation No. 5431. Basic training in Turkey is conducted at the DHMI's training institute and at Anadolu University's Civil Aviation School. These programmes are approved by the DGCA in accordance with Eurocontrol's common core content.

Over the last decade, it was noted that continuous traffic growth had eroded reserve capacity, meaning that the existing system was no longer capable of economic upgrading to satisfy capacity needs. In light of this fact, Turkey has accelerated its Systematic Modernization of Air Traffic Management Resources (SMART) project to allow early implementation of an interim upgrade of ATM systems. SMART was initiated by the DHMI to update the ATC systems procured in 1989, meet future needs for air traffic capacity, increase safety and quality in ATM with new functionalities to the systems, and suit Eurocontrol's one-sky concept. SMART consists of three sub-projects: (i) establishing a central Ankara air traffic control centre (ACC) and other ACCs, (ii) replacing existing radar and procuring additional radar, and (iii) procuring advanced-surface movement guidance and control systems for Atatürk, Esenboğa, and Antalya airports. During the peak tourist season, Istanbul's Atatürk Airport would regularly experience delays due to the large increase in air traffic. These delays have now been virtually eliminated thanks to the interim SMART system; the average en-route delay per flight was reduced to 0.1 minutes in summer 2009.

Finally, note that discussions are ongoing regarding making the DGCA the national supervisory authority, adopting Commission Regulation 2096/2005, laying down common requirements for providing air navigation services, establishing a certification scheme compliant with SES regulations, and certifying national air navigation service providers.

6.4.5 Air Safety

Safety regulations for civil aviation in Turkey have their legal basis through: (i) the organization and functions of the MoTMC, (ii) Turkish Civil Aviation Law, (iii) the Law on the Organization and the Duties of the DGCA, (iv) the Chicago Convention, and (v) the Eurocontrol Convention. Implementing all six Eurocontrol Safety Regulatory Requirements (ESARR) was delayed for some time in Turkey, but the DGCA and the DHMI have worked together to adopt them in full. The ESARR 1 is on safety oversight in ATM, ESARR 2 is on reporting and assessment of safety occurrences in ATM, and ESARR 3 is on use of safety management systems by ATM service providers. The ESARR 4 is on risk assessment and mitigation, ESARR 5 on ATM service personnel, and ESARR 6 on software in ATM systems. Recently, ESARR 2 to ESARR 6 have been enacted. Progress is being made on enacting ESARR 1.

The DHMI Safety Commission, which is responsible for all ATM safety matters, was established in conjunction with the safety management system (SMS). Generic safety management manual guidelines are used for updating local guidelines for SMSs and quality management systems (QMSs) are adapted to Turkish requirements. The DHMI Safety Commission promotes awareness and implementation of SES safety provisions. Oversight activities conducted by the DGCA are presently confined to airports and ATM units.

Civil ATM incidents are investigated by the Investigation and Assessment Commission, which reports incidents and investigation findings to the DGCA. The commission is formed from experts with sufficient qualifications. The DGCA experts may also join the commission in accordance with the Regulation on Reporting and Assessment of ATM Related Safety Occurrences (SHY 65-02), which was aligned with the EC directives on investigations of civil aviation accidents. For each incident, an investigation team is formed to investigate the incident, determine the causal factors, and propose necessary measures to avoid the repetition of such incidents in the future.

Regarding runway safety, local runway safety teams have been formed for all airports, which report and disseminate information to the DHMI and the DGCA. Airport-related personnel have been kept fully aware of all runway incursion matters. Suitable training in line with Eurocontrol's action plan for the prevention of runway incursions has been implemented, and airport runway incident guidelines have also been prepared. Runway safety teams have been carrying out training and awareness campaigns in accordance with the ICAO runway safety toolkit in all aerodromes, which are regularly checked for compliance with the ICAO's Annex 14. Finally, we note that the implementing regulation on approved overhaul administrations, in line with the *acquis*, was published in 2004. Similarly, instructions on licensing plane and helicopter pilots in line with the *acquis* were issued in 2005.

Lately, the DHMI has taken measures to ensure that airport systems have the capacity to work safely and reliably. Communication and surveillance infrastructures have been improved substantially and additional controllers have been recruited. New theoretical capacity and bottlenecks have been identified, and the latter have been further investigated. Collaborative decision-making gap analysis has also commenced to enhance airport productivity.[27] We also note that the number of Safety Assessment of Foreign Aircraft (SAFA) inspections increased from 150 in 2006 to 511 in 2011, and the number of Safety Assessment of National Aircraft (SANA) inspections increased from eighty-five in 2006 to 390 in 2011. These statistics reflect more an increased number of aircraft to inspect rather than an increased number of inspections on the same aircrafts.

6.5 Conclusion

Economic liberalization of air transport services means not only liberalizing the transportation of passengers and freight from one point to another by aircraft, but also liberalizing whenever possible ancillary services, such as air traffic control, airport services, aircraft repair, computer reservation systems, ground handling, and aircraft repair and maintenance, subject to the conditions that minimal safety, security, and environmental considerations are secured. Since air transport is inherently international in character and carriers must operate under the regulatory requirements of many jurisdictions, there is a need for harmonizing those rules and regulations across countries. States have tried to achieve air transport liberalization through multilateral and bilateral liberalization, but on the whole, attempts have not been very successful. Turkey has achieved the liberalization of air transport services in the domestic market mainly through adopting the EU's air transportation *acquis*.

---

[27] Gap analysis is the comparison of actual performance with potential or desired performance.

7

Liberalizing Transport Sectors and the Effects of Infrastructure Development

The Turkish Case

Co-authored with Güzin Bayar

Economic theory emphasizes that countries can derive welfare gains from freer trade, and that the proposition applies to both goods and services.[1] But the types and forms of services liberalization are quite different from those of merchandise liberalization. Barriers to the flow of goods typically arise as customs and non-tariff barriers (NTBs), and hence for goods trade most discussion of liberalization focuses on tariffs and NTBs. On the other hand, barriers to trade in services are typically regulatory in nature, and outcomes of services liberalization depend heavily on the regulatory environments.

Recent research indicates that barriers to global services trade remain prevalent, and that service barriers in both high-income and developing countries are higher than those for trade in goods. Policies are more liberal in OECD countries, Latin America, and Eastern Europe, whereas quite restrictive policies are observed in Middle Eastern and North African (MENA) and Asian countries. The overall pattern of policies across sectors is increasingly similar in developing and industrial countries. Telecommunications and banking services are more competitive while transport and professional services remain bastions of protectionism.[2]

Barriers to services trade lead to inefficiencies in service sectors and to high costs of services. Since the productivity and competitiveness of goods and

---

[1] Güzin Bayar contributed mainly to section 7.4 'The Economic Impact of Liberalizing Transport Services' and section 7.5 'The Economic Impact of Transport Sector Infrastructure Development'.
[2] See Gootiiz and Mattoo (2009).

services firms depend largely on access to low-cost and high-quality producer services such as transportation, distribution, telecommunications, and finance, and since those producer services have a powerful influence on economic growth, it is of utmost importance for countries to increase the efficiency of service industries, which can largely be achieved through liberalization.

This chapter, studying the effects of liberalization in Turkish transportation sectors, is structured as follows: While Section 7.1 concentrates on the opening up of Turkish transport sectors, Section 7.2 discusses the World Bank's new Services Trade Restrictions Database as well as the OECD's Services Trade Restrictiveness Index and the OECD's Indicators of Product Market Regulations. Section 7.3 determines the tariff equivalents of barriers to trade quantitatively in Turkey's different transport sectors as well as in Turkey's major export markets using the approach developed by Chen and Novy (2011). Section 7.4 analyses the effects of liberalization in Turkey's transport service sectors using a computable general equilibrium model and Section 7.5 discusses the economic impact of infrastructure development. Finally, Section 7.6 concludes.

7.1 Opening up the Transport Sectors

Although transport sectors have been and still are regulated for justifiable reasons such as the need for safety, security, technical harmonization, fair competition, and sustainability, there are in each country also many regulations aiming to limit competition in the marketplace. Opening up transport sectors by doing away with overregulation on entry into a profession and easing access to markets leads to healthier competition, which will result in higher efficiency, better service and goods quality, and lower prices. But *opening up* is conducted in general by reinforcing regulations on safety, security, sustainability, and social considerations, which may raise prices.

7.1.1 Opening up the Road Transportation Sector

During the last decade Turkey has undertaken comprehensive reform in the road transport sector. It has introduced criteria for access to the profession, roadworthiness tests for vehicles, social legislation, professional training requirements for drivers, and a licensing system. Retail prices are no longer regulated. The result of such reforms has been the creation of a competitive road transport industry, especially for domestic operations. There are still limitations, however. Turkey, as emphasized by the World Bank (2014a), maintains a large number of different types of licenses for access to its road haulage market. In the regulations, each type of transport activity is specified in detail, and if a particular road transport operator wants to perform different tasks, he/she must apply for each type of license separately. Furthermore, a truck carrying commercial goods cannot re-run with household goods.

Although the domestic road transport market has been liberalized to a large extent, there are still limitations in trade with EU countries due to lack of alignment in the fields of technical conditions, road safety, and sustainability with the relevant EU *acquis*. The Republic of Turkey Ministry for EU Affairs (2014, 2015) states that preparations are ongoing for aligning the rules and regulations with the EU *acquis* on driver licenses; data collected on people who have lost their lives in traffic accidents; combined transport; roadside inspections of commercial vehicles; inspection of the transport of dangerous goods; safety of tunnels; and road infrastructure safety.

In addition, there is the issue of cabotage for foreign operators in the road freight transportation sector. But the main problem is faced in the international market related to the access to the EU market in mode 1. Turkey has about 1,300 firms with a fleet of 45,000 vehicles active in international operations (World Bank, 2014a). The country has been one of the largest users of TIR Carnets in the world for the last twelve years and is participating in the European Conference of Ministers of Transport (ECMT)'s Multilateral Quota System.[3]

In the EU, bilateral road transport agreements remain a sovereign attribute of individual EU members. The main export market for Turkish goods is Germany, and transit countries limit the number of Turkish vehicles that can carry goods in their territory. When carrying goods in the EU by road, Turkish operators must transit through either Greece or Bulgaria. While Greece exchanges 35,000 transit permits every year with Turkey for a fee of €100 per round trip, in Bulgaria Turkish road transport operators receive 250,000 transit permits per year at a cost of €86 per round trip. In Austria, Turkish carriers are obliged to use RO-LA (truck-on-train) transport due to the scarcity of permits exchanged with Austria on the grounds of environmental protection. From Hungary, Turkish carriers receive 24,000 permits free of charge and 16,400 paid permits (€500/round trip transit). On the other hand, approximately 100,000 Turkish trucks transit through Italy every year, of which 70 per cent travel north and 30 per cent travel west. For Romania, if the free quota is exhausted, Turkey can purchase as many transit permits as needed for €1,200/round trip.[4] Some transit quotas for some countries are free if the journey time is fewer than thirty-six hours. However, in several EU member states, when permits are exhausted trade by Turkish road transport operators is effectively closed.

---

[3] For an explanation of TIR Carnets see Chapter 3, 'The Regulatory Framework in Road Freight Transportation'.
[4] See the World Bank (2014a).

Road transport permits are required for Turkish vehicles to enter EU markets, and the number of permits that are issued though bilateral agreements and ECMT's Multilateral Quota System compared to the Turkish demand for them is rather small. The quota regime applied by EU member states limits the number of Turkish-registered vehicles that can carry goods through member countries' territories. The International Transporters' Association of Turkey gives the following example in one of its PowerPoint presentations. A truck has an average capacity of 95 cubic metres (in volume) and 20 tonnes (in weight). If an EU Member State imposes a quota of 10,000 for bilateral road transport operations from Turkey, then permission will be given for entry of Turkish goods by Turkish trucks up to 950,000 cubic metres and 200,000 tonnes. In 2007 because of the quota France was allowing 540,000 tonnes of Turkish goods by road, Austria 360,000 tonnes and Spain 81,000 tonnes of goods. On the other hand the transit permit quota allocated by Italy to Turkish transporters for operations to Switzerland, France, Spain, and Portugal was limited to 6,000. Thus with 6,000 permits Turkish trucks could undertake 6,000 trips for transiting Italy to arrive at France, Spain, or Portugal. If the Turkish trucks would use the quota-free route, then costs increase considerably. Thus, an EU member state setting limits on Turkish goods that can be transported to the EU by Turkish road transport operators raises the transport costs for Turkish exporters. According to Ülengin et al. (2015) the loss of Turkish exports to EU countries over the period 2005–12 has amounted to $10.6 billion.

The World Bank (2014a), noting that road quotas and transits permits create obstacles to the free movement of goods between Turkey and the EU, proposes that those restrictions be eliminated at least for goods covered by the 1995 Customs Union Decision between Turkey and the EU. Alternatively, the European Commission could request a mandate from the twenty-eight member states to negotiate on their behalf regarding road transport quotas and transit permits with Turkey. Other ways to liberalize trade in road transport services between Turkey and the EU is to negotiate a road transit agreement similar to those concluded by the European Commission with Hungary and Romania, or to negotiate a Land Transport Agreement similar to that signed between EU member states and Switzerland as long as the EU would be willing to sign such an agreement. Turkey could also propose a free trade agreement with the EU covering certain services, including road transport. In such a case, Turkey would have to adopt and implement the EU *acquis* on road freight transport, including the EU regulations on market access and competition, prices and fiscal conditions, social conditions, technical conditions, road safety, and international transport networks, as summarized in Chapter 3 on 'The Regulatory Framework in Road Freight Transportation'.

7.1.2 Opening up the Rail Transportation Sector

In rail transport sector, the market structure takes two basic forms: vertical integration and vertical separation. While under vertical integration the same entity operates both infrastructure and services operations; under vertical separation the infrastructure manager is separated from the train operator. Separation takes three forms: accounting separation, functional separation, and organizational/institutional separation. Under accounting separation the infrastructure management and services operations are kept in separate accounts within the same entity; under functional separation the infrastructure manager and services operations are in different divisions of the same legal entity; and under organizational/institutional separation the infrastructure manager is a separate entity from the train operators.

Until recently, Turkish State Railways (TCDD) was operating under vertical integration. Noting that there are both benefits of and costs to vertical integration and vertical separation, and that the benefits derived from increased competition and better performance incentives in downstream operations would exceed the costs associated with coordination and operation, the Turkish Parliament adopted the vertical separation model by passing the Turkish Rail Liberalization Law on 1 May 2013. There is a five-year transition period, during which the government will be establishing the regulations necessary to implement the law, and then the TCDD will complete its transformation into an infrastructure and train-operating company. By the end of the transition period, TCDD trains will compete with private operators for freight service, and passenger services will be provided under public service obligation (PSO) contracts. Since the transition period will end in 2018, the liberalization of the rail transportation sector in Turkey will effectively begin in 2019.

The Republic of Turkey Ministry for EU Affairs (2014, 2015) points out that preparations are ongoing for aligning the rules and regulations with the EU *acquis* on safety on railways; licensing of railway undertakings; registration of railway vehicles; access to railway infrastructure and allocation of railway infrastructure capacity; PSO; certification of train drivers; railway interoperability; passenger rights; construction and maintenance of the rolling stock; infrastructure standards; environmental impact of rail transport; meeting the needs of persons with reduced mobility; and transport of dangerous goods by railway.

In addition, a major problem confronting the liberalization of the rail transport sector in Turkey is the worsening financial performance of TCDD. TCDD has been the largest loss-making state-owned enterprise in the Turkish system due to the pricing policy of TCDD, reductions of revenues from privatized ports, and increases in infrastructure expenditures such as high-speed train (HST) investments. According to World Bank (2014b) construction costs of

HST tracks range between €9 million to €40 million per km depending on the geography and terrain conditions while the maintenance costs add another 10 per cent to the core investment costs. On the other hand, the estimated acquisition cost of rolling stock per seat amounts to €33,000 to €65,000; operating costs per seat goes from €41,000 to €72,000; and maintenance costs of rolling stock varies between €3,000 and €8,000.[5] As a result, the full cost of a return ticket on HST on a 500 km route could be as high as €418. But, to attract riders, the HST services need to be priced to compete with buses. Since bus prices are much lower than €418, HST will require substantial subsidies when the HST network reaches 10,000 km by 2023.

These are some of the problems related with the opening up of the rail transport sector. Since there is too much uncertainty about future developments in the sector, we shall refrain from further discussion of the liberalization of the rail transport sector.

7.1.3 Opening up the Maritime Transportation Sector

Barriers to trade affecting maritime transport are related mainly to cabotage; restrictions and barriers to competition in ports; stricter regulations on safety, security, sustainability, and social considerations of the main trading partners; and sometimes to cargo reservation schemes. While the UN liner code of conduct and its cargo-sharing provisions are still in force, very few states are applying it, and reserving cargoes under bilateral agreements or government-linked or national security-linked cargoes happens infrequently. Thus, opening up trade in maritime transport services can be discussed mainly in terms of cabotage, restrictions and barriers to competition in ports, and stricter regulations on safety, security, sustainability, and social considerations of the main trading partner.

7.1.3.1 CABOTAGE

Maritime cabotage refers to the trade or navigation in coastal waters between two points within a country. It also refers to the right to engage in trade and navigation in coastal waters and to the restriction of that right to domestic carriers. As emphasized by Petrova (1997), the term in essence denotes the discriminatory practice of keeping foreign flags out of coastal waters, and thus often constitutes an element of a government's maritime policy as a category of flag preference. The idea behind cabotage restrictions is to promote the development of national merchant fleets.

---

[5] See World Bank (2014b).

In Turkey, maritime freight cabotage is restricted to ships with a national flag, and as emphasized in Chapter 5, Turkey also imposes requirements on the foreign operator to grant majority control to local citizens, and establishes minimum percentages for crews of Turkish origin. In addition, to promote the development of a national merchant fleet, Turkey has been providing subsidies to shippers navigating in coastal waters between two points within the country since the beginning of 2014. According to the Ministry of Transportation, Maritime Affairs, and Communications (MoTMC) (2015), the annual subsidy provided between January and September 2014, which is to eliminate the special consumption tax on fuel consumed by Turkish shippers, has amounted to $175.4 million.

When market access is denied and the maritime freight cabotage market is protected from foreign competition, there is little incentive for domestic shippers to compete. In such a case, the sole competition comes from other equally protected firms, resulting in no positive change in the sector. Thus, the primary benefit of opening up the maritime freight cabotage market is to gain competitively priced transport and also to encourage a shift from road to ship for reasons of environmental impact, such as greenhouse gas reductions.

7.1.3.2 PORTS

Ports play a key role in the Turkish economy; in 2013 the share of sea transportation in exports amounted to 54.6 per cent, and in imports to 55.6 per cent. Since ports provide the linkages from international to local transport systems and supply chains, the expansion of international trade calls for higher efficiency within seaports. Thus, achieving efficiency in Turkish ports is very important for increasing the country's competitiveness at the international level.

Table 7.1 shows Turkey's and the world's top ten container terminals. In terms of throughput, Turkey's top ten terminals form on average 3.3 per cent of the world's top ten terminals, indicating the production scale effects between Turkish ports and global ports. The table also shows port productivities as calculated by Merk and Dang (2013), who measure port efficiency using a data-envelope analysis. They define an efficient port as one that maximizes output level for the same level of inputs across all observed ports, or one that minimizes quantity of inputs for a given level of output. According to the authors, there are three different types of efficiency: overall efficiency, technical efficiency, and scale efficiency. The overall efficiency indicator, derived from a model assuming constant returns to scale (CRS), provides a measure of overall port efficiency. Technical efficiency is derived from a model assuming varying returns to scale (VRS), and it recognizes that smaller ports may face disadvantages caused by production scale effects. Finally, scale inefficiencies arise when the scale of production is inappropriate, which is

Table 7.1 Container terminals, their throughput (thousand TEUs), and their productivity in 2013

| | | WORLD | | |
Port name	Throughput	Productivity CRS	Productivity VRS	Productivity SE
Shanghai	36,617	1.000	1.000	1.000
Singapore	32,600	0.915	1.000	1.000
Shenzhen	23,279	1.000	1.000	1.000
Hong Kong	22,352	1.000	1.000	1.000
Busan	17,686	0.781	0.783	0.781
Ningbo	17,351	–	–	–
Qingdao	15,520	–	–	–
Guangzhou	15,309	1.000	1.000	1.000
Dubai	13,641	0.365	0.461	0.461
Tianjin	13,000	1.000	1.000	1.000
Total	207,355			

| | | TURKEY | | |
Port name	Throughput	Productivity CRS	Productivity VRS	Productivity SE
Ambarli Marport	1,686	0.483	0.486	0.483
Mersin	1,364	0.197	0.199	0.197
Ambarli Kumport	1,276	0.483	0.486	0.483
Izmir	683	–	–	–
Kocaeli Evyap	455	–	–	–
Ambarli Mardas	354	0.483	0.486	0.483
Gemlik	332	–	–	–
Kocaeli Yilport	305	–	–	–
Aliaga Akdeniz	254	–	–	–
Antalya	216	–	–	–
Total	6,925			

identified when a difference appears between efficiency achieved at the technical and overall levels. According to the authors, scale efficiency (SE) is calculated by the ratio SE = CRS/VRS, where CRS and VRS are the efficiency estimates derived from assuming constant and varying returns to scale, respectively. When SE<1, ports face scale inefficiency, driving higher overall inefficiency compared to pure technical inefficiency. By contrast, when SE=1, ports operate at efficient scales, producing at the optimal level for which they were designed.

Merk and Dang (2013) normalize the efficiency scores by assigning the value of unity to ports with the highest efficiency scores and reporting the efficiency of all other ports relative to the scores of the benchmark group. Table 7.1 reveals that the largest ports in China and Hong Kong are efficient, and that there are potential gains to be achieved by increasing efficiency in the ports of Busan (Korea) and Dubai (United Arab Emirates). Similarly, there are considerable gains to be achieved by increasing efficiency in the ports of Ambarlı and Mersin in Turkey. Focusing on port efficiency, Clark et al. (2004) show that if a country like Turkey improved seaport efficiency to a level similar to Australia, it would be able to increase trade by roughly 25 per cent. Micco and Perez (2001) note that port handling changes are lower in more-efficient ports.

Determinants of port efficiency are the market structure of port services and the quality of port infrastructure. Regarding the former, we note that during the last two decades the Turkish port sector has undergone extensive privatization with the hope of improving port operations by attracting private investments and eliminating the state's financial responsibility for them. In 1994, Turkey adopted the Privatization Act, according to which public ports could be given to private operators by granting operating rights for a certain period of time. As a result, private operators of previously state-owned ports function under a concession agreements generally undertaken for thirty to fifty years, directly employ and coordinate the work of crane operators and dock workers answerable to management, and invest in superstructures such as stacking areas, cranes, forklifts, and so on. The concession agreements usually contain clauses for establishing healthy port operations. However, Merk and Dang's (2013) study reveals that Turkey by following appropriate policies could increase its ports' competitiveness.

According to the World Bank (2014b) competition among Turkish ports is limited. The Transfer of Operating Rights' model used in the privatization of TCDD ports did not allow for intra-port competition. Since all facilities within a port were concessioned to a single entity the TCDD monopoly was transferred into a private monopoly. Since competition between ports is limited except in the Marmara region, there is need for regulation in order to increase the efficiency of ports. But currently, the port sector is not regulated. The World Bank (2014b) points out that there are two forms of regulation in the port sector, namely technical regulation and economic regulation. While technical regulation enforced by a port authority manages the port space and controls port operators, economic regulation regulates the operation of markets controlling market entry and exit and sees to it that fair and competitive behavior are maintained within the sector. Thus, to increase the port efficiency both forms of regulation enforced by an independent entity are needed that will encourage more domestic competition as well as more international liberalization.

Liberalizing maritime services also requires, whenever possible, liberalizing port services such as pilotage, towage, mooring, dredging, bunkering, cargo handling, passenger services, and environmental services. According to a 2013

PricewaterhouseCoopers (PwC) survey, when a port managing body in the EU prevents other providers from entering the market, shipping lines start to complain, and price turns out to be the main problem.[6] From the PwC's survey, the percentage of respondents not satisfied with port services in the EU was 45 per cent in the case of pilotage, 42 per cent in the case of towage, 35 per cent in the case of cargo handling, 29 per cent in the case of dredging, 28 per cent in the case of passenger services, 22 per cent in the cases of mooring and bunkering, and 17 per cent in the case of environmental services. No such survey has been undertaken in Turkey and it is thus difficult to assert the level of stakeholder satisfaction with different port services. However, since by related regulations most of these services can be executed only by Turkish economic units, opening these markets to international competition would lead to efficiency gains in Turkey's port sector.

Table 7.2 gives the costs for shipping a standard (fully loaded 20-foot-equivalent-unit (TEU)) container, where the first column shows the cost to export, the second column the cost to import, and the third column the average cost of exporting and importing a container. The table reveals that the cost to trade in Turkey is much higher than the costs to trade in Malaysia, Israel, Vietnam, Indonesia, China, Korea, Finland, Sweden, Denmark, Germany, and the United Kingdom. While the average freight cost for a 20-foot container is $450 in Singapore, $540 in Malaysia, and $592 in Israel, the cost amounts to about $1,120 in Turkey. The data in the table are based on World Bank surveys of freight forwarders in each country, and are updated annually. Note that there is considerable scope for improvement in Turkey.

7.1.3.3 SAFETY AND SEA POLLUTION PREVENTION

Until recently, Turkey faced serious difficulties in meeting its international requirements for safety and sea pollution prevention. As emphasized by the Delegation of the European Union to Turkey (2012), the country had no efficient legislation on issues such as ship inspection, ship pollution prevention, seamen's working conditions, or of sea casualty investigation. Moreover, most of the regulations at the time did not comply with the relevant EU criteria. According to statistics from the Paris Memorandum of Understanding on Port State Control (Paris MoU), during 2001 about 25 per cent of the Turkish fleet (211 ships) was detained at European ports, and Turkish ships were included on the Paris MoU black list. Turkey had problems not only with fleet inspection, but also with meeting its international commitments regarding foreign ship inspection in its ports. Between 2004 and 2005, Turkey

---

[6] See PricewaterhouseCoopers (2013).

Table 7.2 Cost of trading (US$ per container)

Economy	Cost to export US$ per container	Cost to import US$ per container	Average cost to trade US$ per container
Singapore	460.0	440.0	450.0
Malaysia	525.0	560.0	542.5
Hong Kong SAR, China	590.0	565.0	577.5
Israel	620.0	565.0	592.5
Vietnam	610.0	600.0	605.0
Indonesia	571.8	646.8	609.3
Myanmar	620.0	610.0	615.0
China—Shanghai	620.0	615.0	617.5
Finland	615.0	625.0	620.0
Sri Lanka	560.0	690.0	625.0
United Arab Emirates	665.0	625.0	645.0
Thailand	595.0	760.0	677.5
Korea, Rep.	670.0	695.0	682.5
Taiwan, China	655.0	720.0	687.5
Egypt, Arab Rep.	625.0	790.0	707.5
Sweden	725.0	735.0	730.0
Denmark	795.0	745.0	770.0
Lithuania	750.0	800.0	775.0
Estonia	765.0	795.0	780.0
Morocco	595.0	970.0	782.5
China	823.0	800.0	811.5
Philippines	755.0	915.0	835.0
New Zealand	870.0	825.0	847.5
Portugal	780.0	925.0	852.5
Tunisia	805.0	910.0	857.5
Pakistan	765.0	1,005.0	885.0
Japan	829.3	1,021.3	925.3
Cyprus	865.0	1,010.0	937.5
Netherlands	915.0	975.0	945.0
Qatar	927.0	1,050.0	988.5
United Kingdom	1,005.0	1,050.0	1,027.5
Germany	1,015.0	1,050.0	1,032.5
Greece	1,040.0	1,135.0	1,087.5
Turkey	990.0	1,235.0	1,112.5

Source: World Bank Doing Business 2015.

implemented the EU project titled Support to the Enhancement of Safety of Maritime Transport in Turkey. With the help of this project, the share of detained Turkish ships was reduced to 7 per cent (43 ships) in 2006 and Turkish ships formerly on the black list had moved up to the grey list. Between 2011 and 2013, 1,650 inspections were conducted of Turkish ships in foreign ports. While sixty-nine detentions were observed, in 133 cases Turkey was in the black-to-grey limit, and in ninety-eight cases in the grey-to-white limit. As a result, since 2009, Turkish-flagged ships have been included on the white list of the Paris MoU. Although these are important achievements, there is still considerable scope for improvements in the sector regarding safety, security, sustainability, and social considerations.

7.1.4 Opening up the Air Transportation Sector

Liberalizing air transport services, which started in Turkey in 1983, has generated business opportunities for the industry, created competition for air transport services supply, delivered new employment possibilities, and benefitted the consumer through price reductions and quality increases. In this context, Turkey has adopted a step-by-step liberalization approach. In the past, Turkey had one state-owned air carrier, with overpriced services, which offered the only option for passenger flights. However, within the last decade, the market and the sector have been restructured and reorganized. The first step involved opening up the internal market to competition in domestic airlines, and the second step was to privatize the state-owned air carrier. Third, international flights were opened to competition for all domestic carriers, and fourth, additional traffic rights were granted to international carriers and more liberal bilateral air transport agreements were implemented. The final step involves regional/multilateral liberalization of foreign markets, which Turkey aims to achieve through a case-by-case approach with stakeholder consent.

According to InterVISTAS-EU Consulting Inc. (2009), most of the international air service agreements to which Turkey is a signatory are restrictive. The WTO's QUASAR database reveals that in 2005 Turkey was party to forty-six bilateral air services agreements (ASAs), recorded by the International Civil Aviation Organization (ICAO). Of the top twenty origin/destination markets, nineteen have ASAs, which restrict the airports airlines can fly to, place some kind of restriction on capacity and pricing practices, and in some cases designate only one airline to operate services between two countries. Turkey has concluded only one ASA that can be qualified as open-sky, which was concluded with the United States and signed on 24 March 2000.

The 2000 Turkey–US Open Skies Agreement replaced their 1990 agreement and gives both nations unrestricted rights to transport passengers directly between the two countries. It also allows airlines from either country to transport passengers from third countries on through routes to the US or Turkey. Access to gateway and code-share points was fully liberalized after a three-year transition period. As a result, carriers from both countries can provide services to any number of gateway or code-share points in the other country, and code-sharing with third-country carriers is now permitted. Furthermore, cargo and charter services are now fully liberalized. The new agreement provides for open designations, open route descriptions, and unrestricted frequencies and service points.

Turkey initialized a civil aviation agreement with the EU on 25 March 2010. The new agreement does not replace existing bilateral agreements between Turkey and individual member states, but aligns them with EU law. A de facto open-sky agreement also exists between Turkey and Germany, due to the large Turkish population living in Germany. The EU Commission maintains that under bilateral agreements signed with member states, Turkey should allow Community air carriers to operate from EU member states to Turkey and not discriminate among them on the basis of nationality. As emphasized above, cabotage in air transport in Turkey is not open to competition from foreign companies.

On the other hand, the Republic of Turkey Ministry for EU Affairs (2014, 2015) points out that preparations are ongoing for aligning the rules and regulations with the EU *acquis* by amending the by-law on general aviation; the by-law on licensing of aeroplane pilots; the by-law regulating requirements for aviation data and aviation information quality; the by-law regulating the requirements for coordinated allocation and use of Mode S Interrogator Codes; the by-law regulating the aeroplane ID requirements in surveillance systems; the by-law regulating the requirements for the performance and the interoperability of surveillance; the by-law on licensing of aeroplane pilots; instructions concerning the rights of and arrangements for disabled persons and persons with reduced mobility; instructions on aligning the legislation on aviation health; instructions on the procedures and principles of commercial air transport operations through aircraft; instructions on the flight duty and rest time of flight crew; instructions on the licensing of helicopter pilots; and instructions laying down requirements on air-ground voice channel spacing. But the National Action Plan did not mention any preparations Turkey is conducting for joining the Single European Sky (SES).

The full harmonization with the EU *acquis* would incorporate Turkey within the SES. In such a case EU carriers would begin to service the Turkish market, including flying between domestic destinations, and Turkish carriers would be able to operate between and within EU countries with no discrimination. This freedom would translate into increased competition in Turkish skies, with ensuing benefits for the Turkish consumer in terms of lower prices and wider consumer choice, as witnessed by the experience in EU countries. Thus, as emphasized by Button (2014), the economic arguments for removing the remaining restrictions on foreign competition are compelling. According to the IATA (2014), 35 to 40 per cent of the value of world trade goods is transported by air. Since air transportation is an intermediate input, reductions in the cost of air transportation via liberalization will get passed down the supply chain, and ultimately benefit consumers. Hence, international competition will reduce the cost of doing business in Turkey, leading to more value-added and employment opportunities. Furthermore, competition may increase the likelihood that airline services will become more responsive to consumer demands.

7.2 Trade Restrictiveness in Transportation Sectors

A high-quality transport infrastructure with major international gateways and corridor infrastructures such as airports, harbours, railways, and highways facilitates economies' participation in international trade. On the other hand, restrictive land, air, and sea transport regulations add to exporters' shipping costs, adversely affecting country competitiveness. Because transport services efficiency can be increased largely through liberalization, it is necessary to quantify barriers to trade in services before designing successful reform strategies.

The simplest approach to measuring barriers to services trade involves using the frequency measures developed by Hoekman (1995).[7] A more elaborate restrictiveness measure has been constructed for different service industries by the Australian Productivity Commission (APC) in collaboration with the University of Adelaide and the Australian National University. To develop these indices, the actual restrictions on trade in a service industry were compiled from specifically designed questionnaires using a number of different sources.[8] These restrictions were then assigned scores and grouped into categories, each of which was assigned a numeric weight. These scores and weights were based on subjective assessments of the costs of restrictions to economic efficiency. Finally, the sectoral indices were computed using these scores and weights. This methodology was later extended by the World Bank and the OECD to obtain services trade restrictiveness indices and indicators of product market regulations. We now turn to examination of these indices and indicators.

---

[7] Hoekman (1995) constructs frequency ratios on the basis of commitments scheduled in the GATS. Concentrating on the four modes of GATS supply, and noting that the WTO's services sectoral classification list (MTN.GNS/W/120) differentiates between 155 non-overlapping service sectors, Hoekman emphasizes that a total of 620 potential commitments exist for each member country. As commitments scheduled in the GATS apply to national treatment and market access separately, there are potentially 1,240 data cells for each member. Commitments were then classified into three categories, and each category was assigned a numerical score, as follows: (i) if no restrictions were applied for a given mode of supply in a given sector ('none' in GATS jargon), a value of 1 was assigned; if no policies were bound for a given mode of supply in a given sector ('unbound' in GATS jargon), a value of 0 was assigned; and if restrictions or limitations were listed for a given mode of supply in a given sector ('bound' in GATS jargon), a value of 0.5 was assigned. The value of these indicators was chosen so as to allow aggregation across sectors and countries. The higher the number, the greater the implied extent of openness-cum-binding. Using these scores, Hoekman calculated three indicators: (i) the number of sector/mode of supply combinations (cells) where a commitment was made (as a share of the maximum possible, 620 for market access and 620 for national treatment); (ii) the 'average coverage' of each schedule of commitments, defined as the arithmetic mean of the scale factors allocated to each cell; and (iii) the share of 'no restriction' commitments in (a) a member's total commitments, and (b) relative to the 155 possible sectors of the classification list. The higher the number, the more 'liberal' service regime the country has.

[8] See, for example, Findlay and Warren (2000).

7.2.1 *The World Bank's Services Trade Restrictions Database*

The World Bank's Services Trade Restrictions Database provides new data on services trade policies across 103 countries, eighteen service sectors from within five broad industries (financial, telecommunications, retailing, transportation, and professional services), and three modes of delivery (cross-border, commercial presence, and presence of natural persons).[9] In this section we concentrate only on the transportation sector.

The database is provided mainly from the perspective of a foreign supplier who wishes to provide services in a particular country, and it focuses on policy measures that discriminate against foreign services or service providers. The questionnaire that the database draws upon is based on questionnaires used in the context of WTO services negotiations, and related work at institutions such as the Australian Productivity Commission and the OECD.[10] The set of standardized policy measures with regard to mode 3 is divided into four broad categories: (i) legal form of entry and restrictions on foreign equity, (ii) licensing limits and transparency of licensing requirements, (iii) restrictions on operations, and (iv) relevant aspects of the regulatory environment.

7.2.1.1 ROAD TRANSPORT

The questionnaire on which the database for road transportation services was based distinguishes between four ways of establishing a commercial presence: (i) establishing a new branch, (ii) establishing a new subsidiary, (iii) acquiring an existing private company, and (iv) acquiring an existing publicly owned company in the event of privatization.[11] All of the questions in the questionnaire on road transport concern mode 3.

In the case of Turkey, foreign (domestic) firms are allowed to enter the road transport market as a branch, as a locally incorporated subsidiary, or by acquiring part or all of a private local firm. In the case of a greenfield subsidiary and acquiring a domestic private entity by a single foreign entity or by a group of entities, the maximum ownership allowed is 100 per cent, and in the case of acquiring a domestic private entity, securing a controlling stake is allowed.[12] Acquiring an existing publicly owned company is also allowed, but the

---

[9] Qualitative and quantitative information on the Services Trade Restrictions Database is available at http://iresearch.worldbank.org/servicetrade/ (accessed 9 February 2016). A detailed account of the database is provided in Borchert et al. (2012a) and Borchert et al. (2012b).

[10] See OECD (2009), Kalinova et al. (2010), and Findlay and Warren (2000).

[11] See 'Survey on Impediments to International Integration' available at World Bank's Services Trade Restrictions Database at http://iresearch.worldbank.org/servicetrade/WB_Survey_Services_Version_2010.pdf (accessed 9 February 2016) to examine the questions asked in the questionnaire.

[12] Note that a greenfield investment is a cross border investment where the parent firm builds from scratch and fully owns its subsidiary, and hence a greenfield subsidiary is the subsidiary resulting from greenfield investment.

provisions of the privatization process will state the conditions of maximum foreign ownership. Joint ventures are allowed, with a foreign company authorized to hold a controlling stake, and maximum ownership in a joint venture by a single foreign entity or by a group of entities is 100 per cent. To enter the market, the entities must acquire licenses. Although there are no limits on the number of licenses that can be issued, the MoTMC is entitled to limit the number of licenses according to supply-and-demand conditions, capacity, and security. The criteria for license allocation are not specified. A license is granted for five years, and license renewal is required and not automatic. The issuing authority is required by law to inform applicants for initial or renewal licenses on decisions regarding the application within a certain number of days after receiving the application. The authority is obliged to inform applicants of the reasons for rejecting a license. Regarding operation conditions, we note that there are no nationality requirements for employees or boards of directors; and the number of national employees and national board members could be zero. Furthermore, there are no domestic residency requirements for boards of directors. In addition, there are no restrictions on repatriating earnings in the case of foreign firms. According to Turkish regulations, there is a regulatory authority for the sector but the authority is not independent from the sector ministry, and prior notice of regulatory changes to firms is not required. Finally, there is a right of appeal of regulatory decisions.

7.2.1.2 RAIL TRANSPORT

The rail transportation services questionnaire was identical to the road transportation questionnaire except that the first question was expanded. While the original question was stated as: 'Is entry of firms with foreign ownership and/or control allowed?', the additional questions concern the separation between the network operator and a service provider. If there is no separation, the questionnaire asks whether the network operator can lease part of the network to private and/or foreign service providers. If there is separation, the questionnaire asks whether the network operator is private, inquires about the number of service providers, and queries the number of foreign service providers in the sector. All the questions in the rail questionnaire again concern mode 3.

When the Services Trade Restrictions Database was prepared by the World Bank, the Turkish Rail Liberalization Law of 1 May 2013 had not yet been passed. At that time, the state-owned TCDD was, by law, the monopoly provider of railway passenger and cargo transportation. Hence, the World Bank database states that in Turkey rail freight services cannot be provided by private entities. Since greenfield investment in domestic rail freight as a branch or subsidiary, and entry into the sector through acquisition and joint venture were not allowed, all questions in the rail questionnaire were not applicable.

7.2.1.3 MARITIME TRANSPORT

The maritime transportation services questionnaire distinguished between 'international maritime shipping services' and 'maritime auxiliary services'. In each case, the questions on entry and establishing a commercial presence as well as on obtaining a license were similar to the questions in the road transportation survey. Regarding regulation of the sector and operating conditions, the survey distinguished between maritime transport and maritime auxiliary services. Again, the questions were similar to those for road transportation. Finally, the maritime questionnaire had a section on Maritime Shipping Services: Cross Border, which did not exist in the questionnaire on road transport services. Thus, the maritime questionnaire considers issues related to mode 1 as well as mode 3.

The World Bank database reveals that in Turkey, market entry is allowed for international maritime shipping services. For liner and bulk shipping there are no quotas for private and government cargoes. Exemptions of carrier agreements from competition law have not been granted. Foreign firms are allowed to enter the market as a branch, as a locally incorporated subsidiary, by acquiring part or all of a private local firm, or by acquiring part or all of a public local firm. In the case of greenfield subsidiaries and acquiring domestic private entities by a single foreign entity or by a group of entities, the maximum ownership allowed is 100 per cent, and thus in both cases, acquiring a controlling stake is allowed. When a foreign firm acquires a public entity, the provisions of the privatization process will state the conditions of maximum foreign ownership. Joint ventures are allowed in Turkey, and holding a majority stake in such cases is authorized. The country authorizes up to 100 per cent participation in joint ventures by a single entity or group of entities, and acquiring a controlling stake in both cases is allowed. When a foreign firm acquires part or all of a local firm, a license is required. Ship agencies need to obtain a work permission certificate and a certificate of authorization, which is automatically renewed after five years. The licensing criteria are publicly available, and there are no differences in the criteria for foreign or domestic applicants. There are also no limits on the number of licenses available. Regarding operation conditions, we note that there are no nationality requirements for employees (the minimum number could be zero), but there are nationality requirements for boards of directors. Furthermore, there are no domestic residency requirements for boards of directors, and there are no restrictions on repatriating earnings for foreign firms. There is a regulatory authority for the sector, which is not independent from the sector ministry. Prior notice of regulatory changes to firms is not required, and there is a right of appeal of regulatory decisions.

In the case of maritime auxiliary services, foreign firms are allowed to enter the market. Some Turkish ports have been privatized, and in some ports private sector entry is not allowed and in some ports it is. The scope of permissible activities depends on the port. In the case of greenfield investments, foreign firms are allowed to enter the market as a branch, as a subsidiary, or by acquiring part or all of a private local firm. In the case of subsidiaries and acquiring a domestic private entity by a single foreign entity or by a group of entities, the maximum ownership allowed is 100 per cent, thus acquiring a controlling stake is allowed. Joint ventures are allowed in Turkey, and in such cases, foreign companies holding a majority stake is authorized. Since Turkey authorizes 100 per cent participation in the case of a single entity as well as by a group of entities, acquiring a controlling stake in both cases is allowed. When a foreign firm acquires part or all of a local firm a license is required. However, ship agencies also need to obtain a work permission certificate and a certificate of authorization, which is automatically renewed after five years. The licensing criteria are publicly available, and there is no difference in the criteria between foreign and domestic applicants. There are no limits on the number of licenses available. Regarding operation conditions, we note that there are no nationality requirements for employees, but there are for boards of directors. The minimum percentage, the number of national employees, and the number of domestic residents on boards of directors are zero, and there are no domestic residency requirements for boards of directors. Finally, there are no restrictions on repatriating earnings for foreign firms. There is a regulatory authority for the sector, which is not independent from the sector ministry. Prior notice of regulatory changes to firms is not required, and there is a right of appeal of regulatory decisions.

Maritime cargo handling at the main ports of ships owned by Turkish nationals and of other ships; using container stations/depots of ships owned by Turkish nationals and of other ships at main ports; maritime agency services of ships owned by Turkish nationals and of other ships at main ports; and freight forwarding of ships owned by Turkish nationals and of other ships by foreign firms are allowed. On the other hand, storage/warehousing of ships owned by Turkish nationals and of other ships at main ports as well as customs clearance of ships owned by Turkish nationals and of other ships at main ports can only be done by Turkish firms. There is a regulatory authority for the sector, which is not independent from the sector ministry. Prior notice of regulatory changes to firms is not required, and there is a right of appeal of regulatory decisions.

7.2.1.4 AIR TRANSPORT SERVICES

The questionnaire on air transport services distinguished between domestic and international air transport services. In the case of international (domestic) air passenger services, domestic and foreign firms are allowed to enter the air transport market as either locally incorporated subsidiaries or by acquiring part of a local private firm. Thus, in the case of greenfield investments, opening a branch is not allowed, but opening a subsidiary or acquiring a domestic private entity by a single entity or by a group of entities is allowed. In those cases, maximum ownership allowed for foreign firms is 49 per cent, and the acquisition of a controlling stake by foreign companies is not allowed; a foreign company must be established as a joint stock company. Acquiring an existing domestic publicly owned company by a single foreign entity or by a group of entities is allowed, but a foreign firm is required again to be established as a joint stock company. Joint ventures are allowed, and in those cases the foreign company is required to be established as a joint stock company. Holding a controlling stake is not authorized, and maximum ownership in a joint venture by a single foreign entity or by a group of foreign entities is 49 per cent. To enter the market, the entities must acquire licenses. There are no limits on the number of licenses and the licensing criteria are publicly available. Licensing is not automatic even if the publicly available criteria are fulfilled, and there are no differences in licensing criteria for foreign and domestic applicants. The license is granted for one year. License renewal is required, and the license can be renewed for a maximum three-year period, but renewal is not automatic. The issuing authority is not required by law to provide a licensing decision within a certain time frame, but it is obliged to inform applicants of the reason(s) for rejecting a license. Regarding operation conditions, we note that there are nationality requirements for employees and for boards of directors, and there are no domestic residency requirements for boards of directors. The minimum number of domestic residents on a board of directors is zero. Finally, there are no restrictions on repatriating earnings in the case of foreign firms. There is a regulatory authority for the sector but it is not independent from the sector ministry, and prior notice to firms of regulatory changes is not required. Finally, we note that there is a right of appeal of regulatory decisions.

7.2.1.5 ASSESSMENT OF POLICY REGIMES

Borchert et al. (2012a) assess policy regimes for each sub-sector mode and classifies them into five broad categories: completely open (no restrictions at all); completely closed (no entry allowed at all); virtually open but with minor restrictions; virtually closed but with very limited opportunities to enter and operate; and allowing entry and operations but imposing restrictions that are neither trivial nor stringent. The five regimes are assigned values on an openness scale from 0 to 100, with intervals of 25. Policy measures are divided into two tiers. The first-tier measures include those that affect market entry decisions most significantly, such as a limit on foreign ownership and the number of licenses, and the second-tier measures include those that affect operations of service providers, such as restrictions on the repatriation of earnings. Note that second-tier measures do not contribute to overall restrictiveness when first-tier measures are prohibitive. On the other hand, if first-tier measures are not prohibitive then second-tier measures are considered in determining the overall restrictiveness score. This quantification method is called the Services Trade Restrictions Index. Thus, the index focuses on measures that discriminate against foreign services and providers, and in the absence of any discriminatory measures, the index takes the value of 0, which is associated with the greatest level of openness.

Given the questionnaire results on, for example, road transportation, Borchert et al. (2012a) select first the policy measures that go into building the Services Trade Restrictions Indices for each sub-sector mode combination. For each sub-sector mode they focus on measures that affect the entry and operation of foreign entities most significantly. Next, by consulting private sector representatives in the related countries, they determine the level of restrictiveness of different measures by assigning values from 0 to 100 in intervals of 25.

Table 7.3 shows the trade restrictiveness index scores for Turkey's transport sub-sectors. The table reveals that while the domestic rail freight sector (with a score of 100) is completely closed, the domestic road freight sector (with a score of 0) is completely open. While the score of international maritime shipping is 0 for mode 1, it is 25 for mode 3. On the other hand, the score of maritime auxiliary services is 25. The score of domestic air passenger services is 50 for mode 3, and the score of international air passenger services is 25 in the case of mode 1 and 50 in the case of mode 3.

Table 7.3 Services Trade Restrictions Index

	Overall	Mode 1	Mode 3
Air passenger domestic			50
Air passenger international	32.5	25	50
Maritime shipping international	7.5	0	25
Maritime auxiliary services	25		25
Road freight domestic	0		0
Rail freight domestic	100		100

Source: World Bank's Services Trade Restrictions Database available at the website http://iresearch.worldbank.org/servicetrade (accessed 8 February 2016).

7.2.2 *The OECD's Services Trade Restrictiveness Index Project*

The OECD's Services Trade Restrictiveness Index (STRI) project has two distinct but complementary instruments: a services trade regulatory database and a services trade restrictiveness index. The database is a resource providing internationally comparable current information on regulatory policies affecting trade in services, and the data are presented across forty countries (thirty-four OECD members as well as Brazil, the People's Republic of China, India, Indonesia, the Russian Federation, and South Africa) and eighteen services sectors from eight broad sectors (computer services, construction, professional services, telecommunications, transport, distribution, audiovisual services, and financial services). In the following we concentrate only on the transport sector.

The measures included in the services trade regulatory database for transport services have been divided into five categories: restrictions on foreign market entry; restrictions on the movement of people; other discriminatory measures and international standards; barriers to competition and public ownership; and regulatory transparency and administrative requirements. While *restrictions on foreign entry* contains barriers to foreign ownership, nationality, and residency requirements for boards of directors, quotas regarding the number of firms permitted to practice, and conditions regarding transfer of capital, *restrictions on the movement of people* includes measures affecting the movement of labour, market tests, and durations of stay for different categories of providers. *Other discriminatory measures and international standards* take the form of discrimination between national and foreign providers, discriminatory taxes and subsidies, government procurement, imposition of national standards that may deviate from international ones, and regulation of fares and tariffs. *Barriers to competition and public ownership* reveals discriminatory measures where foreign suppliers' rights are considered inferior to those of local companies, and where state-owned enterprise privileges may put foreign entrants at a competitive disadvantage. The criteria also contain measures relating to the regulation of dominant firms to ensure market access for new entrants, including foreign firms. Finally, *regulatory transparency and administrative requirements* include measures relating to the timely publication of regulations, availability of single contract points and a period for comments on draft regulations, time necessary to obtain a visa, and costs related to registering a company. Thus, the first three categories cover measures related to market access and national treatment, the fourth entails information on the lack or availability of pro-competitive regulation, and the fifth category provides information on administrative procedures.

The services trade regulatory database records policy measures applied on a most-favoured-nation (MFN) basis, records the level of openness toward third countries, and in general does not take into account preferential agreements. The database documents the source by law, regulation, rule, or administrative decision. Each measure has been verified with the country under consideration and peer reviewed by other countries.

7.2.2.1 RESTRICTIONS ON FOREIGN ENTRY

The Services Trade Restrictiveness Index Regulatory Database is the main source of information for derivation of the STRI.[13] Analysis of the database reveals that the requirements on foreign ownership, licensing, nationality, and residency for boards of directors, and conditions regarding transfer of capital, are similar to those considered under the World Banks' Services Trade Restrictions Database. Therefore there is no need to repeat those arguments.

Under *restrictions on foreign entry* in the case of road transport services there is no need for foreign investors to show net economic benefits, no need to have approvals unless contrary to national interest, no need for notification, and no restrictions placed on cross-border mergers and acquisitions. On the other hand, in the case of rail services, provision is not reserved for statutory monopolies and is not granted on an exclusive basis. While access rights for domestic rail transport are not provided to foreign firms, transit rights for international rail transport, access rights for international combined transport, and access rights for international rail transport are provided to foreign firms. We note that commercial presence is required in order to provide rail freight transport.

In the case of maritime transport, Turkey does not have a unilateral/pluri-lateral cargo reservation system, nor any other cargo reservations and preferential schemes, and Turkey is not party to any bilateral/pluri-lateral cargo-sharing agreements. Furthermore, no preference is given to government cargo. In addition, feedering and repositioning of equipment is not allowed, there is no monopoly on port services, there are no restrictions on the type of vessel, no restrictions on the type and quantity of cargo transported, and no restrictions on vessel chartering. But foreign-flagged ships are excluded from cabotage and there are restrictions on establishing and operating representative offices. Finally, in the case of air transport note that the Eighth and Ninth Freedoms of the Air are not granted by Turkey in any one of the bilateral agreements.[14]

---

[13] The Services Trade Restrictiveness Index Regulatory Database is available at http://qdd.oecd. org/subject.aspx?Subject=063bee63-475f-427c-8b50-c19bffa7392d (accessed 7 January 2016).
[14] The eighth freedom (consecutive cabotage) refers to the right or privilege, in respect to scheduled international air services, of transporting cabotage traffic between two points in the territory of the granting party for a service that originates or terminates in the home country of the foreign carrier or (in connection with seventh freedom) outside the territory of the granting party. The ninth freedom (stand-alone cabotage) refers to the right or privilege of transporting cabotage traffic of the granting party for a service performed entirely within the territory of the granting party.

7.2.2.2 RESTRICTIONS TO MOVEMENT OF PEOPLE

No quotas are imposed by Turkey on contractual service suppliers, or independent service suppliers, nor are these workers required to take labour market tests. Turkey does, however, impose a limitation on duration of stay to twelve months for such workers.

7.2.2.3 OTHER DISCRIMINATORY MEASURES

Foreign suppliers are not treated less favourably regarding taxes and eligibility for subsidies. In public procurement, explicit access discrimination favours local firms, but the public procurement process does not skew the conditions of competition in favour of local firms.

In the case of maritime transport, the public procurement process does not affect the conditions of competition in favour of local firms for domestic and international traffic. There are no formal requirements to consider international standards/rules before setting new domestic standards. In Turkey, national standards do not deviate from international standards. Turkey does not impose discriminatory access requirements to port services and installations, nor any discriminatory port tariffs or other port-related tariffs, or any discriminatory environmental and/or security standards. Finally, note that the country imposes obligations to use local maritime and port services.

In the cases of road and air transportation, national standards do not deviate from international standards. In the case of rail transport, however, while discriminatory criteria are not imposed for issuing licenses, interoperability/interlinking is required.

7.2.2.4 BARRIERS TO COMPETITION

In Turkey, the government controls at least one major firm in rail transport and air transport, but does not do so in road and maritime transport. There are minimum capital requirements in all the four transport sub-sectors, and publicly controlled firms are not subject to an exclusion or exemption from the general competition law. Finally, we note that available appeal procedures in domestic regulatory systems are also open to affected foreign parties.

In the road freight transport sector, the government provides pricing guidelines, freight carriers are required to file tariffs, retail prices of road freight services are regulated, but industry representatives are not involved in setting entry and pricing regulations.

In the rail sector, competitive entry/exit is allowed, but rail rates are regulated, and the publication and filing of rail rates are required. The country imposes obligations on the level of services to be provided. Running rights are mandated, confidential contracts are allowed, terminal running rights are in place, the rates for terminal running rights are regulated, interswitching is mandated, interswitching rates are regulated, and bottleneck services are regulated. Although vertical separation is required, there is no monopoly on infrastructure, and hence there is no market dominance. Access to railway infrastructure is mandated at the national level, and access fees are regulated. Access capacity is not regulated, transfer infrastructure capacity trading is not prohibited, access fees and conditions are not developed in advance, nor are they made public in advance. Functions relating to infrastructure access are provided by rail firms. Transfer of public funds between services and infrastructure management activities is not prohibited and independence of infrastructure managers is not required. Track access for supply of services to terminals is not required.[15] Finally, note that a dispute resolution mechanism is available, that the government can overrule the decision of the regulator, and that decisions of the infrastructure manager can be appealed.

In the maritime sector, price fixing or quantity regulations are not allowed, and there are no restrictions on container-station and depot services. In the case of shipping agreements, the right of independent action is not mandated, and confidential service contracts are not mandated. Although there is no obligation to use a local maritime port agent, there is an obligation to use local tug and tow services, and there are restrictions on cargo handling, but there are no restrictions on storage and warehouse services. Finally, there are no restrictions on sales, marketing, or organizing the ship's call.

In the air transport sector, there is no price regulation for domestic use. Contracts for universal service obligations are not awarded through competitive bidding. Slot trading is not allowed, and there are no schedules for airport use. Finally, note that air carrier alliances are not exempt from competition law.

7.2.2.5 REGULATORY TRANSPARENCY

In Turkey, public comment procedures are open to interested persons including foreign suppliers, but regulations are not communicated to the public prior to entry into force. While registering a company takes six business days, the cost to complete all official procedures for registering a company amounts to 12.7 per cent of the income per capita. It takes about two days for customs clearance, and visa processing time amounts to one business day.

7.2.2.6 ASSESSMENT OF POLICY REGIMES

The information provided in the OECD's services trade regulatory database summarized above for Turkish transport services is qualitative. To make

---

[15] Note that as of the beginning of 2015 Turkey, as indicated previously, has not published yet the by-laws on Allocating Railway Infrastructure Capacity and Levying Charges for Using Railway Infrastructure, Rail Safety, Licensing, and Interoperability. Hence, it is difficult to foresee how the final by-laws that will be published in the *Official Gazette* will look like.

comparisons between sectors and between countries the information needs to be translated into quantitative measures. This is achieved by aggregating regulations that are potentially trade restricting into a composite measure of restrictiveness. The OECD's Services Trade Restrictiveness Index Regulatory Database consists of mainly Yes/No questions. Hence, it is easy to assign for each type of impediment a score of 0 or 1, with 0 representing the absence of restrictions and 1 the presence of restrictions. On the other hand, information given in percentages (such as limits on foreign equity) are transformed into binary variables by introducing multiple thresholds.[16]

Having transformed the qualitative database into a quantitative one, the OECD uses an elaborate scoring and weighting mechanism to derive its STRI. Each measure is assigned a weight within the category it belongs to, such as *barriers to competition*. The next step involves aggregation into the overall STRI. A number of weighting schemes have been explored to develop the STRI, including equal weights, expert judgement, and random weights. The weighting scheme used for the calculation relies on expert judgement,[17] with the STRIs calculated by taking the weighted average of the scores. The composite indices quantifying restrictions across five standard categories vary between 0 and 1. Complete openness to trade gives a score of 0 and being completely closed to foreign service providers yields a score of 1. Furthermore, note that, as emphasized by the OECD (2014), a sector score of 0.1 is significant, and scores between 0.2 and 0.3 represent quite significant restrictions on international trade.

Table 7.4 shows the trade restrictiveness index scores for the transport sub-sectors in Turkey. The table reveals that the road transport sector is moderately restrictive, with an average STRI index of 0.18. According to Grosso et al. (2014), the most restrictive sector in Turkey is air transport, with an average STRI value of 0.45, while significant restrictions are present in the maritime and rail transport sectors, both with average STRI scores of 0.32.

---

[16] Grosso et al. (2014) emphasize that the restrictiveness of an equity limit of 49 per cent compared to a limit of 70 per cent is captured by introducing multiple thresholds. For foreign equity the thresholds are lower than 33 per cent, lower than 50 per cent, and lower than 100 per cent. A country with a limit of 49 per cent will receive a score of 1 on the lower-than-50-per-cent threshold as well as on the lower-than-100-per-cent threshold, while a country with a limit of 70 per cent will receive a score of 1 on the lower-than-100-per-cent threshold.

[17] As explained by the OECD (2009), a large number of experts were asked to allocate 100 points among the five policy areas presented above. Those points were translated into weights by assigning weight experts to the policy area to calculate each measure that falls under it and correct for differences in the number of measures under the policy areas.

Table 7.4 Index values for Turkey by policy area

	Restriction on foreign entry	Restriction to movement of people	Other discriminatory measures	Barriers to competition	Regulatory transparency	Overall indicator
Road transport	0.07	0.03	0.02	0.04	0.01	0.18
Rail transport	0.03	0.02	0.02	0.21	0.04	0.32
Maritime transport	0.2	0.04	0.03	0.04	0.02	0.32
Air transport	0.25	0.01	0.03	0.13	0.02	0.45

Source: Grosso et al. (2014).

7.2.3 Indicators of the OECD's Product Market Regulations

Since the 1990s, the OECD has been constructing a system of indicators to measure ongoing developments in product market regulation (PMR) across OECD countries. The OECD publishes two kinds of indicators: an economy-wide PMR indicator and sectoral indicators covering several non-manufacturing sectors, called non-market regulation (NMR) indicators. The economy-wide PMR covers general regulatory issues in the fields of public ownership, involvement in business operations, complexity of regulatory procedures, regulatory protection of incumbents, explicit barriers to trade and investment, and other barriers to trade and investment. This information is grouped first into the broad domains of *state control, barriers to entrepreneurship* and *barriers to trade and investment,* and thereafter into the overall PMR indicator, which was computed for the years 1998, 2003, 2008, and 2013. The NMR indicators cover network industries such as energy, transport, and communication, as well as retail trade and professional services. In the following we are only concerned with the indicators developed for the transport sector.

As indicated by Wölfl et al. (2009), the PMR indicators are based on a large amount of information on regulatory structures and policies that is collected through a questionnaire sent to OECD governments and to selected non-OECD governments.[18] The questions can either be answered with numerical values or by selecting an answer from a pre-defined set of menu options. The qualitative information is transformed into quantitative information by assigning a numerical value to each possible response to a given question. The coded information is then normalized over a 0-to-6 scale, where a lower value reflects a more competition-friendly regulatory stance. Table 7.5 shows the PMR indicators for the Turkish road, rail, and air transport sectors between 1975 and 2013.

---

[18] For the latest version of the questionnaire, see OECD (2012).

Table 7.5 Indicators of Product Market Regulation

	Road			Rail					Airlines		
	Overall	Entry	Prices	Overall	Entry	Public ownership	Vertical integration	Market structure	Overall	Entry barriers	Public ownership
1975	3.00	6.00	0.00	6.00	6.00	6.00	6.00	6.00	6.00	6.00	6.00
1976	3.00	6.00	0.00	6.00	6.00	6.00	6.00	6.00	6.00	6.00	6.00
1977	3.00	6.00	0.00	6.00	6.00	6.00	6.00	6.00	6.00	6.00	6.00
1978	3.00	6.00	0.00	6.00	6.00	6.00	6.00	6.00	6.00	6.00	6.00
1979	3.00	6.00	0.00	6.00	6.00	6.00	6.00	6.00	6.00	6.00	6.00
1980	3.00	6.00	0.00	6.00	6.00	6.00	6.00	6.00	6.00	6.00	6.00
1981	3.00	6.00	0.00	6.00	6.00	6.00	6.00	6.00	6.00	6.00	6.00
1982	3.00	6.00	0.00	6.00	6.00	6.00	6.00	6.00	6.00	6.00	6.00
1983	3.00	6.00	0.00	6.00	6.00	6.00	6.00	6.00	6.00	6.00	6.00
1984	3.00	6.00	0.00	6.00	6.00	6.00	6.00	6.00	6.00	6.00	6.00
1985	3.00	6.00	0.00	6.00	6.00	6.00	6.00	6.00	6.00	6.00	6.00
1986	3.00	6.00	0.00	6.00	6.00	6.00	6.00	6.00	6.00	6.00	6.00
1987	3.00	6.00	0.00	6.00	6.00	6.00	6.00	6.00	6.00	6.00	6.00
1988	3.00	6.00	0.00	6.00	6.00	6.00	6.00	6.00	6.00	6.00	6.00
1989	3.00	6.00	0.00	6.00	6.00	6.00	6.00	6.00	6.00	6.00	6.00
1990	3.00	6.00	0.00	6.00	6.00	6.00	6.00	6.00	6.00	6.00	6.00
1991	3.00	6.00	0.00	6.00	6.00	6.00	6.00	6.00	5.94	6.00	5.88
1992	3.00	6.00	0.00	6.00	6.00	6.00	6.00	6.00	5.94	6.00	5.88

Year										
1993	3.00	6.00	0.00	6.00	6.00	6.00	6.00	5.94	6.00	5.88
1994	3.00	6.00	0.00	6.00	6.00	6.00	6.00	5.94	6.00	5.88
1995	3.00	6.00	0.00	6.00	6.00	6.00	6.00	5.94	6.00	5.88
1996	3.00	6.00	0.00	6.00	6.00	6.00	6.00	5.94	6.00	5.88
1997	3.00	6.00	0.00	6.00	6.00	6.00	6.00	5.94	6.00	5.88
1998	0.00	0.00	0.00	6.00	6.00	6.00	6.00	5.94	6.00	5.88
1999	1.00	2.00	0.00	6.00	6.00	6.00	6.00	5.94	6.00	5.88
2000	1.00	2.00	0.00	6.00	6.00	6.00	6.00	4.94	4.00	5.88
2001	2.00	4.00	0.00	6.00	6.00	6.00	6.00	3.94	2.00	5.88
2002	2.00	4.00	0.00	6.00	6.00	6.00	6.00	3.94	2.00	5.88
2003	2.25	4.50	0.00	6.00	6.00	6.00	6.00	3.95	2.00	5.89
2004	3.25	4.50	2.00	6.00	6.00	6.00	6.00	3.95	2.00	5.89
2005	4.00	6.00	2.00	6.00	6.00	6.00	6.00	3.26	2.00	4.51
2006	4.00	6.00	2.00	6.00	6.00	6.00	6.00	2.47	2.00	2.95
2007	4.00	6.00	2.00	6.00	6.00	6.00	6.00	2.47	2.00	2.95
2008	4.00	6.00	2.00	6.00	6.00	6.00	6.00	2.47	2.00	2.95
2009	4.00	6.00	2.00	6.00	6.00	6.00	6.00	2.47	2.00	2.95
2010	4.00	6.00	2.00	6.00	6.00	6.00	6.00	2.47	2.00	2.95
2011	3.25	4.50	2.00	6.00	6.00	6.00	6.00	2.47	2.00	2.95
2012	3.25	4.50	2.00	6.00	6.00	6.00	6.00	2.47	2.00	2.95
2013	4.00	6.00	2.00	6.00	6.00	6.00	6.00	2.47	2.00	2.95

Source: Indicators of Product Market Regulation website, OECD, http://www.oecd.org/economy/growth/indicatorsofproductmarketregulationhomepage.htm (accessed 8 February 2016).

7.3 Quantification of Policy Restrictiveness in Turkish Transport Sectors

The World Bank's Services Trade Restrictions Database, OECD's Services Trade Restrictiveness Index and OECD's Product Market Regulation Indicators provide information that is useful for comparing trade restrictiveness across countries, over time, and across sectors. The indices can help identify which policy measures restrict trade and help governments identify best practices relative to global practices. Policymakers can then focus reform efforts on priority sectors and measures. But at this stage the indices cannot be used to measure the impact of changes in regulations on different economic variables in the economy. Such an analysis will require first the determination of tariff equivalents in different transport sectors and second the determination of the effects of policy reforms using generally computable general equilibrium models. Since the determination of tariff equivalents in different transport sectors can be studied using the gravity model, we turn to the discussion of the gravity model.

The *gravity equation* in international trade, deriving its name from Newton's Law of Gravitation, specifies that the flow of commodities from one country to another is related multiplicatively to the product of the economic sizes of two countries and the distance between the economic centres of the two countries. The model has been used intensively in empirical models of bilateral trade flows since Tinbergen's (1962) seminal work. The popularity of the gravity equation, stemming from its empirical success, led to interest in formal theoretical economic foundations for it. A review of the existing theoretical literature on the gravity equation is provided by Anderson and van Wincoop (2003, 2004).

Using a model based on product differentiation with a constant elasticity of substitution (CES) specification of within-class expenditure shares, Anderson and van Wincoop (2004) show that in the context of a world of Z countries the gravity equation takes the form:

$$x_{ij}^k = \frac{Y_i^k \, e_j^k}{Y^k} \left(\frac{t_{ij}^k}{\Pi_i^k \, p_j^k} \right)^{1-\sigma_k} \tag{4a}$$

$$(\Pi_i^k)^{1-\sigma_k} = \sum_{j=1}^{Z} \left\{ \frac{t_{ij}^k}{p_j^k} \right\}^{1-\sigma_k} \frac{e_j^k}{Y^k} \tag{4b}$$

$$(P_j^k)^{1-\sigma_k} = \sum_{i=1}^{Z} \left\{ \frac{t_{ij}^k}{\Pi_i^k} \right\}^{1-\sigma_k} \frac{Y_i^k}{Y^k}, \tag{4c}$$

where x_{ij}^k denotes the bilateral trade flow between the exporting country i and the importing country j in industry k, Y_i^k is the output of exporting country i in industry k, e_j^k is the expenditure of importing country j on industry k, $Y^k = \sum_{i=1}^{z} Y_i^k$ is the global output of industry k, $t_{ij}^k - 1$ is the ad valorem tax equivalent of trade costs associated with exporting commodity k from country i to country j, Π_i^k is the average outward multilateral resistance term, P_j^k is the average inward multilateral resistance term, and σ_k is the constant elasticity of substitution in industry k. Note that Π_i^k captures the fact that exports from country i to country j depend on trade costs across all possible export markets, and P_j^k captures the dependence of imports into country i from country j on trade costs across all possible suppliers. Thus, the model picks up the fact that changes in trade costs on one bilateral route can affect trade flows on all other routes because of relative price effects.

Since the variables Π_i^k and P_j^k are unobservable because they do not correspond to any price indices collected by national statistical agencies, we write the domestic trade flows in country i for industry k goods following Chen and Novy's (2011) approach:

$$x_{ii}^k = \frac{Y_i^k \, e_i^k}{Y^k} \left(\frac{t_{ii}^k}{\Pi_i^k p_i^k} \right)^{1 - \sigma_k},$$

where t_{ii}^k denotes the domestic trade costs such as transportation for industry-k goods. Solving this equation for the product of average outward trade barrier and average inward trade barrier, we get:

$$\Pi_i^k P_i^k = \left(\frac{Y_i^k e_i^k}{x_{ii}^k Y^k} \right)^{\frac{1}{1 - \sigma_k}} t_{ii}^k. \tag{5}$$

Next, we multiply the gravity equation (4a) for x_{ij}^k by the corresponding gravity equation for trade flows in the opposite direction x_{ji}^k to obtain the equation:

$$x_{ij}^k \, x_{ji}^k = x_{ii}^k \, x_{jj}^k \left(\frac{t_{ij}^k \, t_{ji}^k}{t_{ii}^k \, t_{jj}^k} \right)^{1 - \sigma_k}.$$

Solving for the trade cost factors we obtain:

$$\frac{t_{ij}^k \, t_{ji}^k}{t_{ii}^k \, t_{jj}^k} = \left(\frac{x_{ii}^k \, x_{jj}^k}{x_{ij}^k \, x_{ji}^k} \right)^{\frac{1}{\sigma_k - 1}}.$$

Chen and Novy (2011) next define the variable as:

$$\theta_{ij}^k = \left(\frac{t_{ij}^k \, t_{ji}^k}{t_{ii}^k \, t_{jj}^k} \right)^{\frac{1}{2}} = \left(\frac{x_{ii}^k \, x_{jj}^k}{x_{ij}^k \, x_{ji}^k} \right)^{\frac{1}{2(\sigma_k - 1)}}, \tag{6}$$

as a micro-founded measure of bilateral industry specific trade frictions. The measure reveals that as long as the two countries trade more with each other so that $x_{ij}^k x_{ji}^k$ is large, then the measure of relative trade frictions will be low. On the other hand, if the two countries trade more domestically so that $x_{ii}^k x_{jj}^k$ is large, then the measure of relative trade frictions will be high. Equation (6) can be used to estimate the trade costs using trade flow data. The tariff equivalent of bilateral trade costs from here on is easy to obtain by deducting 1 from θ_{ij}^k:

$$T_{ij}^k = \theta_{ij}^k - 1.$$

Note that the precise estimate of the level of trade cost T_{ij}^k for commodity k exported from country i to country j depends, among other factors, on the value of the elasticity of substitution σ_k. While Park (2002) and Fontagne et al. (2011) use the value of 5.6 for service sectors, Walsh (2006) assumes that the value of elasticity of substitution is 1.95, and Novy (2013) and Arvis et al. (2013) use the value of 8 for the elasticity of substitution. Anderson and Wincoop (2004) survey estimates the value of σ_k, and they conclude that it typically falls in the range of 5 to 10. In the following, we use Novy (2013) and Arvis et al.'s (2013) measures and set the elasticity of substitution σ_k for the commodities under consideration as equal to 8, which according to Arvis et al. (2013), represents about the mid-point of available estimates.

In the estimation of trade costs we use the dataset provided by the Global Trade Analysis Project (GTAP) for the year 2007 in the GTAP 8 Data Base. The database provides data for fifty-seven commodities, such as textile and machinery. In the following, we concentrate on service sectors only, and in particular on transportation services. The GTAP 8 Data Base divides transportation services into land transport (Sector 48 of GTAP 8 Data Base), water transport (Sector 49 of GTAP 8 Data Base), and air transport (Sector 50 of GTAP 8 Data Base). The database provides data for 129 GTAP regions, such as Germany, Turkey, and the US. Thus, we have data on bilateral trade flows for each of the transport sectors k among the 129 regions. The data allow us to determine the values of bilateral trade flows x_{ij}^k and x_{ji}^k (i = 1, ..., 129; j = 1, ..., 129; k = 48, 49, 50). The GTAP 8 Data Base also has information on the values of domestic demand x_{ii}^k (i = 1, ..., 129; k = 48, 49, 50), defined for commodity k as the sum of intermediate demand, consumption demand (public and private), and investment demand (public and private) minus the value of imports.

To analyse the effects of trade liberalization in transportation services we consider three scenarios, namely unilateral liberalization, liberalization within a regional context, and liberalization within multilateral context.

During the last two decades there has been significant unilateral liberalization in service sectors by different countries, driven by the prospects of large welfare gains. Many countries have taken action to increase competition in service markets by liberalizing FDI and privatizing state-owned or controlled service providers. But such liberalization may be constrained as emphasized in Chapter 1 by the fact that a country cannot on its own gain improved access to larger foreign markets, and to derive efficiency gains the country must implement and follow appropriate competition policies, appropriate domestic regulations, and good governance. However, under unilateral liberalization the country may have difficulty in increasing competition, and may also lack the expertise and resources to devise and implement the appropriate domestic regulatory policies.

On the other hand, the multilateral approach to services liberalization under GATS may lead not only to efficiency gains but also to improved access to larger foreign markets, and to a reduction in compliance costs. In fact, multilateral negotiations on services began during the Uruguay Round of the initial GATS negotiations, which culminated in signing the GATS in 1995. Article XIX required members to launch new negotiations on services no later than 2000, and periodically thereafter. Initial negotiations of the Uruguay Round were launched in 2000, which later became part of the Doha Round. Between 2000 and the end of 2005, WTO members pursued a bilateral approach to negotiations, submitting requests to others and responding to requests with offers. But large asymmetries in interest across the membership have impeded progress.

In 2006, WTO members launched an effort to complement the bilateral request offer process with a pluri-lateral or 'collective' approach. In this context, the US, the EU, and Australia have been leading negotiations on services, known as the Trade in Services Agreement (TiSA). Formal negotiations on TiSA began in early 2013 between a relatively small number of WTO members interested in services trade liberalization. As of the beginning of 2015, participation in TiSA has expanded to twenty-four members, with the EU representing its twenty-eight member states, for a total of fifty-one WTO members, and the European Commission negotiating on behalf of the EU.[19] The purpose of TiSA is to create trading conditions that will enable service industries to achieve their full potential by opening up markets and improving trading rules on issues such as licensing, state-owned enterprises, regulatory barriers, business operations, cross-border data flows, and dispute settlement. TiSA will

---

[19] The twenty-four TiSA parties comprise Australia, Canada, Chile, Chinese Taipei, Colombia, Costa Rica, the EU, Hong Kong, Iceland, Israel, Japan, Liechtenstein, Mexico, New Zealand, Norway, Pakistan, Panama, Paraguay, Peru, the Republic of Korea, Switzerland, Turkey, the US, and Uruguay.

be based on the GATS so that the former can be multi-lateralized once a critical mass of membership is achieved. The twenty-four WTO member countries, accounting for around 70 per cent of global trade in services, concluded their tenth round of negotiations in February 2015. In the case of transport, the TiSA negotiations cover maritime transport services and air transport services, and since April 2015, new proposals have been discussed for road transport.[20]

Achieving liberalization of services within a multilateral context has its own problems, as negotiations in the WTO context have shown. Therefore we abstract from consideration of multilateral liberalization in the following, and concentrate on unilateral liberalization and regional liberalization. Here we note that in recent years the number of regional trade agreements has increased significantly. Many provide for free trade in goods but also include some measures to facilitate trade in services. Such regional agreements can conceivably lead to gains from trade liberalization; in reality, however, little has been achieved in terms of actual market liberalization, with the exception of the EU and a small number of agreements between high-income countries.

To study the effects of unilateral and regional liberalization of transportation services we need estimates of tariff equivalents for Turkey as well as for each of the EU countries. In the following we consider the case of road transportation (Sector 48 of the GTAP 8 Data Base), and concentrate on the estimation of tariff equivalents applied by Turkey and by each of the EU countries.

Given the data on bilateral trade flows on road transportation services for the year 2007 we concentrate on the exports of road transportation services from each of the EU countries to Turkey. We order these data starting from the country with the highest value of exports of road transportation services to Turkey. We consider the twenty largest EU exporters of road transportation services to Turkey and then estimate the tariff equivalent of restrictions in road transportation services applied by Turkey for each of the twenty countries using Equation (6), when $\sigma_k = 8$. Thus we derive twenty different tariff equivalent values T_{ij}^k ($i = 1, \ldots, 20$; $j =$ Turkey; $k = 48$) applied by Turkey on imports of road transportation services. We weight each of these estimates by the share of a country's exports of road transportation services to Turkey in the total exports of road transportation services to Turkey of the twenty countries, and determine the tariff equivalent applied by Turkey on imports of road transportation services as the weighted average of these twenty tariff equivalents.

Next, we consider the determination of tariff equivalents for each of the EU countries. Given the data on the exports of road transport services of Turkey to EU countries, we order these data starting from the country with the highest value of imports of road transportation services from Turkey, and choose

---

[20] On TiSA, see Sauve (2013), Marchetti and Roy (2013), and the Department of Foreign Affairs and Trade of the Australian Government (2015).

fifteen EU countries as the largest importers of road transportation services from Turkey. Next, for each of these fifteen countries we estimate the tariff equivalent applied by those countries on the imports of road transportation services, following a procedure similar to the estimation of tariff equivalents for Turkey.

Thereafter, we consider the case of maritime transportation, and last, the case of air transportation. The results of these calculations are reported in Table 7.6, which reveals that tariff equivalents on road and maritime transportation services applied by Turkey are relatively high. They amount to 154.51 per cent in the case of road transportation services, and 170.73 per cent in the case of maritime transportation services. The tariff equivalent on air transportation services is relatively lower, but still considerable, at 77.07 per cent. The table further reveals that tariff equivalents applied by the fifteen countries on imports of road transportation services are also relatively high. In the case of road transportation services, while the tariff equivalent applied by Germany is 114.6 per cent, the tariff equivalent applied by France is 116.25 per cent. The highest value of tariff equivalents applied by the fifteen EU countries on imports of road transportation services is 147.06 per cent, which is applied by Poland. The tariff equivalents applied by the fifteen countries on imports of maritime and air transportation services are relatively lower, but still very high. In the case of maritime transportation services, the tariff equivalent applied by Germany is 37.73 per cent and the tariff equivalent applied by France is 45.12 per cent. In the case of air transportation services, the tariff equivalent applied by Germany is 57.87 per cent and the tariff equivalent applied by France is 60.67 per cent.

Table 7.6 Tariff equivalents within a regional context when elasticity of substitution is eight

Road		Maritime		Air	
Turkey	154.51	Turkey	170.73	Turkey	77.07
Germany	114.60	Germany	37.73	Germany	57.87
Britain	125.94	Italy	38.63	Britain	51.50
Czech Republic	128.37	Britain	47.61	Spain	49.34
Sweden	138.40	France	45.12	Italy	66.77
Belgium	105.36	Czech Republic	117.58	France	60.67
France	116.25	Belgium	46.76	Austria	78.23
Netherlands	114.29	Sweden	69.08	Belgium	77.82
Austria	113.25	Netherlands	45.52	Portugal	67.31
Italy	124.96	Austria	99.27	Czech Republic	89.48
Spain	129.40	Denmark	59.64	Netherlands	71.02
Denmark	121.97	Greece	20.24	Greece	86.28
Greece	124.58	Romania	71.48	Sweden	50.04
Bulgaria	150.04	Spain	63.31	Hungary	68.77
Ireland	137.93	Bulgaria	85.06	Denmark	48.10
Poland	147.06	Portugal	98.44	Bulgaria	94.41

Source: Own calculations.

Note that the tariff equivalents reported in Table 7.6 represents the trade costs defined by Anderson and van Wincoop (2004) as costs related to policy barriers (such as tariffs and non-tariff barriers (NTBs)), transportation costs (consisting of freight and time costs), contract enforcement costs, costs associated with the use of different currencies, legal and regulatory costs, and local distribution costs (such as wholesale and retail costs). These costs are much larger than the tariff equivalents of transportation costs that we are interested in. Anderson and van Wincoop (2004) report that the tax equivalent of trade costs for goods trade in industrial countries is about 170 per cent and transportation costs represent 21 per cent. But unfortunately we do not have similar data for services trade in developing countries. Hence we shall make some rather restrictive assumptions about the size of tariff equivalents of barriers to trade in transportation services.

7.4 The Economic Impact of Liberalizing Transport Services

In the case of unilateral liberalization, we assume that Turkey is reducing the tariff equivalents reported in Table 7.6 by 50 per cent, and that there is no change in the tariff equivalents of other countries. In the case of regional liberalization, we assume that negotiations between Turkey and the EU will result in the opening up of transportation sectors in trade between Turkey and the EU, and that there is no change in the tariff equivalents of other countries. Hence, we assume that while Turkey reduces its tariff equivalents reported in Table 7.6 by 50 per cent, the EU countries also reduce the tariff equivalents reported in Table 7.6 by 50 per cent. These are quite restrictive assumptions, but they can be justified as we are mainly interested in ordering the alternative scenarios.

The analysis uses the multiregional, multi-sectoral GTAP model, which is a computable general equilibrium model (CGE). The model is based on the GTAP 8 Data Base with the reference year 2007, and documentation on the model and the database is provided on the GTAP website.[21] The bilateral Turkish export and import figures for road transportation services reveal that while total exports of road transport services amounted to $10.6 billion, total imports of road transport services were worth only $1 billion. On the other hand, total exports of maritime services amounted to $104.2 million and total imports to $77.4 million. Total exports of air transport services amounted to $4.5 billion and total imports to $1.97 billion. While the EU share in Turkish exports of road transport services was 44.3 per cent, its share of Turkish exports

---

[21] See https://www.gtap.agecon.purdue.edu (accessed 8 February 2016).

of maritime transport services was 40.9 per cent and of air transport services 44 per cent. While the EU share in Turkish imports of road transport services was 32.2 per cent, its share of Turkish imports of maritime transport services was 17.7 per cent and of air transport services was 38 per cent.

7.4.1 Unilateral Liberalization

As emphasized above, we assume that Turkey is reducing the tariff equivalents reported in Table 7.6 by 50 per cent, and that there is no change in the tariff equivalents of the other countries. The key findings from the simulations are reported in Table 7.7.

The simulation results in unilateral liberalization in road transport services show positive welfare effects of $280.5 million for Turkey. While the output of the road transport sector in Turkey decreases by 0.6 per cent, the output of the Turkish maritime transport sector increases by 0.07 per cent and the output of Turkish air transport sector by 0.17 per cent. The unilateral liberalization of road transport services by Turkey decreases Turkish real GDP by 0.06 per cent

Table 7.7 Effects of unilateral liberalization by Turkey

Only road transportation

	% Change in GDP	Change in equivalent variation (US$ million)	Change in trade balance (US$ million)
Turkey	−0.0603	280.49	84.26
Germany	0.0002	6.89	−5.66
Britain	0.0007	8.67	−5.68
France	0.0003	2.94	−2.91
Austria	0.0015	2.40	−1.35
Only maritime transportation			
Turkey	0.0006	24.81	−3.12
Germany	−0.0001	0.20	0.22
Britain	0.0000	0.18	0.28
France	−0.0001	0.17	0.36
Austria	−0.0001	0.02	0.04
Only air transportation			
Turkey	−0.0837	116.40	38.50
Germany	0.0009	19.20	−7.98
Britain	0.0004	8.75	−3.00
France	0.0002	2.78	−0.75
Austria	0.0006	1.57	−0.27
Simultaneously in road, maritime, and air transportation			
Turkey	−0.14	404.17	119.97
Germany	0	26.64	−14.67
Britain	0	18.15	−9.63
France	0	6.61	−4.53
Austria	0	4.49	−1.72

Source: Own calculations.

while resulting in a trade surplus of $84.4 million. Furthermore, Turkish liberalization has positive but very minor effects on the GDPs of EU countries. The simulation results for the impact of unilateral liberalization in maritime transport services also show positive welfare effects for Turkey of $24.8 million. While the output of the Turkish maritime transport sector decreases by 0.9 per cent, the output of the Turkish road transport sector increases by 0.004 per cent and the output of the Turkish air transport sector by 0.005 per cent. Turkish unilateral liberalization of maritime transport services increases the country's real GDP by 0.0006 per cent while resulting in a trade deficit of $3.1 million. Furthermore, such liberalization has very minor effects on EU GDPs. Finally, unilateral liberalization in air transport services shows positive welfare effects of $116.4 million for Turkey. While the output of the Turkish air transport sector decreases by 4.3 per cent, the output of Turkish maritime transport sector increases by 0.04 per cent, and the output of the Turkish road transport sector by 0.03 per cent. Turkish unilateral liberalization of air transport services decreases real GDP by 0.08 per cent while resulting in a trade surplus of $84.5 million. In addition, liberalization has positive but very minor effects on EU GDPs.

Finally, we assume that while Turkey reduces simultaneously the tariff equivalents in road, maritime, and air transport services by 50 per cent, there is no change in the other countries' tariff equivalents. Such a policy has positive welfare effects of $404.2 million for Turkey and results in decreases in the outputs of Turkish road, maritime, and air transport sectors by 0.72 per cent, 1.13 per cent, and 12.5 per cent, respectively. In addition, the unilateral liberalization of transport services by Turkey leads to a decrease of Turkish real GDP by 0.14 per cent while the trade surplus increases to $119.97 million. Finally, we note that the unilateral liberalization by Turkey has very minor but positive welfare effects for other countries, and no effect on the GDPs of those countries.

7.4.2 Regional Liberalization

In the case of regional liberalization, we assume that negotiations between Turkey and the EU result in the opening up of transportation sector trade between Turkey and the EU, and that there is no change in the tariff equivalents of other countries. Thus, Turkey reduces the tariff equivalents reported in Table 7.6 by 50 per cent and EU countries reduce the tariff equivalents reported in Table 7.6 by 50 per cent. There is no change in the tariff equivalents of the other countries. The key findings from the simulations are reported in Table 7.8.

Liberalization of trade between Turkey and the EU in road transport services has positive welfare effects of $1.44 billion for Turkey. While the output of the

Table 7.8 Effects of liberalization in transport sectors between Turkey and the EU

Only road transportation

	% Change in GDP	Change in equivalent variation (US$ million)	Change in trade balance (US$ million)
Turkey	0.7621	1,438.33	–1,050.40
Germany	–0.0095	201.28	–297.51
Britain	–0.0148	93.68	–43.84
France	–0.0160	–64.24	93.76
Austria	–0.0299	–26.91	4.40
Only maritime transportation			
Turkey	0.0037	10.39	–6.27
Germany	0.0000	–0.82	–0.74
Britain	–0.0001	–0.62	–0.07
France	–0.0001	–0.64	0.47
Austria	–0.0001	–0.16	–0.09
Only air transportation			
Turkey	0.1748	370.48	–272.35
Germany	–0.0033	4.06	–28.32
Britain	–0.0098	–38.46	21.12
France	–0.0037	–15.00	11.95
Austria	–0.0069	–4.96	–5.51
Simultaneously in road, maritime, and air transportation			
Turkey	0.9466	1,831.60	–1,338.79
Germany	–0.0132	196.99	–330.20
Britain	–0.0249	51.43	–22.97
France	–0.0203	–87.54	105.27
Austria	–0.0413	–45.24	–2.11

Source: Own calculations.

road transport sector in Turkey increases by 4.4 per cent, the output of the Turkish maritime transport sector decreases by 0.6 per cent and the output of the Turkish air transport sector by 1.5 per cent. Regional liberalization of road transport services between Turkey and the EU increases Turkish real GDP by 0.76 per cent while resulting in a trade deficit of $1.05 billion for Turkey. Furthermore, liberalization has minor negative effects on EU GDPs. On the other hand, the impact of trade liberalization in maritime transport services between Turkey and the EU has positive welfare effects of $10.4 million. While the output of the Turkish maritime transport sector increases by 0.2 per cent, the output of the Turkish road transport sector decreases by 0.0005 per cent and the output of the Turkish air transport sector by 0.007 per cent. Regional liberalization of maritime transport services between Turkey and the EU increases Turkish real GDP by 0.004 per cent while resulting in a trade deficit of $6.3 million. Furthermore, liberalization has extremely small effects on EU GDPs. Next, we note that regional liberalization in air transport services between Turkey and the EU has positive welfare effects of $370.5 million for Turkey. While the output of the Turkish air transport sector increases by

15.8 per cent, the output of the Turkish maritime transport sector decreases by 0.16 per cent and the output of the Turkish road transport sector by 0.07 per cent. Regional liberalization of air transport services between Turkey and the EU increases Turkish real GDP by 0.17 per cent while resulting in a trade deficit of \$272.4 million. In addition, liberalization has minor negative effects on EU GDPs.

Finally, we assume that Turkey reduces simultaneously by 50 per cent the tariff equivalents reported in Table 7.6 in road, maritime, and air transport services in trade between Turkey and the EU, and that the EU countries follow suit. But there is no change in the tariff equivalents of the other countries. Such a policy has positive welfare effects of \$1.83 billion for Turkey. While the outputs of the Turkish air and road transport sectors increases by 14.3 per cent and 4.3 per cent, respectively, the output of the Turkish maritime transport sector decreases by 0.6 per cent. Regional liberalization of transport services between Turkey and the EU increases Turkish real GDP by 0.95 per cent and results in a trade deficit of \$1.34 billion. Regional liberalization has relatively minor but mixed effects on EU GDPs.

7.4.3 Assessment of Policy Scenarios

Unilateral liberalization and regional liberalization of transportation services have different economic effects on the economies considered. Of the different options considered for Turkey, the best policy alternative seems to be to pursue liberalization simultaneously in road, maritime, and air transport by following the regional model. In such a case, we assume that Turkey and the EU countries succeed in reducing simultaneously the tariff equivalents in road, maritime, and air transport sectors by 50 per cent, while countries other than Turkey and EU members do not change their tariff equivalents. Transport services liberalization between Turkey and the EU may not be easy to achieve, but it is certainly an option worth pursuing.

7.5 The Economic Impact of Transport Sector Infrastructure Development

When analysing the effects of infrastructure on trade costs, and thus on trade, Limao and Venables (2001) express the unit cost of transporting a particular good from country i to country j, t_{ij}, as a function of a vector of characteristics relating to the journey between i and j, z_{ij}; a vector of the characteristics of country i, Z_i; and a vector of the characteristics of country j, Z_j, that is:

$$t_{ij} = f(z_{ij}, Z_i, Z_j).$$

Assuming that t_{ij} can be approximated by a log linear function up to some measurement error u_{ij}, the average observed trade costs appear as follows:

$$\ln t_{ij} = \alpha + \beta_1 \ln z_{ij} + \beta_2 \ln Z_i + \beta_3 \ln Z_j + u_{ij}.$$

Limao and Venables (2001) then write the bilateral export of a particular commodity from country i to country j, X_{ij}, as a function of the GDPs in countries i and j, Y_i and Y_j, and the transport cost factor t_{ij}:

$$X_{ij} = g(Y_i, Y_j, t_{ij}).$$

In the empirical trade literature, a popular model in the analysis of the export function is the gravity model, specified as:

$$\ln X_{ij} = \gamma + \delta_1 \ln Y_i + \delta_2 \ln Y_j + \delta_3 \ln t_{ij}.$$

The rationale behind the gravity model is that trade is generated among others by economic size, which is proxied by GDP. A high level of income in the exporting country indicates a high level of production, which increases the availability of products for export, while a high level of income in the importing country suggests higher imports due to higher purchasing power. We therefore expect the coefficients δ_1 and δ_2 to be positive. On the other hand, since an increase in trade cost t_{ij} is expected to decrease trade, the coefficient δ_3 is expected to be negative.

Inserting the first relation into the second relation we get:

$$\ln X_{ij} = \alpha + \beta_1 \ln Y_i + \beta_2 \ln Y_j + \beta_3 [\alpha + \beta_1 \ln z_{ij} + \beta_2 \ln Z_i + \beta_3 \ln Z_j + u_{ij}].$$

For the vectors of characteristics relating to the journey between i and j, z_{ij}, we follow the approach of Limao and Venables (2001) and consider two variables. While the first variable is the shortest distance between the two countries, denoted by D_{ij}, the second variable indicates whether the countries share a common border. On the other hand, for country characteristics Limao and Venables (2001) concentrate on geographical and infrastructural variables. The main geographical measures are whether the country is landlocked, and the main infrastructural measure is shown by the quantity of infrastructure. It is common to add other variables, such as dummy variables on common language and members of a trading block such as free trade or a customs union.

We estimate the above model for Turkey's exports to its 183 trade partners, with annual data using a dataset covering the period 1993 to 2012. Regression equation is given by the relation:

$$X_{jt} = a + \mu_j + \mu_t + a_1 \ln(Y_t) + a_2 \ln(Y_{jt})$$
$$+ a_3 \ln(D_j) + a_4(border_j) + a_5(landlocked_j) + a_6(INF_t) + a_7(CU_{jt})$$
$$+ a_8(FTA_{jt}) + a_9 \ln(POP_t) + a_{10} \ln(POP_{jt}) + u_{jt}$$

where j denotes its trade partner country j; X_{jt} denotes exports of Turkey to country j at time period t; Y_t Turkish GDP; Y_{jt} GDP of country j; D_j distance between Turkey and country j; $border_j$ common border dummy taking the value of 1 if Turkey has a common border with country j and 0 otherwise; $landlocked_j$ landlocked country dummy taking the value of 1 if country j has no access to the sea and 0 otherwise; INF_t infrastructure variable of Turkey; CU_{jt} customs union dummy taking the value of 1 if Turkey has a customs union with country j and 0 otherwise; FTA_{jt} free trade agreement dummy taking the value of 1 if Turkey has a free trade agreement with country j and 0 otherwise; POP_t Turkish population; and POP_{jt} population of country j. Country dummies (μ_j) and time dummies (μ_t) were added to the model to account for some possible omitted variables. Exports of Turkey to 183 countries over the period 1993–2012 and GDP per capita of Turkey are taken from data reported by the Statistical Institute of Turkey (TUIK). GDP per capita and population (POP) data of the 183 trade partners were taken from United Nations 'Global Indicators Data Base', and the list of the landlocked countries was taken from Wikipedia. Information on Customs Union and Free Trade Agreements of Turkey was taken from Republic of Turkey Ministry of Economy website (http://www. ekonomi.gov.tr, accessed 9 February 2016). Flight distance between the capital of Turkey, Ankara, and capital city of the trade partner were obtained from (http://www.timeanddate.com, accessed 9 February 2016).

Next, we have to come up with a measure of transport infrastructure. For this purpose we build a synthetic index summarizing information on the quantity of different types of transportation infrastructure assets. We denote the synthetic quantity index as INF which is expressed as linear combinations of the under-lying sector-specific indicators with weights determined according to a standard principal-components statistical procedure. The variables considered are the length of road network in km per square km of arable land, the length of rail network in km per square km of arable land, and total freight volume trans-ported through air. Data on length of road network has been obtained from Directorate General of Highways, data on length of rail network from Turkish State Railways, data on arable land from TUIK, and data on freight volume transported through air from Directorate General of Civil Aviation. The princi-pal components are then computed over the entire sample with each variable expressed in its natural logarithm and standardized by subtracting its mean and dividing by its standard deviation. The estimated equation is expressed as:

$$INF = 0.34\,X_1 + 0.33\,X_2 + 0.334\,X_3$$

Table 7.9 Poisson Pseudo Maximum Likelihood (PPML) regression results

	Coefficient	Standard error	z-value	P-value
Infrastructure	2.197*	1.214	1.81	0.070
Income	0.845***	0.051	16.59	0.000
Population	0.696***	0.137	5.08	0.000
Common border	−0.607*	0.334	−1.82	0.069
Landlocked country	−3.107***	0.250	−12.41	0.000
Custom Union	0.356***	0.065	5.43	0.000
Free Trade Agreement	0.252***	0.049	5.11	0.000

Note: *, **, *** indicate that statistics are significant at the 10 per cent, 5 per cent, and 1 per cent level respectively. Statistics about time and country dummies can be obtained from the authors.
Source: Own calculations.

where X_1 refers to standardized quantity of road infrastructure, X_2 standardized quantity of rail infrastructure, and X_3 standardized quantity of air infrastructure.[22]

The model is estimated using Poisson Pseudo Maximum Likelihood (PPML).[23] The estimations revealed that the coefficients of variables like Turkish GDP, distance, and common language were insignificant. Therefore these variables have been removed from the regression equation. In addition, we have added to the equation country dummies and time dummies to account for at least some of the omitted variables and feedback effects. The regression results are given in Table 7.9.

The estimates reveal that a 1 per cent increase in infrastructure index of Turkey results in 2.2 per cent increase in exports. Increases in GDP of trade partner of Turkey lead to increases in Turkish exports with an elasticity of 0.845, and a 1 per cent increase in population of trade partners increases

---

[22] We do not consider maritime infrastructure as data on maritime infrastructure started to be collected only recently.

[23] Santos Silva and Tenreyro (2006) showed that, OLS estimates of gravity equations in logarithmic form are biased, since, if the trade data series have zeros in it (which is common, in some time periods, there may be no trade between some of the countries) deleting these information biases results if the 'zeros' are not randomly distributed. Moreover, even if there are no zeros in the data, when you estimate gravity model in logarithmic form, the dependent variable you estimate is not the trade, but its logarithm; since $E(\ln y) \neq \ln E(y)$ (Jensen's inequality), estimation is biased. Furthermore, even if there are no zeros in the data, since logarithm of the error term depends on higher moments of the data, including its variance, if there is heteroscedasticity, there can be correlation between the independent variables and the expected value of the logarithmic error, which makes OLS estimator inconsistent (Santos Silva and Tenreyro, 2006). Silva and Tenreyo established that, if you estimate the equation in multiplicative form, you can both include zero observations and eliminate biases originating from Jensen's inequality. Among non-linear methods, Poisson Pseudo Maximum Likelihood (PPML) gives the best results (Santos Silva and Tenreyro, 2006). Moreover, although the dependent variable for the poisson regression is specified in levels rather than logarithms, coefficients of the independent variables which are taken in logarithmic form can still be interpreted as elasticities (Shephard (2012)).

Turkish exports by around 0.7 per cent. Turkey exports more to countries that it has customs union and free trade agreements with. But Turkey exports less to its neighbours largely due to economic and political problems in its neighbouring countries.

7.6 Conclusion

Transport costs have been and still are an important component of trade costs defined by Anderson and van Wincoop (2004) as costs related to policy barriers, such as tariffs and non-tariff barriers (NTBs), transportation costs consisting of freight and time costs, as well as communication costs, information costs, contract enforcement costs, costs associated with the use of different currencies, legal and regulatory costs, and local distribution costs such as wholesale and retail costs. Trade costs are important as these costs turn out to be one of the major determinants of the volume of trade as shown by Jacks et al. (2008). According to the authors the enormous rise in trade experienced between 1820 and 1913 was a consequence of sharply declining trade costs, and the trade boom experienced between 1950 and 2000 is also explained by a fall in trade costs. Thus, decreases in trade costs increases trade which in turn increases not only the GDP of the country but also the rate of economic growth of the country as pointed out in Chapter 1.

Studies reveal the main determinants of transport costs are transport infrastructure, the regulatory framework in transport sectors, geography, technological change, trade facilitation, fuel costs, and product characteristics. Of these determinants we have concentrated in this study on only two factors, namely the transport infrastructure and regulatory framework in transport sectors. Empirical study of Turkish transport sector infrastructure development reveals that a 1 per cent increase in infrastructure index results in a 2.2 per cent increase in exports. Since an increase in exports leads to increases in GDP one could thus state that infrastructural developments in Turkey will result in higher Turkish GDP over time as shown by Esfahani and Ramirez (2003), Calderón and Servén (2010), and Limao and Venables (2001) for a large number of countries. On the other hand the present chapter has also shown that economic liberalization pursued unilaterally or regionally has beneficial effects for the country, and that the best alternative for Turkey is to pursue liberalization of trade with the EU in road, maritime, and air transport services that will lead to simultaneous reduction of trade costs in Turkey as well as in the EU member countries.

How can Turkey pursue with the EU such liberalization of trade in road, rail, maritime, and air transport services? But before answering this question let us consider the state of trade relations between Turkey and the EU in general terms. These relations are determined by the Association Agreement (Ankara Agreement) of 1963; the Additional Protocol and Financial Protocol of 1970; the EU-Turkey Association Council Decision 1/95 forming the EU-Turkey customs union (CU) covering industrial goods including the industrial component of processed agricultural commodities but excluding European Coal and Steel Community (ECSC) products; Commission Decision 96/528/ECSC of 29 February 1996 on the conclusion of an Agreement between ECSC and the Republic of Turkey on trade in products covered by the Treaty establishing the ECSC; and the Decision of the Turkey-EU Association Council No 1/98 relating to agricultural products.

The EU-Turkey Association Council Decisions 1/95 together with Decision 96/528/ECSC have been major instruments of integration for Turkey into the EU and global markets, offering the country powerful tools to reform its economy. Under the CU and free trade agreement (FTA) Turkey and the EU preferentially grant tariff-free market access to each other's imports of industrial goods including processed agricultural products. The parties agreed to apply the EU's Common External Tariff to those industrial imports from the rest of the world. In addition Turkey had to adopt and effectively apply the EU rules on modernization of customs; elimination of TBTs; competition policy; intellectual property rights; anti-dumping, countervailing duties, surveillance and safeguards measures. Fulfilling the requirements of the CU has been quite challenging for Turkey. The country faced major difficulties when trying to eliminate the TBTs in trade with the EU, adopting and implementing the EU's competition policy provisions on state aid and ensuring adequate and effective protection of intellectual property rights. In those cases, the process of fulfilling the requirements of the CU even after twenty years is still not complete.[24]

As a result of the CU Turkey was credibly locked into a liberal foreign trade regime for industrial goods. Turkish producers of industrial goods have become exposed to competition from imports from the EU and they operate within one of the largest free trade areas for industrial products in the world. They are now protected by tariffs from external competition to exactly the same extent as EU producers are and as such, face competition from duty-free imports of industrial goods from world-class pan-European firms. In return, Turkish industrial producers have duty-free market access to the European Economic Area.

The above considerations reveal that services and hence transportation services are not covered by the CU and the FTA. To open up trade in transportation

---

[24] See Togan (2014).

services between Turkey and the EU, Turkey has two options. Turkey could either negotiate separate agreements for road, rail, maritime, and air transportation with the EU on liberalization of those sectors similar to the Land Transport Agreement signed between the EU and Switzerland, or it could deepen the EU-Turkey economic integration further as advocated by the recent World Bank study commissioned by the European Commission.[25]

The present study concentrates on the liberalization of transportation services and shows that achieving liberalization for Turkey in trade with the EU is a challenging task requiring not only the elimination of barriers to cross-border trade between the parties but also harmonization of the rules and regulations of different parties pertaining to market access and competition conditions, prices and fiscal conditions, social conditions, technical conditions, and safety, as well as eliminating restrictions to modes 3 and 4. A comprehensive FTA between the EU and Turkey covering services will have to specify which services will be covered by the FTA. In the EU services are classified under three headings: (i) services where EU wide regulations apply such as financial services, telecommunication services, energy services, and transportation services; (ii) services regulated by Services Directive 200/123/EC such as legal services, accounting services, business related services, and construction services; and (iii) services regulated by national regulations such as public services including health services, education services, and social services. A future FTA between the EU and Turkey covering services will most probably include services in the first group and some of the services in the second group, but will exclude services regulated nationally. Since Turkey in those cases will have to adopt and implement the EU rules and regulations, the liberalization of services will be quite challenging for Turkey.

It is the hope of the author of this study that the present book will be helpful for policymakers and academicians when Turkey and possibly other countries in the neighbourhood of the EU will be confronted with the prospect of concluding a FTA with the EU covering services.

---

[25] See World Bank (2014a).

Bibliography

Abu-Lughod, J. L. (1989). *Before European Hegemony: The World System A.D. 1250–1350*. Oxford: Oxford University Press.

Akhtar, S. I. and V. C. Jones (2014). 'Transatlantic Trade and Investment Partnership (TTIP) Negotiations'. Congressional Research Service. Washington, DC: CRS.

Amos, P. (2009). 'Freight Transport for Development Toolkit: Rail Freight'. Department for International Development. Washington, DC: World Bank.

Anderson, J. E. and E. van Wincoop (2003). 'Gravity with Gravitas: A Solution to the Border Puzzle'. *American Economic Review* 93: 170–92.

Anderson, J. E. and E. von Wincoop (2004). 'Trade Cost'. *Journal of Economic Literature* 42: 691–751.

Aperte, X. G. and A. J. Baird (2013). 'Motorways of the Sea Policy in Europe'. *Maritime Policy & Management* 40: 10–26.

Arvis, J.-F., Y. Duval, B. Shepherd, and C. Utoktham (2013). 'Trade Costs in the Developing World 1995–2010'. World Bank Policy Research Working Paper No. 6309. Washington, DC: World Bank.

Aschauer, D. (1989). 'Is Public Expenditure Productive?' *Journal of Monetary Economics* 23: 177–200.

Baldwin, R. (2006). 'Globalization: The Great Unbundling(s)'. In *Globalization Challenges for Europe*, edited by the Secretariat of the Economic Council. Helsinki: Finnish Prime Minister's Office, 5–47.

Baldwin, R. (2011a). '21st Century Regionalism: Filling the Gap between 21st Century Trade and 20th Century Trade Rules'. World Trade Organization Staff Working Paper ERSD-2011-08. Geneva: WTO.

Baldwin, R. (2011b). 'Trade and Industrialization after Globalization's 2nd Unbundling: How Building and Joining a Supply Chain Are Different and Why It Matters'. National Bureau of Economic Research Working Paper No. 17716. Cambridge: NBER.

Baldwin, R. (2013). 'Global Supply Chains: Why They Emerged, Why They Matter, and Where They Are Going'. In *Global Value Chains in a Changing World*, edited by D. K. Elms and P. Low. Geneva: WTO, 13–59.

Baldwin, R. (2014). 'WTO 2.0: Global Governance of Supply Chain Trade'. *Review of International Organizations* 9: 261–83.

Behar, A. and A. J. Venables (2011). 'Transport Costs and International Trade'. In *A Handbook of Transport Economics*, edited by A. de Palma, R. Lindsey, E. Quinet, and R. Vickerman. Cheltenham: Edward Elgar Publishing, 97–115.

Bernadet, M. (2009). 'The Construction and Operation of the Road Freight Transport Market in Europe'. International Transport Forum. Paris: OECD.

Bernard, A. B., J. B. Jensen, S. J. Redding, and P. K. Schott (2007). 'Firms in International Trade'. *Journal of Economic Perspectives* 21: 105–30.

Blonigen, B. A. and W. W. Wilson (2008). 'Port Efficiency and Trade Flows'. *Review of International Economics* 16: 21–36.

Blyde, J. (2010). 'Paving the Road to Export: The Trade Impacts of Domestic Transport Costs and Road Quality'. Inter-American Development Bank.

Boeing (2014). 'World Air Cargo Forecast 2014–2015'. Seattle: Boeing.

Borenstein, S. and N. L. Rose (2007). 'How Airline Markets Work... or Do They? Regulatory Reform in the Airline Industry'. National Bureau of Economic Research Working Paper No. 13452. Cambridge: NBER.

Borchert, I., B. Gootiiz, and A. Mattoo (2012a). 'Policy Barriers to International Trade in Services: Evidence from a New Database'. World Bank Policy Research Working Paper No. 6109. Washington, DC: World Bank.

Borchert, I., B. Gootiiz, and A. Mattoo (2012b). 'Guide to the Services Trade Restrictions Database'. World Bank Policy Research Working Paper No. 6108. Washington, DC: World Bank.

Bougheas, S., P. O. Demetriades, and E. L. W. Morgenrouth (1999). 'Infrastructure, Transport Costs and Trade'. *Journal of International Economics* 47: 169–89.

Boylaud, O. (2000). 'Regulatory Reform in Road Freight and Retail Distribution'. Economics Department Working Papers No. 255. Paris: OECD.

Braithwaite, J. and P. Drahos (2000). *Global Business Regulation*. Cambridge: Cambridge University Press.

Breinlich, H. and C. Criscuolo (2011). 'International Trade in Services: A Portrait of Importers and Exporters'. *Journal of International Economics* 84: 188–206.

Button, K. (1990). 'Environmental Externalities and Transport Policy'. *Oxford Review of Economic Policy* 6: 61–75.

Button, K. (2001). 'Deregulation and Liberalization of European Air Transport Markets'. *Innovation* 14: 255–75.

Button, K. (2002). 'Environmental Externalities and Transport Policy'. *Oxford Review of Economic Policy* 6: 61–75.

Button, K. (2014). 'Opening the Skies: Put Free Trade in Airline Services on the Transatlantic Trade Agenda'. Policy Analysis, CATO Institute. Washington, DC: CATO.

Çakmak Avukatlık Bürosu (2013). 'Liberalization of Turkish Railway Sector', Ankara.

Calderon, C. and L. Servén (2010). 'Infrastructure and Economic Development in Sub-Saharan Africa'. *Journal of African Economies*, Supplement 19: i13–87.

Campos, J. and P. Cantos (1999). 'Regulating Privatized Rail Transport'. World Bank Policy Research Working Paper No. 2064. Washington, DC: World Bank.

Canning, D. (1999). 'The Contribution of Infrastructure to Aggregate Output'. World Bank Policy Research Working Paper No. 2246. Washington, DC: World Bank.

CE Delft, Infras, and Fraunhofer ISI (2011). *External Cost of Transport in Europe: Update Study for 2008*. Delf: CE Delft.

Cella, G. (1984). 'The Input-Output Measurement of Interindustry Linkages'. *Oxford Bulletin of Economics and Statistics* 46: 73–84.

Chen, N. and D. Novy (2011). 'Gravity, Trade Integration, and Heterogeneity across Industries'. *Journal of International Economics* 85: 206–21.

Clark, X., D. Dollar, and A. Micco (2001). 'Maritime Transport Costs and Port Efficiency'. World Bank Policy Research Working Paper No. 2781. Washington, DC: World Bank.

Clark, X., D. Dollar, and A. Micco (2004). 'Port Efficiency, Maritime Transport Costs, and Bilateral Trade'. *Journal of Development Economics* 75: 417–50.

Coe, D. T. and E. Helpman (1995). 'International R&D Spillovers'. *European Economic Review* 39: 859–87.

Combes, P.-P. and M. Lafourcade (2005). 'Transport Costs: Measures, Determinants, and Regional Policy Implications for France'. *Journal of Economic Geography* 5: 319–49.

Commission of the European Communities (1995). 'Green Paper—Towards Fair and Efficient Pricing in Transport Policy—Options for Internalizing the External Cost of Transport in the European Union'. COM (95) 691 final. Brussels.

Commission of the European Communities (1996). 'Air Traffic Management: Freeing Europe's Airspace'. White Paper. COM(1996) 57 final. Brussels.

Commission of the European Communities (1997). 'Trans-European Rail Freight Freeways'. Communication from the Commission to the Council, the European Parliament, the European Economic and Social Committee and the Committee of the Regions. COM(1997) 242 final. Brussels.

Commission of the European Communities (1998). 'Fair Payment for Infrastructure Use: A Phased Approach to a Common Transport Infrastructure Charging Framework in the EU'. White Paper COM(1998) 466 final. Brussels.

Commission of the European Communities (1999). 'The Creation of the Single European Sky'. Communication from the Commission to the Council and European Parliament. COM(1999) 614 final/2. Brussels.

Commission of the European Communities (2003a). 'European Road Safety Action Programme: Halving the Number of Road Accident Victims in the European Union by 2010: A Shared Responsibility'. Communication from the Commission. COM (2003) 311. Brussels.

Commission of the European Communities (2003b).'Proposal for a European Parliament and Council Regulation on the Negotiation and Implementation of Air Service Agreements between Member States and Third Countries'. Communication from the Commission on relations between the Community and third countries in the field of air transport. COM(2003) 94 final. Brussels.

Commission of the European Communities (2006). 'Background Paper No. 9 on Multilateral and EC Instruments Related with the Seas and the Oceans'. Background documents for the Green Paper 'Towards A Future Maritime Policy for the Union: European Vision for the Oceans and Seas', SEC(2006) 689. Brussels.

Commission of the European Communities (2008a). 'Communication from the Commission Providing Guidance on State Aid Complementary to Community Funding for the Launching of the Motorways of the Sea', *Official Journal of the European Union* OJ C 317: 10–12.

Commission of the European Communities (2008b). 'Single European Sky II: Towards More Sustainable and Better Performing Aviation'. Communication from the

Commission to the European Parliament, the Council, the European Economic and Social Committee and the Committee of the Regions. COM(2008) 389 final. Brussels.

Commission of the European Communities (2009a). 'A Sustainable Future for Transport: Towards an Integrated, Technology-led and User-friendly System'. European Communities. COM(2009) 279 final. Brussels.

Commission of the European Communities (2009b). 'Communication and Action Plan with a View to Establishing a European Maritime Transport Space without Barriers'. Communication from the Commission to the European Parliament, the Council, the European Economic and Social Committee, and the Committee of the Regions. COM (2009) 11 final. Brussels.

Commission of the European Communities (2010). 'Development of a Single European Railway Area'. Communication from the Commission. COM(2010) 474 final. Brussels.

Commission of the European Communities (2011a). 'Turkey 2011 Progress Report' SEC (2011) 1201. Brussels.

Commission of the European Communities (2011b). 'Airport Policy in the European Union—Addressing Capacity and Quality to Promote Growth, Connectivity and Sustainable Mobility'. Communication from the Commission to the European Parliament, the Council, the European Economic and Social Committee, and the Committee of the Regions. COM(2011) 823 final. Brussels.

Commission of the European Communities (2011c). 'Setting up an Aviation Safety Management System for Europe'. Communication from the Commission to the Council, and the Parliament. COM(2011) 670. Brussels.

Commission of the European Communities (2015). 'Test Case on Functional Equivalence: Proposed Methodology for Automotive Regulatory Equivalence'. EU Position Paper tabled for discussion with the US in negotiating round of 29 September 2014–3 October 2014 and made public on 7 January 2015. Available at http://trade.ec. europa.eu/doclib/docs/2015/january/tradoc_153023.pdf, accessed 29 December 2015.

Commission of the European Communities (various years). *Turkey Progress Reports*. Brussels.

Cooper, J. C. (1946). 'The Bermuda Plan: World Pattern for Air Transport'. *Foreign Affairs* 25: 59–71.

COTIF (1999). Convention Concerning International Carriage by Rail (COTIF) of 9 May 1980 in the version of the Protocol of Modification of 3 June 1999.

De La Cruz, J., R. B. Koopman, and Z. Wang (2012). 'Estimating Foreign Value-added in Mexico's Manufacturing Exports'. Office of Economics Working Paper No. 2011-04A, US International Trade Commission. Washington, DC: USITC.

Delegation of the European Union to Turkey (2012). 'Support to the Enhancement of Safety of Maritime Transport in Turkey', Ankara.

Dempsey, P. S. (2008). 'Air Traffic Rights'. PowerPoint presentation prepared by the Institute of Air & Space Law at McGill University.

Department of Foreign Affairs and Trade of the Australian Government (2015). 'Trade in Services Agreement'. Available at: http://dfat.gov.au/trade/agreements/trade-in-services-agreement/Pages/trade-in-services-agreement.aspx, accessed 16 April 2015.

Directorate-General for Civil Aviation (2013). *Activity Report 2013*. Ankara: DGCA.

Dornbush, R., S. Fisher, and P. A. Samuelson (1977). 'Comparative Advantage, Trade, and Payments in a Ricardian Model with a Continuum of Goods'. *The American Economic Review* 67: 823–39.

Dutz, M., A. Hayri, and P. Ibarra (2000). 'Regulatory Reform, Competition, and Innovation: A Case Study of the Mexican Road Freight Industry'. World Bank Policy Research Working Paper No. 2318, Washington, DC: World Bank.

Esfahani, H. S. and M. T. Ramirez (2003). 'Institutions, Infrastructure, and Economic Growth'. *Journal of Economic Development* 70 (2): 443–77.

Estache, A., J. C. Carbajo, and G. de Rus (1999). 'Argentina's Transport Privatization and Re-Regulation: Ups and Downs of a Daring Decade-Long Experience'. World Bank Policy Research Working Paper No. 2249, Washington, DC: World Bank.

European Conference of Ministers of Transport (1997). 'Framework for Bilateral Agreements in Road Transport—Recommendation'. Document CEMT/CM(97)21—CM(97)21/ADD1. Paris: ECMT.

European Conference of Ministers of Transport (2001). *Regulatory Reform in Road Freight Transport*. Paris: ECMT.

Eurostat (2015). *EU Transport in Figures*. Luxembourg: Publications Office of the European Union.

Findlay, C. and T. Warren (eds) (2000). *Impediments to Trade in Services: Measurement and Policy Implications*. Sydney: Routledge.

Findlay, R. and K. H. O'Rourke (2007). *Power and Plenty: Trade, War, and the World Economy in the Second Millenium*. Princeton: Princeton University Press.

Fink, C., A. Mattoo, and H. C. Neagu (2002). 'Trade in International Maritime Services: How Much Does Policy Matter?' *The World Bank Economic Review* 16: 81–108.

Fontagne, L., A. Guillin, and C. Mitaritonna (2011). 'Estimation of Tariff Equivalents for the Services Sectors'. CEPII Working Paper 24. Paris: CEPII.

Francois, J., M. Manchin, and P. Tomberger (2013). 'Services Linkages and the Value Added Content of Trade'. World Bank Policy Research Working Paper No. 6432, Washington, DC: World Bank.

Frankel, J. A. and D. Romer (1999). 'Does Trade Cause Growth'. *The American Economic Review* 89: 379–99.

Freund, C. and S. Oliver (2015). 'Gains from Harmonizing US and EU Auto Regulations under the Transatlantic Trade and Investment Partnership'. Policy Brief No. PB15-10, Washington, DC: Peterson Institute for International Economics.

Fujita, M., P. R. Krugman, and A. Venables (1999). *The Spatial Economy: Cities, Regions and International Trade*. Boston: MIT Press.

Gerede, E. (2010). 'The Evolution of Turkish Air Transport Industry: Significant Developments and Impact of 1983 Liberalization'. *Yönetim ve Ekonomi* 17: 63–91.

Ghosh, A. (1958). 'Input-Output Approach to an Allocation System'. *Economica* 25: 58–64.

Golub, S. S. and B. Tomasik (2008). 'Measures of International Transport Cost for OECD Countries'. Organisation for Economic Co-operation and Development Economics Department Working Paper ECO/WKP(2008)17, Paris: OECD.

Goodwin, P. B. (2002). 'Demographic Impacts, Social Consequences, and the Transportation Policy Debate'. *Oxford Review of Economic Policy* 6: 76–90.

Gootiiz, B. and A. Mattoo (2009). 'Services in Doha: What Is on the Table?'. *Journal of World Trade* 43: 1013–30.

Gönenç, R. and G. Nicoletti (2000). 'Regulation, Market Structure and Performance in Air Passenger Transportation'. Organisation for Economic Co-operation and Development, ECO/WKP(2000) 27. Paris: OECD.

Grosso, M. G., H. K. Nordas, A. Ueno, F. Gonzales, I. Lejarraga, S. Miroudot, and D. Rouzet (2014). 'Services Trade Restrictiveness Index (STRI): Transport and Courier Services'. OECD Trade Policy Papers, No. 176. Paris: OECD Publishing.

Gunder Frank, A. (1998). *ReORIENT: Global Economy in the Asian Age*. Berkeley: University of California Press.

Hall, R. E. (1988). 'The Relation between Price and Marginal Cost in U.S. Industry'. *Journal of Political Economy* 96: 921–47.

Hanaappel, P. P. C. (1980). 'Bilateral Air Transport Agreements—1913–1980'. *Maryland Journal of International Law* 5: 241–67.

Hewing, G. J. D. (1982). 'The Empirical Identification of Key Sectors in an Economy: A Regional Perspective'. *Developing Economies* 20: 58–64.

Hoekman, B. (1995). 'Assessing the General Agreement on Trade in Services'. In *The Uruguay Round and the Developing Countries*, edited by W. Martin and A. L. Winters. Cambridge: Cambridge University Press, 88–124.

Hoekman, B. (2014). 'Governance of Deeper Economic Integration in a Supply Chain World'. Robert Schuman Centre for Advanced Studies. Florence: European University Institute.

Hubner, W. and P. Sauve (2001). 'Liberalization Scenarios for International Air Transport'. *Journal of World Trade* 35: 973–87.

Hummels, D. L. (1998). 'Towards a Geography of Transport Costs'. Department of Economics, University of Chicago. Mimeo.

Hummels, D. L. (1999). 'Have International Transport Costs Declined?' University of Chicago, unpublished paper.

Hummels, D. L. (2007). 'Transportation Costs and International Trade in Second Era of Globalization'. *Journal of Economic Perspectives* 21: 131–54.

Hummels, D. L. and G. Schaur (2013). 'Time as a Trade Barrier'. *American Economic Review* 103: 2935–59.

Ibn Battuta (1929). *Travels in Asia and Africa 1325–1354*. Translated by H. A. R. Gibb, London: Broadway House.

Intergovernmental Organization for International Carriage by Rail (2014). 'Annual Report 2013'. Berne: OTIF.

International Air Transport Association (2014). *Air Cargo: Delivering the Modern World*. Geneva: IATA.

International Civil Aviation Organization (2009). 'Overview of Trends and Developments in International Air Transport'. Montreal: ICAO.

International Energy Agency (2008). 'Worldwide Trends in Energy Use and Efficiency: Key Insights from IEA Indicator Analysis'. Paris: OECD.

International Transport Forum (2009a). 'Report on European Road Freight Transport Markets and ECMT Multilateral Quota Perspectives'. Report prepared by PROGTRANS AG. Paris: ITF.

International Transport Forum (2009b). *Intermodal Transport: National Review Turkey.* Paris: OECD.

InterVISTAS (2009). 'The Impact of International Air Service Liberalization on Turkey'. InterVISTAS-EU Consulting Inc.

Investment Support and Promotion Agency (2013). 'The Logistics Industry in Turkey'. PowerPoint presentation prepared by Deloitte for the Investment Support and Promotion Agency of the Republic of Turkey Prime Ministry, Ankara.

Jacks, D. S., C. M. Meissner, and D. Novy (2008). 'Trade Costs, 1870–2000'. *The American Economic Review: Papers and Proceedings* 98: 529–34.

Jones, L., W. Powers, and R. Ubee (2013). 'Making Global Value Chain Research More Accessible'. Office of Economics, Washington, DC: US International Trade Commission. Washington, DC: USITC.

Kalinova, B., A. Palerm, and S. Thomsen (2010). 'OECD's FDI Restrictiveness Index: 2010 Update'. OECD Working Papers on International Investment 2010/03. Paris: OECD Publishing.

Kessides, I. N. and R. D. Willig (1995). 'Restructuring Regulation of the Rail Industry for the Public Interest'. World Bank Policy Working Paper No. 1506. Washington, DC: World Bank.

Koopman, R., W. Powers, Z. Wang, and S. J. Wei (2011). 'Give Credit where Credit Is Due: Tracing Value Added in Global Production Chains'. National Bureau of Economic Research Working Paper No. 16426. Cambridge: NBER.

Kowalski, P., J. L. Gonzales, A. Ragoussis, and C. Ugarte (2015). 'Participation of Developing Countries in Global Value Chains: Implications for Trade and Trade Related Policies'. OECD Trade Policy Papers No. 179. Paris: OECD Publishing.

Kruk, C. B. and M. Donner (2009). *Freight Transport for Development Toolkit: Ports & Waterborne Freight.* Washington, DC: World Bank.

Krugman, P. R. (1979). 'Increasing Returns, Monopolistic Competition, and International Trade'. *Journal of International Economics* 9: 469–79.

Krugman, P. R. (1991). 'Increasing Returns and Economic Geography'. *Journal of Political Economy* 99: 483–99.

Krugman, P. R. and A. J. Venables (1995). 'Globalization and the Inequality of Nations', *Quarterly Journal of Economics* 110: 857–80.

Kunaka, C., V. Tanase, P. Latrille, and P. Krausz (2013). *Quantitative Analysis of Road Transport Agreements (QuARTA).* Washington, DC: World Bank.

Levinson, M. (2006). *The Box: How the Shipping Container Made the World Smaller and the World Economy Bigger.* Princeton: Princeton University Press.

Limao, N. and A. Venables (2001). 'Infrastructure, Geographical Disadvantage, Transport Costs, and Trade'. *The World Bank Economic Review* 15: 451–79.

Liu, Z. and E. L. Lynk (1999). 'Evidence on Market Structure of the Deregulated US Airline Industry', *Applied Economics* 31: 1083–92.

Londono-Kent, P. (2009). *Freight Transport for Development Toolkit: Road Freight.* The World Bank and Department for International Development. Washington, DC: World Bank.

Lopez, R. S. (1987). 'The Trade of Medieval Europe: the South'. In *The Cambridge Economic History of Europe,* ii: *Trade and Industry in the Middle Ages,* 2nd edition, edited by M. M. Postan and E. Miller. Cambridge: Cambridge University Press, 306–401.

Low, P. (2013). 'The Role of Services in Global Value Chains'. In *Global Value Chains in a Changing World*, edited by D. K. Elms and P. Low. WTO, Fung Global Institute and Temasek Foundation Centre for Trade & Negotiations. Geneva: WTO, 61–82.

Lundgren, N. G. (1996). 'Bulk Trade and Maritime Transport Costs: The Evolution of Global Markets', *Resources Policy* 2: 5–32.

Maddison, A. (2005). *Growth and Interaction in the World Economy: The Roots of Modernity*. Washington, DC: American Enterprise Institute (AEI) Press.

Maibach, M., C. Schreyer, D. Sutter, H. P. van Essen, B. H. Boon, R. Smookers, A. Schrotten, C. Doll, B. Pawlowska, and M. Bak (2008). *Handbook on the Estimation of External Costs in the Transport Sector*. Karlsruhe: Fraunhofer Institut System- und Innovationsforschung.

Marchetti, J. A. and M. Roy (2013). 'The TiSA Initiative: An Overview of Market Access Issues'. WTO Economic Research and Statistics Division Staff Working Paper ERSD-2013-11. Geneva: WTO.

Martins, J. O., S. Scarpetta, and D. Pilat (1996). 'Mark-up Ratios in Manufacturing Industries'. Organisation for Economic Co-operation and Development Economics Department Working Papers No. 162. Paris: OECD.

Matsuyama, K. (2009). 'Competitive Trade: Ricardian Theory', work in progress, Northwestern University.

Mayer, T. and G. I. P. Ottaviano (2007). 'The Happy Few: The Internationalization of European Firms'. Bruegel Blueprint 3. Brussels.

Melitz, M. J. (2003). 'The Impact of Trade in Intra-industry Reallocations and Aggregate Industry Productivity'. *Econometrica* 71: 1695–725.

Melitz, M. J. and G. I. P. Ottoviano (2008). 'Market Size, Trade, and Productivity'. *Review of Economic Studies* 75: 295–316.

Melitz, M. J. and S. Redding (2013). 'Heterogeneous Firms and Trade'. In *Handbook of International Economics*, iv, edited by G. Gopinath, E. Helpman, and K. Rogoff. Elsevier: North Holland, 1–54.

Melitz, M. J. and D. Treffler (2012). 'Gains from Trade when Firms Matter'. *Journal of Economic Perspectives* 26: 91–118.

Merk, O. and T. T. Dang (2013). 'Efficiency of World Ports in Container and Bulk Cargo (Oil, Coal, Ores and Grain)'. OECD Regional Development Working Papers 2012/09. Paris: OECD.

Messerlin, P. (2014). 'The Transatlantic Trade and Investment Partnership and the Developing Countries'. Unpublished paper.

Micco, A. and N. Perez (2001). 'Maritime Transport Cost and Port Efficiency'. Mimeo prepared for the seminar 'Toward Competitiveness: The Institutional Path'. Santiago, Chile.

Ministry of Transport (2007). 'Transport Operational Programme'. CCI No: 2007 TR16IPO002. Ankara: MoT.

Ministry of Transport (2010). 'Transportation and Communications Strategy—Target 2023'. Ankara: MoT.

Ministry of Transportation, Maritime Affairs, and Communications (2013). 'Deniz Ticareti 2013 İstatistikleri'. Ankara: MoTMC.

Ministry of Transportation, Maritime Affairs and Communications (2015). 'Ulaşan ve Erişen Türkiye 2014'. Ankara: MoTMC.

Mirza, D. and H. Zitouna (2010). 'Oil Prices, Geography and Endogenous Regionalism: Too Much Ado about (almost) Nothing'. CEPREMAP Working Papers No. 1009. Paris: CEPREMAP.

Monsalve, C. (2011). *Railway Reform in South East Europe and Turkey on the Right Track*. Washington, DC: World Bank.

Nordas, H. K. and R. Piermartini (2004). 'Infrastructure and Trade'. Staff Working Paper ERSD-2004-04. Geneva: WTO.

Norton Rose Fulbright (2013). 'EU Liberalization: The Fourth Package of 2013—Reaching the Final Destination'. London.

Novy, D. (2013). 'Gravity Redux: Measuring International Trade Costs with Panel Data'. *Economic Inquiry* 51: 101–21.

Office of Technology Assessment (1982). 'National Airspace System'. In *Airport and Air Traffic Control System*, National Technology Information Service No. PB82-207606. Washington, DC: US Government Office, 25–42.

O'Rourke, K. H. and J. G. Williamson (1999). *Globalization and History: The Evolution of a Nineteenth-Century Atlantic Economy*. Cambridge, MA: MIT Press.

Organisation for Economic Co-operation and Development (2000a). 'Recommendations of the Council Concerning Common Principles of Shipping Policy for Member Countries'. OECD document number C(2000) 124/Final. Paris: OECD.

Organisation for Economic Co-operation and Development (2000b). 'Airline Mergers and Alliances'. Directorate for Financial, Fiscal and Enterprise Affairs Committee on Competition Law and Policy. Paris: OECD.

Organisation for Economic Co-operation and Development (2001). *Regulatory Issues in International Maritime Transport*. Paris: OECD.

Organisation for Economic Co-operation and Development (2003). 'Cost Savings Stemming from Non-Compliance with International Environmental Regulations in the Maritime Sector'. Maritime Transport Committee DSTI/DOT/MTC(2002)8/FINAL. Paris: OECD.

Organisation for Economic Co-operation and Development (2009). 'Methodology for Deriving the STRI'. Paper presented at the OECD Experts Meeting on the Services Trade Restrictiveness Index. Paris: OECD.

Organisation for Economic Co-operation and Development (2011). 'The Shipbuilding Industry in Turkey'. OECD Council Working Party on Shipbuilding. Paris: OECD.

Organisation for Economic Co-operation and Development (2012). 'The OECD Regulatory Indicators Questionnaire 2013'. Economics Department Working Party No. 1 on Macroeconomic and Structural Policy Analysis ECO/CPE/WP1(2012)28. Paris: OECD.

Organisation for Economic Co-operation and Development (2013). *Interconnected Economies: Benefitting from Global Value Chains*. Paris: OECD.

Organisation for Economic Co-operation and Development (2014). 'Services Trade Restrictiveness Index: Policy Brief '. Paris: OECD.

Organisation for Economic Co-operation and Development, WTO, and the World Bank (2014). 'Global Value Chains: Challenges, Opportunities, and Implications for

Policy'. Report prepared for submission to the G20 Trade Ministers Meeting, Sydney, Australia. Paris: OECD.

Parameswaran, B. (2004). *The Liberalization of Maritime Transport Services*. Berlin: Springer.

Park, A., G. Nayyar, and P. Low (2013). *Supply Chain Perspectives and Issues: A Literature Review*. Geneva: WTO and Fung Global Institute.

Park, S.-C. (2002). 'Measuring Tariff Equivalents in Cross-Border Trade in Services'. KIEP Discussion Paper 02-15. Seoul.

Petrova, R. (1997). 'Cabotage and European Community Common Maritime Policy: Moving Towards Free Provision of Services in Maritime Transport'. *Fordham International Law Journal* 21: 1019–92.

Pietrantonio, L. D. and J. Pelkmans (2004). 'The Economics of EU Railway Reform'. Bruges European Economic Policy Briefings. Bruges: College of Europe.

Pilat, D., N. Yamano, and N. Yashiro (2012). 'Moving up the Value Chain: China's Experience and Future Prospects.' In *China in Focus: Lessons and Challenge*. Paris: OECD, 72–88.

Polo, M. (1992). *The Travels of Marco Polo*. Ed. and trans. Henry Yule and Henri Cordier. New York: Dover Publications.

Powers, W. (2012). 'The Value of Value Added: Measuring Global Engagement with Gross and Value Added Data'. *World Economics* 13: 19–38.

PricewaterhouseCoopers (2013). *Final Report: Study Aimed at Supporting and Impact Assessment on 'Measures to Enhance the Efficiency and Quality of Port Services in the EU'*. London: PwC.

Ramsey, F. (1927). 'A Contribution to the Theory of Taxation'. *Economic Journal* 37: 47–61.

Rasmussen, P. (1956). *Studies in Inter-Sectoral Relations*. Copenhagen: Einar Harks.

Republic of Turkey Ministry for EU Affairs (2007). Presentations prepared within the Screening Process, Ankara. Available at: http://www.ab.gov.tr/files/tarama/tarama. htm, accessed 29 December 2015.

Republic of Turkey Ministry for EU Affairs (2014). *National Action Plan for EU Accession: Phase I (November 2014–June 2015)*. Ankara.

Republic of Turkey Ministry for EU Affairs (2015). *National Action Plan for EU Accession: Phase II (June 2015–June 2019)*. Ankara.

R&H Consultants (2009). 'TCDD Maintenance Review'. Ankara.

Rodrigue, J.-P., C. Comtois, and B. Slack (2006). *The Geography of Transport Systems*. Oxford: Routledge.

Roeger, W. (1995). 'Can Imperfect Competition Explain the Difference between Primal and Dual Productivity Measures? Estimates for U.S. Manufacturing'. *Journal of Political Economy* 103: 316–30.

Sachs, J. and A. Warner (1995). 'Economic Reform and the Process of Global Integration'. *Brookings Papers on Economic Activity* 1: 1–95.

Samuelson, P. A. (1952). 'The Transfer Problem and Transport Costs: The Terms of Trade when Impediments Are Missing'. *Economic Journal* 64: 264–89.

Samuelson, P. A. (1964). 'Theoretical Notes on Trade Problems'. *The Review of Economics and Statistics* 46: 145–54.

Santos Silva, J. M. C. and S. Tenreyro (2006). 'The Log of Gravity'. *The Review of Economics and Statistics* 88: 641–58.

Sauve, P. (2013). 'A Plurilateral Agenda for Services? Assessing the Case for a Trade in Services Agreement (TiSA)'. Swiss National Centre of Competence in Research Working Paper No. 2013/29. Berne: SNSF.

Shephard, B. (2012). 'The Gravity Model of International Trade: A User Guide'. United Nations. ESCAP.

State Airports Authority (2013). '2013 Annual Report'. Ankara: DHMI.

State Planning Organization (various years). Pre-Accession Economic Programme. Ankara: DPT.

Steensgaard, N. (1973). *Carracks, Caravans and Companies: The Structural Crisis in the European-Asian Trade in the Early 17th Century*. Lund: Studentliteratur.

Stopford, M. (1997). *Maritime Economics*. London: Routledge.

TINA Turkey Joint Venture (2008). *Technical Assistance to Transportation Infrastructure Needs Assessment: Turkey*. Vienna: TINA Vienna Transport Strategies Ges.m.b.H.

Tinbergen, J. (1962). *Shaping the World Economy*. New York: Twentieth Century Fund.

Togan, S. (2010). *Economic Liberalization and Turkey*. London: Routledge.

Togan, S. (2014). 'The EU-Turkey Customs Union: A Model for Future Euro-Med Integration'. In *Economic and Social Development of the Southern and Eastern Mediterranean Countries*, edited by R. Ayadi, L. De Wulf, and M. Dobrowski. Heidelberg: Springer, 37–61.

Togan, S. (2015). 'Silk Road: Past and Present', *The Problems of Oriental Studies* 3(69): 32–7.

Trujillo, L. and G. Nombela (1999). 'Privatization and Regulation of the Seaport Industry'. Policy Research Working Paper No. 2181. Washington, DC: World Bank.

Turkish State Railways (2013). *İstatistik Yıllığı 2009–2013*. Ankara: TCDD.

Turkish State Railways (2015). 'Sivil Toplum Kuruluşları Diyalog Toplantısı'. Restructuring Commission. Ankara: TCDD.

Ülengin, F., B. Çekyay, P. T. Palut, B. Ülengin, Ö. Kabak, Ö. Özaydin, and Ş. Ö. Ekici (2015). 'Effects of Quotas on Turkish Foreign Trade: A Gravity Model', *Transport Policy* 38: 1–7.

United Nations Conference on Trade and Development (2013). *World Investment Report 2013*. Geneva: UNCTAD.

United Nations Conference on Trade and Development (2014). *Review of Maritime Transport 2014*. Geneva: UNCTAD.

United Nations Economic Commission for Europe (2012). 'Openness of International Road Freight Transport Markets in the UNECE Region'. Working Party on Road Transport. Geneva: UNECE.

United Nations Economic Commission for Europe and United Nations Economic and Social Commission for Asia and the Pacific (2008). *Joint Study on Developing Euro-Asian Transport Linkages*. Geneva: UNECE.

Van Biesebroeck, J. (2005). 'Exporting Raises Productivity in Sub-Saharan African Manufacturing Firms'. *Journal of International Economics* 67: 373–91.

Walsh, K. (2006). 'Does Gravity Hold? A Gravity Model Approach to Estimating Barriers to Services Trade'. Institute for International Integration Studies No. 183. Dublin: IIIS.

Warziarg, R. and K. H. Welch (2003). 'Trade Liberalization and Growth: New Evidence', NBER Working Paper No. 10152. Cambridge, MA: NBER.

Wilson, J. S., C. L. Mann, and T. Otsuki (2003). 'Trade Facilitation and Economic Development: A New Approach to Quantifying the Impact'. *World Bank Economic Review* 17: 367–89.

Wilson, J. S., C. L. Mann, and T. Otsuki (2005). 'Assessing the Potential Benefit of Trade Facilitation: A Global Perspective'. *The World Economy* 28: 841–71.

Wölfl, A., I. Wanner, T. Kozluk, and G. Nicoletti (2009). 'Ten Years of Product Market Reform in OECD Countries—Insights from a Revised PMR Indicator'. OECD Economics Department Working Papers No. 695. Paris: OECD.

World Bank (1994). *World Development Report 1994: Infrastructure for Development*. Oxford: Oxford University Press.

World Bank (2007). *Port Reform Toolkit: Effective Decision Support for Policy Makers*. Washington, DC: World Bank.

World Bank (2011). *Railway Reform: Toolkit for Improving Rail Sector Performance*. Washington, DC: World Bank.

World Bank (2014a). 'Evaluation of the EU-Turkey Customs Union'. Poverty Reduction and Economic Management Europe and Central Asia Region. Washington, DC: World Bank.

World Bank (2014b). *Turkey Transport Sector Expenditure Review Synthesis Report*. Report No. 62581-TR. Washington, DC: World Bank.

World Economic Forum (2006). *The Global Competitiveness Report 2006–2007*. Geneva: WEF.

World Economic Forum (2012). *The Global Enabling Trade Report 2012: Reducing Supply Chain Barriers*, edited by R. Z. Lawrence, M. D. Hanouz, and S. Dohery. Geneva: WEF.

World Economic Forum (2014a). *Global Competitiveness Report 2014–2015*. Geneva: WEF.

World Economic Forum (2014b). *The Global Enabling Trade Report 2014*, edited by M. D. Hanouz, T. Geiger, and S. Dohery. Geneva: WEF.

World Health Organization (2013). *Global Status Report on Road Safety 2013*. Geneva: WHO.

World Trade Organization (1991). 'Services Sectoral Classification List'. Document MTN.GNS/W/120. Geneva: WTO.

World Trade Organization (1998). 'Maritime Transport Services'. Background Note by the Secretariat S/CSS/W/106. Geneva: WTO.

World Trade Organization (2000). *Guide to the GATS: An Overview of Issues for Further Liberalization of Trade in Services*. The Hague: Kluwer Law International.

World Trade Organization (2002). *The Legal Texts: The Results of the Uruguay Round of Multilateral Negotiations*. Geneva: WTO.

World Trade Organization (2006a). *Air Transport and the GATS: Documentation for the First Air Transport Review under GATS 1995–2000 in Review*. Geneva: WTO.

World Trade Organization (2006b). *Air Transport and the GATS: Documentation for the Second Air Transport Review under GATS 2000–2005 in Review*. Geneva: WTO.

World Trade Organization (2008). *World Trade Report 2008: Trade in a Globalizing World*. Geneva: WTO.

World Trade Organization (2010a). 'Road Freight Transport Services: Background Note by the Secretariat'. Council for Trade in Services S/C/W/324. Geneva: WTO.

World Trade Organization (2010b). 'Maritime Transport Services: Background Note by the Secretariat'. S/C/W/315. Geneva: WTO.

World Trade Organization (2013). *World Trade Report 2013: Factors Shaping the Future of World Trade*. Geneva: WTO.

World Trade Organization (2014). *World Trade Report 2014: Trade and Development: Recent Trends and the Role of WTO*. Geneva: WTO.

World Trade Organization Secretariat (2001a). 'Road Transport Services'. In *Guide to the GATS: An Overview of Issues for Further Liberalization of Trade in Services*, edited by WTO Secretariat. The Hague: Kluwer Law International, 501–30.

World Trade Organization Secretariat (2001b). 'Maritime Transport Services'. In *Guide to the GATS: An Overview of Issues for Further Liberalization of Trade in Services*, edited by WTO Secretariat. The Hague: Kluwer Law International, 429–62.

Index